ALSO BY BRIAN TRACY

Maximum Achievement

Brian Tracy

A F I R E S I D E B O O K

Published by Simon & Schuster

New York London Toronto Sydney Tokyo Singapore

ADVANCED *S*ELLING STRATEGIES

*The Proven System
of Sales Ideas, Methods,
and Techniques Used
by Top Salespeople
Everywhere*

FIRESIDE
Rockefeller Center
1230 Avenue of the Americas
New York, New York 10020

Copyright © 1995 by Brian Tracy
All rights reserved,
including the right of reproduction
in whole or in part in any form.

First Fireside Edition 1996

FIRESIDE and colophon are registered trademarks
of Simon & Schuster Inc.

Designed by Karolina Harris
Manufactured in the United States of America

10

Library of Congress Cataloging-in-Publication Data

Tracy, Brian.
  Advanced selling strategies : the proven system practiced by top salespeople /
Brian Tracy.
     p. cm.
  Includes index.
  1. Selling. 2. Success in business. I. Title.
HF5438.25.T7 1995
658.85—dc20   94-36889 CIP
ISBN 0-671-86519-6
ISBN 0-684-82474-4 (Pbk)

ACKNOWLEDGMENTS

This book is a synthesis and consolidation of the best ideas, techniques, and strategies I've learned and practiced over a sales career spanning three decades.

I am therefore indebted and grateful to the thousands of sales professionals I've had the opportunity to work with and learn from over the years.

The subject of sales covers the entire spectrum of human behavior, including psychology, economics, sales and persuasion theory, personality development, and every kind of communications. The people I've learned from are too numerous to mention individually, but you know who you are.

I especially want to thank Dan and Kerima Brattland, my dear friends and partners in promoting sales seminars to many thousands of professionals over the years. The same thanks for the same reasons go to my friends and business associates Tom Gundrum, Jim Kaufman, Ron Marks, Brian Dodge, and the inimitable Charles Whitnell of Nashville.

I owe a great debt of thanks to my friends and associates who have worked with me over the years to develop and polish this material and our sales training programs. I would especially like to mention and thank Voss and Robin Graham, Steve and Diane Muntean, Jeff Gardner, Monte and Kathy Lewis, Mike Pastore, Cynthia Forbes, Brooke Bovo, Chuck Suter, Nick Roosevelt, Cliff Hurst, David Pemberton, Dana Kirby, Mary Jane Arnold, John Carroll, Toni Harkins-Taylor,

Don Klassen, Mark Laughran, Kathy McGovern, Tom Russell, and Dale Wernette.

My international licensees have done extraordinary work to creatively translate and adapt this material and our training programs into foreign languages and cultures. I would especially like to thank Ib Moller and Paul Fergus of Canada, Carlos Dias of Latin America, Sune Gellberg of Sweden, John and Imelda Butler of Ireland, José Marques, Pedro Dionisio, Pedro Matos, Tony Paulo and Vicente Rodrigues—all of Portugal, Thom and Beverley Shields of New Zealand, Bill Natsume of Japan and Taiwan, Robert Yu of Taiwan, Cosimo Chiesa de Negri and Emilio Duro Pamies of Spain, Thrainn Kristjansson and Fanny Jonmundsdottir of Iceland, Enrico Masserini and Carla Cecere of Italy, and David Cheung of Hong Kong.

Finally, and perhaps most important of all, I would like to thank my wonderful literary agent, Margret McBride, for her input, advice, and counsel throughout the writing process, plus my outstanding senior editor, Bob Bender of Simon & Schuster, my Copy Supervisor, Gypsy da Silva of Simon & Schuster, and her remarkable and ever brilliant copy editor, Fred Chase.

To all of you, I express my deepest gratitude and appreciation for everything you have done to make this book possible.

To my wonderful children,
Christina, Michael, David, and Catherine,
the finest salespeople I've ever met.

I've learned more about caring, communication,
persuasion, and the importance of relationships from
you than from all other sources put together.

CONTENTS

INTRODUCTION

This book will do more to help you increase your sales than any other book or article you ever read. It is based on more than thirty years of direct, face-to-face selling of products and services of many different kinds. Everything contained in these pages has been tested and proven in the crucible of real selling experiences. Many thousands of salespeople, from hundreds of different businesses and industries, have used these ideas, methods, and techniques as stepping-stones to become the top salespeople in their organizations.

After many years of direct selling, I began presenting these ideas and methods to salespeople in live seminars in 1981. The seminars became so popular, and the results so immediate, that in 1984 the program was recorded onto audiocassette and assembled in a series entitled *The Psychology of Selling*. This six-cassette program was released in 1985 by Nightingale-Conant Corporation of Chicago and has now sold more than 200,000 sets at up to $70 each, making it the best-selling audio program on sales in history!

In 1987, the seminar was upgraded and videotaped as a thirty-five-part professional sales training program, *The New Psychology of Selling*. Tens of thousands of men and women from companies large and small, throughout the United States and Canada, have now attended this program. Most increased their sales dramatically, sometimes overnight! This powerful, practical approach to selling has now been translated into fourteen languages and is taught in thirty-one countries, including Japan and China. It is perhaps the most popular sales training program in the world.

Since I began teaching these ideas publicly, I have spoken before more than one million men and women from thousands of companies, selling every conceivable product and service, from door-to-door salespeople to economic planners for municipalities. By applying these ideas, countless thousands have gone on to rapidly increase their sales, doubling and even tripling their personal income. I have files of letters from men and women who have revolutionized their sales careers by practicing the methods and techniques you are about to learn.

Before I tell you a bit about *myself*, and the contents of this book, let me tell you about *yourself*. There are three things that I know about you as a salesperson, all of which are predictors of potential greatness for you in this profession. They are indispensable to all success.

First, I know that you have one of the toughest jobs in the world. It may vary in being difficult, *very* difficult, or *extremely* difficult, but it is *always* difficult. Selling is hard work. It always has been and it always will be. And the more difficult the economy, and the more competitive the market, the tougher it becomes.

But you continue to sell nonetheless. You continue to prospect and call on customers, day after day, facing continual rejection, failure, disappointment, disillusionment, and dashed expectations as an inevitable and unavoidable part of your way of making a living. You may complain, but you keep on going. You are a true hero or heroine of our business and social system.

Second, you are an *action* person. You are a doer rather than a talker. You are the kind of person who is a creator of circumstances rather than a creature of circumstances. You take charge of your life. If you are unhappy with your situation, you get busy and do something about it. The very fact that you have picked up this book is proof of your intense action orientation.

The third thing I know about you is that you are committed to your own personal and professional development. You recognize that your life can get better only if you get better. You know that we live in a knowledge-based society and that the height to which you rise will be determined by the depth to which you develop yourself. All top salespeople are avid students of their profession.

There are more than three thousand books on selling, and all of them contain ideas of value, sometimes of great value. Over the past thirty years, I've read as many books and articles as I possibly could in order to improve myself, and to help my students to become better. But this book is different from any of them. It takes the very best ideas and practices discovered in sales since the beginning of the century and synthesizes them into a more comprehensive and effective approach to selling than has ever before been developed. Countless salespeople, using these ideas, have gone from the bottom of their sales force to the top, from beginning salespeople to leaders in their industry; and from being broke and scared to becoming some of the highest paid and most self-confident people in America.

Before we begin however, let me tell you my own story. I was not always a salesman. When I was growing up, the idea of selling for a living never occurred to me. I stumbled into selling when I reached the place in my life where there was nothing else that anyone would hire me to do. I started out so far behind, I thought I was first. I flunked out of high school and got a job washing dishes in the back of a small hotel. When I lost that job, I got a job washing cars. When I lost that job, I got a job washing floors. I thought for a while that my future lay in washing things.

For various reasons, my jobs didn't last very long. With no high school diploma and no marketable skills, I had to take whatever I could get. I worked in a sawmill stacking lumber on the afternoon shift and then on the graveyard shift. When that job gave out, I drove my old car up into the mountains and got a job on a logging crew. It may sound romantic, but there is nothing exciting about working twelve-hour days with a chain saw in 90 degree heat, covered with blackflies and dust, slogging along in the wake of the bulldozers and giant logging trucks.

I even got a job digging wells at one time. That's where you start at ground level and work *down*, rather than *up*. And when you succeed, you fail, because when you find water, they lay you off. It is not a great incentive system.

When the winters came, I drifted back to working in hotel kitchens, where at least it was warm. I worked as a construction laborer and then in a factory, putting nuts on bolts eight hours a day. As these jobs gave out, one after the other, sometimes I went on unemployment, and once, when that ran out, on welfare. I often slept in my car, and occasionally on the ground next to it. When I was twenty-one, I got a job on a Norwegian freighter as a galley boy, the lowest form of laborer on the ship. When I was twenty-three, I was working on a farm during the harvest and sleeping on the hay in the farmer's barn.

Then, when I could no longer get a laboring job, I got into sales. I was new in town, had very little money, and I was a bit desperate, so I took the first commissioned sales job that came along, going from business to business selling office supplies.

Like too many salespeople, I had no training, aside from a little product knowledge. I knew nothing about the profession of selling. I had no idea that it was an art as well as a science. I thought that you just went out and found people who would listen to you talk about your products, and that if you talked to enough people, some of them would buy.

With this mind-set, I walked the streets knocking on doors, hour after weary hour, barely making enough money to keep the wolf away. I could only afford to live in rooming houses, boarding houses, or cheap residential hotels. I began moving from sales job to sales job, always on straight commission, and needing to be paid with every sale so that I could continue to have a roof over my head. I was always broke and I worried about money all the time.

Fortunately, I had two things going for me that eventually saved me from a life of quiet desperation. The first was that I wasn't afraid of hard work. I was willing to get up early and knock on doors all day long, and late into the evening, if that's what it took to find prospects and make presentations.

Second, I was an eager student of selling and I tried to learn from my experiences so I could be better in the future. But nonetheless, at the age of twenty-four, I was still walking the streets making calls in a wash-and-wear shirt I rinsed out in the sink of my rooming house each night and the same clip-on tie I wore every day. I had one pair of used shoes, which were too large for me and which flopped a little as I walked. I was making a living, but just barely.

Then came the turning point in my life. I discovered the law that Socrates had first articulated in 410 B.C. It came to be called the Socratic Law of Causality. We know it today as the Law of Cause and Effect.

The Law of Cause and Effect is devastatingly simple. It says that we live in a universe governed by law, not chance. This law states that everything that happens, happens for a reason. It says that if you can clearly define an *effect* that you desire, such as wealth, health, happiness, or sales success, and then trace that effect back to the actions that *cause* it, and you engage in those same actions, you can achieve the same effect for yourself.

This law was so simple, it was amazing. It said, in effect, that if I (or anyone) wanted to be successful in selling, all I would have to do was find out what other successful salespeople were doing, and then do the same thing, over and over, and I would get the same results.

The top salesman in my company was a fellow named Pete. He wore expensive clothes, lived in a beautiful apartment, drove a nice car, dined at the best restaurants, had a pocketful of $20 bills, and flew around on jets for both business and pleasure. He was getting the kind of effects, or results, that I wanted to get, so I decided to ask his advice.

In my mind's eye, I can still see that time and place many years ago when I approached him and asked for help. He was more than willing. I asked him what it was he did that enabled him to be so successful in selling. He in turn asked me what I was doing. How was I selling on a day-to-day basis?

I wasn't sure what he meant. As I've said, my style of selling at the time was to go out and knock on the doors of offices or apartments until I found someone who would listen to me and then recite all the most positive features of my product as they were described in the brochure. He then asked me this question, "Can you show me your sales presentation?"

I was a bit embarrassed. I had heard about a "sales presentation" but I wasn't sure what it was. So I asked him if he would show me *his* sales presentation instead. He agreed.

He took a blank sheet of paper and sat me on his right side. Pretending that I was a prospect, he began to ask me a series of questions. As I answered, he wrote things down, then asked me more questions and told me about the benefits of the product, getting agreement and confirmation at each stage. I was fascinated. His presentation went from the general to the particular, from the feature to the benefit, from the general interest to the desire to take action and the close of the sale. It was wonderful!

That was the turning point for me. From that moment on, instead of talking incessantly, I would show, tell, and ask questions. I took more time to learn more thoroughly about my customer's situation before beginning to talk about my product. I listened better and took better notes. I suggested ways for my prospects to get the benefits they were seeking and asked questions to isolate major buying desires and critical objections. And my sales started to go up.

When I asked Pete for more advice, he gave me more ideas on how to get appointments, qualify the prospect, present the product in its best light, answer objections effectively, and different ways of closing the sale. He then asked me if I had read a particular book on selling.

Book? Were there books on selling? I had no idea that there were books, much less whole *libraries* on the profession of sales. That was the second turning point for me. I began to haunt the local bookstores, buying and reading everything I could find on how to sell more effectively. I started getting up at five o'clock in the morning and reading for two hours, taking notes and making plans on how to use the ideas I had just read during the coming day. My sales continued to climb.

Shortly after I began to read about selling, I stumbled upon audiotapes. This was another great breakthrough for me and my selling career. I was amazed at the incredible amount of valuable information that was available. I spent hours listening to sales professionals and sales presentations on tape, repeating the best material over and over, and taking careful notes. Soon I had a library of books and tapes. As I learned and practiced, my sales presentations became better polished and more effective in every way. And my sales continued to increase.

Wow! Perhaps the greatest discovery of all time: **you can learn anything you need to learn to achieve any goal you want by finding out what others have done before you to get the results you want to get.**

The key to success is to learn from the experts. Study and copy the very best people in your field. Do what they do, day after day, until it becomes second nature. And then, surprise! surprise! You begin to get the same results.

The third revelation that changed my sales life was the discovery of live seminars and training programs. In a few hours I could get the benefit of what had taken the best sales trainer many years to learn. I could save myself hundreds and even thousands of hours of work trying to learn the same things on my own.

Within a year, after buying every book, listening to every audiotape, and attending every sales training seminar or course I could find, I literally went from rags to riches. I went from living in a boarding house to having a large, beautifully furnished apartment with a maid. I went from worrying about every dollar to never carrying less than $1,000 in my pocket. I flew on jets and dined in the best restaurants in the biggest cities in my market area. Eventually, they made me a sales manager and then a sales executive. They gave me six countries and a development budget, plus overrides on the sales of all my people.

By the time I was twenty-five, I had recruited and built a ninety-five-person sales force, covering six countries and generating millions of dollars per month in sales. I had apartments in three cities and I was living a life I had never dreamed possible. And it was all because I learned what the very best people were doing and did it over and over again myself, until I got the same results.

In time, I moved on. I have now traveled and worked in more than eighty countries on six continents. I've been around the world three times. I have stayed at the best hotels and dined in the finest restaurants, and I own the home and the automobile that I want. Most importantly, I have a beautiful family for whom I can provide all the good things of life. And it is all because I learned and practiced the Law of Cause and Effect as it applies to professional selling.

I have sold mutual funds and other investments. I have sold residential real estate, and real estate syndications, and industrial and commercial real estate. I have developed and leased millions of dollars' worth of office buildings and shopping centers. I have sold printing supplies and advertising, office supplies and typewriters, memberships in discount clubs, Bibles and encyclopedias, door to door. I have sold cars and construction materials. I have sold seminars, consulting and training services. And I have done sales consulting and designed sales training programs for dozens of industries, from A to Z, from airlines to zoological supplies, and almost everything in between.

As a sales consultant and seminar leader, I've had the opportunity to meet and work with thousands of the finest salespeople in America, Canada, Europe, Australia, New Zealand, as well as throughout Asia and many other countries. I have spent countless hours with them, observing their behavior, listening to their stories about how they became successful in their field. I've compared their experiences with my own and with those of thousands of other men and women who are in every level of sales. And I have found that there is a constant thread that runs through the lives and activities of all the highest paid salespeople in every industry.

What I found is that top salespeople are almost identical in many ways. Sometimes, as an exercise in a sales management seminar, I will offer to describe the top salesperson in each person's company. I will explain his or her qualities, characteristics, behaviors, and attitudes in some detail. The sales manager or company owner in the audience will inevitably ask me, "How can you be so accurate in describing my best person?"

Then I tell them that it's because all the best salespeople are cut from the same cloth. They all have pretty much the same temperament. They have the same attitudes and attributes. They trigger the same feelings and responses from their co-workers and their customers. They all do very much the same things in the same ways, over and over, and they get pretty much the same results.

I am an intensely practical person. I always use myself, my customers, and my own sales team as a laboratory to test any new sales idea or concept. I always say, "Is this true for me?" I never accept anything on faith, and I don't expect you to accept anything on faith either. I have been forced to discard many of the sales books and articles I have read over the years because they make recommendations for selling that I don't feel comfortable with. I will not use them, because I do not want to have them used on me.

So, as you read, listen to your heart. Compare the ideas, methods, and techniques taught in this book with your own experience. Be sure that it feels right. If the idea makes sense to you, try it out in a real-life situation with a prospective customer. If it has to do with your own inner development, try that out as well. And be patient. Give these ideas a chance to work. You can only grow by moving out of your comfort zone, by doing things that you've never done before. But only take action if your inner voice tells you that it makes sense in your situation.

The sales system you are about to learn is divided into ten parts. This book is designed to be read one chapter at a time, in order. Please be sure to make notes in the margins and underline key ideas that you want to come back to later. When you have completed the book, you should use it as a reference tool, going back to the specific parts of the particular chapters that can be most helpful to you at that time.

In Chapter 1, you will learn "The Psychology of Selling," the common qualities, attributes, and behaviors of the highest paid salespeople in every industry, and how you can incorporate them into your character and personality. You will learn how to develop the kind of *self-image* and *self-confidence* that will give you the edge in every sales situation.

In Chapter 2, "The Development of Personal Power," you will learn how to develop the qualities of unshakable self-confidence, optimism, and a positive mental attitude, which enable you to bounce back from the inevitable ups and downs of day-to-day selling. You will learn a series of *mental tools and strategies* you can use continually to keep yourself performing at your best. You will learn the little-known techniques of thinking and acting that give you a powerful personality in any sales situation.

In Chapter 3, you will learn the process of "Personal Strategic Planning for the Sales Professional." You will learn how to create a *sales blueprint* that will enable you to meet and exceed your sales goals on schedule. You will take everything you have learned in the previous chapters and develop it into a step-by-step process for every day, week, and month of the coming sales period, to make sure you are among the top producers in your industry.

In Chapter 4, "The Heart of the Sale," you will learn about the central importance of *customer relationships* in achieving sales success. You will learn how to build higher levels of trust with your prospects and customers by focusing your attention and your efforts on the key emotional elements that determine and decide every sale.

In Chapter 5, you will learn "The Profession of Selling" and how to apply the principles of scientific management to becoming better at every aspect of the sales process. You will learn how to approach selling with the same organized and systematic process practiced by all top salespeople. You will learn how to identify the vital functions of sales success and how to develop the *winning edges* that enable you to move to the head of your field. You will learn what you must do to become one of the best paid salespeople in your industry.

In Chapter 6, "Motivating People to Buy," you will learn how to determine the *key motivators* that cause your customer to buy. You will learn why different people respond in different ways to the same offer and how to present your product in such a way that it triggers buying desire. You will learn the key concepts of motivational theory, the role of dissatisfaction in stimulating buying behavior, and how to find and push the "hot button" in each customer.

In Chapter 7, "Influencing the Buying Decision," you will learn how to *influence your prospect* by appealing to his subconscious mind. You will learn how to orchestrate your appearance, body language, voice, and words to ensure an excellent first impression, and how to handle every element of the sales conversation in a way that builds maximum credibility in you and your offering.

In Chapter 8, "Prospecting: Filling Your Sales Pipeline," you will learn how to find *qualified prospects* in any market. You will learn how to analyze your market, define your ideal customer, identify the prospects who can be centers of influence, and get all the appointments you need to be busy every minute of every day. You will learn how to overcome the internal and external obstacles that hold salespeople back, and how to develop a "golden chain" of referrals and repeat sales.

In Chapter 9, "How to Make Powerful Presentations," you will learn how to identify the most pressing need your product can satisfy, position yourself against competition, become the best-choice provider, and demonstrate the specific benefits your customer will enjoy from buying what you are selling. You will learn how to make effective presentations that *arouse buying desire* in the most skeptical customer.

In Chapter 10, "Closing the Sale: The Endgame of Selling," you will learn how to get the customer's commitment to take action on your offer. You will learn how to identify and isolate the various types of questions, concerns, and objections that can stall or stop the sale, and how to respond to them. You will learn a variety of ways to deal with the *price objection* and how to neutralize it. You will learn the most effective ways ever discovered to close the sale.

This book will change your selling life. It will give you the keys to unlock your full sales potential. By practicing what you learn in the coming pages, you, too, can become one of the finest salespeople in America.

"If you believe you can do a thing, or if you believe you cannot, in either case you are probably right."

—HENRY FORD

THE PSYCHOLOGY

OF SELLING

Some salespeople always do well, no matter what is happening around them. They make excellent money, live in nice homes, drive new cars, and dine in fine restaurants. They always seem to have money in their pockets and in their bank accounts. Most of all, they are happy, optimistic, positive, friendly, relaxed, and seem to be in complete control of themselves and their lives. They are the top salespeople in every organization and their companies are dependent upon them for continued sales results.

Thousands of hours and millions of dollars have been spent studying the most successful salespeople in our society. They have been interviewed exhaustively, as have their customers, co-workers, and managers. Today as a result of this research, we know more about what it takes for you to be one of the best in your business than we have ever known before. And the most important thing we have learned in all these studies is that selling is more *psychological* than anything else.

One of the most important principles ever discovered in the field of human performance is called the "winning edge concept." This concept states that "small differences in ability can translate into enormous differences in results." What this means is that if you become just a little bit better in certain critical areas of selling, this slight improvement can translate into a substantial increase in your sales results. You may be on the verge of a major breakthrough in your sales career at this very moment by just learning and practicing one small thing that is new and different from what you have done before. If a racehorse comes in first, even by a nose, it wins ten times the prize money of the horse that comes in second. Does this mean that the horse that wins by a nose is ten times *faster* than the horse that comes in second? Of course not! Is the horse that wins by a nose *twice* as fast, or 50 percent faster, or even 10 percent faster? The horse that wins is only a *nose* faster, but that translates into ten times the prize money.

By the same token, the salesperson who gets the sale for himself and his company gets 100 percent of the business and 100 percent of the commission. Does this mean that his product is 100 percent better than that of the competition, or 100 percent cheaper? Of course not! His product may not even be as good and it may cost more than that of the competitor, but the top salesman gets the sale nonetheless. The person who gets the sale is, in most cases, not a lot better than the person who loses the sale. He or she merely has the winning edge, but that's all it takes to get 100 percent of the business.

This concept is vital to your success. You may have heard of the Pareto Principle, the 80/20 rule, which, as it applies to sales, says that 80 percent of sales are made by 20 percent of the salespeople. Depending upon the sophistication of the industry and the overall level of training, the ratio can be 90/10 or 70/30, but in large national sales forces, the 80/20 rule holds true. Twenty percent of the salespeople make 80 percent of the sales and earn 80 percent of the commissions, while 80 percent of the salespeople make only 20 percent of the sales and share only 20 percent of the commissions.

What this means in dollar terms is remarkable! If ten salespeople are making a total of $1 million in sales in a given period, this means that two of the salespeople are making $800,000 of sales or approximately $400,000 each, and eight of the salespeople are making $200,000 of sales, or $25,000 each on average. This is a ratio of 16 to 1. The top salespeople are outselling the bottom salespeople by sixteen times!

This difference in sales results cannot be explained simply by sales technique and methodology. There is something else going on, and that something else is the mind-set or psychological state of the salesperson.

In every large company, it is common for some salespeople to be earning $25,000 a year while other salespeople are earning $250,000 a year, a difference of ten times. They are all selling the same product, to the same people, at the same price, under the same competitive conditions, into the same market, and out of the same office.

Is the person earning ten times as much as the other working ten times as hard, putting in ten times the number of hours? Does he or she see ten times the number of prospects?

Is it possible for the high-earning salesperson to be ten times better, in any area, than the person earning one tenth as much? Of course not.

In fact, sometimes the person earning ten times as much as the other salesperson in the office is younger, has less education, sees fewer people, works fewer hours, and has less experience than the long-term professional who is barely making a living.

This book will show you how to move into that top 10 percent of salespeople, to become one of the highest paid people in America, and to achieve all of your goals and dreams in this wonderful profession. And this requires, more than anything else, that you develop the winning psychological edge, which we will talk about through the rest of this chapter.

ATTITUDE VERSUS APTITUDE

The 80/20 rule is as applicable to individual salespeople as it is to large sales forces. Fully 80 percent of your success as a salesperson will be determined by your *attitude* and only 20 percent by your *aptitude*.

A positive mental attitude, or a constructive and optimistic way of looking at yourself and your work, goes hand in hand with sales success in every field and in every market. Developing this attitude of unshakable self-confidence and enthusiasm, no matter what is going on around you, is your passport to greatness in selling.

The 20 percent of sales effectiveness that comes from product knowledge and professional selling skills is extremely important as well. It is only when you are thoroughly knowledgeable about what you are selling and thoroughly skilled in your ability to present it effectively that you develop the confidence and self-assurance upon which a positive mental attitude depends. We will talk more about this in later chapters, but for now, let's continue our discussion of attitude.

The quality of your thinking determines the quality of your life. If you improve the quality of your thinking, in any area, you will improve the quality of your life in that area. By using your mind, your ability to think, you take charge of your life and determine your own destiny. You move from being powerless to being powerful. You determine everything that happens to you by the way you think about it, in advance. You may not be what you think you are, but what you think, you are!

The most rapid and positive changes in your personality and your sales results come about when you change your thinking about yourself and your possibilities. When you reprogram your subconscious mind so you feel a sense of personal power and control, every part of your life begins improving immediately. As William James of Harvard wrote in 1905, "The greatest revolution of my generation is the discovery that individuals, by changing their inner attitudes of mind, can change the outer aspects of their lives."

The very best salespeople have an attitude of calm, confident, positive self-expectation. They feel good about themselves and they have a quiet faith that everything they are doing is contributing toward their inevitable success. They are relaxed about their lives and their careers. They know, in their hearts, that they are good at what they do, and their customers know it as well. Often, their customers decide to buy from them even before they've made a sales presentation or described their product or service. They are the champions of selling everywhere. And because of the Law of Cause and Effect, you can become one of them by developing the same attitudes and attributes that they have.

SELF-CONCEPT:
THE MASTER PROGRAM OF PERFORMANCE

One of the greatest breakthroughs in human performance and effectiveness in the twentieth century is the discovery of the **self-concept.** Your self-concept is the bundle of beliefs that you have about yourself and your world. It is the master program of your subconscious computer. These beliefs began forming with your very first experiences as an infant. Over the years, you have absorbed a complex series of interwoven ideas, doubts, fears, opinions, attitudes, values, expectations, hopes, phobias, myths, and other impressions. You have taken them into your mind and accepted them as true. These are the operating instructions of your subconscious computer and they control everything that you say, do, think, and feel. In the absence of any deliberate change on your part, you will continue doing, thinking, saying, and feeling very much the same things indefinitely.

Just as you have an overall self-concept, or composite idea of who you are and what you can do, you also have a **mini-self-concept** for each individual part of your life. These mini-self-concepts determine how you think, feel, and perform with regard to people, sports, health, relationships, work, learning, creativity, and everything else you do.

You have a mini-self-concept for how much money you earn, as well. Whether or not you are happy with your income, it is the amount you have programmed yourself to earn, based on your past earnings and your current belief system. It is your self-concept level of income. It is the cumulative total of all your experiences with earning money since you got your first job. It is a part of your subconscious programming, and you tend to earn that amount even if you change jobs or move to another city. It is locked in.

In fact, this self-concept level of income is so deeply ingrained that if you earn much more or less than your current level of income, you will feel distinctly uncomfortable. Even *thinking* about earning substantially more or less than you're accustomed to will make you uneasy.

For example, if you earn 10 percent or more above this level, you will do everything possible to get rid of the money. You will have an irresistible urge to go out and spend it, even splurge on buying something you don't need. If you earn more than you're comfortable with for any period of time, you will feel impelled to invest in things you know nothing about, lend it to people who won't pay it back, or even give it away.

If you earn *less* than your self-concept level of income, you will start engaging in scrambling behaviors to get your income back up into the range where you feel comfortable. You will start working longer and harder, and maybe upgrading your skills. You may consider second income opportunities, starting your own business, or think about getting a new job where you can earn more.

Any change, or even an attempt to change anything you are doing, makes you uncomfortable. By attempting to change, you move out of your **comfort zone.** You feel increasingly uneasy. You experience stress and tension. If the change is too extreme, your physical and mental health can be affected. You will experience sleeplessness, indigestion, or fatigue. You may react with impatience, irritability or anger. You will often feel as if you are on an emotional roller coaster.

So if you want to sell more and earn more, you must increase your self-concept level of income. You must increase the amount you believe yourself capable of earning. You must raise your aspirations, set higher goals, and make detailed plans to achieve them. You must begin to see yourself and think about yourself as capable of being one of the highest earning salespeople in your field. You must take charge of developing a new self-concept for sales and income that is more consistent with what you really want to accomplish.

Your self-concept determines your levels of performance and effectiveness in everything you do. In sales, you have mini-self-concepts that govern every activity of selling. You have mini-self-concepts for prospecting, for cold calling, for making appointments, for presenting, for closing, for getting referrals, and for making follow-up sales. You have a mini-self-concept for your level of product knowledge, your personal management skills, your level of motivation, and for the way you relate to different types of customers. In every case, you will always perform in a manner consistent with the way you see yourself.

Wherever you have a high self-concept, you perform well. If you enjoy working on the telephone, you look forward to telephone prospecting and selling, and you do it well. If you have a high self-concept for making presentations or for closing sales, you feel comfortable and competent whenever you are doing them.

Wherever you feel tense or uneasy in selling, it means that you have a low self-concept in that area. You do not feel comfortable when you are engaged in that activity. You probably avoid that activity as much as possible.

If you are not particularly skilled at a particular activity, you will feel uncomfortable at the very thought of it. If you are not good on the telephone, you will avoid the telephone as much as possible. If you are not good at prospecting, you will avoid prospecting as much as possible. If you are not good at confirming the sale and closing the order, you will choke up at the end of the sales presentation and avoid asking for a commitment from the prospect. In each case, your income and your sales will suffer until you decide to change.

Some years ago, a young man in one of my seminars told me how moving out of his comfort zone was affecting him. He had come from a small farming community and he was selling large, expensive satellite dishes to wealthy farmers who had just had an excellent harvest. The winter was coming and they wanted television during the cold months ahead. The satellite dishes were new at the time and popular, and he was selling two a week, earning $1,000 commission on each one.

He told me that he had never made so much money in his whole life. His problem was that, after his second sale of the week, he experienced a form of withdrawal, accompanied by a desire to flee. He said that he was so overwhelmed by the amount of money he was making that he would go home after the week's second sale, close all the blinds in his bedroom, and lie on his bed in the darkness for several hours. This was his comfort zone.

Whenever you feel any kind of stress in selling, your natural tendency will also be to return to your comfort zone, at a lower level of performance, rather than to continue at what you're doing until you feel comfortable at that new level. Sometimes this discomfort, which can lead to self-sabotage, is mislabeled the "fear of success." But what it really is is the experience of attempting to achieve at a level beyond what you really believe is possible for you.

It is no surprise, then, that the top salespeople have high self-concepts in every phase of the selling process. They make most of the money that is paid in the sales profession. They are the most respected and esteemed people within their organizations and by the customers they call on. Their high, positive self-concepts for selling translate into excellent sales results and great lives for themselves and their families.

YOUR MENTAL MAKEUP:
SELF-IDEAL, SELF-IMAGE, SELF-ESTEEM

Your self-concept is made up of three parts, each of which affects the others. When you understand the roles of these three aspects of your mental makeup, you can then put your hands on the keyboard of your own mental computer and change your programming. When you learn how to create a new and better self-concept of yourself as a salesperson, you can then control your sales results for the rest of your career.

The first part of your self-concept is your **self-ideal.** Your self-ideal largely determines the direction of your life. It guides the growth and evolution of your character and personality. Your self-ideal is a combination of all the qualities and attributes of other people that you most admire. It is a description of the person you would most like to be if you could embody the qualities that you most aspire to.

Throughout your life, you have seen and read about people who demonstrated the qualities of courage, confidence, compassion, love, fortitude, perseverance, patience, forgiveness, and integrity. Over time, these qualities have formed in you an ideal, or vision, of the very best person you or anyone could possibly become. You may not always live up to the very best that you know, but you are constantly striving, even at a subconscious level, to be more like the kind of person you most admire. In fact, in almost everything you do, you are comparing your activities with these ideal qualities, and you strive continually to behave consistent with them.

Successful salespeople have very clear ideals for themselves and their careers. Unsuccessful salespeople have only fuzzy ideals, if they have any ideals at all. Successful salespeople are clear about wanting to excel in every part of their work and their personal lives. Unsuccessful salespeople don't give the subject very much thought. One of the primary characteristics of successful men and women in every walk of life is that they think continually about whether or not their current behaviors are consistent with their idealized behaviors.

Part of your ideals are your goals. As you set higher and more challenging goals for yourself, your self-ideal improves. When you set clear goals for the kind of person you want to be and the kind of life you want to live, your self-ideal becomes a greater guiding and motivating force in your life.

Perhaps the most important part of developing your self-ideal is for you to realize that whatever anyone else has done or become, you can do or become as well. Improvements in your self-ideal begin in your imagination, and in your imagination there are no limits except the ones that you accept.

What is your ideal vision of the very best person you could possibly become? How would you behave each day if you were already that person? Asking yourself these questions and then living your life consistent with the answers is the first step to creating yourself in your ideal image.

The second part of your self-concept is your **self-image.** Your self-image is the way you *see* yourself and *think* about yourself in the present. It is often called your "inner mirror." You constantly refer to this mirror to see how you should perform or behave in a particular situation. You always behave on the outside in a manner consistent with the picture you have of yourself on the inside.

For example, when you see yourself as calm, confident, and competent in any aspect of selling, whenever you are engaged in that activity, you will feel calm, confident, and competent. You will be positive and happy. You will perform well and get excellent results. If, for any reason, it doesn't go well at that time, you will throw it off and dismiss it as a temporary situation. Your self-image is clear. In your mind's eye you see yourself as good and capable in that area, and nothing can disturb your mental picture.

The most rapid improvements in sales results come from changing your self-image. The moment you see yourself differently, you behave differently. When you behave differently, you feel different. And because you are behaving and feeling differently, you get different results.

Some years ago, when I was selling discount club memberships, I would end my presentation by giving the prospect a booklet outlining the membership benefits and encourage him to "think about it." My self-image was such that I could not bring myself to ask the prospect to make a buying decision.

All day long, I would go from office to office giving my presentation and leaving a little booklet for the prospect to read. And as you might imagine, I was not making any sales. When I called people back after they had time to think about it, they would invariably say they were not interested.

I was getting desperate. I was living from hand to mouth at the time. Although I was seeing lots of prospects, I was making very few sales. Then I had a revelation that changed my career at the time. I realized that it was my fear of asking for the order that was causing all my problems. It was not my prospects. It was me. I needed to change my self-image and thereby change my behavior if I wanted my results to improve.

The very next morning, I made the decision that I would not call back on a prospect. The size of the purchase was small and, when I had completed my presentation, the prospect would know everything that he needed to know to make a decision. There was no benefit or advantage to leaving material behind or giving the prospect several days to think about it.

At my very first call, when I had finished my presentation, the prospect said, "Let me think it over." This time I was ready. I smiled and told him politely that I did not make callbacks because I was too busy making sales to other customers. I then said, "You know everything you need to know to make a decision right now. Why don't you just take it?"

I remember him shrugging his shoulders and saying, "Okay. I'll take it. How would you like to be paid?"

I walked out of that office on a cloud. That very day I tripled my sales. That week, I sold more than anyone else in the company. By the end of the month, I had been promoted to the position of sales manager with forty-two people under me. I went from making one or two sales a week to making ten to fifteen. I went from worrying about money constantly to earning a large salary with an override on the activities of all my salespeople. My sales life took off and, with few exceptions, it never stopped. And the turning point was my decision to change my self-image and make it more consistent with the results I wanted rather than the results that I was getting.

The third part of your self-concept is your **self-esteem.** This is the emotional component of your self-concept. It is the "reactor core" or energy source of your inner power. It is the most important single element determining your attitude and your personality. It is the key to your success in life.

Your self-esteem is best defined as how much you like yourself.

The more you like yourself, accept yourself, and respect yourself as a valuable and worthwhile person, the higher your self-esteem. The more that you genuinely feel you are an excellent human being, the more positive and happy you are.

Your self-esteem determines your levels of energy, enthusiasm, and self-motivation. Your self-esteem is the control valve on your performance and your effectiveness. Your self-esteem is like the fuel in a rocket that blasts it free of the earth's gravity and into orbit. People with high self-esteem have tremendous personal power and do well at just about everything they attempt.

Your self-ideal is the person you most want to be, sometime in the future. Your self-ideal determines the direction of your life, of your growth and evolution as a person. Your self-image, on the other hand, determines the way you perform in the present. Your self-image is the way you see yourself *now*, today, at this moment. Your self-esteem is largely determined by the relationship between your self-image and your self-ideal, or the way you are performing in your day-to-day activities compared with the way you would be performing if you were the very best person you could possibly be.

The more that your day-to-day activities are consistent with the person you want to become, the higher will be your self-esteem. If your ideal is to be well organized, calm, positive, and working progressively toward the achievement of your goals, and in reality you are behaving in a well-organized, calm, positive manner, working step by step toward your objectives, you will have a high level of self-esteem. You will like and respect yourself. You will feel happy, healthy, and optimistic. You will be a high-performance personality.

Self-esteem is the foundation of a positive self-concept. High self-esteem is the critical element in sales success. The more you like and respect yourself, the better you perform at everything you do. Developing and maintaining high levels of self-esteem is the most important thing you can do, every day, in building yourself to the point where you are capable of achieving all your goals.

THE MAJOR OBSTACLES TO SALES SUCCESS

High self-esteem goes hand in hand with great sales success. By the same token, the major cause of sales failure is *low* self-esteem. Low self-esteem translates into feelings of inferiority, unworthiness, and undeservingness. It is manifested in feelings of incompetence and inadequacy. Low self-esteem is a feeling of not being good enough. Low self-esteem is comparing yourself negatively with others, ascribing greater qualities to them than they have, and ascribing to yourself lesser capabilities than you possess. Low self-esteem is seeing the glass as half empty rather than half full. Low self-esteem leads to stress, negativity, pessimism, fearfulness, self-doubt, and the tendency to sell yourself short in almost every situation.

In sales, the negative effects of low self-esteem are experienced in the **fear of rejection.** The fear of rejection is the biggest single obstacle to success in selling. It is the fear of rejection that, more than anything else, holds you back from achieving your full potential. It is the fear of rejection that causes you to settle for far less than you deserve. It is the fear of rejection that causes you to hold back from seeing more and better prospects, and from translating those calls into more and better sales. It is the fear of rejection that acts as the brake on your potential for greatness in the field of sales. And it is the fear of rejection that you must eliminate if you are going to go all the way to the top in your field.

The one good thing about the fear of rejection is that it is an *acquired* fear. No one is born with it. It is learned through a process of conditioning from early infancy onward. It is a negative habit pattern that almost everyone develops during the process of growing up. And because it is a learned condition, it can be unlearned as well, and sometimes quite quickly.

When you were born, you had no fears at all except for two: the fear of falling and the fear of loud noises. Every fear that you have today had to be taught to you by your parents, siblings, and others through repetition and reinforcement as you grew up. Your fears are all learned.

The fear of rejection or disapproval is based on "conditional love." Conditional love occurs, for example, when one or both parents make their love and support conditional upon your behaving in a certain way. At an early age, you learned that if you didn't do what Mommy or Daddy expected of you, they would withdraw their love and approval. They would be angry and negative. They would use destructive criticism and even physical punishment on you to get you to do what they wanted you to do.

As you grew up, your self-image, the way you see yourself and think about yourself, became more and more dependent upon the way you thought others saw you and thought about you. You might even have become hypersensitive to the way people treated you and talked to you. You may have started adjusting your behaviors to get other people to like you, respect you, and approve of you. You started down the slippery slope of compromising your own uniqueness in an attempt to gain the respect and esteem of others.

To a greater or lesser degree, we all have fears and concerns about how other people think about us. Adults with low self-esteem are extremely sensitive to the opinions of others, often to the point where they cannot make a decision without getting the approval of someone else.

A husband will not make a buying decision without getting the approval of his wife, or a wife will not make a buying decision without getting the approval of her husband. Grown children will not make buying decisions without getting the approval of their parents. People will not buy things without asking their friends, lawyers, accountants, or advisors. In business, people will not make decisions without referring the entire matter to one or more other people to gain their approval.

In sales, the fear of rejection manifests itself in a fear of calling on strangers. It is at the root of the reluctance you feel to seek out new prospects for your product or service. Fear of rejection causes stress, anxiety, and even depression. It paralyzes prospecting behavior and undermines a salesperson's effectiveness at every stage of the process. Fear of rejection is the primary reason that so many people drop out of sales, blaming the company and the management, and then take jobs earning far less than they could be. This fear of rejection can manifest itself in different ways, and not all salespeople are subject to the exact same fears.

For example, low self-esteem, and feelings of inferiority leading to the fear of rejection, make some salespeople tense and uneasy about calling on prospects who they feel are better than they are socially or economically. These salespeople will not call on senior executives or professional people because they don't feel good enough.

An older salesman was telling me recently about several people he had gone to school with who were now senior executives in major corporations. He was proud of his friendships with these people, which he had maintained over the years. I then asked him how many of them were customers of his. The answer was none. His particular type of call reluctance was holding him back from approaching them even though he knew they were buying large quantities of the services he sold from other companies.

Many salespeople are afraid to sell to their friends and associates for fear that they will disapprove of them or be critical of their career choices. Sometimes, salespeople are ashamed of being in sales in the first place, and as a result they are afraid to approach almost anyone they know to offer their products or services.

The most common fear of rejection is that associated with approaching strangers, people that you don't know and who you have never spoken to in the past. This generalized fear of disapproval is the greatest destroyer of promising sales careers. It is the fear that a person will say something unkind or "I'm not interested."

The fear of rejection is always the fear of not being liked by the other person. It is the fear of rudeness, criticism, or negativity. It is the fear of hearing the word. "No!" (And, by the way, if you have a fear of the word "No!" you have picked the wrong field in which to earn a living.)

The starting point of overcoming the fear of rejection is to realize this: **rejection is not personal.** Rejection has nothing to do with you as a person. The prospect does not know you well enough to reject you as an individual. The rejection is only associated with the situation and personality of the *prospect*, and has nothing to do with *your* personality, integrity, and competence. To repeat: rejection is simply not personal. It is a standard reaction to almost any sales proposal in a commercial society.

Some of your very best customers will be people who responded negatively to your first approach. This is to be expected. The average American is bombarded by hundreds of commercial messages every single day. Television, radio, newspapers, magazines, mail, and telephones are filled with solicitations for products and services. The prospect's initial reaction to you, even if he wants and needs the product you sell, because of message overload, will almost invariably be negative. Prospective customers are busy, if not overwhelmed, with their activities and the demands on their time. Your job is to be calm, patient, and persistent, and to realize that nothing that a prospect says to you can affect you in any way, because it's not personal.

Not long ago, a man came up to me at a sales seminar in St. Louis and told me that something I said at an earlier seminar had changed his life. His story contained an excellent lesson.

He told me that one year ago he was on the verge of failing out of his sales career. He hated prospecting because he was afraid of it. He had an inordinate fear of rejection based on previous experiences. Because he hated prospecting, he was doing less and less of it, and his sales were decreasing every month. He knew that it wouldn't be long before he would be let go by his company.

He came to my seminar and heard me say, "Rejection is not personal." It hit him like a slap in the face. He realized that his career was going down the drain for no other reason than because of his inordinate fear of calling on people he didn't even know or care about. He was inflicting emotional and financial pain on himself and on his family simply because he had allowed his fears to get the best of him, rather than him getting the best of his fears.

That was his wake-up call! He resolved that very day to do whatever it took to excel at prospecting, both on the telephone and in making cold calls. He began a study program. He began listening in his car to audiotapes on prospecting and selling. He read books and articles on prospecting each day. He started earlier every morning practicing his prospecting skills. Within six months, he was not only the best prospector in his company, but his sales had gone up by more than 400 percent.

Furthermore, he had recently been promoted to the position of sales manager for his company and transferred to St. Louis with a large salary. He had a development budget for a new office, and he received an override on all his salespeople. In less than one year he had transformed his life and his career by going to work on himself and eradicating the fear of rejection that had been holding him back. He changed his self-image and he now saw himself as an excellent prospector. His new self-image determined the way he thought, felt, and behaved, and his prospects responded to him with greater openness and interest. He realized that it had been his attitude, and his attitude alone, that was determining his results.

JOB NUMBER ONE

Fear is and always has been one of the greatest enemies of mankind. It is the greatest obstacle to success in your life and your career. It is both subtle and devastating. It works on you, deep in your subconscious mind, and causes you to see the world negatively instead of positively. Fear makes you interpret events to yourself in a negative way. It causes you to associate only with other people who think and feel the same way. You reinforce each other's fears and beliefs. The cumulative result on your personality and your sales career can be tragic. For you to achieve great success in selling, the eradication of fear as an influence in your life is job number one.

There is an inverse relationship between fear and self-esteem, like a teeter-totter. The greater the fear, the lower your self-esteem. But the higher your self-esteem, the lower will be your fear. Everything you do to raise your self-esteem will decrease the fears that hold you back, and everything you do to decrease your fears will raise your self-esteem and improve your performance.

Since all fears are *learned* by repetition of the fear-inducing event or thoughts of those events, fears are *unlearned* by repeated acts of courage in opposition to the responses of fear. For example, if you are afraid of cold calling, the way to overcome your fear is to confront it repeatedly until it goes away. This is called "systematic desensitization." You keep doing it until it no longer holds any fear for you. It is the very best and most effective way of developing courage and confidence in any area of your life. As Ralph Waldo Emerson said, "Do the thing you fear and the death of fear is certain."

Another way for you to overcome the fear of rejection is to learn to speak on your feet. Certain fears are bundled together, like wires, in the subconscious mind, and the short-circuiting of one fear causes the short circuiting of the others on the same circuit. One of the fears that is bundled with the fear of rejection is the fear of public speaking. Fifty-four percent of American adults rank the fear of public speaking ahead of the fear of death.

When you learn to speak on your feet—by joining Toastmasters International and attending the weekly meetings, or by taking a Dale Carnegie course, for example—you become more confident and self-assured in your interactions with others on a one-to-one basis. When you become a competent public speaker, you simultaneously become more powerful and persuasive in your prospecting and sales activities.

I gave this advice at a sales seminar a couple of years ago. About a year later, a businessman came up to me to tell me how that advice had helped him. He said that when he left the seminar, he had immediately joined a local chapter of Toastmasters and began attending regular meetings. Within six months, he had overcome his lifelong fear of speaking in front of an audience. He worked for an engineering firm in a back-office job, but his increasing confidence came to the notice of his boss. One day, his boss asked him if he would conduct a presentation to the board members of a client corporation on a project they were proposing. He accepted the assignment with a little trepidation, but he prepared thoroughly and then went and gave an excellent presentation. By the time he got back to the office, the prospective client had phoned his boss and told them that the job was theirs, and how impressed they were with the presentation.

Now, he told me, his company sends him out to meet with clients at least twice a week. He had received two promotions and his income had increased 40 percent in the last twelve months. He had his own office with a secretary and was included in all senior staff meetings. His career was on the fast track and he had never been happier since he learned to confront his fear and overcome it. It was the turning point in his life.

Sales success does not necessarily come from prospecting. It comes from being *eager* to call on new prospects. It comes from being eager to present your product or service as the solution to their problem. It comes from being eager to show them why their objections have no merit. It comes from being eager to ask them to make a buying decision right now. It comes from being eager to ask for referrals and to look for ways to sell more to the same customer. And eagerness comes from the self-esteem that emerges naturally when you have confronted and eliminated the fear of rejection.

SELF-IMAGE MODIFICATION

Your level of self-esteem will largely determine your level of sales, and how happy, positive, and optimistic you feel. Your self-esteem is determined by how much you like, accept, and respect yourself, by how much you feel you are a valuable and worthwhile person. Everything you do to boost your self-esteem will improve every part of your life.

The flip side of self-esteem is your self-efficacy. Your level of self-efficacy is determined by how well you feel you perform at the things you do. The better you perform, the better you feel. And the better you feel, the better you perform. Each one feeds on the other. They are mutually supportive and reinforcing. It is not possible for you to to feel good about yourself and perform poorly, nor is it possible to perform poorly and feel good about yourself. The more consistent your current actions are with the very best person that you can imagine yourself becoming, your self-ideal, the higher will be your self-esteem and the greater will be your self-liking and self-respect.

If you consciously and deliberately act in a positive and professional manner, over and over, you will eventually see yourself as being a positive and professional person. You will feel positive and professional in your work with your prospects and customers. Your actions, which are under your control, will generate the feelings and images consistent with them. People judge you by the way you behave toward them. They largely accept you at face value. They form their estimation of you by the way you carry yourself, and by the way you talk and act when you are with them. If you act like a top sales professional, in every sense of the word, people will treat you as if you are one.

You can take a top salesperson out of a good territory, put him into a poor territory, and he will make just as many sales in the poor territory as he made in the good territory. You can also take a poor salesperson out of a poor territory and put him into an excellent territory, and his sales will stay at the same level they were in the poor territory.

Your self-image, how you *see* yourself, determines your performance in the present. If you see yourself as a salesperson earning $50,000 per year, then no matter what happens to the economy, the competition, or the company, wherever you go, under whatever conditions, you will sell enough to earn $50,000 per year. Your sales results will have very little to do with what happens to you on the outside. They will be largely determined by what is happening to you on the inside, within you as a person.

One of my corporate clients had thirty-one branch offices. One of the offices stood head and shoulders above the others. It led the company in sales results year after year, sometimes outselling the number two office by two or three times.

This office was run by an excellent sales manager who hired and trained top people. He was very selective in recruiting. He chose people based on their attitudes and personalities as much as anything else. Over the years, salespeople who had been average performers in other companies or branches became top salespeople within a few months after joining this particular sales office.

What was the reason? It was quite simple. The new salesperson was immediately surrounded by *winners*, by examples of sales superiority and sales excellence. He saw positive, enthusiastic people, coming in earlier, working harder, and staying later. He got caught up in a sense of teamwork and cooperation. He was surrounded by positive, supportive people. Everyone was excited and proud about being among the top people in the top branch. In no time at all, this enthusiasm infected the new salesperson and he or she began acting the same way—and getting the same results.

Self-image modification is the key to unlocking your sales potential. It is the means by which you program into yourself the thoughts, feelings, and behaviors of the best salespeople everywhere. As you change the way you see yourself, your sales results will begin to improve immediately.

There are seven ways the top salespeople in every business and industry see themselves, think about themselves, and respond to their prospects and customers. You can think of these as seven steps to enhanced self-image or self-esteem. As you shape and modify your self-image so that it is similar to that of the best salespeople, you will begin to see improvements in your sales performance faster and more predictably than by anything else you could do. .

1. See Yourself as Self-Employed

The first and most important quality or self-image, from which all the others flow, is the attitude of **self-employment.** The word "attitude" in aeronautical terms refers to the approach or angle of attack of an airplane with regard to the horizon. Your attitude with regard to self-employment is the way you approach your work, your company, your products and services, your prospects and customers, and everything you do. This attitude of being in charge of your own economic destiny is the critical distinction between high performers and low performers in selling and in almost every other field.

Seeing yourself as the *president* of your own professional sales corporation is the natural extension of your accepting total responsibility for the person you are and for everything that happens to you.

If self-esteem is the first pillar of sales success, then self-responsibility is the second. The more you like yourself, the more you accept responsibility for your life, and the more you accept responsibility for your life, the more you like yourself. The two support each other, and each is impossible without the other.

In our legal system, you can become the president of your own company by simply deciding to do it. You don't need permission from anyone. You don't even need to register your company if you name it after yourself, like "John Jones and Associates." You can then have business cards printed and open a bank account. By making yourself president in your own mind, you take complete charge of your own life. You accept complete accountability for your sales results. You become a completely self-reliant individual, in command and in control of your personal and financial destiny.

When you accept complete responsibility for everything that happens to you, you stop making excuses and blaming others. You say, "If it's to be, it's up to me." Like President Harry Truman, when there is a problem, you say, "The buck stops here." You are the boss. You are the final authority. There is no one beyond you to pass it off to. If sales are good, you get the credit. If the sales are poor, you get the responsibility. You "never complain, never explain."

The top 3 percent of Americans, in all fields, act as if they "own the place." They look upon everything that happens in their companies as though they personally owned 100 percent of the company's stock. They feel personally responsible for customers, sales, quality, profitability, distribution, and cost-effectiveness. They are totally engaged with their work and with their products and services.

Some things in life are optional and some things in life are mandatory. Taking your next winter vacation in Hawaii is optional. You may or may not do it, as conditions permit. But being the president of your own company is *mandatory*. It is not a matter of choice. You already are. The biggest mistake you can ever make in life is to think you work for anyone else but yourself! You are always self-employed, from the day you take your first job until the day you retire. You are your own boss. You are on your own payroll. You ultimately determine your own income. You determine the conditions of your work life. If there is anything about your current situation that you don't like, it is up to you to change it. No one else can or will do it for you.

Would you like to make more money? Then go to the nearest mirror and negotiate with your "boss." The person in the mirror is the one who determines how well you do in your profession and how much you get paid for it.

Here's an exercise for you: On the first day of each month, take your own personal checkbook and write out a check for the amount of money you want to earn that month and date it for the last day of that month. Make it payable to yourself. Sign it. Then, for the rest of the month, concentrate on figuring out *how* you are going to make payroll, just like a company president. If you have to increase your sales in order to increase your paycheck, your job is to figure out how to do it. As the president of your own professional sales corporation, your current employer is your best client. You have not always worked for your current employer, and the way the economy is changing, you may not always work for the same company. But you will always be working for yourself. You will always be self-employed.

By making the decision to go from employee status to being the president of your own personal services corporation, you make the decision to become the primary creative force in your own life. You no longer see yourself as a victim or as a passive recipient of what happens in the economy. You are an active agent. You are in charge. You go out into the workplace and you make your own life and your own living. You sell your services to the highest bidder and you deliver the very best services of which your personal sales corporation is possible. Instead of waiting for things to happen, or hoping that things will happen, you instead *make* things happen.

As the president of your own company, you are in charge of every activity of your business. You are in charge of sales, marketing, production, quality control, distribution, and administration. You are in charge of your own training department, constantly working on yourself to increase the value of what you do so that you can charge more for it in the marketplace. You are in charge of every aspect of your life, both personal and professional.

What is one difference between a professional salesperson and a nonprofessional? The professional salesperson, like a doctor, lawyer, architect, engineer, or dentist, has his own library of books and tapes on selling that he continually adds to as his career develops.

Nonprofessional salespeople, those who view themselves passively, as employees, or victims of the economy, seldom invest in themselves and, in many cases, have no books or tapes on selling at all. They are waiting for their companies to take the time and spend the money to train them to be better. They don't realize that they are in business for themselves. And in not realizing that they are self-employed, their futures become more limited with every passing year.

To sum up, the very first and most important self-image that you must develop is that of seeing yourself as self-responsible and self-employed, as the president of your own professional sales corporation. From this moment onward, see yourself as completely in charge of everything that happens to you, and if you don't like what's going on, then it's up to you to change it or improve it in some way.

2. Consulting Versus Selling

The second self-image possessed by high-achieving salespeople is that they see themselves as **consultants** rather than as salespeople. They see themselves as problem solvers with their products or services rather than as vendors looking for someone who will trade them money for what they have to offer. They do not approach their customers with hat in hand, hoping for a sale. Instead, they approach their *clients* with the attitude that they are consultants calling on their prospects to help them solve a problem or achieve a goal.

Seeing themselves as consultants, they ask questions carefully and listen intently. They focus their attention on understanding the customer's situation so that they can make intelligent recommendations based on what the customer really wants and needs.

As consultants, they recognize that they must be experts and authorities in their fields. They invest time to learn their products and services inside and out. They spend many hours familiarizing themselves with every single detail of what they sell, and of what their competitors sell as well. They know the features and benefits, strengths and weaknesses, advantages and shortcomings, of what they are offering. They have excellent product knowledge, which their customers can sense and which gives both themselves and their customers greater confidence throughout the sales conversation.

Top salespeople, positioning themselves as consultants, see themselves as resources for their clients. They see themselves and carry themselves as advisors, mentors, and friends. They become emotionally involved in their sales relationships and they are intensely concerned that their products or services be the ideal solution to the real needs of the prospects they are dealing with. They differentiate themselves from their competitors by being more concerned with helping their prospects than they are with selling their products or services. Their customers often feel that they care more about them than they care about making a sale. And it's true.

The final element in seeing yourself as a consultant rather than a salesperson, as a problem solver rather than as a vendor of goods and services, is that you take the time to fully understand your customer's situation before you make any recommendations as to what he or she should buy. You do your homework prior to the meeting, and you build on that homework by asking the probing questions that help you understand the customer's needs at a deeper level. You sell by tailoring your product or service in such a way that the customer eventually concludes that what you sell is the ideal solution to his or her current problem.

This ability to present your product as the ideal solution comes from your taking the time to understand the customer's business or situation completely before you make any suggestions or recommendations. This is the hallmark of the consulting approach.

3. Become a Doctor of Selling

The third self-image practiced by the top sales professionals is that they see themselves as **doctors of selling.** They see themselves as professionals, acting in their "patient's" best interests, and bound by a high code of ethics.

As a doctor of selling, you follow the same professional conduct and sequence of activities practiced by medical doctors with their patients when you deal with your customers. You do not allow the client to determine your sequence of activities or dictate your sales process.

The medical process is the same everywhere. Whenever you go to any doctor, of any kind, for any condition, he or she will follow the three-part sequence of *examination, diagnosis,* and *prescription.*

Just as a medical professional would never think of treating you without following these three steps in order, you, as a doctor of selling, would never allow a customer to force you to present your product without your going through your three-stage process as well. This is as applicable to selling magazines door to door as it is to selling oil tankers to Exxon.

In the **examination** phase, you ask excellent questions, carefully prepared, in sequence, which are geared to give you a more thorough knowledge of the patient's condition, or the customer's situation. You would not think of proceeding to the second phase until you had done a thorough examination and you were satisfied that what you had uncovered in your examination indicated that a treatable condition existed.

The second phase is that of *diagnosis*. In the diagnosis stage with a customer, you would repeat back the results of your examination and double-check to be sure that the symptoms you had detected were the real symptoms being experienced by the patient. You would ask additional questions to confirm and corroborate. You and the patient would mutually agree that this diagnosis seems to be an accurate description of the condition or problem.

Once this mutual agreement has been reached, that a treatable condition exists and that you have identified it accurately, you can move on to phase three. This is the **prescription** phase, where you show your customer that your product or service is the best available treatment, taking all the factors of the patient's situation into consideration for the ailment that you have diagnosed. You show the customer that this treatment will take away the pain, or solve the condition. You point out the possible side effects and shortcomings in your product or service offering. And you show that, on balance, what you are suggesting is the best of all possible solutions.

Professionals who sell to customers the same way that doctors treat patients find that their sales activities proceed far more smoothly and result in better sales in less time.

4. Becoming a Strategic Thinker in Sales

Top salespeople are **strategic thinkers.** They set clear goals for what they want and they develop organized plans of action to attain it. They think before they act, and then they act decisively. They plan their work and work their plan. They decide in advance exactly how they are going to get from where they are to where they want to go.

Nonprofessionals throw themselves at the marketplace very much the way a dog throws itself at a passing car, barking and running along frantically, consuming a lot of energy, and accomplishing very little.

But this is not for you. As a professional, you take the time, on weekends, or during the evenings, to think about how you are going to accomplish your sales objectives. You know exactly what you are doing every minute of every day. You have a plan for the week, the month, and the year. You know how much you are going to earn in a given period and how much you are going to have to sell to earn it. You know where your prospects and customers are going to come from, and you have a plan for getting them.

A person with a clear blueprint for sales success, covering every aspect of running his or her own sales business, is far more relaxed, confident, and capable than a person who feels that he or she is "too busy" to plan their activities in advance. When you have a good plan, you have a track to run on. Short-term setbacks and disappointments don't bother you. You take the long view. You are more objective and able to detach yourself from any single call, prospect, or sale. You are able to work steadily, systematically, without haste or waste.

One great benefit of strategic thinking and planning is that engaging in them raises your self-ideal and improves your self-esteem. The more you are focused and concentrated on achieving clear, written goals, the happier you will be with yourself and your career.

5. Getting the Job Done

A key quality of top salespeople is that they are intensely **result-oriented.** In the Gallup Organization's study of successful men and women in America, reported in the "Great American Success Story," the researchers found that the most respected and esteemed Americans, in all fields, were known by their friends and colleagues as being very result-oriented. They were the kinds of people that could always be counted on to do the job properly, and on schedule. This is the way you should see yourself as well.

Top salespeople have two qualities, *empathy* and *ambition*. The quality of empathy causes them to be sensitive to the best interests of their customers. The quality of ambition causes them to be focused on making the sales expected of them. And they manage to keep these two qualities in balance. They are both concerned about the customer and concerned about the sale.

People who fear rejection too much become so overly concerned with not offending the customer that they avoid asking for the order. People who care only about making the sale often offend the customer and end up losing it. Successful salespeople keep their eyes on both balls at the same time.

Intense result-orientation requires that you use your time extremely well. You must make every minute count. You must carefully analyze and separate your high-value prospects and customers from those of lesser value. You must discipline yourself to spend more time with the prospects and customers who represent the greatest potential return on time invested. To develop the self-image of intense result-orientation, you must always remember that your primary job is to sell your products or services and to keep your mind focused on that task in everything you do.

6. Being the Best

Top professional salespeople see themselves as capable of **being the very best** in their fields. They have high levels of ambition and their role models are the very best people in their industries. They identify with the most successful salespeople. They read their books, listen to their tapes, and attend their seminars. In their companies, they spend time with the best people and ask for their advice on books to read, tapes to listen to, and things to do.

High self-esteem triggers the desire to be better and better. A person who really likes himself sets excellence as his standard. He is not afraid to shoot for the stars. He looks at the very best people in the business and he thinks every day about how he could be like them. He then backs his ambitions and aspirations with continuous work on himself and on his profession.

The very act of thinking of yourself as capable of being one of the best salespeople in your industry improves your overall self-concept and boosts your self-esteem. Psychologist Nathaniel Branden calls self-esteem "your reputation with yourself." When you set high standards for yourself, your reputation with yourself improves immediately. You like and respect yourself more. You believe yourself capable of greater accomplishments, and your sales performance improves on the outside as your self-image improves on the inside.

Earlier in this chapter, I pointed out that in every large sales organization there are people who earn $25,000 a year and others who earn $250,000 a year or more. It's important to realize that the person earning $250,000 was once earning $25,000 as well, until he or she made a decision to go all the way to the top. And that decision was the turning point in his or her life.

It's the same with you. The starting point of becoming a top salesperson in your industry is your making an unequivocal, do-or-die decision that you are going to be the best at what you do. That is your number one goal. That is where you are going and your decision to be the best then dictates what you will do each day to achieve it. You recognize that excellence is a journey, not a destination. Once you have made that commitment, you back it with persistence and determination and work on it continuously.

7. Practice Golden Rule Selling

The seventh step to building a better self-image and improving your sales performance is to adopt the Golden Rule mentality. The Golden Rule says, "Do unto others as you would have them do unto you." The Golden Rule mentality in sales says simply that you should "Sell unto others as you would have them sell unto you."

What does this mean? Aren't there all kinds of different personalities that require different approaches and techniques? Well, yes and no. Practicing the Golden Rule in selling simply means that you sell with the same honesty, integrity, understanding, empathy, and thoughtfulness that you would like someone else to use in selling to you.

If you would like a salesperson to take the time to thoroughly understand you and your situation before making a recommendation, you do the same thing with your customers. If you would like a salesperson to give you honest information to help you make an intelligent buying decision, you practice the same with your customer. If you would like a salesperson to be thoroughly knowledgeable about the strengths or weaknesses of his or her product or service, and that of his or her competitors, then you do the same with your product or service and your competitors.

Perhaps the most important part of Golden Rule selling is the emotional component contained in the word "caring." Top sales professionals care about their customers. They care about themselves, their companies, their products and services, and they really care about helping their customers make good buying decisions.

If you think about the very best salespeople you know, you will recognize that they are caring individuals. If you think about your very best customers, you will recall that these are invariably people you care about, and who care about you. When you think about the people you buy from, you will recall that they seem to care about you more than the average. In every part of your business life, you will find that the significant people all have the common denominator of caring as part of their character and their personalities.

Only a genuinely honest person can be caring. Only a person with high self-esteem and self-acceptance can reach out and genuinely care about the well-being of others. Only a person who really cares about his or her customer will take the time to thoroughly prepare prior to every meeting. Only a person who really cares about his or her company will take the time and make the effort to be thoroughly knowledgeable about what the company does and how its resources can help customers satisfy their needs. Only a person who really cares about his product or service will take the time to study it from every angle so that he is thoroughly prepared to give good advice when the time comes.

Seeing yourself as a thoroughly prepared, completely competent, intelligent, warm, and caring sales professional will enable you to perform at your best in every situation. You will have the mind-set of the top salespeople in every industry, and you will get the same results.

SUMMARY

Eighty percent of your sales success will be determined by what is going on in your mind. It will be determined by the way you think about yourself and by the way you feel with regard to yourself and your profession. By improving the way you think about yourself and your capabilities, you improve your performance, sometimes overnight!

Your self-concept, the master program that controls everything you say or do, is complex and multifaceted. It is affected by every suggestive influence in your world, by everything that you think, feel, see, hear, read, touch, taste, and the people and influences around you. It is in a constant state of evolution, under your own direction, moving you either toward or away from your goals and aspirations. You must therefore take complete control of your own inner development to make sure you are moving in a direction of your own choosing.

By accepting complete responsibility and seeing yourself as the president of your own professional sales corporation, you take charge of your thinking, your emotions, and your future. You become the primary creative force in your own life. You become proactive rather than reactive. You make things happen rather than being at the mercy of things that happen.

When you see yourself as a consultant, you carry yourself with a high level of competence and professionalism. Your customers will then accept you at your own valuation. You will sell at a higher level and you will sell more of your product or service, easier than you have before. Above all, your customers will respect you more, and you will like yourself more as well.

As a doctor of selling, you see yourself as a thoroughly trained professional, following a specific sequence of examination, diagnosis, and prescription with each prospect. You carry yourself with confidence. You always act in the best interests of your customers and your customers know it when they deal with you.

When you become a strategic thinker and planner you know *what* you are doing and *why* every minute. You know exactly how much money you intend to make and exactly what mix of sales you will have to make to earn it. You feel very much in control of your activities and your career.

Because of your intense result-orientation, you never take your eyes off the ball. You know that your job is to make sales and to bring in the orders. You make every minute count and you measure the value of everything you do against the sales results that are expected of you. Your consistent sales performance makes you feel like a winner and boosts your self-esteem at the same time.

You see yourself capable of being among the very best salespeople in your industry. You emulate the behaviors of the top salespeople around you. You act on the outside as if you were already an outstanding sales professional on the inside, and as a result, you get continually better at everything you do.

Above all, you practice the Golden Rule in selling. You treat your customers the way you would want to be treated if you were a customer. You focus on helping them solve their problems or achieve their goals. You really care about them, and they sense it.

As a result of these ways of thinking, you mold and shape your self-image so that it is the same as that of the most successful and highest paid salespeople in every industry. You see yourself the way the top people do.

This is the psychology of selling.

2

THE DEVELOPMENT OF
PERSONAL POWER

Selling is hard work. It is one of the most difficult jobs in our economy. As a salesperson, you face continual rejection, potential failure, persistent disappointment, setbacks, obstacles, and difficulties not experienced by most people. Selling is not easy and it has *never* been easy. It never will be easy. It will always be characterized by varying degrees of difficulty, from hard to very hard to very, very hard. And to be successful in selling you must be tough enough to deal with this hardship.

When we talked about the *critical success factors* of selling in the last chapter, the first vital function was that of a positive mental attitude. In selling, your attitude accounts for probably 80 percent of your success. Your attitude is the outward expression of everything that you *are*, and everything that you have become over the course of your lifetime. Your attitude has the greatest single impact on the people you deal with. The development of a positive mental attitude is therefore an indispensable prerequisite for success.

Psychologists have defined the "hardy personality" as the type that is most suited to the rigors of the modern business world. The hardy personality, the personality you need to develop, is resilient, optimistic, tough, strong, and capable of bouncing back continually from temporary disappointments and defeats.

A positive mental attitude is best defined as a *constructive response to stress*. It is a solution-oriented, objective approach to the difficulties and challenges you face each day. A positive mental attitude is expressed in a general optimism toward life and the inevitable ups and downs of earning a living. A positive mental attitude is the most outwardly identifiable quality of a winning human being, and it is the characteristic most closely identified with success in selling of all kinds.

To become and remain *physically* fit, you must engage regularly in a course of *physical exercise*. To become *mentally* fit, to develop the kind of attitude that goes along with success and happiness, you must engage in continuous *mental exercise*. It is a never-ending process. Just as you do not achieve physical fitness and then stop exercising, you cannot achieve mental fitness without working on it continuously, every day, like breathing in and breathing out.

Human beings are *emotional*. Your thoughts are largely determined by your feelings. Your emotions dominate and control virtually everything you do. It is how you *feel* at any given moment that determines your health, your happiness, the quality of your relationships, how well you sleep, your stress levels, and how well you do in professional selling.

The true measure of how well you are doing in life overall is largely determined by how you feel at any given moment. Intelligent people are aware of the fact that the quality of their emotions, how they feel, is the key measure of how effective they are in each area of their lives. One of your aims must be to create within yourself the highest quality of positive emotions in everything you do, and that is the focus of this chapter.

Over the years, I have recruited, trained, managed, or motivated thousands of salespeople, all over the United States, Canada, and many foreign countries. This has been an incredible learning experience for me. I have seen salespeople go from rags to riches, from poverty and depression to affluence and self-confidence. I have worked with salespeople who had been at the bottom of their fields for many years and helped them move quickly to the very top. I have taken salespeople from welfare, unemployment, and even out of jail, and with proper training and motivation showed them how to become superstars in their professions. And in every case, the critical factor was the change that took place in their thinking.

Ralph Waldo Emerson wrote, "A man becomes what he thinks about most of the time." You control what happens to you by controlling the thoughts you think about yourself and the people and situations around you. When you begin to understand and apply the power of your mind, in selling and in life, your future becomes virtually unlimited.

The wonderful thing about mental fitness is that it is as readily achievable as physical fitness if you do the right things in the right way. Many people look at those men and women who are doing extremely well in life and envy them, wishing they had the same talents and opportunities. However, mental fitness is amenable to what I call the Schwarzenegger effect. When you look at Arnold Schwarzenegger, bristling with muscles and physical fitness, you do not say, "Wow, he sure is lucky to be born with such a great physique!"

You know that Arnold Schwarzenegger, six times Mr. Olympia and five times Mr. Universe, has worked out for more than twenty years, investing thousands of hours pumping iron to build his body to the point where he wins prizes, and starring roles in high-grossing movies. However, Arnold Schwarzenegger has the same 610 muscles on his body that you and I have. He may have developed his muscles to a far greater degree than we have, but the muscles that he started out with are exactly the same muscles that you and I have, right now. He has simply worked on them far longer and far more seriously than you or I could ever imagine. He has paid an incredible price to develop himself physically, and he is enjoying the rewards, as well he should.

By the same token, you have the same mental muscles as anyone else. You can develop your mental muscles by engaging in mental exercise, over and over, the same way that Schwarzenegger, or anyone else, has engaged in physical exercise to develop his physical muscles. The main difference that sabotages so many people's best intentions is that the results from physical exercise are immediately visible whereas the results from mental exercise are largely unseen, except for their eventual results.

Many salespeople have developed a fatal flaw in their thinking, one that you must be careful to avoid. It is the tendency to look for the quick fix or the magic bullet that will enable them to escape years of poor work habits and insufficient preparation.

In my seminars, people are constantly coming up to me and asking me for the "secret of success in selling." They ask me for the name of a single tape or a single book, or an explanation of a single method or technique that will enable them to leap ahead in the selling of their product or service.

This attitude, even among intelligent people, is fatal to success. If a person is convinced that there is a quick, easy way to circumvent the long, hard process of preparation necessary for success in any field, instead of buckling down and getting to work, he will be continually looking for shortcuts. The belief in some kind of hidden shortcut will take him down a blind alley. He will never put in the sustained efforts in personal development that are necessary.

THE ATTITUDE THAT GUARANTEES SUCCESS

Dr. Edward Banfield of Harvard University conducted several years of research into upward social mobility in America. He was looking for the reasons some people moved up economically from one generation to the next, while others did not. After years of testing various hypotheses, he finally concluded that success in America, and in any other society, is largely *attitudinal*. It is determined by a person's attitude toward time.

Banfield called this "time perspective." He found that people who became successful invariably had a *long* time perspective. They took the long term into consideration when they planned their daily, weekly, and monthly activities. They thought five, ten, and twenty years into the future. They allocated their resources and made their decisions based on how their choices would affect where they wanted to be several years from now.

On the other hand, Dr. Banfield found that unsuccessful people invariably had *short* time perspectives. They gave little thought to the long term. They were more concerned with immediate gratification than with long-term success and accomplishment. They were more concerned with having fun in the short term than enjoying financial security and success in the long term. Because of this attitude, they made short-term choices that led to long-term hardships.

This discovery is one of the most important in all the research on success. What it means is that, for you to achieve everything of which you are capable, you must take a long-term view of your life and your career. You must be prepared to work hard for many months, even years, to build yourself to the point where you are capable of earning the kind of money that is possible for you, and living the kind of life you most desire. You must be willing to pay the price, over and over, for months and even years before you achieve really worthwhile goals. You must develop long-term perspective.

To be successful in *any* field, you must make a minimum five-year commitment to it. Whatever you are doing, you must be prepared to put your whole heart into it for five solid years, if you are ever going to achieve what is possible for you in that area. It takes a long time for you to become proficient enough at selling your product to succeed in a competitive market, and a long time perspective on your career is essential if you want to get to the top.

Now, this doesn't necessarily mean that you must commit to selling your current product or service for your current company for five solid years before you do something else. Because of the rapid changes in technology, products, and services, you may find yourself selling something different for a different organization in a year or two. What long time perspective means with regard to your sales career is that you must be willing to devote five years to becoming the kind of person, both internally and externally, who is capable of enjoying the good life in professional selling. That long-term commitment, all by itself, will completely transform your attitude toward your education, your daily work, your customers, yourself, your community, and everything else you do. All superior men and women in our society have a long-term perspective with regard to themselves and their lives.

THE SEVEN MENTAL LAWS OF SELLING

You are a mental being. Your life is what your thoughts make it. Every aspect of your life is determined and controlled by the way you think. In effect, you have a body to carry your *brain* around. It is the way you use your mind that, more than anything, determines everything that happens to you. If you change the quality of your thinking, you change the quality of your life.

Because you are primarily mental, your success is largely dependent upon your getting the very most out of yourself by understanding your mental processes and making them work for you. From time immemorial, going back hundreds of years before Christ, the wisest men and women have studied the effect of thought on individual experience. They have derived certain laws and principles of mind, or mental activity, that largely explain almost everything that happens to you. When you understand and apply these laws to your life, you find yourself making progress at a rate that is unbelievable to most people.

There are seven mental laws that apply to selling. When you organize your life and your activities in harmony with these laws, your career will take off. You will feel wonderful about yourself. You will sell easily and well to almost any qualified prospect that you speak to. You will sleep well at night, wake happy and refreshed in the morning, and get along well throughout the day with almost everyone you meet. All your success in life comes from living in harmony with the following mental principles.

1. THE GREAT LAW

As discussed earlier, the first of the mental laws is the Socratic Law of Causality, otherwise called the Law of Cause and Effect. It is so profound and powerful that it is often referred to as the "iron law" of human destiny. It explains virtually everything that happens to you. In its simplest terms, the Law of Cause and Effect states that for every effect in your life, there is a specific cause, or causes. What this means is that if there is anything that you want to see in your life, or see *more* of, and you can define it clearly, you can attain it by tracing it back to the things that cause it and by implementing those causes.

Sales success is an effect. It has specific causes. If you find someone else who is successful in selling and you do the same things that he or she is doing, you will get the same results. If you implement the same *causes* in any area, you will ultimately get the same *effects* that others do. It is not a miracle. It is not dependent upon luck. It is not determined by "being in the right place at the right time."

The Law of Cause and Effect in your professional career says that if you want to be one of the most successful and highly paid salespeople in your field, you must find out what other highly paid and successful salespeople are doing, and do the same thing. If you do the same thing they do, over and over, you will eventually get the same results.

This is a *law*, not a theory or an opinion. It is as unchanging and unavoidable as the law of gravity. The reverse of the Law of Cause and Effect says that if you do *not* implement the same causes as those people who are getting the effects that you desire, you will not get those effects. If you don't do what other successful people are doing, you won't get what other successful people are getting.

The sales field is full of people, the vast majority I'm afraid, who don't understand this simple principle. They think that they can start late, manage their time poorly, take long coffee breaks and lunch hours, spend much of their days socializing, reading the newspaper and wasting time, quit early—and still end up making a good living and having a good life. The average salesperson does not understand that the Law of Cause and Effect is working inexorably, minute by minute, leading people on to either success or failure, depending upon the way they apply it to their activities.

You know that a positive mental attitude is essential to sales success. And your attitude is subject to the Law of Cause and Effect. If you do the specific things that other happy, positive people do, you will develop and maintain a positive attitude as well. It is exactly the same as if you went to a gym each day and exercised to build up your body. You would soon get the same results as anyone else who was engaging in the same kind of physical exercises. You would not be surprised, or consider it to be a miracle or a matter of luck. It is simply the application of the Law of Cause and Effect.

The corollary of the Law of Cause and Effect is the Law of Sowing and Reaping. Whatever you sow, whatever you put into your life and work, you will get out, no more and no less. If you put in hard work, self-discipline, willpower, and persistence, you will get out respect, status, esteem, sales success, and financial achievement. You will reap exactly what you sow.

Another way of stating the Law of Sowing and Reaping is that *you are reaping today the results of what you have sown in the past*. When you look around you at every aspect of your life—your health, your relationships, your income, your level of sales, and your relative happiness and security in your career—what you see is the result of what you have sown, what you have put in, in the past.

If, for any reason, you are not happy with what you are *reaping*, it is up to you to begin immediately to change what you are *sowing*. If you want to get something different out of your life, you have to put something different into it. Just as a farmer has to plant different seeds to get different crops, you have to plant different thoughts and activities if you want to reap different results.

2. THE LAW OF COMPENSATION

Ralph Waldo Emerson, in his essay "Compensation," wrote that each person is compensated in like manner for that which he or she has contributed. The second law, the Law of Compensation, is a restatement of the Law of Sowing and Reaping. It says that you will always be compensated for your efforts and for your contribution, whatever it is, however much or however little.

This Law of Compensation also says that you can never be compensated in the long term for *more* than you put in. Your income today is your compensation for what you have done in the past. If you want to increase your compensation, you must increase the value of your contribution.

Your mental attitude, your feelings of happiness and satisfaction, is also the result of the things that you have put into your own mind. If you fill your mind with thoughts, pictures, and ideas of success, happiness, and optimism, you will be compensated by positive experiences in your daily activities.

Another corollary of the Law of Sowing and Reaping is what is sometimes called the Law of Overcompensation. This law says that great success comes from those who make a habit of putting in *more* than they take out. They do *more* than they are paid for. They are always looking for opportunities to *exceed* expectations. And because they are always *over*compensating, they are always being *over*rewarded with the esteem of their employers and customers and with the financial rewards that go along with great sales success.

One of your main responsibilities in life is to align yourself and your activities with the Law of Cause and Effect (and its corollaries), accepting that it is an inexorable law that always works, whether anyone is looking or not. Your job is to institute the causes that are consistent with the *effects* that you want to enjoy in your life. When you do, you will realize and enjoy the rewards you desire.

3. THE LAW OF CONTROL

The third mental law that applies to selling is the Law of Control. The Law of Control says that "You feel good about yourself to the degree to which you feel you are *in control* of your own life."

The reverse of this law states that you feel *negative* about yourself to the degree to which you feel you are *not* in control of your own life. Psychologists call this the "locus of control" theory. They have found that your level of happiness is largely determined by how much you feel you are in charge of the important areas of your life. You are the very happiest and the most confident when you feel that you are the master of your own destiny, when you feel that you are in the driver's seat of your own life in whatever you are doing.

The *key* to a positive mental attitude is a *sense of control*, a sense that you are the primary creative force in your own life. It is a feeling that you are in complete control of what you do and everything that happens to you. The development and maintenance of this sense of control, this feeling of being in charge, is absolutely essential to your being a positive and optimistic human being.

As you can see immediately, the Law of Cause and Effect and the Law of Control fit neatly together. The Law of Cause and Effect states that there is a *reason* for everything that happens. Nothing happens by chance. If you can take full control of the *causes* of the effects that you want, you can take full control of your life. You can create a positive mental attitude in yourself by doing the things that are consistent with what you want to accomplish.

4. THE LAW OF BELIEF

The fourth mental law that applies to selling is the Law of Belief. This states that "Whatever you believe, with emotion, becomes your reality."

The Law of Belief says that you do not necessarily believe what you *see*, but you *see* what you have already decided to believe. Your beliefs *control* your realities. You always act in a manner consistent with your innermost beliefs and convictions. In fact, you can tell what you, or anyone else, believes by simply looking at what they *do*. It is not what a person says, or hopes, or writes, or wishes, or intends that tells what he or she believes. It is only his or her *actions*. It is only what a person actually *does* that tells you what he truly believes.

This Law of Belief is *reversible* as well. Since your actions are an expression of your beliefs, and you can control your actions, you can indirectly shape and control your beliefs. By engaging in the actions that are consistent with the beliefs that you want to develop, you can eventually develop those beliefs, just as you develop muscles by lifting weights.

For example, if you absolutely believe that you are destined to be a great success in your field of selling, and you walk, talk, act, and behave every single day exactly the way a great success would act, you will eventually develop the mind-set of a high performer in selling. And as you develop the mind-set, you will begin to get the results consistent with it. Your beliefs will become your realities.

Many people say, "When I begin to be successful in selling, I'm really going to invest a lot in myself in learning how to be better."

I hear this at my seminars all the time. It is a sad misunderstanding. It is an attempt to reverse the great laws of life. It is an attempt to have effect before cause, to create reality before creating the belief that is essential to it.

If a person genuinely believes that he is going to be a great success in selling, he will invest in himself continually. He will be determined to become better and better. If a person does *not* invest in continually upgrading his skills, he is saying, by his actions, that he doesn't really *believe* that he will ever be successful. This lack of belief will create the negative fact just as the positive belief creates the positive fact.

The most dangerous of all beliefs are *self-limiting beliefs*. These are beliefs of doubt and fear that hold you back from doing the things that you need to do to enjoy the success that you want to enjoy. These are negative ideas you may have about your lack of ability, intelligence, appearance, creativity, energy level, and skills. Whenever you doubt yourself, whenever you allow a self-limiting belief to hold you back, you give power to that belief. And the more you repeat the self-limiting behavior, the more powerful the negative belief becomes.

One of the most helpful decisions you can make is to *challenge* your self-limiting beliefs. Hold them up to the light of scrutiny and examine them carefully. Refuse to accept them as true. Imagine that your limitations exist only in your *mind* and think about what you would do differently if you had all the talent, intelligence, and ability you could possibly want.

Here is an exercise you can do: Determine a goal that you would like to achieve and then go through this process: First, ask yourself a question like, "Would I like to be one of the top 10 percent of salespeople in my field?"

Your answer to this question should be "Yes!"

Then ask yourself, "Why aren't I already?"

Why aren't you *already* in the top 10 percent? Why aren't you already at the top of your field? What is holding you back? What fears, doubts, and limitations are blocking your progress? Why aren't you achieving your goal at this very moment?

You can ask this question after any statement of a goal or desire and the first answers that will pop into your mind will usually be your self-limiting beliefs. Sometimes people will say that they would be a top salesperson except that "Business is tough," or, "I'm too young," or, "I'm too old," or, "I've got too much education," or, "I've got too little education," or, "I don't have enough experience," or, "I have too much experience."

Mark Twain once wrote, "There are a thousand excuses for every failure, but never a good reason." The way you can test whether or not your excuse is valid is by looking around you and asking, "Is there anyone else with my same limitation who is succeeding in spite of it?"

If you are honest, you will immediately recognize that there are people all around you with difficulties far greater than you have ever imagined who are doing well in spite of them. If others are doing well in spite of a particular limitation, it means that you can as well, by *refusing* to accept that that limitation can hold you back. The minute you stop allowing a doubt or a fear to block your progress, it begins to lose its hold over you. In no time at all, you will have left it behind and it will no longer be a factor in your life.

5. THE LAW OF CONCENTRATION

The fifth mental law that applies to selling, the Law of Concentration, states that "Whatever you *dwell* upon grows and expands in your life." This law says that the more you think about something, the more of your mental capacity is assigned to think about that issue. If you think about something often enough, it eventually dominates your thinking and affects your behavior.

This law contains a double-edged sword. If you think continually about your goals and the things you want to accomplish, these thoughts will come to dominate everything you say and do. If you think about increasing your effectiveness as a salesperson, you will actually find yourself doing the things that make this a reality. The more you concentrate on what you want, the more determined and focused you will become to achieve it. The more you think about them, the faster your goals will appear and expand in the world around you.

But if you make the mistake of thinking about the things you fear, worrying about your bills, trembling about the idea of prospecting or asking for the order, these fears will soon expand and dominate your thinking and behavior instead. You will find yourself making every excuse to avoid doing the very things you need to do to achieve the very success you desire. You unwittingly sabotage yourself by thinking continually about exactly the things you *don't* want to happen. Tragically enough, the more you think about negative things, the more they grow and expand in your life as well.

This Law of Concentration is a natural sublaw of the Laws of Cause and Effect, Control, and Belief. Successful people are those who continually think about what they want. Unsuccessful people are those who allow themselves to think about or dwell on the things they don't want. As a result, successful people get more and more of what they want and unsuccessful people get less and less.

You must keep your mind on the person you want to become and the kind of sales success you want to achieve. To properly utilize this law, you must think continually about the things you want and the kind of person you will have to be to achieve them. You must resolutely keep your mind, your conversation, and your activities off and away from anything that is inconsistent with your desires.

6. THE LAW OF ATTRACTION

The Law of Attraction, the sixth law, affects every part of your selling and helps determine your sales success and your income. It states that "You are a living magnet and you inevitably attract into your life people and circumstances in harmony with your dominant thoughts."

Your thoughts create a force field of mental energy around you. When you are positive and optimistic about yourself, and your product or service, you broadcast a form of positive mental energy that attracts back to you an endless chain of leads, prospects, referrals, and sales opportunities. The better you become at serving your customers, the better customers will be attracted to you for you to serve. Nothing succeeds like success. The more you have, the more you get.

Like attracts like. This is one of the great truths of life. Birds of a feather flock together. Everything you have in life today you have attracted to yourself because of the person you are. You can have more in your life because you can change the person you are, by changing your dominant thoughts.

The more emotion you put into your thinking, the more power your thoughts will have in affecting your life. The more positive, optimistic, and enthusiastic you are about what you are doing, the greater will be the magnetic power of your mind and the faster you will attract into your life the people and opportunities you need to achieve the goals that you have set. The key is for you to control your thoughts every minute of every day.

7. THE LAW OF CORRESPONDENCE

The seventh mental law that applies to selling, the Law of Correspondence, is a paraphrase or restatement of the earlier mental laws. The Law of Correspondence states that "Your outer world is a reflection of your inner world." This is a principle for understanding the human condition. It explains almost every aspect of your life. Your outer world is a *mirror* that reflects back to you the person you are, in every respect. It does not necessarily reflect the person that you *want* to be, or pretend to be, but it reflects back to you the person *you really are* at this moment.

The outward expression of your true character is contained in your general attitude toward people and circumstances. People respond to you based on your attitude toward them. The way people treat you is a reflection of the way you think about yourself and the way you think about them. If you want people to treat you well, to have a positive attitude toward you, then you must have a positive attitude toward them.

Your relationships are a reflection of your true personality and character. They correspond to your inner attitudes of mind. The people you choose to spend time with are a reflection of the person you really are inside. As you become a better person, the people around you will become better as well. By altering your thoughts, you alter the outer aspects of your life.

Your level of success in your field is a reflection of your training, experience, and the way you think about yourself as a salesperson. If you have developed yourself through study and practice to a point where you truly believe that you are excellent at what you do, this attitude will be demonstrated in all of your behavior and it will be reflected back to you by your results.

Remember Emerson: "You become what you think about most of the time," said Emerson. Your primary need is to engage in a mental fitness program, as I will explain in the following pages, that ensures that you are thinking about the person you want to be and the goals you want to accomplish most of the time. By taking deliberate, purposeful, systematic control over every aspect of your thinking, you will take complete control over the entire future of your selling career. You will make more progress in a few months than you may have made in several years. You will be using the real "secrets of success."

SEVEN EXERCISES TO ACHIEVE MENTAL FITNESS

Mental fitness can be defined as a general attitude of optimism, self-confidence, and good cheer that positively affects everything you do. It is very much like physical fitness. To achieve it, you must work on it every day until it becomes a part of your character and personality. This process is not easy, but persistence of effort and consistency in practice will reap results out of all proportion to the work you put in. It is not an exaggeration to say that this process will change your entire life for the better.

There are *seven* mental exercises that you can practice throughout the day to keep yourself positive, optimistic, and mentally fit. These are used by all the highest achieving professionals in every field. They are the mental foundation stones, or building blocks, of great success in every area of endeavor.

The first of these seven exercises is **positive self-talk.** Decades of psychological research have concluded that the way that you talk to yourself determines how you feel more than any other single factor. Your emotional life, or "tone," is determined by the words you say to yourself and believe.

Dr. Martin Seligman of the University of Pennsylvania, in his book *Learned Optimism,* calls this your "explanatory style." Your explanatory style is the way you explain or interpret things to yourself. Practitioners of neurolinguistic programming call this "framing." When you change the way you explain an event to yourself, either positively or negatively, it is called reframing. This is the way you interpret what is going on around you. It consists of your inner dialogue, or the words that race through your mind as you take in information from your environment and process it through your thoughts. As Shakespeare said, "There is nothing either good or bad, but thinking makes it so."

The Sufi master Izrat Kahn once wrote, "Life is a continuous succession of problems." You are surrounded by a world that seems preoccupied by negative events. Every radio and television show, news broadcast, newspaper, and news magazine is crammed full of negative and sensational stories. The conversations of the people around you consist largely of problems, negative gossip, worries, and uncertainties about the future. Most of your discussions with customers revolve around the reasons why they can't buy your product or service because of the negative conditions and limitations that exist in their lives or businesses.

If you are not careful, your habitual way of thinking can become negative as well. You will start to see the negative aspect of a situation before you see the positive. You will start to see the glass as half empty rather than as half full.

Your mind has a natural tendency to slip into a negative way of thinking. You may find yourself talking to yourself about the people you are mad at, who you feel have wronged you in some way. You will be continually rehashing your financial worries, your problems, and your fears. Without meaning to, you can develop a negative attitude that will affect your personality and ultimately your sales. Bit by bit, you can easily slip into becoming a negative, skeptical, and cynical human being. And because most people around you think the same way, you will make the mistake of thinking that this is "just the way the world is."

However, you can counteract this negative tendency by *controlling* your inner dialogue and talking to yourself positively rather than negatively. You can *decide* how you are going to talk to yourself, and thereby control your thoughts and your emotions. The very act of deciding to control your inner dialogue gives you a feeling of optimism and personal power.

Simple self-affirmations you say to yourself as you go about your day can be surprisingly powerful. By repeating positive thoughts to yourself, such as "I like myself!" or, "I love my work!" with enthusiasm and conviction, you drive this message deeper and deeper into your subconscious mind. You feel more positive and optimistic, more in control of your life. You feel more capable and confident. You look forward more to the next call and to the next presentation. The more you repeat these words to yourself, the more you believe them. As you convince yourself that you are "the best," your words, actions, and behaviors begin to *correspond* to this message.

For example, you can't say the words "I like myself!" without actually feeling better about yourself. The more you say "I like myself!" the more you will actually like and respect yourself, regardless of what is going on around you. You will feel happier. You will be more positive. You will be more optimistic. You will perform better at everything you attempt.

My favorite combination of affirmations, which I've used for years, is, "I like myself and I love my work!" These words are especially powerful for starting out your day, or mentally preparing yourself for a sales call.

Controlling your inner dialogue, the way you talk to yourself, is a key to peak performance. It is the way you take charge of your mind and keep it focused on the way you want things to be, rather than the way things are at the moment. It is the way you overcome difficulties and obstacles and keep yourself thinking and feeling positive most of the time.

Remember, talk to yourself the way you want to be, not the way you are. Tell the truth, in advance!

The second exercise for building mental fitness is **positive imaging.** Because your outer world is a reflection of your inner world, all improvement in your outer world begins with an improvement in your mental pictures. Positive imaging, or positive visualization, is the way you create clear, vivid pictures in your mind that are consistent with the experiences you want to enjoy in your work.

Visualize yourself as being confident, positive, determined, and completely successful. Visualize yourself living in the kind of house you want to live in. See yourself weighing your ideal weight and dressing in the kind of clothes you most admire. See yourself driving your dream car and taking your dream vacations. Flood your mind with pictures of success and affluence at every opportunity.

When successful, happy, productive people are interviewed, and asked what it is that they are thinking about and visualizing, they always reply that they think about and imagine the things that they want to have in their lives. They are very disciplined in their thinking in that they *refuse* to dwell upon or imagine experiences or outcomes they don't want.

Denis Waitley once said, "Your imagination is your preview of life's coming attractions." Because of the Law of Concentration, you have a natural tendency to think more and more about the things you imagine. And the more you think about these things, positive or negative, the more you will say and do the things necessary to bring them into your reality. Your pictures crystallize and become parts of your life. You control your future by the thoughts you think and the images you hold today.

All improvement in your life and work begins with an improvement in your mental pictures. By the Law of Correspondence, your outer world of experience will tend to mirror back to you your inner images and pictures. If you change your inner pictures, you will change your outer realities.

The third exercise in mental fitness is to feed your mind continually with **positive mental food.** Since you become what you think about, your attitude, your personality, your values, and your emotions are largely the result of the mental "food" that you are feeding into your mind on a minute-by-minute basis.

You know that your physical body, your health, your levels of energy, your digestion, your skin, and so on are all determined by the food you eat. Your thoughts, feelings, attitudes, and expectations are likewise determined by the *mental* food you take in. The way you think and feel will determine your conduct and your behavior, which will in turn dictate your actions and your results. Because of the Law of Cause and Effect, of action and reaction, it could not be otherwise.

Every suggestive influence around you has an impact, great or small, on your thinking and on your subsequent behavior. The television shows you watch, the radio programs you listen to, the newspapers and magazines you read, and all the other influences you pay attention to are having a cumulative impact on the way you think and the person you are becoming.

If you want to be perfectly healthy physically, you would eat only the healthiest and most nutritious foods. If you want to be mentally fit and have a positive mental attitude throughout the day, you must feed your mind with highly nutritious *mental* foods as well.

To perform at your best, you must take in mental protein rather than mental candy. You must take in rich, nourishing, healthy ideas and information from books, tapes, and videos rather than mental junk food from mindless television shows, radio babble (chewing gum for the ears), and the pages of useless information in magazines and newspapers. Be definite, disciplined, and specific about the material that you allow your mind to dwell upon because it is controlling your destiny. The mental food you take into today, by the Laws of Cause and Effect and Correspondence, is determining the person you become and the results you ultimately accomplish.

The fourth exercise in attaining mental fitness is to associate with **positive people.** The people you habitually associate with, both in person and in your thinking, have a tremendous effect on the person you become. Your goal must be to "fly with the eagles." Your aim should be to associate with the very best people you know. You must get around *winners* and simultaneously stay away from people who are going nowhere with their lives.

Perhaps 80 percent of the people around you, because of a variety of factors over which you have no control, are not particularly positive, ambitious, goal-oriented, or successful. They are not accomplishing very much with their lives. They waste their time throughout the day, and they grumble and complain at every opportunity. And if you associate with this type of person, you will become very much like them.

Dr. David McClelland, in his years of research at Harvard, concluded that your choice of a "reference group" would, more than any other factor, determine what happened to you in life. Your reference group is made up of the people you identify with, associate with, and consider yourself similar to.

Your family is your first reference group. They exert an inordinate influence on the way you think about yourself and the world around you. If you were brought up by positive, supportive parents who encouraged you to think highly of yourself and your possibilities, you will naturally seek out and be attracted to other similar people when you grow up. You will identify with them because you feel that you have a lot in common with them. You will refer to them in your thinking when you make decisions or take action. They will be your reference group.

When you get older, your peers at school and college become the members of your reference group. The people at your church and at your place of work are members of your reference group. The social activities and political parties that you get involved in become part of your reference group. Over time, you develop a picture in your mind of the person you are, and of the kind of people who are similar to yourself. You then take on the same values, attitudes, behaviors, manners of dress, philosophies, ideologies, and beliefs of these people.

Associating with positive people makes you more positive. Associating with negative people will make you more negative. A successful, achievement-oriented reference group, either in person or in the people you read about and think about, will cause you to be successful and achievement-oriented as well. A negative, aimless reference group will cause you to be negative and aimless, just as they are. Your choices of friends and associates largely determines your future.

Because of the inordinate influence of your reference group, you must get away and stay away from negative people. You must make a conscious decision to avoid people you neither respect, admire, or want to be like. You must choose the people you spend time with carefully because they are having an effect on your thinking, your personality, and on everything that happens to you.

Almost all successful salespeople are described by their peers as loners. This does not mean that they are *lonely*, or that they spend their time alone. It simply means that they are very selective about the people they associate with. They refuse to spend time with negative people. They avoid them at all costs. They realize that negative people, "toxic people," actually *drain* them of energy and enthusiasm and make them feel tired and pessimistic.

Positive people, on the other hand, make you feel happy and optimistic. They are positive and cheerful. They are upbeat and encouraging, and they are always talking about opportunities and possibilities. You enjoy their company and you come away from them feeling better about yourself and your work.

Your goal should be to become the kind of person that others enjoy being around. As you become a more positive and attractive person, you will find yourself attracting other positive, attractive people to you.

The fifth exercise in developing mental fitness is **positive training and development**. The more new ideas and information that you take in about how to be more effective in selling, and the more you *think* about these ideas, the more you will embody them in everything you do. Your outer world will become like your inner world. You will become what you think about. Whatever you concentrate on will grow and expand in your reality. The more you read books, listen to tapes, and attend seminars to learn to be a better salesperson, the more you will walk, talk, think, and feel like one of the best in your field. And it will be no surprise that you begin to get the same results that outstanding salespeople get.

School is never out for the professional. You never stop learning. In fact, it is only when you finish your formal education that your real schooling begins. At the end of high school or college, you go through a *commencement* ceremony. To "commence" means to begin, not to end. Many people, when they leave school, resolve to never read another book as long as they live. I have met salespeople who are thirty-five and forty years old who have *kept* that promise. They stopped learning and growing when they left school because they didn't realize that education is a lifelong process. And in most cases, they plateaued in their careers years ago.

Continuous training and development makes you more optimistic, gives you a greater sense of competence and control, attracts better prospects and customers into your circle of influence, and increases your belief in yourself and your future. And by working on yourself, you can learn anything you need to know to achieve any goal you can set for yourself. Continuous self-improvement is your springboard to the future.

The sixth exercise in achieving mental fitness is to practice **positive health habits.** Selling is an extremely demanding job. It requires enormous amounts of physical, mental, and emotional energy to do it well day after day. Because of this, virtually all successful salespeople seem to have higher than average levels of energy and enthusiasm. To be among the best, you must take excellent care of your health throughout your career. You must organize your activities to make sure you have high levels of energy and vitality every minute of every sales day. Sometimes, even just a small change in your diet or exercise regimen can produce a substantial increase in your energy level.

First, *eliminate* as many *fats* of all kinds from your diet as quickly as possible. Fats have been found to be the biggest single enemy of healthy living. They are closely associated with a variety of degenerative illnesses, as well as obesity, high blood pressure, heart problems, and overall feelings of fatigue and depression. To reduce your fat intake, use the principle of substitution and instead eat more low-fat or nonfat foods, such as fruits, vegetables, pastas, and whole grain products.

The second key to higher levels of health and energy is *regular exercise*. You can get all the exercise you need by going for a two-mile walk, five days a week. You can also swim, run, cycle, play tennis, downhill ski, go cross-country skiing, or a combination of these at a health club or on equipment that simulates these exercises.

When you combine physical exercise with a lighter, leaner diet, you will feel healthier, happier, and more energetic. You will sleep better and wake more refreshed. You will be brighter and more alert. You will perform at your best. When you feel happy and energetic, you will be more positive and optimistic with your customers. You will be a more likable person. This positive personality will translate into more and better sales almost immediately.

The third key to higher levels of energy is to *drink lots of water* during the course of the day. The average person loses a gallon or more (eight glasses) of water a day in normal activities. When you drink lots of water, you irrigate and cleanse your whole body, flushing away toxins, salts, sugars, and other impurities, improving your health and increasing your energy. You need to replace this water to avoid dehydration and the tiredness that accompanies it.

The fourth key to high levels of health and energy is *ample rest*. You need seven to eight hour of sleep each night if you are going to sell effectively during the day. You need adequate sleep to replenish the mental and physical energy you burn up in highly demanding sales activities. You need sufficient sleep to build up your immune system so that you do not catch colds or other illnesses.

Discipline yourself to turn off the television, put away the newspapers, and go to bed *early* enough to get sufficient rest the night before every selling day. This, as much as anything else, will ensure that you maintain the energy and enthusiasm you need to continue performing at your best in the face of the inevitable rejections and disappointments you experience each day.

The seventh exercise for mental fitness is **positive action.** The *faster* you move, the more energy you have. The faster you move, the more positive you feel. The faster you move, the more people you see and the more experience you get, and therefore the faster you learn. The faster you move, the more prospects you talk to and the more of them that will turn into customers. The faster you move, the more enthusiastic you will be and the more you will feel in control of your life.

Fast tempo is essential to success. Set your pace for action. Develop a sense of urgency. When you have a job to do, get on with it. Do it now! Get going! Move fast, and then faster!

By moving faster, you will achieve greater success in a shorter period of time. This success will motivate you and make you more positive and enthusiastic about what you do. And this enthusiasm will then cause you to move faster, which will in turn increase your sales success, and so on. The very decision to start a little earlier, work a little harder, stay a little later, and move a little more quickly through the day will reinforce all the other methods for achieving mental fitness ideas discussed here. It will guarantee you a great career in professional selling.

THE CARDINAL RULE OF SELLING

The Law of Accumulation says that all great success and achievement is an accumulation of hundreds, if not thousands, of efforts that most people never see or appreciate. This law states that your great successes in life will come as the result of weeks, months, and even years of hard work preparing yourself and developing your skills in ways that no one is even aware of.

The corollary of the Law of Accumulation is that everything counts. This is the cardinal rule of selling. Everything counts! Successful men and women are those who believe and accept that everything counts, and they live their lives accordingly. Unsuccessful men and women hope that it doesn't. They try to convince themselves that it doesn't matter. And they find themselves experiencing endless frustration and difficulties.

Robert Ringer, author of *Million Dollar Habits*, calls this the "reality habit." He says that successful people are those who refuse to engage in self-delusion. They refuse to try to believe things that are not true. They make a habit of facing reality as it is, not as they wish or fantasize it could be.

Abraham Maslow, the groundbreaking psychologist, in his study of self-actualizing men and women, concluded that one of their predominant qualities was that of intellectual honesty, or objectivity. Highly developed men and women tended to be completely straightforward with themselves and their lives. They were rigorously objective and honest about their strengths and weaknesses. They knew what they needed to learn and who they had to become to achieve the things they wanted to achieve. They avoided all temptations to fool themselves or to pretend that things were not as they were. And as a result of this attitude, they were some of the healthiest, happiest, and highest performing men and women in society.

Often salespeople come to me and complain that being successful in selling seems to be extraordinarily difficult. They complain that there are too many things that they would have to do if they wanted to move to the top of their fields. They ask me why it is that it is so complicated, and isn't there an easier way?

The fact is that success in any field is very *rare*. Only one in twenty people working today will be financially independent when they retire. The other nineteen will either have some savings put aside, be dependent on relatives or pensions, or be flat broke and still working. The odds against you achieving your goals of financial independence are therefore twenty to one. You need to do everything you possibly can during your prime working years to put the odds in your favor. And perhaps the most important thing you can do is to realize, from this moment forward, that *everything counts*.

When you fully accept this rule for success in selling and in life, you take complete control of your future. You stop relying on luck or chance. Instead of hoping that you will have a good day, you instead go out and *make* it a good day.

THE DEVELOPMENT OF PERSONAL POWER

Selling is a mental game. To succeed at it you need mental strength, mental power. You need to exercise for strength, endurance, and mental flexibility every single day. Here are several things you can do to develop the kind of personal power that you need to be more persistent and persuasive.

First, as we discussed in Chapter 1, **you must take full responsibility for yourself.** You must accept that you are where you are and what you are because of yourself. You are completely responsible for your results. You are totally accountable for your level of sales. You are the president of your own life, your own career, and your own professional sales corporation.

The most powerful words you can use to take control of your thoughts and emotions are "I am responsible!" These words short-circuit any anger you may experience, and neutralize your negative emotions. They eliminate worry and make you start thinking in terms of being proactive rather than reactive. "I am responsible" enables you to seize the reins of your own life.

As a fully responsible person, you refuse to make excuses, or to blame anyone else for anything. If you are successful, you take the credit, and if you are unsuccessful, you accept the responsibility.

Responsibility always looks *forward*, to the future. Responsibility always thinks in terms of solutions rather than problems. A responsible person focuses on fixing the problem rather than the blame. As a completely responsible person, when things go wrong, you immediately stop and say, "I am responsible," and then you begin thinking not about what has happened but about what you can do next.

Responsible people focus on the opportunities of the future rather than the problems of the past. They don't cry over spilled milk. They realize that very little can be done about what has happened. They look into every setback or obstacle for the valuable lesson and they say, "Next time, I'll . . . "

The motto of the responsible person is "If it's to be, it's up to me." This attitude of self-responsibility goes hand in hand with high performance and personal effectiveness in every area of professional selling.

The second requirement for the development of personal power is **a positive explanatory style.** This simply means that you make a point of interpreting the things that happen to you in a positive way. You explain away difficulties and setbacks as containing valuable lessons or opportunities. You refuse to see problems as permanent, or indicative of a personal lack of ability. You shrug your shoulders and tell yourself and others, "Next time it will be different."

Optimistic people make a habit of explaining things to themselves in a positive way. Pessimistic people explain things to themselves in a negative way. Optimistic people brush problems aside and refuse to dwell upon them. Pessimistic people consider problems to be proof of their shortcomings or evidence of the failings of their product or service. Optimistic people think about what they can do to make things better while pessimistic people dwell on what went wrong, becoming demoralized and depressed in the process.

The third step in developing personal power is for you to make a **commitment to excellence.** You must be determined to be the best in your field. You must set excellence as your standard and strive toward it continually.

Most people, because of low self-esteem, never allow themselves to think about being really good at their work. Even when they make the extra effort necessary to achieve some sort of success, they tend to dismiss it or downplay it as being lucky or accidental. They don't like and respect themselves enough to embrace the idea that they have the capacity to be outstanding in their chosen field of selling.

One of the worst aspects of our upbringing revolves around the question of *deservingness.* Many of us don't feel that we deserve the kind of success that we desire. We work hard on the outside to achieve our goals, to make our quotas, and to earn our incomes, but on the inside, we don't really feel that we are entitled to it. We are often held back by feelings of inferiority and inadequacy. In some cases, these feelings can be so overwhelming that we don't even try in the first place.

Deservingness is an issue you must address and deal with sooner or later. You must accept that you deserve all the success that you can honestly acquire through hard work and determination. You deserve all the good things that you can hope for and imagine for yourself. You deserve all the rewards that you can earn through self-development and applied effort. You are as good as anyone else and everything that anyone else can achieve is possible for you. The only obstacles to the health, happiness, and prosperity you desire are within you, not without.

Life is a process of two steps forward and one step back. We make a little progress and we make a little regress. We advance and we stall. We do a few right things and we do a few things wrong. But the commitment to excellence is a lifelong quest. It is a road that you set off on and stay on throughout your career.

I have worked with many of the top salespeople in America, as well as in many other countries. Every one of them became successful only after they made the conscious commitment to be the best in their field. Once they had made that decision and that commitment, they put their heads down and went to work.

Sometimes it took months, and even years, for them to gradually move ahead of the other salespeople in their field, but move ahead they eventually did. Once they got ahead, they kept working on themselves, widening the lead. Eventually they moved to the top of their fields where they were honored and esteemed by everyone around them. And it all began with their making a conscious commitment to excellence.

The fourth requirement for personal power is **persistence.** It is your willingness to stay at it longer and work at it harder than anyone else that often makes the critical difference in your life. The person with greater persistence will gradually pass every other person in the business for no other reason than that he or she is too determined to give up.

Persistence is really a combination of many qualities condensed into one. Persistence is your measure of your belief in yourself and your ability to succeed. You can tell how much faith you have in yourself by observing your willingness to persist when the going gets tough.

Persistence is self-discipline in action. It is the measure of your character. You can tell how much self-discipline you have by watching what you do when you are tired and discouraged and you feel like throwing in the towel.

Persistence is allied with courage. If the first part of courage is the ability *to begin* in the face of uncertainty, then the second part of courage is the ability *to endure* when you have no assurance of success. And as C. S. Lewis wrote, "Courage is not simply one of the virtues, but the form of every virtue at its testing point." Without persistence there can be no success.

The fifth requirement for personal power is **integrity,** being perfectly honest with yourself and others. Honesty requires that you be true to yourself and to the very best that is in you. Only then can you be completely straightforward with everyone else.

Honesty is the most important quality that customers look for when deciding on a long-term purchase. This is why all top salespeople are completely honest in everything they do and say. They would never sell a product or service they did not believe was right for a particular customer. And their customers know it.

Just as trust is the foundation quality of all relationships, integrity is the practice and expression of that trust. All top salespeople have such good relationships with their customers that often their customers buy from them without even asking the price. Their customers know that, whatever the price, it is fair and honest or the salesperson would not recommend the purchase.

Integrity is essential to building *self-confidence*. It is amazing how much better you feel about yourself when you are being true to yourself and everyone around you. Men and women with integrity develop a deep and abiding belief in themselves and in the value of what they are doing. They become formidable salespeople who are continually recommended and referred to others.

The sixth requirement for personal power is an **attitude of gratitude.** This attitude is based on the Law of Increasing Returns, which states, "The more you give thanks for what you *have*, the *more* you will have to give thanks for."

An attitude of gratitude is a hallmark of the fully integrated personality. A person with an attitude of gratitude goes through his daily life looking for the good in every situation, and giving thanks for his blessings rather than grumbling about his problems.

An attitude of gratitude goes hand in hand with a positive mental attitude. The salesperson with this attitude is deeply appreciative for the many aspects of his life. He appreciates his health, his family, his home, his car, and his work. He appreciates his company and the products and services that he represents. He appreciates the opportunity he has to serve his customers and to make a good living at it. He continually says "thank you" to other people for the little things they do for him.

A thankful person is essentially an optimistic person. He or she is continually cheerful. No matter what happens, the thankful person always has something kind or positive to say. Even with the most difficult prospects, the thankful person is always friendly and appreciative. He or she is the kind of person who sends a thank-you card to even the most difficult person for even the must cursory contact.

Luckily, an attitude of gratitude is habit forming. When you practice being thankful and appreciative, even for a short time, thankfulness begins to become a part of your personality. You become a warmer and more friendly person. You find yourself more welcome wherever you go. People want to do business with you and your friends want to socialize with you. You are recommended and referred to other prospects. Every aspect of your life improves.

When you are with your prospects or customers, never give in to the temptation to share your problems or personal concerns with them. Even if you are going through a difficult period in your personal or business life, keep it to yourself. When people ask you how things are going, tell them that "Business is wonderful." Tell them that you "Couldn't be better." Tell them that you "Really enjoy what you do." And the more you tell people how happy you are with your life and your work, the more you will come to believe it as well. Soon, you will be unable to tell the difference between your attitude and your reality.

The seventh requirement for personal power is **clear, specific goals.** To achieve your personal best, you need written sales and income goals for each month, each quarter, and each year. You need goals for your health, your home, and your family. You need financial goals, personal development goals, and spiritual goals. You need a blueprint for your life just as you would have a blueprint for a new home. You need a plan that you work on every single day.

The predominant characteristic of the best salespeople in all fields is **intensity of purpose.** Holding equal for age, education, experience, and intelligence, the salesperson who moves to the front is always the one who desires success *more* than the other person. Intensity of purpose goes hand in hand with great success and achievement in sales and in all walks of life. And you develop this intense desire by writing your goals down, making written plans for their accomplishment, and then working your plan every day.

A beneficial aspect of goals is their incredible power to make you an irresistible force in selling. Goals unlock your positive mind. They release energy and ideas for goal attainment. Clear goals enable you to focus your attention and concentrate your energies. Goals give you vision and clarity. They give you the courage to begin and the persistence to endure. With clear, written goals, you can accomplish more in a year or two than the average person might accomplish in ten years, or twenty.

Goals have other powers as well. They enable you to align your life in harmony with all the mental laws. Goals enable you to apply the Law of Cause and Effect to your greatest advantage. Your goal is the definition of the effect you desire, and when you are clear about the effect, it is relatively simple to trace back to the causes you will have to implement to achieve it.

Goals give you control over your life. With goals, you can control the direction of change. With goals you can make better decisions and better choices. Goals enable you to more intelligently allocate your time and your resources. When you are absolutely clear about what you want, you are more calm and confident in everything you do.

Goals intensify your belief that success is possible for you. When you crystallize a goal and write it down, you overcome your natural doubts and fears. You begin to believe that it is possible for you to achieve it. As your belief begins to grow, you do more and more of the things consistent with making your goal a reality. Soon, the line blurs between your hope of achieving the goal and your belief that it is attainable. Your conviction and your commitment deepen, and in no time at all your goals begin to appear in the world around you.

The Law of Concentration says that "Whatever you dwell upon grows and expands in your reality." What should you dwell upon? Your goals! The more you think about your goals, the more of your mental powers are assigned to making those goals a reality.

When Sir Isaac Newton was asked why it was that he had made such great contributions to physics and mathematics in his lifetime, he said, "By thinking of nothing else." When you also reach the point where you think of nothing else but your goals, you will stop having them, and your goals will have you. From that point forward, you will accomplish more than you ever have before.

Your attitude of confident expectations also influences the behavior of the people around you. You activate the Law of Attraction by becoming a living magnet for the people and circumstances that can help you achieve your goal. The more you think about your goals, the more you intensify your mental vibrations. You send out waves of thought energy that attract into your life opportunities and events that help make your goals a reality. Your customers will often buy from you just because you so confidently expect them to.

By the Law of Correspondence, your outer world will come to reflect your dominant thoughts, ideas, and pictures. Your outer world will correspond to your inner world. Whatever you hold in your mind on a continuing basis will begin to materialize in the world around you. The more you think about your goals, about how you can achieve them, and about how much you will enjoy them when they are accomplished, the more your outer world of realization will conform to your inner world. "As within, so without."

Happiness has been defined as "the progressive realization of a worthy ideal or goal." Every step that you take in the direction of your goal increases your happiness, your enthusiasm, and your self-confidence. By working on your goals every day, you gradually develop within yourself an absolute conviction that you will attain them. Your daily progress enables you to brush your fears aside and crush your doubts underfoot. You move from positive thinking to positive knowing. Nothing can stop you.

PEAK PERFORMANCE SELLING

In 1895, at his clinic in Geneva, Switzerland, a man named Dr. Emile Coué developed a psychological technique for his patients that began a revolution in modern medicine. It was simple but it proved to be very powerful. He taught each of his patients to repeat regularly, "Every day in every way, I'm getting better and better."

Although this method of positive self-talk, or affirmation, was initially dismissed as being simplistic and ineffective, the results were undeniable. Dr. Coué's clinic began to experience cure rates as much as 500 percent greater than those being experienced by similar patients with similar illnesses at other clinics and hospitals throughout Europe.

In 1905, a German doctor, Johannes Schultz, building on the work of Emile Coué, developed a treatment process called "autogenic conditioning." He combined relaxation, positive affirmations, and creative visualization to help patients reprogram their subconscious minds. These improvements in thinking brought about rapid changes in their attitude toward themselves, which translated into rapid improvements in their condition.

Over the years, especially in Eastern Europe and Russia, Dr. Schultz's work led to the development of more advanced methods of autogenic conditioning, especially in the areas of teaching and sports.

Today, autogenic conditioning is a part of what is called sports psychology, and virtually all top athletes, in every sport, are taught mental conditioning techniques to improve their performance in competition. An Olympic sports psychologist wrote recently, "By the end of this century, there will be those athletes who are using sports psychology and there will be those athletes who are no longer in competition."

All top athletes use advanced forms of autogenic or psychological conditioning to give them the winning edge in world-class competition, where success can be determined by fractions of an inch or a second. Top "sales athletes" can use these same techniques as well to dramatically improve their performance in selling situations.

Everything we've talked about in this chapter so far is a form of *mental conditioning*. Every recommendation has been a particular exercise that you can use to develop a stronger and more powerful sales personality. Every idea has been aimed at helping give you the winning edge that will enable you to perform at superstar levels in selling in competitive markets.

MENTAL REHEARSAL IN SELLING

The technique of **mental rehearsal** that you are about to learn can be practiced in a variety of situations. It is simple, straightforward, and effective. It brings about immediate improvement in performance. It increases your self-confidence, your sense of control, and your creativity. It enables you to be calm, poised, and relaxed in any sales situation. It prepares you to perform at your best when you meet with a prospect.

You should use mental rehearsal prior to every sales call. It is the same as warming up physically before an athletic competition. It is a way of warming up mentally before calling on a customer.

Here's how it works, in five steps: First, take a few seconds to *think about a recent sales success*. Recall a sales conversation that ended exactly as you wanted it to. Let your mind dwell on a time when you performed at your best. Think about the positive way the customer responded to you. Remember how the meeting ended with the customer signing the contract or the check and your leaving with the sale.

Your subconscious mind cannot tell the difference between a real experience and one that you vividly imagine, or remember. If you have *one* successful selling experience, and you think about it repeatedly, each time you recall it your subconscious mind records it as a new experience. When you recall a specific success experience repeatedly, your subconscious mind believes that you are having an entire series of success experiences.

This remarkable aspect of the way your mind works can help you or hurt you. All salespeople have negative experiences of rejection, rudeness, and temporary failure, but instead of brushing them aside, many make the mistake of continually thinking about them. Sometimes they review and rehash them with others. They go home and talk about them with their spouses. And each time they think about the unsuccessful experience, their subconscious mind records it as though they were having it again. Soon the very thought of selling triggers fears of failure and rejection.

The first step in mental rehearsal is therefore for you to think about a sales experience, or even imagine a sales experience, that makes you feel happy and successful. *Dwell* on a sales experience where you felt calm, confident, and in control. Feed that success experience into your subconscious mind by reliving it repeatedly in as vivid detail as possible in your conscious mind. This mental picture will eventually be accepted as a command by your subconscious mind to repeat the success experience in your next sales call.

Second, prior to the sales call, close your eyes, *breathe deeply*, and relax. You can do this wherever it's convenient—in your car, before you leave the office, before you leave home, or even in the washroom.

Deep breathing is a powerful form of mental control that relaxes both your mind and your body, gives you greater clarity and creativity, and prepares you to be at your best when you go into the sales meeting. When you breathe deeply, fill your lungs completely so that you can feel them pressing on your diaphragm. Hold this breath for a few seconds and then let it out slowly. Repeat this exercise five to seven times and you will become completely calm. Your mind will relax. You will then be ready to program yourself for how you want to perform in the upcoming sales call.

Step three is for you to *visualize* the exact desired outcome of the coming meeting. With your eyes closed, see yourself performing at your best. See your customer smiling and relaxed. Picture yourself in complete control of the situation and, especially, see the end of the conversation with the customer signing the order or check, or confirming his or her decision to make the purchase.

It's very important that you see the final outcome that you desire, not just the process. When you visualize the ideal outcome, you instruct your subconscious mind to guide you to do and say whatever is necessary to make the sale. If you only visualize the sales process, you could find yourself having a very pleasant sales conversation that ends with no sale.

Step four is for you to create an *affirmative statement* describing what you want to achieve. Say something like, "I believe this meeting will turn out perfectly!" Sometimes, prior to a sales call, I will visualize and affirm several times, "This is going to be a great meeting!" Whichever words you choose, repeat them a few times while you hold the picture of the ideal sales call in your mind. Keep the words and the picture clear until you can recall them at will.

The fifth step in mental rehearsal, the key to making the whole process work, is for you to *get the feeling*. Exhale, smile, relax, and *release* the entire process. Imagine that the sales call has already ended exactly as you visualized. The transaction has concluded successfully and you have achieved all your goals. Smile to yourself and feel the exact same pleasure you would experience if the customer had already bought and you were on your way to your next call.

The most important part of this entire mental conditioning process is your bringing yourself to the point where you convince your subconscious mind that you have already made a successful sales call. This mental image, and the *feeling* that goes with it, will make you more calm and confident. You will be less anxious and stressed. You will find yourself doing and saying exactly the right things at the right time to bring about the desired results that you have already prepared for.

When you go into the meeting with the prospect, you should keep your physical movements consistent with the feelings of calmness and confidence you have practiced during mental rehearsal. Lift your head, raise your chin, and smile. It is impossible to feel nervous and anxious when you hold your head high. Straighten your back and shoulders and you will feel ready for anything.

As you travel to each sales meeting, imagine that you have just closed a million-dollar sale. Think about yourself as one of the finest salespeople in your industry. Relax and release any tension you may have about the outcome of this presentation. If you feel any nervousness returning, take a deep breath, hold it, and let it out slowly. See yourself performing at your best. Remember, you will always behave on the outside consistent with the picture you have of yourself on the inside.

When you combine your internal preparation with your external behavior, by the Law of Correspondence, each will be an expression of the other. Your subconscious mind will then coordinate your thoughts, feelings, and words so that you will perform like a top salesperson.

This process of mental rehearsal is very powerful. You should go through the five steps prior to every sales call. Take a few moments to prepare mentally and emotionally before you go in. To review: First, think of a recent success experience, real or imagined. Second, close your eyes, take a deep breath, and relax. Third, visualize yourself performing perfectly in the sales meeting. Fourth, describe exactly the result you desire. And fifth, get the feeling of success and the satisfaction that goes with it. Then, exhale deeply, relax, smile, and open your eyes. You are now ready for one of the best performances of your life.

If you have a major sales presentation coming up in a few days, you can practice this exercise each night before you go to sleep. Every time you think about the upcoming meeting, take a few seconds to breathe deeply and visualize perfect performance. Affirm exactly the outcome you want. Get the feeling. The more often you go through this process of mental rehearsal, the more relaxed and confident you will become. At the actual meeting, you will be ready to perform at your best.

Mental rehearsal is a breakthrough technique that will give you the winning edge in selling. Because it unlocks the powers of your subconscious mind, mental rehearsal enables you to be the very best salesperson you can possibly be in every situation.

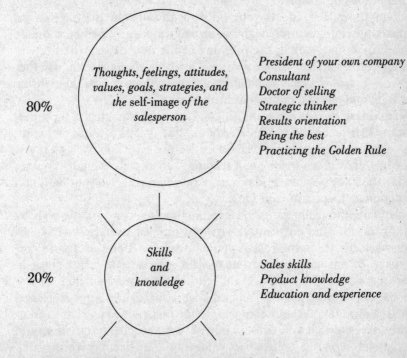

Selling is 80% psychological, only 20% technical

SUMMARY

Selling today is an incredibly complex process, and it will only become more so in the months and years ahead. Fully 80 percent of your success in selling will derive from the quality of your personality in your interactions with your prospects and customers. People will buy from you because they like you and because they feel good being around you. And people will always respond to you in direct proportion to the kind of person you are. Their attitude toward you will be determined by your attitude toward yourself.

The cardinal rule of selling is that everything counts. In mentally preparing yourself to be an Olympic *sales* champion, a top performer in your field, you must work like an Olympic *sports* champion works on his or her specialty. Just like an athlete in sports, you are engaged in an extraordinarily competitive field. The difference between you and the sports athlete is that you are in competition continuously, five and six days a week, and it never stops. Because of this unrelenting pressure, it's even more important for you to train intensively than it is for a professional athlete.

Everything that affects your thinking throughout the day has an impact on your personality and your performance. Whether you read an inspirational book in the morning or the newspaper, whether you listen to the radio in your car or to a learning audiocassette, whether you eat a salad at lunch or a hamburger, everything counts. Everything adds up and either helps you or hurts you.

The mark of the true professional, and the completely honest person, is that he or she recognizes that nature is both neutral and completely fair. Nature plays no favorites. Nature gives you back what you put in. All of life is sowing and reaping, action and reaction. You get what you give, no more and no less. And when you give your best, you experience the best in your life.

Anyone who really wants to can build themselves a fantastic body by lifting weights and engaging in vigorous physical exercise three times per week. By the same token, you can develop a powerful sales personality by engaging in vigorous *mental* exercise every day. You can become positive, optimistic, and enthusiastic by practicing mental rehearsal, positive self-talk, and creative visualization of your desired goals. You can build your character to the point where you can accomplish any goal that you can confidently set, thoroughly plan for, and completely commit yourself to achieving. The factors constraining your performance today will fall away and your future will be unlimited.

3

PERSONAL STRATEGIC PLANNING FOR THE SALES PROFESSIONAL

Personal strategic planning is the process you use to attain your goals and achieve your objectives. It is the vehicle that takes you from wherever you are to wherever you want to go. Personal strategic planning is the accelerator that enables you to dramatically increase your speed of accomplishment in every area of your life. It is a powerful process for harnessing your mental and physical energies and putting them behind clear aims and purposes. It makes sure you earn the highest return on energy in everything you do.

As I described in Chapter 1, the most important attitude you can develop in selling is that of seeing yourself as *self*-employed, as the *president* of your own professional sales corporation. By doing this, you accept complete responsibility for yourself and for everything that happens to you. You become the master of your own fate. You stop making excuses and blaming other people for your problems and difficulties. You take charge of your life and you take control of your future. By accepting complete responsibility for your life and your career, you move into the top ranks of sales professionals everywhere.

Jack Welch, CEO of General Electric, has said, "Control your destiny or someone else will!" By taking the time to think carefully and plan thoroughly before acting, you greatly increase your likelihood of hitting your sales and income targets on schedule. Personal strategic planning is perhaps the most important single skill you could ever develop in ensuring that you achieve the success of which you are capable.

The story is told that in 1953, a questionnaire was circulated to the graduating seniors at Yale University. They were asked the question, "Do you have clear, specific, written goals for your life, and have you developed complete plans for their accomplishment after you leave this university?"

The results of the survey were surprising. Only 3 percent of the seniors had clear written goals and plans for what they wanted to do when they left school. Thirteen percent had goals, but had not written them down. The other 84 percent had no goals at all, except to get out of school and enjoy the summer.

Twenty years later, in 1973, the surviving members of that Yale graduating class were surveyed again. Among other questions, they were asked, "What is your net worth today?"

When they totaled and averaged the results of this survey, they found that the 3 percent who had clear, written goals and plans when they left the university twenty years before were worth more, in dollar terms, than the other 97 percent put together! And *goal setting* was the only characteristic that the top 3 percent had in common. Some had earned good grades and some had received poor grades. Some had worked in one industry and some in another. Some had moved across the country, and some had stayed in the same city. The one common denominator of the most successful graduates was that they had been intensely goal-oriented from the very beginning.

In my conversations with hundreds of top salespeople over the years, I have found that they all have *one* thing in common. They all have clear, written goals. They have taken the time to sit down and create a blueprint for themselves and their future lives. Every one of them has been amazed at the incredible power of goal setting and strategic planning. Every one of them has accomplished far more than they ever believed possible in selling. And almost every top salesperson credits his or her success to the process of thinking through their lives and their work in advance, and then developing a detailed, written road map to get them to where they wanted to go.

Happiness, as I've mentioned, has been defined as, "the progressive realization of a worthy ideal or goal." When you are working progressively, step by step, toward something that is important to you, you experience a continuous feeling of success and achievement. You feel more in control of your own life. You feel happier and more fulfilled. You feel like a *winner*, and you soon develop the psychological momentum that enables you to overcome obstacles and plow through adversities that would stop the average person. When you are working toward the accomplishment of something that is important to you, you develop the kind of personal power and persistence that enables you to push beyond anything you've achieved before.

VALUES AND VISION

Personal strategic planning begins with your determining what it is you believe in and stand for, your *values*. Your values lie at the very heart of everything you are as a human being. Your values are the unifying principles and core beliefs of your personality and your character. The virtues you believe in and the qualities that you stand for are what constitute the person you have become from the beginning of your life to this moment. Your values, virtues, and inner beliefs are the axle around which turns the wheel of your life. All improvement in your life begins with your clarifying your true values and then committing yourself to live consistent with them.

In Chapter 1, I talked about the importance of the self-ideal. Your self-ideal is composed of the values you hold most dear and the qualities you most admire in yourself and others. Successful people are successful because they are very clear about their values. Unsuccessful people are fuzzy or unsure. Complete failures have no real values at all.

Values clarification is the starting point of building greater self-confidence, self-esteem, and personal character. When you take the time to think through your fundamental values, and then commit yourself to living your life consistent with them, you feel stronger and more confident. You feel more secure. You feel more centered in the universe and more capable of accomplishing the goals you have set for yourself.

VALUES CLARIFICATION

What *are* your values? What do you stand for? What are the organizing principles of your life? What are your core beliefs? What virtues do you aspire to, and hold in high regard when you see them demonstrated by others? What will you *not* stand for? What would you sacrifice for, suffer for, and even die for?

These are extremely important questions that are only asked by a very few people, and these few tend to be the most important and influential people in every society.

When I first began this values clarification exercise some years ago,

I wrote out a list of 163 qualities that I aspired to. I think I eventually came up with every virtue, value, or positive descriptive adjective in the dictionary that referred to personality and character in any way. I felt that they were all important and I wanted to incorporate every single one of them into my character.

But then reality set in. I realized that it is very hard to develop even *one* new quality, or to change even one thing about myself, let alone dozens of things. So I scaled down my ambitions and began condensing my list of values to a small number that I could manage and work with. Once I had settled on about five core principles, I was then able to go to work on myself and start making some progress in character development.

You should do the same. You should write down your five most important values in life. Once you have those five values, you then organize them in order of priority. Which is the most important value in your hierarchy of values? Which would be second? Which would be third, and so on?

Every choice or decision you make is based on your values. Whenever you decide between alternatives, you invariably choose the alternative that you value the most. Because you can only do one thing at a time, everything you do is a statement of what you consider to be most important at that moment. Therefore, organizing your values in order of priority is the starting point of personal strategic planning. It is only when you are clear about what you value, and in what order you value it, that you are capable of planning and organizing the other activities of your life.

Here's a key point. A *higher*-order value always takes precedence over a *lower*-order value. If you place one value higher than another in your personal hierarchy, and you have to choose between doing one thing or doing another, you will always select the action that is consistent with your higher value. Therefore, once you are clear about your order of values, you can make better decisions, faster than ever before.

How can you determine what your values really are today? Simple. Just observe your *behaviors*, especially the things you do when you are *under pressure*. Your *values* are always expressed in your *actions*. It is not what you say, or wish, or hope, or intend that expresses your true values. It is only what you *do*. If you want to know what your values are at this moment, you can examine your recent past actions and notice the choices you made when you could have gone one way or another. Your choices, and your subsequent actions, demonstrated to yourself and others what was of greatest value and importance to you.

Here is an example. Imagine you have two people who have the same three values of family, health, and career success. The only difference between these two people is the order of importance that they place on these values, their priorities. The first person, Bill, says, "My family comes first, my health is second, and career success is third."

Tom, on the other hand, has the same values, but he says, "Career success comes first for me, then my family, and then my health."

Would there be a difference in character and personality between these two people? Of course there would! Would there be a *small* difference or a *large* difference? Would you be able to tell these two people apart in conversation? Which one do you think you would like and trust more? Which of these two people would you like to get to know and become friends with?

The answers to these questions are obvious. The person with their values in a better order of priority will invariably be a better person than the person whose values are in a different order.

Your choice of values determines the quality of your character. When you select values such as integrity, love, courage, honesty, excellence, or responsibility, and you live your life consistent with those values, every hour of every day, you actually become a better person. It is your values that determine the quality of the person you really are.

What is character? Your character is the degree to which you live your life consistent with positive, life-enhancing values. A person who lacks character is one who compromises on higher-order values in favor of short-term advantages or benefits, or who has no values at all. How strongly you adhere to what you believe to be right and true is the real measure of your character and the person you have become to this moment.

You can tell how strong a value is in your personal hierarchy when it costs you time, money, or emotion (ego) to practice it. Many people espouse fine and noble values until they are put between a rock and a hard place and they have to choose. If they choose the higher value, it may cost them something, maybe a lot. If they choose the lower-order value, they may get away scot-free, materially if not emotionally. But whenever you have to choose, you always demonstrate what is truly important to you.

Let us say that one of your values is excellence. Your definition of excellence could be, "Excellence means that I set the highest standards for myself in everything I do. I do my very best in every situation and under all circumstances. I constantly strive to be better in my work, and to be a better person in my relationships. I recognize that excellence is a lifelong journey and I work every day in every way to become better and better."

With a definition like this, you have a clear organizing principle for your actions. You have set a standard by which you can evaluate your behavior. You have created a framework within which you can make decisions. You have a measuring rod against which you can compare yourself in everything you do. You can continually grade your activities in terms of "more" or "less." You have a clear target to aim at and to organize your work around.

It's the same with each of your other values. If your value is your family, you could define this as, "The needs of my family take precedence over all other concerns. Whenever I have to choose between the happiness, health, and well-being of a member of my family, and any other interest, my family will always come first."

From that moment onward, it becomes easier for you to choose. Your family comes first. Until you have fully satisfied the needs of your family, no other time requirement will sidetrack you into a lower-value activity.

The wonderful thing about values clarification is that it enables you to take charge of developing and shaping your own character. When your values and goals, your inner life and your outer life, are in complete alignment, you feel terrific about yourself. You enjoy high self-esteem. Your self-confidence soars. When you achieve complete *congruence* between your values and your goals, like a hand in a glove, you feel strong, happy, healthy, and fully integrated as a person. You develop the kind of courage that makes you unafraid to make decisions and take action. Your whole life improves when you begin living your life by the values that you most admire.

THE IMPORTANCE OF VISION

Your **vision** flows from your values. In Proverbs it says, "Where there is no vision, the people perish." In reviewing more than 3,300 studies examining the personalities of leaders, the one quality that they all had in common was found to be that of vision. It was their ability to imagine an ideal future well in advance of creating it that enabled ordinary men and women to rise to unprecedented levels of personal and professional leadership. And it is the same with you.

Henry David Thoreau wrote, "If you have built castles in the air, your work need not be lost. That is where they should be. Now put foundations under them." Your vision is an imaginary creation of the ideal life you would like to live, in every respect. You create it as an expression or an embodiment of the values you hold most dear. From the very day that you develop a clear vision for who you are and where you are going in life, you begin to become a superior person, and soon you begin to accomplish superior results.

One of the great secrets of success is to "dream big dreams." It is to let your mind float freely into the future and imagine that you have no limitations on what you can be, have, or do. Imagine for the moment that you have all of the resources that you would ever need to achieve the highest goals to which you could ever aspire. Imagine you have all the time, money, people, contacts, and intelligence that you could ask for to become everything that you could ever become.

Make a *dream list*. Let yourself fantasize, and project yourself into the future. What would you like to do? Where would you like to go? What would you like to accomplish? And most of all, what kind of person would you like to become? Since you attract into your life people and situations that are in harmony with the person you really are, what kind of attributes and qualities would you like to develop in yourself so that you can live the very best life you can imagine, surrounded by the kind of people you would most enjoy?

All the great movers and shakers of the sales industry, and of every other field, have been visionaries and dreamers. They have practiced what is called "back from the future" thinking. They have projected themselves forward three to five years, and then, looking around from that imaginary vantage point, they have begun thinking of the things they would have to do in order to get there. They have started with their goals in mind, and then worked backward. With their vision clear before them, they gain a better and better idea of the things they will have to do and the people they will have to become to make their future vision into their current reality.

What is your vision for yourself? What would you do differently if you had no limitations at all? How would you answer this question: "What one great thing would you dare to dream if you knew you could not fail?" If you were absolutely guaranteed of success in anything, what goals would you set for yourself, and what changes would you make in your life? These are not easy questions, but as you answer them, your vision will begin to crystallize and your life will begin to change forever.

THE IMPORTANCE OF A MISSION STATEMENT

All successful companies have clear mission statements. All successful salespeople have clear mission statements as well. As the president of your own company, in charge of your own life and career, you need *two* separate mission statements, each of which supports and reinforces the other. The writing out of your mission statements is the logical next step that follows from the definitions of your vision and values. It becomes your personal credo and determines your future. It is the organizing statement that serves as the directional mechanism for everything you do.

Your personal mission statement is a definition of the kind of person that you wish to become, in every respect, sometime in the future. Your business mission statement defines how you want to be known to your customers.

For example, a personal mission statement could be:

> "I am an outstanding human being in every respect. I am warm, loving, compassionate, sincere, and forgiving in all my relationships with the important people in my life, my family, and others. I am an honest person, a good friend, and known for my qualities of generosity, helpfulness, sincerity, understanding, and patience. I am positive, enthusiastic, happy, and fully engaged with life. I am liked, admired, and respected by everyone who knows me."

Your business mission statement might read as follows:

> "I am an outstanding sales professional in every respect. I am extremely knowledgeable about my products and services, and about my customer's situation, and I am thoroughly prepared for each appointment. I am possessed of the finest character, known for my honesty, dependability, reliability, and determination. I am a warm, friendly, likable human being who takes excellent care of each customer and I am a pleasure to deal with in every way."

This is a definition of how you wish to be seen and thought about by your customers. It is the way you want others to talk about you and describe you to other people. As the president of your own professional sales corporation, once you have developed your business mission statement, you will have a set of guidelines that will help you do and say the right things in all your business activities.

A mission statement is always written in the present tense, as though you have already become the person that you have described. It is always positive rather than negative. It describes the qualities you desire to have rather than the weaknesses you wish to overcome. And it is always personal. It begins with the words, "I am," "I can," "I achieve."

Your subconscious mind can only accept your mission statement as a set of commands when you phrase it in the present, positive, and personal tenses. "I am an exceptional salesperson," is a perfect example. After every sales call, you should quickly reread your mission statement and ask yourself if your recent behavior was more like the person you want to be, or less. As a top sales performer, you are always comparing your sales activities against a high standard and adjusting your activities upward. You are continually striving to be better. Every day in every way, you are deliberately working to become more like the ideal person you have envisioned.

Your goal is that, a year from today, if not earlier, when one of your customers has lunch with one of your prospects, and your prospect asks your customer to describe you as a salesperson, your customer will describe you in terms of your business mission statement. Without even knowing what it contains, he will use the words you have chosen to describe yourself. This will happen because you have treated your customer in a manner consistent with your mission statement.

Once you have developed your mission statements, you can read them, review them, edit them, and upgrade them regularly. You can add additional qualities to them and more clearly define the qualities you've already listed. They become your personal credos, your philosophy of life, your statement of beliefs and guides to your behavior in all your interactions with others. Each day, you can evaluate your behaviors and compare them against the standards that you have set for yourself in these statements.

Over time, a remarkable thing will happen. As you read and review your mission statements, you will find yourself, almost unconsciously, shaping your words and conforming your behaviors so that you are more and more like the ideal person you have defined. People will notice the change in you almost immediately. You will find that you are actually creating within yourself the kind of character and personality that you most admire in others and desire for yourself. You will have become the molder and the shaper of your own personal destiny.

Fully 84 percent of sales in America take place as the result of word-of-mouth of some kind. Some of the most important sales promotion sales activities are those that take place between customers and prospects, between friends and colleagues, in the form of advice and recommendations on what to buy, or not buy, and who to buy or not buy from.

The only way you can be among the top 10 percent of salespeople in your industry is by having your existing customers selling *for* you on every occasion. Because of the importance of *mega-credibility* in selling, your customers must be eager to open doors to new customers for you wherever you go. All top salespeople eventually reach the point where they seldom have to prospect because their customers do much of their selling for them. When you live your life consistent with your personal and business mission statements, each reinforcing the other, your sales career will soar, as will your sales results and your income.

One important point with regard to vision, values, and mission statements: be *gentle* with yourself. It has taken you your whole life to become the person you are today. If you are like everyone else, you are not perfect. You have lots of room to grow and improve. There are many changes you can make in your character and personality in the course of becoming the excellent human being you aspire to. But change in your personality will not come easily, and it won't come overnight. You must be patient.

The reason people grow and become better and better over the course of time is because they persist gently in the direction of their goals and dreams. They don't expect overnight transformations. When they don't see results immediately, they don't get discouraged. They just keep on. And you must do the same.

Once you have a clear idea of the person you want to be, and the kind of life and career you want to create for yourself, just take the first step. Read your mission statements each day as you go about your activities. Think of the different ways that you could practice the virtues and qualities that you are in the process of incorporating into your own personality. Remember, it is only your *actions* with regard to other people that really demonstrate the kind of person you have become. And if you persist long enough, you will eventually shape yourself into the exact person that you have imagined.

SITUATION ANALYSIS

There are four basic steps to achieving big goals in life. First, you must clearly define exactly where you are and what you are doing at the moment. Second, you must examine your past and determine how you got to where you are today. Third, you must decide where you are going, and where you want to be, one, two, three, and five years from now. Finally, you must decide how you are going to get from where you are to where you want to be in the future.

When I conduct strategic planning sessions for the executives of large corporations, we spend a good deal of time analyzing the company as it exists today. Sometimes, a thorough analysis of the current situation can generate valuable insights into what the company should be doing in the future. In your personal strategic planning exercise you must do the same. You must stand back and take a look at your sales career, as well as your personal life as it is now, and honestly evaluate yourself in terms of the larger picture.

Here's an example of how you can analyze your current situation: Imagine that you begin walking from City A to City B, a distance of thirty miles. At the half way point, fifteen miles out, you will be in neither city. When you look backward toward City A, you would no longer be able to see it. When you look forward to City B, it will not yet be visible. This is similar to your situation at this initial phase of personal strategic planning.

City A represents the *past* and City B represents the *future*. Where you are at this moment represents the present. Now, imagine that you could rise above yourself, way up into the air, thousands of feet. At a certain height, you would be able to see City A—where you came from; yourself on the road—your present situation; and City B—your possible future, all at once. You would be able to see yourself and your career within the context of your past, your present, and your future.

By the same token, situation analysis enables you to see the past, present, and future of your life and career, and how they affect each other, with greater clarity. When you are clear about where you are coming from, where you are at the moment, and where you are going, you become much more focused and effective in your planning and goal setting.

Begin with your current sales and income. How much are you selling today and how much are you earning? How much were you selling and earning one year ago? How much were you selling and earning two years ago? Three years ago? What trends do you see in your selling career? Are your sales and income moving gradually upward, increasing each year? Or have they leveled off, or declined?

One of the key thinking skills of the superior person is that he practices the "tip-of-the-iceberg" technique of situation analysis. As you know, 90 percent of the bulk of an iceberg is below the waterline and therefore invisible. When a sailor sees the tip of an iceberg, he knows that most of the ice is not visible to the naked eye, and he adjusts his course accordingly.

The tip-of-the-iceberg rule is that, whenever something happens in your business or personal life, you should *assume a trend* until proven otherwise. You should assume that this event, either an increase or decrease in sales, or a change in your life, is the tip of an iceberg. It is indicative of a deeper trend, or tendency, most of which cannot be seen or explained at the moment.

You may, however, find that a canceled order, or an increase in sales, is a one-time event, with no connection to anything else happening in the marketplace. But you may find that it is a sign of a larger trend that can have a major impact on your future. Superior salespeople are sensitive to the possibility of trends and they are constantly looking for evidence, one way or another, to prove or disprove that a trend is taking place in their sales activities.

In the course of your career, your sales should be tracking upward each year. Your income should be tracking upward as well. You should have a goal to increase your income 10 percent to 20 percent every year, and your personal strategic plan is the way that you achieve that goal.

What has been the trend in your income over the last three to five years? If you are not happy with the trend, your job is to make a new plan and change its direction. Remember the old saying, "If you keep going in the same direction, you are going to end up where you are heading."

The next step in situation analysis is for you to look at the products or services that you are currently selling. Analyze their proportions. Applying the Pareto Principle to your sales work, you will find that 80 percent of your sales are coming from 20 percent of your products. At the same time, 80 percent of your time is being consumed by activities that only yield 20 percent of your business. What products or services are you selling, and in what proportion, relative to the way you use your time? And what are the trends? What were you selling last year and the year before? If things continue as they are, what will you be selling next year, and the year after?

Analyze your existing customer base as well. Who are your major customers, and your minor customers? What do they have in common? In what sort of companies do your customers work and what types of positions do they have?

Especially, how have your customers *changed* over the last one or two years? Do you develop all new customers each year, or do you do most of your business with repeat customers? Which of your customers represent the lion's share of the business you are doing? If trends continue, who will you be selling to in the months and years ahead? Is this trend healthy or unhealthy for the success of your sales career?

One of the important aspects of selling is for you to recognize that you are most successful selling to a particular kind of person. There may be many potential prospects in the marketplace, but they will not all be *your* prospects. Because of your unique character and personality, you are most comfortable with a specific type of person, and the more of those people you deal with, the more you will sell.

Smart salespeople are those who are aware of their own strengths and shortcomings with regard to the kinds of people who buy from them. They structure their activities so they spend more and more time with the kind of people who are most likely to buy from them the earliest.

What are the common denominators of *your* customers, the ones who represent the bulk of your sales?

The next step in situation analysis is for you to examine your personal financial history. Just as though you were going to apply for a bank loan, make out a statement of your assets, your liabilities, and your net worth. Make a list of everything you own and put its value next to it. Make a list of everything you owe, and those amounts as well. Subtract your liabilities from your assets to find out what you are worth in financial terms. This number can be very revealing and helpful to you in planning for the future.

Around 70 percent of salespeople have *no* discretionary income. They spend everything they make, every month, and a little bit more besides. Similarly, according to one study, the average young married couple spends approximately 110 percent of their income, making up the difference with credit and loans from their parents.

As a business, one of your major concerns is net profits. When you put together your personal balance sheet, the amount of money you are worth today, net of liabilities, is your "retained earnings." It is the measure of how profitably you have been operating your personal business over the course of your career. It is a measure of your efficiency and effectiveness as the president of your own corporation.

You can take the amount that you are worth today and divide it by the number of years you have been working. That will give you the amount of "profit" that you have made since you began your career. If your net worth is $20,000 and you have been working for ten years, you have achieved a profit on your efforts of about $2,000 per year. If there are 250 working days in a year, this means that you are making an average of $8 per day, after expenses. Is this a good investment of your life? Or could you be operating your personal business more profitably? Conducting a financial analysis of your situation is the starting point of achieving your own financial independence.

YOUR CAREER PATH

A part of situation analysis is the evaluation of your career path up to the present day. Take some time to think about your first job. Your second job? Your third job? Make a list of every job you have ever held. Next to each job you should ask, "What were my key result areas?" What were you hired to do? What did they pay you for? What particular skill or ability did you have that qualified you for that job in the first place? Was there a common denominator in the various jobs you've had up to now?

What has been the trend over the course of your career? Have each of your jobs become more complex, requiring greater knowledge and skill and paying more money? Or have you been doing pretty much the same thing and getting pretty much the same results for the last couple of years?

If current trends continue, what are you likely to be doing a year from now? Two years from now? Five years from now? Are you becoming better and better at what you do, and therefore more and more valuable and more highly paid? If not, what could you do to begin increasing the speed at which you grow and develop in your career?

Analyze your education. Make a list of all of your educational accomplishments. If you finished high school, or college, or university, write it down and write out the most important things you learned as they have affected your career. You will probably find that 80 percent of everything you ever learned in your formal education has been of little use to you in the world of work. But what were the subjects that most prepared you for what you are doing today?

What kind of on-the-job training have you had that has proved to be particularly helpful? What have you learned over the years that has represented the biggest payoff to you in terms of sales results and personal income? What kinds of opportunities to learn are there for you in your company today that you might take advantage of?

In terms of self-study, what books have you read that have been most helpful to you in your sales career? What audiotapes do you listen to on a regular basis to keep your mind fully engaged when you drive? What outside sales seminars have you taken to broaden your skills?

What are your *natural* talents and abilities? What skills have been most responsible for your success in your career to date? What have you found to be both easy to *learn* and easy to *do* that other people may have found difficult or challenging? What skills and abilities will you need in the future to ensure an upward trend line in your sales and income?

One of the most important lessons you can ever learn is this: **Your *life* can only get better when *you* do.** You can't accomplish anything more on the outside until you have achieved something more on the *inside*. This means that if you want your customers to get better, you must become a better salesperson. If you want your staff to become better, you must become a better manager. If you want your family to become better, you must become a better spouse and parent. If you want your relationships to improve, you must become a better human being. Your world only gets better if you do.

In what areas of your work and personal life do you need to improve, if you want things to improve for you?

BUNDLE OF RESOURCES

A strategic way of thinking about yourself and your sales career is to view yourself as a *bundle of resources*. See yourself as having a combination of talents, abilities, and competencies that you can use to get a variety of results. You have the capacity to achieve a multiplicity of goals.

One of the marks of leaders in every study is that they carefully deploy themselves to their very best advantage. They are always thinking about what might be the highest and best use of their time in fulfilling their responsibilities and in getting the results that are expected of them. In terms of your sales career, how could you better use your mental, emotional, and physical resources for maximum accomplishment?

PERSONAL SITUATION

Your sales career and your work life are intertwined with your personal life and activities. They are inseparable in that you are usually thinking about both of them most of the time. The most successful salespeople tend to be fully integrated. There seems to be a natural flow between their personal lives and their sales work. The dividing line between the two is very faint. Like trading off from one hand to another, their sales and personal activities are extensions of each other.

In personal situation analysis, you must therefore stand back and take a look at your family and your relationships. Are you married or single? Separated, divorced, or widowed? Are you happy? Do you intend to stay in your current situation or relationship for the rest of your life? If so, what are your plans to ensure the greatest amount of happiness and satisfaction from what you're doing? If you are not planning to stay in your current situation indefinitely, what are your plans to change it? What are you doing on a day-to-day basis that will lead to your being in a different situation a month or a year from now?

You are responsible for whatever situation you find yourself in. You are in charge of your own life. Wherever you are and whatever you are doing, and whoever you are doing it with, you have decided to be there. Your life today is a result of your personal choices. And this life is not a *rehearsal* for something else. This is the real thing. It's not possible to improve your sales life substantially if you have unresolved problems in your personal life.

Do you have any children? What are their ages? How well are they doing in their education and personal lives? If your children are young, what plans do you have for them in the future? Do you want them to go to college? Do you have an organized savings plan to make sure they can get the best education possible when they finish high school? If you don't, when were you planning to start? One of the greatest motivations for doing anything is our children. We will sometimes make superhuman efforts to assure a better life for them. What physical, financial, and emotional needs do your children have that you could become more active in satisfying?

What about your home? Everybody dreams of having the ideal home sometime, somewhere. How are you doing? Do you own your own home, or are you renting? Do you have an apartment, or a condominium? Are you happy with your current living situation, or do you aspire to something more? If you do, what are your plans to accomplish it? Where do you plan to be in two, three, and five years? You know that nothing happens all by itself. If you want things to get better for you, you must *make* them better.

Make a list of all your possessions. What kind of car do you have? Are you happy with it? Do you want a bigger, better, faster car sometime in the future? What are your plans to acquire it? What about your clothes, your furniture, your appliances, your jewelry, and your other personal possessions?

As an exercise, make a list of everything you could ever think of that you could ever want to own and enjoy in your personal life. Don't worry about how you are going to pay for it at the moment. The most important part of this exercise is for you to let your mind flow freely and dream big dreams.

If you are married, sit down with your spouse and write down everything you could think of that you could ever want to have or enjoy. The longer and more extensive your lists, the more focused you will become and the more energy you will have in the attainment of the sales and income goals that will make them possible.

Imagine that the answers to all of these questions so far are pieces of a jigsaw puzzle that you are shaking out of a box onto a flat surface. Just as you assemble a jigsaw puzzle by laying all the pieces out in front of you and then beginning to put them together, one by one, you assemble a great life by laying out all the ingredients of your past, present, and your desired future and then assembling them into a single blueprint for accomplishment. As your personal strategic plan comes together, you will begin to accomplish goals at a rate that will astonish you.

ZERO-BASED THINKING

This is a vital part of strategic thinking. Zero-based thinking is an extension of zero-based accounting, where every expenditure has to be justified every single year or it is automatically canceled. In zero-based thinking, you justify every decision that you have ever made, by subjecting it to rigorous analysis. You ask, "Knowing what I *now* know, would I make this decision over again, in the same way?"

Almost every person is involved in one or more situations that he would not get into in the first place if he had to do it over again. These negative situations act as obstacles to your creating your ideal life. You cannot achieve the high levels of success and satisfaction that are possible for you if there are major parts of your life that you would change if you possibly could. They often act as shackles on your possibilities. They cause you to sell yourself short. They undermine your self-confidence and self-esteem and often make you feel helpless or trapped. They often act on you unconsciously to put the brakes on your potential for greatness in personal selling.

It takes courage for you to face the fact that you are in a situation that you wouldn't get into in the first place if you had to do over again. It takes courage to admit that you feel trapped. It takes courage for you to confront the fears of failure, rejection, and confrontation that hold you back. It takes courage for you to make the decision to get yourself free, but if you are going to become everything you are capable of becoming, you must deal with the negative situations in your life that you wouldn't get into today if you had the decision to make over again.

There are three major areas where zero-based thinking is most helpful. The first place is in your relationships. Is there any relationship, personal or business, that you would not get into if you had to do it over again? Many people, for example, are in a wrong marriage and all their energies are spent trying to keep the marriage together, even though they are not happy.

If you're a manager, is there any employee you wouldn't hire if you had it to do over? Many managers have hired the wrong people and are continually frustrated at their lack of results. Knowing what they now know, they would never hire that person again. And as long as they keep him on the payroll, they are going to feel stressed and dissatisfied.

Are there any people in your life that you don't enjoy? Do you associate with anyone whose effect on you is negative? Many people are in bad social relationships that they feel obligated to continue even though they get nothing out of them. Is there anyone you spend time with today who you wouldn't get involved with in the first place if you were starting over?

If there is, you should make the decision to break off your association with these people. You must accept the general fact that *people rarely change*, that the situation is not going to get better unless you make it better. Getting yourself free of a bad situation almost invariably involves walking away, or encouraging the other person to walk away.

We had a woman working for us not long ago who was doing a poor job and causing a good deal of trouble as well. My wife, who is the president of our company, was talking about various ways we could move this person to another position and hire someone else to do her current job. Then I asked my wife the key question, "Would you hire her again, if you had it to do over?"

She immediately said, "Absolutely not!" And at that moment, she realized what she would have to do. If she wouldn't hire her *back*, it meant that the employee should be let go as soon as possible. And that's exactly what she did.

Every manager I have ever met has someone back at the office that they would not hire again. The best advice I can give to executives is that you can't get on with the job of building an exceptional organization if you feel saddled with people that you wouldn't hire in the first place. You have to go back and deal with *old* people problems before you can get on to creating *new* and better people situations.

The second place you apply zero-based thinking is with regard to your investments. Are you invested in anything today that, knowing what you now know, you wouldn't get into in the first place? If so, your question should be, "How can I get out of it, and how fast?"

One of the characteristics of the fully functioning person is that he is willing to be honest and objective with himself and his life, and cut his losses when necessary. He has the character to admit that he made a mistake. He doesn't try to fool himself, or hope for miracles. He accepts that he has made a bad investment, of time, money, or emotion, and he does whatever he needs to do to minimize his losses.

The third area for you to apply zero-based thinking is with regard to your activities. Is there anything that you are committed to doing, either in terms of your work, your social activities, or your community affairs, that, if you had it to do over, you wouldn't get into in the first place? Examine your life and analyze every single activity that consumes time or money against this question. Is there anything, anywhere that you are doing that you would get out of if you could?

You will always know where to apply the concept of zero-based thinking by the stress test. The areas of greatest stress in your life are the areas where you are in a situation you should get out of. You always experience anxiety, frustration, anger, resentment, and even depression when you feel trapped into something that you wouldn't get into if you had it to do it over. Wherever this type of situation exists, it is absolutely essential that you go back and straighten it out if you are really serious about making the kind of progress that is possible for you.

SELF-ANALYSIS

Your great goal must be complete freedom and self-expression. Your aim in life should be to fulfill your full potential as a human being and become everything that you are capable of becoming. Your work on yourself and your career must be dedicated to greater self-actualization, on becoming a fully mature, fully functioning, fully integrated personality. In your career, you must be committed to being one of the top salespeople in your field.

This journey to self-realization in the world of professional selling requires careful and honest evaluation of your actual skills and competencies in every part of the business of selling. Self-delusion regarding the true state of your abilities can be fatal to long-term success. If you can't honestly face the areas where you may be weak, you can never become very strong.

We are very sensitive about being evaluated or criticized by others.

This fear of being judged makes us hypersensitive to the comments and remarks of others, even when they're trying to help us. Salespeople hate to have their sales managers come along to observe the call and give feedback on it afterward. Because we are so sensitive to failure and rejection, we do everything possible to avoid and evade facing the possibility that we may not be particularly competent in certain areas.

One of the most important practices of personal leadership, especially in sales, is the application of the "reality principle." Your ability to deal honestly and objectively with yourself and your life is a mark of the superior person. The psychologist Abraham Maslow found that *self-actualizing* men and women were able to be completely frank and honest with themselves. Psychologist Carl Rogers called this the "fully functioning person," the person who was completely self-accepting and nondefensive. The most advanced person seems to be the individual who can see himself with complete honesty and feel no need to explain or make excuses.

The reality principle says that you must deal with the world as it is, not as you wish it were. Living with reality, which is an extension of personal honesty, means refusing to engage in self-deception. It means accepting your weaknesses as well as your strengths. It means dealing with life exactly as it is, not as you wish, or hope, or pray it could be.

CRITICAL SUCCESS FACTORS

Everything that happens is subject to the Law of Cause and Effect. Everything happens for a reason. There are no accidents. Success is an effect with specific causes and so is failure. Sales success is also a desirable *effect* that can be traced back to the *causes* we've discussed in earlier chapters. It is largely predictable as well.

One of the greatest advances in personal and business success has been the discovery of the "critical success factors" concept. These are the factors that determine the success or failure of the enterprise or the individual. Poor performance in any area is enough in itself to sabotage the entire enterprise. Fortunately, there are seldom more than five to seven of these factors. But wherever there are problems in your business or in your work, the primary cause is usually a weakness in one of these areas.

We've talked about the critical success factors of selling throughout this book. Some of them are: prospecting, establishing rapport, problem identification, selling solutions, positioning against competition, overcoming concerns and gaining confirmation, follow-up and follow-through, and personal management. A weakness in any one of these areas can undermine or even be fatal to sales success. Each of these skills must be performed at a high level of competence for you to take full advantage of your skills in the other areas.

The idea of *critical success factors* can be applied widely. They exist for a business, a family, a marriage, health and fitness, financial success, and so on. To achieve excellence in any of these areas, you must identify the critical success factors for that area, honestly analyze how you score on a one-to-ten scale on each of those factors, and then create a plan to bring up your scores in the factors where you may be falling behind. You cannot allow yourself to be deficient in any key area.

As you'll remember, the most important part of critical success factors is the discovery that your weakest important area determines the height at which you can use all your other talents and abilities. For example, you could score at a seven or above in all your areas save one, but be at a three in that one area. That three score would determine the height to which you could use all your other skills. It would set the limit on your sales and income. Your weakest critical success factor would determine your success in all your other activities.

For example, you could be scoring very high in every area of selling except for personal time management. Your inability to manage your time properly, however, would negatively effect your overall sales results. Poor time management would lead to your spending too much time in nonproductive activities, too little time in genuine sales activities, and too little time with high-quality prospects and customers. A deficiency in personal time management could be enough to sabotage your entire sales career.

It would be the same for prospecting. You could be absolutely excellent at every part of selling but if you were poor at new business development, this weakness alone could be enough to end your sales career.

What are the critical success factors of your job? Of these factors, how do you score on a scale of one to ten? What is your *strongest* area? What is your *weakest* area? If you have any questions about this, ask your sales manager, your co-workers, or even your customers. You must put your ego aside. Your career depends on your getting an accurate answer to this question.

A salesman who graduated from one of my seminars took this advice to heart. He went back to a customer he trusted and asked him where he was the weakest in the sales process. When the customer saw that he sincerely wanted to know, and wouldn't be upset or offended, he told him: "You ask questions well but when I begin to answer, you interrupt and go on talking about your product or yourself."

The salesman was surprised. He had no idea he was interrupting. He was completely unaware of his behavior, as most of us are. But he double-checked with another customer and was told the same thing. That one piece of information helped him make an important adjustment in his behavior and led to a substantial improvement in his sales results.

When you ask for feedback and you get responses you don't particularly enjoy, instead of arguing or defending, simply say, "Tell me more." If the person accuses you of doing or not doing something with which you disagree, instead of arguing just say, "For example?" And don't feel that you have to argue or defend yourself. Just listen and take the comments away with you.

When you train yourself to use one or both of these statements on a regular basis, you will be amazed at the quality of candid feedback that you will get from others. With this feedback, you can immediately begin improving your performance in those areas. You don't have to spend enormous amounts of energy defending or justifying yourself.

In terms of self-analysis, what is your personal *area of excellence?* What is your unique selling proposition as a salesperson? What makes you different from and better than your competitors? What is your personal competitive advantage? What is your *tangible* competitive advantage? What is your *intangible* competitive advantage? Why should someone buy from you rather than from someone else in your company, or from someone in some other company?

Every person has the capacity to be excellent in his or her field. You can become very good as a salesperson by identifying the potentially excellent parts of your character and personality and then working to improve them. You can dedicate yourself to study and practice in those areas. You can practice those skills in your sales conversations.

It may be that the quality of your personality and your attentiveness to the needs of your customers is your unique intangible competitive advantage. Good salespeople will often say, "Mr. Prospect, you may be able to get this product from someone else but there is *one* thing no one else can offer you. Me! When you buy this product from me, you get me as part of the package. If you can get a better deal than that from anywhere else, I would advise you to take it."

You should analyze your personal image as well. How do you *appear* to the prospect? Evaluate your clothing, your grooming, and your accessories. Look in the mirror and ask yourself, "Do I look like one of the top sales professionals in my industry?" If you have any questions or uncertainties, ask for advice from other people. Ask others how you could improve your appearance. As long as you are not defensive, others will tell you things you can do to greatly improve the impression you are making and leaving with your customers.

The foundation of personal strategic planning is your taking the time to carefully determine and define your values, your vision, and your mission statements. You then analyze every aspect of your personal situation as it applies to selling. Like taking inventory of a large warehouse, you take personal inventory of every single aspect of your personal life and your professional skills. The more honest and accurate you can be in objectively analyzing exactly where you are, where you are coming from, and the things you will need to do to get to where you want to go, the faster you will progress and the more sales you will make.

COMPANY ANALYSIS

Top sales professionals take the time to become thoroughly familiar with every aspect of their companies. They know how and when their company started. They know who the key players are in the organization. They understand the power relationships and the people who have influence on various kinds of decisions. They understand the interrelationships between the various executives in various departments. They are alert and aware and extremely well informed about the company they represent.

Whatever the size of your company, you need to know its main products, its major customer groups, and the markets it serves. How did the company start and what did it sell at that time? Especially, what have been the predominant products, customers, and markets in the last three to five years? How are they different from what the company is doing today? What are the trends within the company? What will be the major products, customer groups, and markets served by the company in the future?

It's been said that there are three types of people. There are the small few who *make* things happen; there are a larger number who *watch* what is happening; and then there are the vast majority who simply ask, "What happened?"

As you move toward being one of those people who *make* things happen, you must be observant about what is actually going on around you.

What is your company's corporate strategy? What is your company committed to achieving, avoiding, or preserving in the current marketplace? What are the values of your company? What does your company stand for? These values may be written or unwritten, but they exist nonetheless. They are demonstrated in the way the company treats its people and treats its customers. What are they?

Your values are the core of your personality. The values of your company are the core of its corporate personality. Ideally, your personal values and your company's values should be in harmony. There should be no conflict or contradiction. In fact, it's difficult for you to sell at your best if you find yourself working for a company that has values with which you don't agree. So decide what your values are, and then find out what your company's values are. Make sure they fit together.

What is your company's marketing strategy? What is your company's unique selling proposition? What is its area of competitive advantage? What is its area of uniqueness or excellence? What does your company do better than any other company?

Each individual and each company is built around specific core competencies. These are the things that the company does well, usually better than any other company. All processes, functions, products, and services flow outward from the company's core competencies. Just as you have core skills, your company has certain areas in which it excels in the marketplace. What are they?

What is your company's positioning in the current market? This will have as much of an impact on your sales as any other single factor. One of the major reasons why people buy or refuse to buy anything is because of the *reputation* of the company. When you represent a company with an excellent reputation, it is much easier to get in to see people and to make sales. If you are representing a company with a poor reputation, it can interfere with the best sales efforts you can make.

Dr. Theodore Levitt of the Harvard Business School wrote in his book *The Marketing Imagination* that "A company's most valuable asset is how it is *known* to its customers." Often, a company's reputation with its customers is so valuable that another company will pay millions of dollars for the goodwill associated with the name.

How do people think about and talk about your company? Especially, what is its *quality* ranking? According to the PIMS Studies on strategy and profitability, analyzing 620 companies over many years, the most important single variable determining corporate profitability is its quality rating among its competitors.

Imagine that your company is ranked number four out of ten companies in your business. That means that there are three companies that are perceived to be better than your company in terms of quality products or services, and there are six companies that are perceived to be worse. This ranking will usually determine the sales and profitability of each of the companies. Where does your company score?

By the way, quality is defined by the customer. It is what the customer says it is. And the customer's definition of what constitutes the quality he will pay for in comparison with other competitive offerings changes over time. Basically, it is composed of the product itself plus the associated services that accompany the product, and even the way the product is sold. The relationship between price and perceived value may also be part of his or her quality assessment. In other words, a fair price may add to the perception of quality while a higher price lowers it. In any case, you must find out how the customer defines quality before you attempt to appeal to it in your product as a selling feature.

You also have a *personal* quality ranking within your organization. All the salespeople within the company are ranked, either formally or informally, from the best to the worst. What is your personal quality ranking? Who is ahead of you and who is behind you? And here's the key question: How can you improve your quality ranking? What can you do to get better?

There is a direct relationship between your sales, your income, and your quality ranking. One of your goals must be to move up toward the top position. And you don't have to jump from number five to number one overnight. All you have to do is go from number five to number four. Then you can move up to number three, and so on. Your commitment to improving your quality ranking in your company is just as important to your personal success as your company's commitment to improving its quality ranking in the marketplace is important to its success. How can you do it?

MARKET ANALYSIS

All strategy is ultimately market strategy. All strategic planning, in the final analysis, is aimed at the marketplace and at improving relative results in competitive markets. It is focused outward, toward the customers and the competition. It is aimed at the future and at changing the results that would occur in the absence of the strategy. It is organizing and reorganizing resources so as to increase your sales above what they would have been if you had not engaged in the personal strategic planning process.

Most salespeople are in what is called an "operating mode." They are focused on doing their jobs, day by day, with very little thought to what is likely to take place one month, or one year from now. But when you do a market analysis, combined with personal strategic planning, you move into a "managing mode." You take charge of the direction of your sales career rather than allowing yourself to be swept along with the current, as most other salespeople seem to be.

In Chapter 8 on prospecting, I will detail at length the questions you must ask to analyze your product or service in the marketplace, and especially in comparison with other products and services available. Ongoing market analysis, like a radar scanning the horizon, will enable you to focus your efforts and pinpoint better-quality prospects that you can sell to faster and more easily. Be sure to review that chapter a couple of times until you have a very good sense for the concepts and questions it contains.

INCREASING YOUR RETURN ON ENERGY

The basic organizing principle of strategic planning is **return on energy.** The purpose of continuous market analysis is so that you can deploy yourself in the best possible way. It is to assure that you achieve the maximum results in return for the amount of energy you put out.

The two concepts that enable you to maximize your sales results in your territory are the "money tree concept" and the "farmer concept." The money tree concept consists of your looking at every prospect as a prospective money tree, with many different branches that can lead to sales and referrals not only within that company but within other organizations.

Sometimes, this is called the "salami-slice concept." When you approach a prospect for the first time, instead of trying to get a large share of his business, you concentrate instead on getting the prospect to give you a small slice of the business that he is currently giving to another supplier. With this small slice, you have an opportunity to perform for the customer in terms of better customer service, quicker response to requests, better quality products, more reasonable prices, and whatever other competitive benefits your company offers.

You now have your hand on one branch of the money tree. Once you have satisfied the customer, you immediately go back to him and look for new ways to provide new products or services to him. You look for new applications for other products within his existing operations.

You ask for testimonials and referrals that you can use to open doors to other companies.

If you had to learn a lot about the customer's business to get the first sale, you have begun building up a data base of knowledge and information that you can use to sell to similar prospects in similar companies or similar situations. Look at your most recent customers and ask, "What industries are they in?" Then begin to think of how you could help other people in those same industries with the same products or services.

Many salespeople have made a sale to a customer in a particular industry and then parlayed that sale into an entire sales career. A friend of mine was an accountant who helped doctors set up their bookkeeping and accounting systems. Because there was nothing else on the market, he developed a computer program to automate patient records and billing. For his computer program to work, each doctor's office required a certain configuration of computers, terminals, other software, printers, forms, and a variety of other items.

It took him almost a year to put together the combination of products that his client required to run his office efficiently. His first customers reported improvements in their billing and office operations almost immediately. He realized that he had created a potential money tree. He asked his doctor clients for referrals to other doctors. He began selling the entire office automation process to other medical professionals, and before long he had a multi-million-dollar business with sixteen sales professionals working throughout the western half of the United States.

You may not be able to achieve the same kind of results, but you may be swinging in the branches of a potential money tree right now. In a money tree, every sale can lead to other sales and referrals, to the same customer and to other customers in similar situations.

With the farmer concept, you look upon your sales territory the way a farmer would look upon his land. Your job is to cultivate, prepare, plant, seed, water, fertilize, weed, protect, grow, develop crops, harvest, and then prepare to repeat the process all over again.

Cultivating your market means to network as much as possible and learn everything you can about the customers you want to call on.

Preparing your market can refer to telephone calls, sales letters, advertising, promotion, and even testimonials that you obtain to put yourself in better position for when you call on the customer.

Planting your market can refer to meeting with the prospect initially and helping the prospect to realize he has a problem for which your product or service might be a solution.

Seeding your market is equivalent to the sales presentation where you demonstrate conclusively to your prospect that your product or service can be the best choice solution to his problem.

Watering your market can refer to providing testimonials, assurances, and guarantees to your prospect to lower his fear of making a mistake in purchasing your product or service.

Fertilizing your market could refer to selling your product into a large organization and getting them to attest to the efficacy of what you sell to other prospective customers.

Weeding your market can refer to keeping your competitors out of the same account. This is also a good definition of **protecting** your market as well.

You **grow** and **develop** your market by continuous new business development, by continually seeing new and better prospects, and by never hanging all your hopes on one large sale coming through.

You **harvest** your market by actually getting the sale, by doing everything that we will discuss in the following chapters and bringing the customer to the point where he accepts your recommendation to go ahead with your product or service.

Continuous harvesting requires that you maintain excellent customer relations, and that you take special care of the relationship that has developed between you and the customer over time. In this way, you make sure this customer continues to buy from you for as long as he is in the market for your product or service.

Finally, there is the issue of resales, or expanding your farming activities into other organizations to which your customer can refer you.

The whole concept of farming your territory requires that you see it as a vast area of potential sales and financial possibilities for you. You do everything possible to maximize the dollar value of sales you can get from a particular customer or geographical area.

Market analysis never stops. You are always looking for better, faster, more convenient, higher-value, lower-cost ways to position yourself positively in the minds of your customers, and to simultaneously undermine the strengths of your competitors by emphasizing their weaknesses and vulnerabilities. Ongoing market analysis enables you to sell more and more of your product in your particular marketplace.

STRATEGIC PLANNING MADE SIMPLE

Essential to effective strategic planning is breaking the entire process down into its constituent parts and then reassembling them into a smooth-running, efficient strategic sales machine. This is precisely what you have done by analyzing every aspect of your business and by answering the questions that have appeared throughout this chapter. You are now ready to pull it all together and propel your sales results into the stratosphere.

The simplest of strategic planning approaches is the GOSPA model. GOSPA stands for goals, objectives, strategies, plans, and activities. This chapter is concerned with the first four steps. We'll deal thoroughly with step number five, activities, throughout this book.

You set your **goals and objectives** by determining exactly what you want to accomplish as a result of your sales activities. You set long-term, medium-term, and short-term goals, each of which flows into the other. You set goals and objectives for both your personal and business life. You draw up a blueprint so that you know exactly *what* you are doing, *why* you are doing it, *what* you want to accomplish, *when* you want to accomplish it and *what it will look like* when you are successful. By putting these ingredients together into a written plan, your success will be virtually assured!

Goals are the specific, long-term, measurable, time-bounded targets that you are aiming to accomplish. A specific level of sales in a specific sales period, such as a year, would represent a goal.

Objectives refer to the interim goals that you will have to accomplish in order to achieve your overall goal. For example, in order to develop a certain level of business, you will have to call on a certain number of new prospects. The number of prospects you will have to call on in a particular sales period represents an objective that must be achieved if your long-term goal is to be realized.

Begin with your income goal for the next one, two, three, four, and five years. How much do you want to personally earn each year? Determine how much you are earning today and then extrapolate out five years ahead. Increase your income goal by 10 percent to 25 percent for each subsequent year, starting with today. This gives you specific, personal targets to aim at.

Then examine your company's compensation plan. It has been designed to reward you for making a certain level of sales of a certain variety of products and services. Your job is to maximize the compensation plan to make sure your activities are generating the very highest sales results for yourself and your company. Determine exactly how many dollars of sales, and what particular mix of products or services, you will have to sell to earn your desired annual amount for the coming year. You can determine the sales mix for the coming years as you get to them.

Once you have written down your sales and income goals for the foreseeable future, make a list of all the reasons why you want to achieve those goals. "Reasons are the fuel in the furnace of motivation." The more reasons you have, the more motivated and determined you will be.

A friend of mine is a sales manager for a large national corporation. At the beginning of each year, he helps his salespeople strategically plan for the months ahead. He has found, year after year, that the salespeople who have very clear reasons for achieving their income goals are invariably the salespeople who meet and exceed their quotas. The salespeople who have fuzzy reasons for selling a certain amount, or no reasons at all aside from paying bills, seldom make their quotas or do particularly well.

Make a list of every single thing you would like to do or acquire as a result of achieving your income goals for the next year. Make a list of the things you would like to do for yourself, your spouse, your children, your family and friends, and your community.

Your chief financial goal in professional selling is to ultimately reach the shores of financial independence, climb up onto the high ground, and build a financial fortress. Perhaps the biggest single responsibility you have to yourself, aside from your health, is to provide for your financial well-being. One of the reasons you are working, and one of the reasons that we analyzed the financial aspects of your life earlier in this chapter, is to help you create a blueprint for financial accomplishment.

Just as your company aims to make a profit and to continue growing in a competitive market, you must aim to make a profit as well and to put it away for the long term. Your objective must be to reach the point, sometime in your career, where you never have to worry about money again.

The only way to achieve financial independence is for you to begin saving and investing from every paycheck. The key to financial success has always been: "Pay yourself first." Pay yourself a certain percentage, off the top, of every paycheck. Put it away in a savings account for long-term investment and never ever touch it for any reason.

The great destroyer of financial independence is called Parkinson's Law. This law says, "Expenses rise to meet income." It states that, no matter how much you earn, your expenses eventually rise and consume it all, if not a little bit more besides.

All financial success comes from consciously and deliberately *violating* Parkinson's Law. It comes from driving a wedge between your increasing income and your increasing cost of living. If you earn 10 percent more as the result of becoming better in your field, you can allow your living standard to rise, but only by 5 percent. Take the other 5 percent and save or invest it for financial freedom.

As the years pass, drive this wedge deeper and deeper between your income and your living costs until you are saving 10 percent, 15 percent, and eventually 20 percent of your total salary. If you pay yourself first, and learn to live on the balance, rather than paying all your bills and saving what is left over, you will eventually be out of debt and building a considerable nest egg. This is the only absolutely guaranteed route to financial independence ever discovered.

Your ability to save money is a measure of your character. It is a test of your self-discipline and willpower. It makes a statement about your fundamental values as a human being. If one of your values is to be self-reliant and self-responsible, you have no choice but to build up a cash reserve of three to six months of income as rapidly as possible. As insurance company founder W. Clement Stone once wrote, "If you cannot save money, then the seeds of greatness are not in you."

Five percent of self-made millionaires in America today are *salespeople* who got there by working hard, continually upgrading their skills, earning very good livings, and then saving substantial amounts every month.

There is no reason why you cannot do the same. There is no reason why you cannot achieve financial independence by becoming an outstanding salesperson and then by putting away every month some of what you earn until you have assured your financial future.

Your **strategy and plans** are how you are going to accomplish your objectives and achieve your goals.

There are usually a variety of ways to approach any goal or objective, just as there are usually several ways to climb a mountain. The purpose of strategy is to enable you to achieve your goals by getting the highest return on your expenditure of personal time and energy. Once you have determined your strategy, or route to the top, you then lay out your plan, or the steps that you are going to take every day, week, and month, to scale the heights.

For example, in personal strategic planning, you would carefully examine your sales cycle, and the buying process. How long does it take for a qualified prospect, on average, to make a buying decision, take delivery, and pay for your product?

Many companies have long sales cycles that take several months. If an average sales cycle is seven months, for example, the salesperson must have made all his initial contacts by the end of May for all the sales he is going to achieve in that particular year. Instead of coasting through the first few months of the year, the professional with a clear sales goal must go to work on January 2 and get every single prospect lined up and organized by May if he is going to achieve his quotas for the coming year.

With smaller sales, made to a large number of prospects, the key selling strategy is **activity.** Your strategic planning would involve organizing your activities so that you see as many prospects as possible every working day. The more people you see, the more sales you make.

With a larger sale and longer sales cycle, the key to sales success lies in carefully planning the approach and penetration of the customer account.

Some salespeople may have only ten potential customers in their entire market area. Every potential customer is therefore extremely valuable. The salesperson and the company cannot afford to lose or alienate a single one as the result of a sloppy sales effort. Considerable thought and planning must go into every aspect of the approach, the proposal, the presentation, and the follow-up work that leads to the sale. No detail is unimportant.

THE MILESTONE METHOD

When dealing with larger, multi-call sales, the "milestone method" of selling is very helpful. With the milestone method, you make a list of all the things that have to happen before the customer can make a final buying decision. You analyze the situation from the viewpoint of the customer. What problems does he have? What needs? What questions does he have that need to be resolved? What competitors need to be outflanked or outmaneuvered to win this account? What must happen, from the precontact stage of the sale, all the way through to the delivery and installation, for this customer to be completely satisfied? What must he know and be convinced of before he can buy?

The answers to these questions may consist of as many as thirty different items. You may be able to accomplish only one item on one sales call. You may be able to cover several items in another sales call. But all the items must be covered, and usually in a particular order or sequence, before the prospect will be ready to make the buying decision.

With the milestone method, you can track your progress in every customer interaction. If your sales manager asks you "How are you doing?" you can say that you are now at milestone number 17 and that you have an appointment coming up in which you hope to cover milestones 18, 19, and 20. In other words, you know exactly what you are doing. You know exactly why you are doing it. You know what you are trying to accomplish and what you need to do before you move to the next step. You are in complete control of the process.

Remember also the importance of "experience curve theory." This says that the more you do of a particular job or activity, the better you get at it. The better you get at it, the fewer mistakes you make and the more of it you can do.

With experience curve theory, when you become absolutely excellent in servicing a particular customer in a particular situation, you learn an enormous number of things that you can use to service similar customers in similar situations. It may take six months for you to make a sale in a particular industry, but then it may only take three or four months, then one or two months, to make subsequent sales in the same industry. You may have to invest large amounts of time and effort to penetrate a new customer type, but this effort can pay off in larger and easier sales later on.

SUMMARY—PUTTING IT ALL TOGETHER

You are now ready to create your own personal strategic plan. You have decided upon your values and defined them. You have developed a vision for who you are and where you want to go. You have written out clear personal and business mission statements to give you guidance and direction in your activities in the months and years ahead.

You have conducted a thorough situation analysis. You have looked at every aspect of your life as a person and as a sales professional. You have examined the past, present, and future of your sales career, where you are coming from, where you are now, and where you are going.

You have thought through how you can best deploy yourself to achieve your highest return on energy, and maximum sales results. You have thought through every aspect of your personal life as well. You have applied zero-based thinking to your life and made some clear decisions about people and situations that you are going to change so that you can begin making progress in other areas.

You have conducted a thorough self-analysis. You have honestly evaluated your strengths and weaknesses. You have defined the critical success factors of your work and you have identified your weakest important area. You have looked at every aspect of your person, your health, your appearance, and your behavior to find ways to improve in everything you do.

You have conducted a thorough company analysis. You have taken the time, asked the questions, and read the materials so that you have an in-depth understanding of your company. You know how it was formed, what it sells, where it sells the most, and a lot about its past, present, and future. You have asked questions both internally and externally and you have a good idea of where your company is positioned in the marketplace, and why. You know your company's market strategy and you are clear about its area of excellence and its unique selling proposition. You know why your company is better than its competitors and how to emphasize your company's strengths in any sales situation.

You have done a complete market analysis and begun to look at your prospective customer base in terms of maximizing your sales and your income over the months and years ahead. You have applied both the money tree concept and the farmer concept to your sales territory, and you are continually thinking about ways to plant and harvest a richer crop from your sales activities.

You have identified your goals and objectives for the months and years ahead. You know how much you want to earn, how much you will have to sell, and especially, you have determined why you want to be successful.

You are internally motivated to achieve goals and objectives of your own choosing. You accept complete responsibility for yourself and your results.

Finally, you are ready to assemble your strategy and plans. You pull everything we have talked about in this book together into a blueprint that you can follow each day to turn your plans into realities.

You are now ready for the final letter in the GOSPA model, activities. In the coming chapters, you will learn every aspect of the professional selling process and how to incorporate them into your sales work. You will learn how to become one of the most effective and efficient salespeople in your industry. You will learn how to accomplish your goals and objectives with a minimum of effort and a maximum of personal effectiveness.

4

THE HEART OF THE SALE

What is selling? In its simplest terms, selling is the process of persuading a person that your product or service is of greater value to him than the price you are asking for it. Our market society is based on the principles of freedom of choice and mutual benefit. Each party to a transaction only enters into it when he feels that he will be better off as a result of the transaction than he would be without it. In a free market, the customer always has three options with any purchase decision. First, the customer can buy your product or service. Second, the customer can buy the product or service from someone else. Third, the customer can decide to buy nothing at all, or something else completely different.

For the customer to buy your particular product or service, he or she must be convinced not only that is it the best choice of product or service available but also that there is no better way for him to spend the equivalent sum of money that it costs. Your job as a salesperson is to convince the customer that these conditions exist and then to elicit a commitment from him to take action on your offer.

The field of professional selling has changed dramatically since World War II. In a way, selling methodologies are merely responses to customer requirements. At one time, customers were relatively unsophisticated and poorly informed about their choices. Salespeople catered to this customer with carefully planned and memorized sales presentations, loads of enthusiasm, and a bagful of techniques designed to overcome resistance and get the order at virtually any cost.

But the customer of the 1950s has matured into the customer of the 1990s. Customers are now more intelligent and knowledgeable than ever before. They are experienced buyers and they have interacted with hundreds of salespeople. They are extremely sophisticated and aware of the incredible variety of products and services that are available to them, as well as the relative strengths and weaknesses of those products. Many of them are smarter and better educated than most salespeople and they are far more careful about making buying decisions of any kind.

In addition, they are overwhelmed with work and other responsibilities, and undersupplied with time. Because of the rapidly increasing rate of change, downsizing, restructuring, and the competitive pressures surrounding them, customers today are harried and hassled. They are impatient and demanding. To sell to today's customer requires a higher level of sales professionalism than has ever before been required. And it is only going to become tougher and more competitive in the months and years ahead.

The entire process of selling today is more complex than it has ever been. It used to be that we would make a single call on a single buyer who would make a single decision on our product or offering. In this uncomplicated world of selling, we used the four-part AIDA model (attention, interest, desire, action) and focused on different ways of closing the sale. Once we had made the sale, in most cases we never needed to see the customer again.

Today, however, everything is different. In most cases, we must make multiple calls, an average of five or six, in order to make a sale. We deal with multiple decision-makers in an organization, each of whom can influence the purchase. Much of the sale takes place when we are not present. Sometimes we never even meet the final decision-maker who signs the check. And it is not unusual for a sale to be derailed at the last minute by something completely unexpected.

If that weren't enough, there is more competition today than ever before and it is more determined and resolute than it has ever been. Not only must we compete on the basis of price, quality, service, capabilities, financing, warranties with many other vendors of similar products or services, but we must also compete with every other vendor of every other product or service who is striving to get the same customer dollar that we are after. Our competitors are driven by the same forces we are, by tighter markets, fewer sales, and more discriminating customers. Our competitors are committed to starting earlier, working harder, and staying up later thinking of ways to take our customers away from us.

Our prospective customers are beset on all sides by every conceivable sales offering. Because they are drowning in details, options and choices, they are in no hurry to make up their minds. With markets changing and contracting, the amount of discretionary funds they have available has shrunken and they are more cautious today than they have ever had to be in the past.

The purpose of a business is to create and keep a customer. If a business does this in sufficient quantity and with proper cost controls, it will make a profit. The profit is the result of creating and keeping customers efficiently.

As the president of your own professional sales corporation, your job is to create and keep customers as well. And just as a company must continually restructure and redesign its product and service offerings to satisfy the changing tastes of a demanding and competitive customer marketplace, you as a salesperson must constantly upgrade the quality and sophistication of your sales procedures and approaches if you are going to create customers in sufficient quantity.

MAJOR OBSTACLES TO BUYING

Two of the greatest enemies of mankind are and always have been fear and ignorance.

Fear feeds on itself. It holds us back. It causes us to question our own potential and possibilities. It leads us to interpret events and circumstances negatively rather than positively. It eats away at us silently, deep inside, and keeps our foot on the brakes of our own hopes and aspirations.

Ignorance is often the breeding ground of fear. When you don't understand something, or you don't know how to do something, you tend to feel uneasy and even fearful about it. Much failure and frustration is based in ignorance and uncertainty. On the other hand, the better you become at something, the less you fear it. You can eventually reach the point where you have such complete confidence in yourself that you have no fear at all. Knowledge and skill override fear and ignorance and make all things possible for you.

If the biggest obstacle to selling is the **fear of rejection**, experienced by the salesperson, then the biggest obstacle to buying is the **fear of failure**, experienced by the customer. The fear of failure is probably the greatest single obstacle to success of all kinds in our society today. The fear of failure does more to hold people back and paralyze their decision-making abilities than any other factor.

The reason that qualified customers do not buy is because they are afraid of making a mistake. They are afraid of being stuck with the wrong item. They are afraid of paying too much, or finding it at a lower price elsewhere. They are afraid of being criticized for making a poor purchase decision. They are afraid that if the product or service doesn't work, you or your company will not service it and they will be left hanging. They are afraid that your product or service will not do the things that you claim it will do, and will not yield them the benefits that you tell them they will enjoy. In short, when a customer thinks about buying your product, he or she is often overwhelmed with a wave of fear that triggers the response of "Let me think it over."

My son David, six years old, came home from the supermarket with my wife, Barbara, the other day. He gets a small allowance each week and he had insisted on spending a dollar of his allowance on a cheap plastic gun from the toy department. Barbara tried to talk him out of it by telling him that the gun was cheap and flimsy and would fall apart as soon as he started playing with it. But David was adamant. He wanted the gun and he kept bothering her until she finally allowed him to buy it with his own money.

When they got home, David immediately pulled the gun out of the package and began playing with it. After just a few minutes, the trigger broke and the handle cracked. The mechanism came apart inside the transparent plastic gun so that you could see the pieces rattling around. It was finished.

With an angry look on his face, David said, "Look at this gun; it's just a piece of junk!" With that, he marched over to the trash compactor and threw it in. He said, "I'll never buy another piece of junk like that again!" He then stomped out of the room.

David's education as a consumer in our commercial society has begun. He has had one of what will eventually turn into hundreds, if not thousands, of experiences as the result of his buying decisions. Many of these buying decisions will be mistakes and leave him wishing he had never bought the item in the first place. And each time he has a negative buying experience, he files away the combined emotions of anger and fear that go with it. The anger, for having been taken for a ride, and the fear of having it happen to him again. By the time he reaches adulthood, David will be thoroughly programmed to be a customer in today's complex society.

Every day, you as a salesperson are dealing with a similar David when you approach a customer. Because of a lifetime of experience, the prospect's *instinctive* reaction to you as a salesperson is to see you as someone who will attempt to sell them something that costs too much and that doesn't work as promised. He or she will respond with skepticism, suspicion, hostility, resistance, and tension. To escape from a potentially negative experience, they will say things like:

"We're not in the market right now."
"I can't afford it."
"It costs too much."
"I'm not interested."
"I can get it cheaper from your competitor."
"It's not in our budget."
"We are quite happy with our existing product or supplier."
"We are going through a reassessment of our needs and we are not in a position to consider it at this time."
"Business is bad; our cash flow is too low to consider at this time."
"I have to talk it over with someone else who isn't here at the moment."
"Why don't you leave me some material and I'll get back to you later."

You've heard these responses, and many more besides, many times. But think about this. If they were all true, no sales would ever take place to anyone, because almost all customers respond to an initial sales offering with one or more of the above statements. Initial sales resistance is to be expected because of the fear of failure, the fear of making a bad buying decision. It is always easier to say, at the outset, "I'm not interested," than it is to make a mistake and end up feeling angry and frustrated.

In most sales conversations, you have the worst of both worlds. You have the salesperson, who is paralyzed by the fear of rejection, dealing with the prospect, who is paralyzed by the fear of failure. The salesperson is anxious not to incur the disapproval of the prospect and the prospect is anxious not to make a buying mistake.

Most salespeople and prospects in this situation enter into an unspoken agreement not to put each other on the spot. They exchange social niceties and courteously end the conversation without either one saying or doing anything to hurt the feelings of the other.

You've heard the story of the two salespeople who arrive back at the office at the end of the day. The first one says, "Boy, did I have a lot of good interviews today!"

The second one replies, "Yeah, I didn't sell anything either."

THE CRITICAL FACTOR: RISK

The critical factor in selling today is **risk**. Because of continuous change, rapid obsolescence, and an uncertain economy, the risk of buying the wrong product or service has become greater than ever before. One of our powerful needs is for security, and any buying decision that represents uncertainty triggers the feeling of risk that threatens that security.

There are four main factors that contribute to the perception of risk in the mind and heart of the customer. The first is the *size* of the sale. The larger the sale, the more money involved, the greater the risk. If a person is buying a package of Lifesavers, the risk of satisfaction or dissatisfaction is insignificant. But if a person is buying a computer system for their company, the risk factor is magnified by hundreds of thousands of times. Whenever you are selling a product that has a high price on it, you must be aware that risk enters into the buyer's calculations almost immediately.

The second factor contributing to the perception of risk is the *number of people* who will be affected by the buying decision. If you go out for lunch alone to a new restaurant, the risk is very low. If the food or service is poor, you are the only one involved. The experience can be quickly forgotten. But if you invite a group of business customers to a restaurant to discuss a large transaction the risk factor is very high.

Almost every complex buying decision involves several people. There are the people who must use the product or service. There are the people who must pay for the product or service. There are the people who are dependent on the results expected from the product or service. There is the reputation of the person making the final buying decision. If a person is extremely sensitive to the opinions of others, this factor alone can cause him or her to put off a buying decision indefinitely.

The third factor contributing to the perception of risk is the *length of life of the product*. A product or service that, once installed, is meant to last for several years, generates the feeling of risk. The customer thinks, "What if it doesn't work and I'm stuck with it?"

How many times have you bought something that turned out to be the wrong item and you were stuck with it? You couldn't replace it with something more appropriate because of the amount you had already paid.

The fourth major risk factor is the customer's *unfamiliarity* with you, your company, and your product or service. A first-time buyer, one who has not bought the product or service before, or who has not bought it from you, is often nervous and requires a lot of hand-holding. Anything new or different makes the average customer tense and uneasy. This is why a new product or service, or a new business relationship with your company, has to be presented as a natural extension of what the customer is already doing.

In every case, you must overcome the customer's fear of risk if you are going to make the sale. Everything you do, from the first contact, through to the closing, the delivery and installation of the product or service, and the follow-up to the sale, must be done with the customer's perception of risk uppermost in your thinking.

Successful salespeople are those who position their products or services as the lowest-risk product or service available to satisfy the particular need or achieve the particular goal of the customer. Your job is to be the *low-risk provider*, not necessarily the low-price vendor. Your job is to demonstrate clearly that your product or service represents the safest and most secure purchase decision rather than merely being the least expensive or the highest quality.

Volvo manufactured and sold hundreds of millions of dollars of cars for decades by emphasizing how safe they were to drive because they were so well made. Mercedes-Benz emphasizes that they included certain safety features as standard items years before they were introduced into other cars. Neither company ever attempted to compete on the basis of price.

When a prospect has a choice between two products, one that is lower priced but represents a *higher* degree of risk and a second that has a higher price but that represents a *lower* degree of risk, which do you think the customer will choose to relieve the tension involved in the buying decision? Whenever possible, the customer will move up to higher price and lower risk to relieve buying tension, rather than moving down to lower price and higher risk to save money.

Our customers today are the most experienced customers in history. They know that there is usually a close correlation between higher price on the one hand and greater security and after-sales satisfaction on the other. Your task is to make this differential clear in your sales presentation, especially when positioning your product or service against lower-priced competition.

THE NEW MODEL OF SELLING

What if there were a way of selling you could use to simultaneously reduce your fears of rejection, reduce your prospect's fear of failure, and dramatically diminish the perception of risk associated with any significant buying decision? Well, there is such a way and that is what we are going to discuss for the rest of this chapter. It is the key to increased sales, higher income, and greater satisfaction from your selling career than you may have ever imagined possible.

The profession of selling, like any other profession or area of technology, has been evolving more rapidly in the last few years than at any other time in history. When I first started selling investments, I had to learn how to use a slide rule to multiply and divide share value into the proposed investment amount. I still remember when the first handheld calculators came out. I eagerly paid $200 for one in 1972. As calculators became more sophisticated and less expensive, computers entered the market. Today I have the latest portable computer with a modem that gives me access to an entire world of information almost instantaneously. And the changes that will take place in the next ten years in the way we process information of all kinds are beyond the imagination of the average person.

The profession of selling has changed as well. The new model of selling is a disarmingly simple way of looking at how selling has changed in the past twenty-five years. It enables you to analyze your strengths and weaknesses and make adjustments in your performance so that you can achieve better results.

The new model of selling must be contrasted with the old model of selling to understand its simplicity, its power, and its importance. The old model of selling emerged in the years prior to World War II when customers responded to a basic form of sales presentation. After this period, sales trainers began to share their experiences in the form of lessons for other salespeople to follow. Over time, most of these sales trainers borrowed from one another and blended their sales methods and techniques together into a relatively homogenous and straightforward approach to selling anything, epitomized by the work of the sales trainer J. Douglas Edwards.

The descendants of J. Douglas Edwards, most of them over forty and many in their fifties and sixties, still teach and attempt to practice the old methods of selling. But like dinosaurs, they are gradually dying out in the face of the new customer. All the sales research based on actually sitting in on the sales conversations of top professionals in various industries demonstrates that the best salespeople use the new model of selling rather than the old. Neil Rackham found, in his research for *S.P.I.N. Selling*, that even if they had been trained in the old model of selling, top salespeople were successful by deliberately *not* using it with customers.

What I've found in my sales seminars with thousands of salespeople from hundreds of different industries is that a transition from the old model to the new model of selling leads to an immediate improvement in sales results, sometimes overnight and often that very same day. To understand why the new model is so effective, however, we should first take a look at the old model.

The old model of selling divided the sale into roughly four parts, like a triangle divided into four sections with horizontal lines.

The first part of the sale, the tip, represented 10 percent of the total sales transaction. This part consisted of approaching and getting the attention of the prospect. Usually, this was accomplished with a bold statement or a strong question. When I was just learning how to sell, it was called preoccupation breaking. It was likened to the process of hitting a donkey between the eyes with a two-by-four to get its attention. Only, as salespeople, we did it with words, or sometimes with tricks or gadgets.

I worked with a very successful salesman in the 1960s, Joe Grundel, who was fondly nicknamed the "Gadget Man." He would greet a prospect and place a three-minute egg timer on his desk. He would then say, "If you will give me just three minutes, at the end of that time, when the last grain falls through the glass, if you don't ask me to continue, I'll leave."

He would use egg timers, alarms, $20 bills, puzzles, pictures, and a

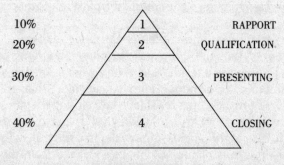

Old Model of Selling

variety of other devices to get the prospect to stay still and listen to him long enough for him to get the prospect interested in what he was selling.

In the old model, we were taught to get right down to the purpose of your visit. Don't waste time. Don't bother the prospect with too much small talk. Ask about the weather, the latest football game, or the wife and kids and then immediately launch into the sale.

The second part of the old model, 20 percent of the sales process, was the qualification phase. In this phase we were instructed to use a variety of techniques to determine whether the prospect had the money before we gave a presentation. We were told, "Don't waste time on a prospect if he doesn't make it clear that he can part with the money when you come to the close."

We would ask questions like, "Mr. Prospect, if I showed you the very best product or service in this area, are you in a position to make a buying decision today?" This approach, also called the qualification close, was designed to avoid having the prospect say at the end of the presentation, "I can't afford it," or, "I have to talk it over with someone else before I make a decision."

The third part of the old model, taking up 30 percent of the sales process, was presenting. The purpose of the presentation was to show the features of the product or service and the benefits that the prospect would enjoy as a result of purchasing. Often, salespeople were taught to use clever, manipulative phrases and techniques to weaken sales resistance and build a propensity or desire to buy. They were taught to raise or lower their voices, shift their bodies, and ask leading questions that the prospect would have to answer in a certain way.

The fourth part of the sale in the old model of selling was the close. This was 40 percent of the traditional sales process. Countless books, articles, and seminars are devoted to the subject of closing, and to the various ways of extracting a commitment from a reluctant or indecisive prospect.

Well into the 1970s, most salespeople, sales managers, and sales trainers believed that the close was the most important part of the entire sales process. As a result, salespeople were trained in a variety of closing techniques. Some books claim to teach more than one hundred different ways of overcoming resistance and closing the sale.

The overemphasis on closing was only valid, and is only really valid today, in the case of the single, simple sale, to a single person on whom the salesperson is only planning to make a single call. In this case, the product is usually small, the need is clear, all the information necessary for a decision can be presented at one time, and the only thing to be overcome at the end of the process is the natural resistance experienced by every customer when contemplating a new product or service.

However, in the 1970s, a revolution occurred in the selling process. The selling triangle flipped over and the entire process of selling changed forever. *This is the most significant and meaningful transformation of basic selling techniques that has ever taken place, and the mastery of this new model is your key to outstanding sales performance for the indefinite future.*

In the *new* model, which is like an upside-down triangle, there are also four parts of the selling process, just as there are four parts in the old model. The four steps are the process by which all top salespeople sell today.

The first part of the new model, 40 percent of the sales process, is building **trust**. The level of trust between you and the prospect is the ingredient that makes the rest of the sales process possible. If for any reason you fail to establish a certain level of trust at the outset, the sales relationship will probably never get off the ground. Because customers today are bombarded by so much conflicting and often contradictory product information, the element of trust becomes the indispensable ingredient in all sales relationships.

The second part of the new model, 30 percent of the process, consists of identifying the real **needs** of the prospect as they relate to your product or service offering. Needs identification requires that you ask well-prepared questions and listen carefully to the answers. It requires that you read between the lines and feed back the prospect's words and concerns to check for understanding. Only then can you be sure that the prospect has a clearly definable need that you can satisfy in a cost-effective way with what you are selling.

These two elements, building trust and clarifying needs, constitute

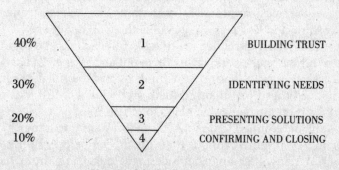

New Model of Selling

fully 70 percent of the sales conversation. If they are accomplished skillfully and professionally, the sale will come together smoothly with low levels of fear or tension on the part of either the salesperson or the customer.

The most wonderful part of this new approach to selling is that it is based on the establishment of a high-quality relationship between the buyer and the seller. It is a process of asking questions, listening carefully, and seeking for a way to genuinely help the prospect achieve a goal or solve a problem. Building a relationship in this way alleviates most of the tension and stress that generates the fear of rejection in the salesperson and the fear of failure on the part of the customer.

When you focus your attention on the customer and his or her genuine needs and wants, when you ask questions and listen carefully to the answers, the customer naturally relaxes and trusts you more. When the customer starts to feel that you are there to help him, the customer opens up to you more honestly and completely with his genuine problems and concerns. When you listen carefully as he talks, the customer trusts you more and tells you more. If you listen long enough and hard enough during these first two stages of the sales conversation, the customer will eventually tell you everything that you need to know to either make the sale or to determine that this person is not a good prospect for what you are selling.

Some years ago, on a visit to New York, I wanted to buy one or two dress shirts to go with a couple of new suits. I had some time between appointments so I stepped into a men's wear store in Manhattan and began looking around. I was a young man in a big city and I was a little bit tense and uneasy about being taken advantage of.

In the first store, and then in the second and third, the salespeople came up to me and said something like, "What can I do for you?" or, "May I help you?"

I explained tentatively that I was looking to buy a shirt or two. In each case, the salesman would say something like, "Great, let me show you our shirts and let's pick out a couple that you might like."

They would then introduce me to racks full of shirts and begin pulling them off the shelves and laying them out and saying, "What do you think of this?" or, "What do you think of that?" until I became so overwhelmed that I just thanked them and said, "I'm just looking; I'll be back." I then hurried away, never to return.

I was still determined to buy two shirts so I went into a fourth men's wear store, even more cautious than I had been before. In this store, however, I remember an older salesman looking up from halfway across the floor, making direct eye contact with me and smiling. He then said warmly, "Thank you for coming in; please feel free to look around."

As I began looking around, he approached me and stopped about twelve feet away. "Is there anything particular that you were looking for today?" he asked.

I told him that I wanted to buy a couple of shirts. Then he did something that I hadn't seen before, and which I subsequently learned is the modus operandi of all top salespeople.

He asked me, "What will you be wearing the shirts for?" When I explained to him that I was in sales, he then asked, "What color of suits would you be wearing the shirts with?"

When I told him the colors of my suits, he asked me, "What kind of shirts do you prefer, and do you have a price range in mind?"

I explained to him that I wasn't too sure about the types of shirts and that I hadn't really thought about how much to spend. He then said, "Well, let me show you some shirts and explain the differences in price and fabric and you can decide for yourself which are most appropriate."

By this time, I was so happy at finding a salesman who was genuinely concerned about helping me get what I needed that I followed him willingly. He showed me an entire selection of shirts and explained the differences in fabric, cut, stitching, cuffs, price, and care. He showed me how different colors and combinations of colors went with different suits and the different ties that could be mixed and matched with the shirts and the suits for maximum attractiveness. I was fascinated and I asked him question after question, all of which he answered in a very low-key, professional way.

I walked out of the store half an hour later with two large bags full of shirts and ties. As he showed me to the door, he gave me his card and invited me to call or come back and see him anytime if I had questions or concerns or if there was anything else he could do for me.

I remember standing on that busy New York sidewalk looking at his business card and looking up at the sign over the door of the store at the same time. The business card said, "Harry Rosenman, Clothier to Gentlemen," and the sign over the store read, "Harry Rosenman, Clothiers."

My salesman was the *owner* of the store! There wasn't the slightest question in my mind why it was he was so successful that he could have a major clothing store on a busy New York street. He was a master of the craft of selling.

What he did was to focus on the first two parts of the new model of selling. He concentrated all his attention on helping me relax by directing the conversation to my situation and my needs. He then listened patiently and pleasantly while I talked. He never tried to sell me anything. He asked questions, listened carefully, and then *taught* me how my needs could be met in various ways with the clothes he was selling. That was many years ago and I still remember the experience. I wouldn't be surprised if he retired a very wealthy man. He deserved it.

The third part of the sales presentation in the new model, representing only 20 percent of the entire process, is **presenting.** The presentation part of the sales process is relatively simply if the first two parts of the new model have been carried out completely. In the presentation, the salesperson shows the prospect how his or her needs can be ideally satisfied by the product or service offering.

Top salespeople match products to needs more skillfully than poor salespeople. They present only those elements of the product or service that the prospect has made clear are of concern or interest to him. If the product or service consists of a dozen features but only two of the features were determined to be of importance during the questioning process, these are the only two the salesperson emphasizes. He focuses his efforts on showing the prospect that his primary needs in these two areas will be fulfilled by the purchase.

The final part, the remaining 10 percent, of the new model of selling is **gaining confirmation and commitment** to action. In gaining a commitment to take action, the salesperson asks such questions as, "Does this make sense to you so far?" Or, "Is this what you had in mind?" He checks and double-checks to make sure that what he is selling and what the customer wants are the same.

Instead of the close of the sale being a painful process disliked by both the salesperson and the customer, it becomes a natural conclusion to a professional sales conversation. In many cases, if the sales process has been followed correctly, the customer will come right out and ask, "How long does it take to get this?" Or even, "I'm sold; let's get on with it."

Often, the customer will buy without even asking how much it costs. His level of trust and confidence in you will be so high that he absolutely knows that, whatever you charge, it will be a fair and reasonable price. If he does ask the price, it will often be just for the sake of information, or to have something to write down on the check or purchase order.

Using the new model of selling makes the profession of sales more enjoyable. It removes most of the anxiety and stress associated with trying to "sell" something to somebody.

According to consumer studies conducted by the University of Chicago, people today do not like to be "sold" anything. They like to be helped to make intelligent buying decisions, but they do not want to feel for a minute that they are being persuaded or manipulated into doing something that may be contrary to their best interests.

Top salespeople know this intuitively and they are always aware that their job is to help, not pressure. Their job is to give good advice and make professional recommendations on the use and enjoyment of their products or services.

LISTENING: A KEY TO SALES SUCCESS

A vital key to sales success is **listening.** The ability to listen well is absolutely indispensable for success in all human relationships. The ability to be a good listener in a sales conversation is perhaps the critical skill of the new model of selling. Active, sincere listening leads to easier sales, higher earnings, and greater enjoyment from the sales profession.

Many salespeople have been brought up with the idea that, in order to be good at your profession, you must be a good talker. You have even heard people say, "You have the gift of gab; you should be in sales!"

Nothing could be further from the truth. As many as 75 percent of top salespeople are defined as introverts on psychological tests. They are low-key, easygoing, and other-centered. They are interested in the thoughts and feelings of others and they are comfortable sitting and listening to their prospects. They would much rather listen than talk in a sales situation. Poor salespeople dominate the *talking*, but top salespeople dominate the *listening*.

Listening has even been called "white magic." It exerts an almost magical effect on human relationships. It causes people to relax and open up. When a salesperson is an excellent listener, prospects and customers feel comfortable and secure in his or her presence. They buy more readily, and more often.

You've heard it said that God gave man two ears and one mouth, and he is supposed to use them in that proportion.

Top salespeople practice the 70/30 rule. They talk and ask questions 30 percent or less of the time while they listen intently to their customers 70 percent or more of the time. They use their ears and mouth in the right ratio.

Many years ago, when I was just starting out, I worked with one of the best salesmen I ever met, a man named Leon Cahan. He would take me with him when he visited his prospective clients. I remember that he would sit down directly in front of the prospect like a boulder, and stare intently into his face.

When the silence became almost unbearable, Leon would lean forward, watching the prospect intently, and ask him a very deliberate question about his current situation as it related to the product we were selling. As the prospect began answering, Leon would lean forward even more with his eyes boring into the prospect's face. With Leon listening intently, the prospect would begin elaborating on his situation, on what he was doing, and what his concerns or problems were. Leon would listen and nod, and occasionally smile, with his attention never wavering from the prospect's face and words.

I would sit quietly on the side of this interaction. To this day, I have never seen a better use of silence in a sales conversation. We were selling mutual funds and while I was trying to sell a $5,000 investment program, Leon would be uncovering both needs and resources that would enable him to make sales of $25,000, $50,000, and even $100,000 to the same prospect that I had been struggling with for weeks or even months. He listened himself into the top 10 percent of salespeople in the mutual fund industry.

THE BENEFITS OF GOOD LISTENING

There are several benefits to listening that can never be gained by talking. First, **listening builds trust.** This is one of the most important truths in professional selling. Talking does not build trust; listening builds trust. There is no faster way for one person to gain the trust of another than by listening intently to what the other person has to say. Remember, the first 40 percent of the new model of selling is the development of a trust bond between the prospect and the salesperson, and the very fastest and most predictable way to do this is simply to listen intently to every word the customer says.

On the other hand, there is no faster way to undermine trust and irritate the prospect than by talking too much and listening too little. According to the Purchasing Manager's Association of America's annual survey, year after year, the biggest single complaint of professional purchasers is that salespeople talk too much.

Professional purchasing managers report in the same surveys that the salespeople they like the *most* are good listeners who seem genuinely concerned with understanding their real needs and helping them to purchase the products they need in a cost-effective way.

The second benefit of good listening is that **listening lowers resistance.** It reduces tension and defensiveness on the part of the customer. It diminishes the natural nervousness customers have in dealing with any salesperson where the possibility of paying out money and making a mistake exist simultaneously. The more you listen to a prospect, the more comfortable and relaxed the prospect feels, and the more open he or she becomes to considering your offer seriously.

Third, **listening builds self-esteem.** It has been said that "Rapt attention is the highest form of flattery." When you listen intently to another person and it is clear that you genuinely care about what that other person is saying, his or her self-esteem goes up. His or her feeling of personal value increases. You can actually make another person feel terrific about him- or herself by listening in a warm, genuine, caring way to everything he or she has to say.

When a man and a woman go out for the first time, they spend a great amount of time talking and listening to each other. They look into each other's eyes and hang on each other's every word. They are each fascinated by the personality of the other. The more each listens to the other, the more positive and happy each of them feels and the stronger become the bonds of affection between them.

The opposite of listening is *ignoring*. You always listen to that which you most value. You always ignore that which you do not value. The fastest way to turn a person off, to hurt his feelings, and make him feel slighted and angry is to simply ignore what he is saying or interrupt him in the middle of a thought. Ignoring or interrupting a person is the equivalent of an emotional slap in the face. Men especially have to be careful about their natural desire to make a remark or an observation in the middle of a conversation. This can often cause the sales conversation to come to a grinding halt.

Fourth, **listening builds character and self-discipline.** You can listen and understand at the rate of 500 to 600 words per minute, but the average person only speaks at the rate of 125 to 150 words per minute. This means that two thirds of your listening time is available for you to think of other things. You must discipline yourself continually to concentrate on the prospect or your mind will drift. You will start thinking about your bills, your problems, your financial situation, or the coming weekend.

You require tremendous self-mastery and self-control to keep focused on the words and meanings of the prospect when he is answering questions and explaining his situation. (And the more and better you listen, the better a person you become.) All great leaders, and outstanding men and women in every field, have trained themselves to be excellent listeners. This skill is especially necessary in the field of professional selling.

Interestingly enough, the *higher* your personal self-esteem, the easier it is for you to listen calmly and comfortably to another person. When you genuinely like and accept yourself, you are less preoccupied with your own thoughts and feelings and more relaxed in your interactions with others. This is very important in sales because, in order for you to be truly effective, you must be able to get *out* of yourself and *into* the mind and feelings of your prospect. You must be able to see yourself and your product or service offering from his point of view. As motivational speaker Ed Foreman says, "If you can see Joe Jones through Joe Jones's eyes, you can sell Joe Jones what Joe Jones buys."

The more comfortable you are with yourself, the more readily you will be able to put yourself in the shoes of your prospect. It will be easier for you to "walk a mile in his moccasins." You will be more sensitive to your prospect and more aware of what he is really saying. Especially, you will be better able to determine what your prospect is afraid of or worried about. When you can correctly identify your prospect's true emotional agenda, you can then present your product in such a way that you address his or her true concerns.

HOW TO LISTEN FOR SALES SUCCESS

There are books, articles, and multiday courses on listening. There are audio and video learning programs that include hours of instruction and a variety of exercises. They are all helpful, but what they teach can be distilled down into four basic skills. Your mastery of these skills, through discipline and practice, is all you need to become an excellent listener, with all that that entails.

The first listening skill is to **listen attentively.** Lean forward and face the prospect directly, rather than at an angle. Focus your attention on the prospect's face, and on his or her mouth and eyes.

Listen without interruption. Listen as though you were hanging on every word the prospect was saying. Listen as if the prospect were about to give you the winning lottery number and you would only hear it once. Listen as if this were a million-dollar prospect who was just on the verge of giving you a major order. Listen as if there were no one else in the world to whom you would rather listen at this moment than this prospect, and to what this prospect is saying.

The ability to pay close, uninterrupted attention to a person when he is speaking is the primary listening skill. It is the hardest facility to develop and is simultaneously the most important of all. It requires continuous practice and discipline. And it's not easy. It is hard to keep your thoughts from wandering, but the payoff can be tremendous.

The second skill of listening is simply to **pause before replying.** When the prospect finishes talking, rather than jumping in with the first thing you can think to say, take three to five seconds to pause quietly and wait.

All excellent listeners are masters of the pause. They are comfortable with silences. When the other person finishes speaking, they take a breath, relax, and smile before saying anything. They know that the pause is a key part of good communications.

Pausing before you speak has three specific benefits. The first is that you avoid the risk of interrupting the prospect if he or she has just stopped to gather his or her thoughts. Remember, your primary job in the sales conversation is to build and maintain a high level of trust, and *listening builds trust.* When you pause for a few seconds, you will often find that the prospect will continue speaking. He will give you further opportunity to listen, enabling you to gather more of the information you need to make the sale.

The second benefit of pausing is that your silence tells the prospect that you are giving careful consideration to what he or she has just said. By carefully considering the other person's words, you are paying him or her a compliment. You are implicitly saying that you consider what he or she has said to be important and worthy of quiet reflection. You make the prospect feel more valuable with your silence. You raise his self-esteem and make him feel better about himself.

The third benefit of pausing before replying is that you will actually *hear* and understand the prospect better if you give his or her words a few seconds to soak into your mind. The more time you take to reflect upon what has just been said, the more conscious you will be of its real meaning. You will be more alert to how his words connect with other things you know about him in relation to your product or service.

A very important quality of successful men and women in every field, and especially in sales, is the quality of thoughtfulness. Successful people are more thoughtful than others. They take more time to think before they speak or act. They are more deliberate and they carefully consider the ramifications of a particular reaction or response before they do or say anything.

When you pause, not only do you become a more thoughtful person, but you convey this to the customer. By extension, you become a more valuable person to do business with. And you achieve this by simply pausing for a few seconds before you reply after your prospect or customer has spoken.

The third skill of listening is to **question for clarification.** Prospects often say things that are subject to misinterpretation. Often they are vague or unclear, even to themselves. Your basic operating principle should be that, if there is *any* doubt at all as to what the prospect has said, then you *didn't* really understand.

When you question for clarification, you not only get an opportunity to listen more while the prospect is answering the question, but you also make sure that what the prospect said and what you heard are the same. Questioning for clarification slows the conversation down, increases the clarity of the communication, and builds greater trust.

My favorite question in selling is, "How do you mean?" Or, "How do you mean, exactly?"

You can use this question after almost any statement by the prospect. It is an irresistible question and it is virtually impossible for a person to hear it without expanding on what he is thinking or what he previously said. Whenever you have any doubts at all, or whenever the prospect objects to any part of your offering, simply pause, smile, and ask, "How do you mean, *exactly?*"

Never assume that you know or understand before you have questioned and received an accurate clarification of exactly what the prospect meant when he or she asked a question or offered an objection. Always ask.

The fourth key to skillful listening is to **paraphrase** what the prospect has said and feed it back to him in your own words. This is where you demonstrate in no uncertain terms to the prospect that your listening has been real and sincere. This is where you show the prospect that you were paying complete attention to what he or she was saying. Paraphrasing is how you prove it.

When the prospect has finished explaining his or her situation to you, and you have paused, and then questioned for clarification, you paraphrase the prospect's primary thoughts and concerns, feeding them back to him or her in your own words.

For example, you might say, "Let me make sure I understand exactly what you are saying. It sounds to me as though you are concerned about two things more than anything else, and that in the past you have had a couple of experiences that have made you very careful in approaching a decision of this kind."

You then go on to repeat to the prospect exactly what he or she has told you, pausing and questioning for clarification as you go, until the customer says words to the effect of, "Yes, that's it! You've got it exactly."

Only when you and the customer have completed a thorough "examination," and have mutually agreed on the "diagnosis," are you in a position to begin talking about your product or service. In general terms, this means that you cannot bring out your brochures and price lists and begin telling the customer how your product or service can solve his problems or achieve his goals until about seventy percent of the way through the sales conversation. Until then, you have not yet *earned* the right. Until then, you don't even know enough to begin an intelligent presentation without embarrassing yourself.

You can become an excellent listener by practicing these four key skills. You can practice them every day, everywhere, with your friends and family, with your boss and co-workers, and especially with your prospective customers. Incorporate the 70/30 rule of active listening into everything you do, making it a habit to dominate the listening and letting others dominate the talking.

The more and better you listen, the more and better people will like you, trust you, and want to do business with you. The more they will want to get involved with you as a person and the more popular you will be with them. Excellent listeners are welcome everywhere, in every walk of life, and they eventually and ultimately arrive at the top of their fields.

THE IMPORTANCE OF THE LONG-TERM RELATIONSHIP

If you could take everything we have talked about in this chapter so far and put it into a large pot, boil it down, and distill it into its critical essence, it would emphasize the importance of relationships in successful selling. Building and maintaining long-term selling relationships is the key behavior and skill of the top 10 percent of the money earners in sales, in every field, selling every product and service.

Most of your success in life will depend on your ability to get along well with other people, and on the quality of your relationships. Psychologist Sidney Jourard found that 85 percent of a person's happiness in life comes from happy interactions with other people. The reverse holds true as well: 85 percent of a person's unhappiness or problems in life come from difficulties in getting along with others.

Anyone can sell to a few people, some of the time. But only the very best human relations experts can sell to a wide variety of people, and sell to them repeatedly, most of the time. The only way you can make the kind of sales you are capable of is by selling more easily, and more often, to the prospects you talk to, and by having those prospects open doors to others through testimonials and referrals. This is why all top salespeople build and maintain high-quality business relationships with their customers and sell to them repeatedly year after year.

We are all sensitive to the quality of our relationships with other people. We are primarily emotional and we make most of our decisions on the basis of how we feel inside. We may carefully consider all of the logical and practical reasons why or why not with regard to buying a product or service, but in the final analysis we tend to go with our gut feelings. We listen to our inner voices. We obey the dictates of our hearts. We buy on the basis of how we feel about the relationship that we have with the other person. Where there is no relationship, there is no sale.

Everything that you ever learn in the profession of selling, about your product or service or personality, is only helpful to the degree to which it contributes to the building of high-quality relationships with customers. There is an old saying, "The fox is clever because he knows many things; but the hedgehog is smarter because he knows *one* big thing."

The one big thing that the top sales performers know is that everything in their selling lives is dependent upon their relationships with their customers and they allow nothing to interfere with the cultivation and maintenance of those relationships.

Today, the decision to buy a larger product or service, one that costs a good deal of money, or involves a lot of people, or lasts a long time, or requires a departure from what the prospect has done in the past because it is new or different, requires the decision to enter into a long-term relationship with the salesperson and his or her company. As you know from your own experiences, relationships are very important things. We commit ourselves to relationships very carefully. We are extremely sensitive to how well our relationships are doing, especially in the critical areas of our lives.

The key emotional element of a long-term relationship is dependency. Before the customer buys from you, he or she is independent of you. The customer may like you or dislike you, but he or she can take you or leave you. However, when the customer makes a buying decision and gives you money for your product or service, the customer is stuck. The customer is now completely dependent upon you to fulfill the promises you made in your presentation. The customer is now dependent upon you for prompt delivery of the product or service. He or she is dependent upon you for installation and maintenance, and for the warranties you have made. Once he or she has made the buying decision and given you the money, the customer's hands are tied.

People do not like to be dependent on others. Customers are hesitant about getting into a long-term relationship with a vendor of any kind. Every customer you deal with has purchased a product or service in the past that turned out to be a disappointment. Customers are nervous about getting into the same situation again.

This is why trust is so important. Trust is an extremely rare commodity, built up slowly and painstakingly. It is fragile. It is capable of being shaken or even destroyed by a single mistake. Building and maintaining trust is the essential precondition for continuing or building a relationship of any kind.

Products and services today are increasingly complex and are changing very fast. There is no way that your customer can accurately assess the quality and dependability of the product or service you are selling. There is no way your prospect can assess all the components of your product or service offering, much less the management, administration, production, quality, services, integrity, distribution, delivery, billing accuracy, and follow-up support of your company.

In addition, 95 percent or more of all the contact that your customer has with your company will be represented by *yourself*. The customer, in the final analysis, is buying *you*, and when he or she makes a buying decision, he or she is trusting and believing in *you* to fulfill the commitments that you have made with regard to what you sell.

This commitment to a long-term relationship, with all that that entails, is often an enormous choice on the part of the customer. A mistake in placing his bet on the wrong person and the wrong company can lead to financial loss, criticism from superiors, delays and additional costs in satisfying his own customers, embarrassment, frustration, and aggravation of all kinds. The risk involved in a large buying decision can be huge. Your failure to allay this risk can be the primary reason why qualified prospects do not buy from you.

Because there are so many unknown factors involved in the purchase of any product or service, the relationship is often *more important* to the customer than the product or service itself. The prospect may not be able to assess the inner workings of your company or what you are selling but he or she can make a decision about *you*.

Your job at this stage is to assure the customer that it is safe to do business with you and your company. The establishment of the sales relationship upon a foundation of trust is the starting point of alleviating anxiety and lowering the perception of risk that is the major obstacle to sales success.

Relationship building in sales is subject to the Law of Indirect Effort. This law states that you acquire things through people more often indirectly than directly. For example, you get people interested in you by being *interested* in them, the indirect way. You impress people by being *impressed* by them. You get people to like you by first *liking* them. The best way to have a friend is to *be* a friend, and so on.

The Law of Indirect Effort in selling says that the more you concentrate your attention on the relationship, the more likely it is that the sale will take care of itself, indirectly. But, if you focus your attention on the sale, and ignore the relationship, you will almost invariably fail to make the sale. Like the hedgehog, you must know one big thing: you must know that the relationship is everything, and without it there will be nothing.

A long-term selling relationship is seldom established in a single meeting. Many factors are involved. The bigger the product or service offering, the newer your company, the higher the level of satisfaction that your prospect has with his existing supplier, or the amount of competition there is for the same sales dollar, the greater will be the amount of time that it takes to build the trust in the relationship to the point that the prospect will seriously consider doing business with you.

You may have to call on the prospect several times before he reaches the psychological point where he is prepared to enter into a long-term relationship with you and your company. You must often be patient and persistent, like the force of erosion, and wear down the natural resistance that almost every prospect has when you approach him for the first time.

When you call on a prospect, you should expect him to say something like, "I'm not interested." This is perfectly normal and natural. Don't be discouraged. How could he possibly be interested if he's never seen or heard of you before? If he says that he is already buying from another supplier, this simply means that he is comfortable with the relationship he already has.

Customers fall easily into a *comfort zone* with an existing supplier and prefer to continue buying a particular product or service from the same supplier, even if it is of lower quality or higher price, rather than go through the discomfort and inconvenience of changing to someone new and better. This is not personal. It is just the way it is in the world of buying and selling. You must take it into consideration in everything you do.

Once you begin to establish a relationship with a prospect, or anyone else, *consistency* is absolutely essential to maintaining momentum. If you tell a person that you will be in touch with him every two weeks, or once a month, it is essential that you do so. Whatever you say you will do, you must do. If you say that you will send a person a new brochure or a cutting from a newspaper, the customer will remember, like an elephant, and will judge your character and integrity by how rapidly and readily you fulfill your promise.

If you dress well, prepare thoroughly, and arrive punctually for your first appointment with the prospect, you must remain consistent with that approach for the rest of your relationship. You cannot later dress casually, come late, or be unprepared. Inconsistency undermines trust and credibility. It weakens confidence in the relationship. Inconsistency in the salesperson creates an expectation of inconsistency in the company, and the product or service.

All top salespeople think of themselves as relationship experts. They think continually about their relationships with their customers. They are always looking for ways to strengthen the relationship, knowing that their best and easiest sales will come from their satisfied customers, and from referrals given by those satisfied customers. Top salespeople know that the beginning of a sales relationship is like the thin edge of the wedge. It is often the hole in the dike, or the crack in the egg. If the trust established at the beginning of the relationship can be built upon and expanded, it can often lead to sales that multiply and increase over the months and years ahead.

When salespeople are asked why people buy or don't buy their products or services, the majority will say that it is because of *price*. However, when customers themselves are asked why they bought or didn't buy a particular product or service, they seldom mention price. They almost invariably say that they bought something because of the reputation of the company and because of the relationship they have established over time with the salesperson. They will also mention the importance of product quality, the services included, the reliability of the person and the company, the responsiveness of the salesperson and the organization, and the support that the company offered.

But when the customer makes a decision to buy, these are all merely *promises* of things to come. At the moment of making the buying decision, what determines the customer's decision is the deep-down trust and confidence in the quality of the relationship that he has with you, and through you, with your company and your products and services.

In fact, it may be that the primary reason that people do *not* buy your product or service is because they don't trust you. It may be because they don't like you or believe in you. It may be because they lack confidence in you. It may be because they feel there is too much of a risk involved in dealing with you.

After all, if a prospect absolutely believed you and your claims about your products or service, and was completely confident that he or she would get everything that you promised, what would stop a qualified prospect from going ahead with a purchase decision?

The answer is that, if the prospect believed in you completely, and needed the product or service you were selling, and could afford to pay for it, there would be *no* reason for not proceeding. So the primary reason that the prospect does not proceed is because he or she is still afraid of making a mistake. You have not yet allayed that fear to the point where he or she feels confident enough to go ahead.

I cannot emphasize too strongly that *you are in the relationship business.* The old model of selling was based on the "hit-and-run" approach. The salesperson saw himself pitted against the prospect in an adversarial relationship. It was a fight for the checkbook. Salespeople were taught to look upon the prospect as the enemy and to plan every element of the sales process so as to "defeat" him and get the money. In the old model, we were taught, "Buyers are liars, so close them early and often."

In the new model, your approach is cooperative rather than confrontational. It is based on the establishment of long-term, mutually beneficial selling relationships rather than a quick, one-time sale where you don't anticipate seeing the prospect again. In the new model, your focus is on building trust and on maintaining the quality of the relationship that exists between you and each of your customers. The new model is collaborative and conversational and based on the friendship factor in sales.

THE FRIENDSHIP FACTOR

The **friendship factor** underlies all great sales success. It is based on the fact that a person will not buy from you until he or she is convinced that you are his or her friend and acting in his or her best interests. A person cannot buy from you unless he likes you. And you cannot sell to someone that you do not like. You cannot even buy from someone you do not like. This emotional connection between you and your prospect is the catalyst that causes the sale to come together.

The friendship factor is based on the three elements of *time, caring,* and *respect.* You build a business friendship by investing **time** in the prospect and in the prospect's situation. When you are with the prospect, you never hurry. You make it clear that you are willing to spend as much time as is necessary to help the prospect make the correct buying decision. You are never impatient. You are relaxed, easygoing, and customer-focused. You act as though you have all the time in the world—even if you are busy every minute of the day. You focus on building the relationship.

Some years ago, when I decided to move to San Diego, I brought my family down to spend a week looking at homes. We called several real estate agencies and I was honest with them up front. I told them that I wouldn't be ready to buy for at least a year, but I wanted to get an idea of what was available in the market and what it would cost. They each offered to mail me some information and asked me to call them when I was ready to make a purchase, except for one woman.

Joan told me that she understood we were not buyers at the moment, but she was nonetheless willing to invest some *time* showing us some of the homes that were available in our price range. For the next three days, she acted as though we had a briefcase full of money ready to plunk down at the first house we liked. She treated us as though we were hot prospects and eagerly set up appointments and showed us houses in a variety of neighborhoods, sometimes ten and fifteen houses in one day. By the time we had finished looking around with her, we had a pretty good feeling for where we would eventually settle and we thanked her for her time.

We returned to San Diego fourteen months later as customers. We phoned her in advance and told her our expected time of arrival. This time, we went out with her and stayed with her until we found the home we wanted. We bought it through her and she made about $20,000 in commissions. I later calculated that she had earned more than $200 for every hour she had invested with us over the previous fourteen months. Not a bad payoff! But the critical factor was that she had been willing to invest the time with us, and by so doing, she had built up her emotional credit with us to the point where we would not have considered buying a house through anyone else.

On the other hand, last year I decided to buy a new car. I knew exactly the car I wanted, the model, the accessories, the color, everything. There were two major dealerships in San Diego that sold this car. I decided, being in sales management myself, to buy it through the sales manager of one of the dealerships. When I phoned the first dealership, I asked to speak to the sales manager. When they put me through, I explained that I was going to come in and buy that car on this particular day, and that I would pay cash. Would he be available to sell me the car?

To my amazement, he told me he was far too busy to deal with an individual customer. If I came in, he would be pleased to turn me over to one of his salespeople but he couldn't take the time to deal with me personally. Wow! What an amazing response!

I then called the other dealership and went through the same routine. In this case, however, the sales manager treated me as though I was going to come down and buy *ten* cars that day. He offered to make an appointment at any time that was convenient for me and be available for the entire process. He assured me that he would personally handle all the documentation on the car. Well, you can imagine who I eventually bought the car from. But here's the interesting part.

I decided to check out both dealerships to be sure that I was getting the best deal. In the first dealership, where the sales manager said that he was far too busy to talk to me, the showroom was empty. I was the only customer in the place. When I asked the salesman how business was, he said that it was terrible and they were worried about it. He blamed it on the economy, the recession, the import duties, and a variety of other things.

When I went down to the second dealership, it looked like a fire sale was going on. People were driving in and out from all directions. Every closing room had a salesperson and customer filling out orders. The service people were driving new cars up to the front and taking used cars out for test drives. I asked them how business was and they said that they were so busy, they didn't have enough hours in the day to process all the sales.

These dealerships were both selling the same cars, at the same prices, in the same marketplace, about fifteen minutes away from each other. They were advertising in the same newspapers and were offering the identical models with identical features. But one of them was swamped with business because they made it clear that they had all the time that a customer wanted or needed to make a buying decision. The other place was empty because they were "too busy."

The second element of the friendship factor is what we discussed in Chapter 1. It is the factor of **caring.** The more you care about your prospects, the more interested they will be in doing business with you. The emotional element of caring is so powerful that it can often overwhelm concerns about price, relative quality, deliverability, size of company in the market, and so on. Caring is evident to others in your attitude toward your work and toward your customers. Once the customer is convinced that you genuinely care about him or her and his or her situation, the customer will want to buy from you, no matter what the details of the sale or the arguments of the competition.

The third element of the friendship factor is **respect.** It has been said that everything you do, or refrain from doing, is to earn the respect of the people you respect. Your own personal pride, dignity, and self-esteem is largely determined by the amount of respect that you feel other people have for you. And the more you value the opinion of another person, the more influence his or her respect will have on your behavior.

Whenever we feel respected by someone else, we see that person in a better light. If a person respects us, we consider him or her to be a better person, to have better judgment, to have greater insight, and to have finer character. When you show that you genuinely respect your customer, by practicing the essential listening skills, by being courteous, patient, and attentive, and by admiring the customer and his accomplishments, you make the customer feel better and happier about himself. And the better you make the customer feel about himself, the more the customer will like you and want to do business with you.

THE SEVEN STEPS TO RELATIONSHIP BUILDING

There are seven proven, tested steps to relationship building that have been around since Dale Carnegie wrote *How to Win Friends and Influence People*, and for many years before. They have always worked, and they always will. I have been at conferences where the entire room was full of salespeople earning more than $1 million a year on straight commission in extremely competitive businesses. And they all had these qualities in common.

First, **never criticize, complain, or condemn.** This is as good a piece of advice as when it was first written by Dale Carnegie in 1936. Be a positive, upbeat, cheerful person. Be optimistic and encouraging. Be happy and easygoing. Be the kind of person that other people are attracted to. No matter what is going on in your own personal life, never share it with your prospects. Behave as though you haven't a care in the world aside from how you can help your prospect achieve his goals or solve his problems.

Never criticize anyone or anything, either politically or religiously. Never criticize or bad-mouth your competitors. Whenever the name of your competitor comes up, you simply smile and say, "That is a very fine company." And then go on with your presentation. If people tell you of criticisms that your competitors have expressed about you, you just smile and let it pass.

Never condemn anyone or anything else, either in your business, your company, or in the industry in general. People are surrounded by negative influences and they don't need a salesperson to add to the chorus. As the Frank Sinatra song says, "If you can't say something *nice*, don't talk at all, is my advice."

If someone asks you how sales are going in your company, always say, "They couldn't be better! We're having our best month of the year!" Even if it's not exactly true, remember that no one wants to deal with a person or company that is doing poorly. No one wants to buy a product from a company whose sales are down. Even if business is soft for some legitimate reason, always talk optimistically about the future by talking optimistically about the present.

The more positive you are about yourself, your company, and your industry, the more confident will be the prospect in doing business with you.

The second step to relationship building is just plain **acceptance**. One of the deepest of all subconscious needs that people have is for unconditional acceptance from others. You express acceptance to others by smiling at them and by being a warm and friendly person. People like to be around people who accept them for the way they are, without judgment or criticism. And the more accepting you are of other people, the more accepting they will be of you.

The third step to relationship building is **approval**. Your expression of approval toward anyone satisfies another deep subconscious need, the need to be recognized and respected for our accomplishments. Whenever you give praise and approval to another person for anything, he feels happy inside. His energy levels rise. His heart rate increases. He feels good about himself. When you continually look for ways to give praise and approval of others on every occasion, you'll be welcome wherever you go.

The fourth step is **appreciation**. Appreciation is expressed by the magic words "Thank you." Whenever you thank another person for anything, you cause his or her self-esteem to go up. You make him or her feel more valuable and important.

You should get into the habit of thanking everybody for everything they do. Especially, thank people for things that you'd like to see them repeat. Thank secretaries, thank prospects, thank customers, thank co-workers, thank bosses, thank your spouse and children, thank waitresses and waiters, and thank anyone else who does anything for you, for any reason.

Perhaps the most wonderful benefit of thanking people is that every time you express your appreciation, your own self-esteem goes up as well. You feel happier and more positive. You feel more confident and courageous. You feel more effective and efficient. You feel more in control of your own destiny and you feel better toward everyone you meet. And you get all these benefits from the continual use of the words "Thank you."

The fifth step to relationship building is **admiration**. Whenever you admire a person's accomplishments, traits, or possessions, you raise his self-esteem and make him feel better about himself. As long as your admiration, approval, appreciation, and acceptance is *sincere*, people will be positively influenced by you. They will feel good toward you to the very degree to which you make them feel good about themselves and their lives.

Abraham Lincoln once said, "Everybody likes a compliment." Whenever you see anything that anyone has done or achieved that is worthy of a compliment, be sure to point it out and tell them how much you admire it.

I was sitting next to a businessman at a city council meeting some years ago when I noticed he had a beautiful, complicated multidial watch on his wrist. It calculated the date, day, month, year, hour, minute, and second. It included a barometer, a stop watch, and a compass. It was an astonishing creation. I remember leaning over to him and saying, "That is an amazing watch!"

He turned to me enthusiastically and spent about five minutes telling me about the watch, what it did, and how he had wrestled with the idea of paying the amount of money that it had cost. He told me how delighted he was with it and how he used it in a variety of ways during the day.

Over the next twelve months, I ended up doing more than half a million dollars' worth of real estate development and sales with this businessman. He came to me continuously on a variety of deals, each of which netted me and my company many thousands of dollars in commissions. Some years later, I ran into him at a meeting and he told me he still remembered that day I complimented him on his watch. He said, "In all the time I owned that watch, you were the only person who ever said anything nice about it, or noticed it at all."

The sixth step in relationship building is **agreeability**. This simply means that you never argue with a prospect. Whatever the prospect says, you nod, smile, and agree pleasantly.

Customers like to deal with agreeable people. Conversely, they do not like to deal with argumentative people. Even when it's obvious that a person is dead wrong, he will resent it if you point it out. If a person makes a mistake of any kind, unless it is absolutely earthshaking, simply let it pass. Keep your eyes focused on the relationship. Remember, as author and philanthropist Dr. Gerald Jampolski once asked, "Do you want to be *right*, or do you want to be *happy?*"

In some cases, you cannot be right and happy at the same time. You have to make a choice. In the interests of relationship building, you must often bite your lip and go along with statements that you know are not quite accurate.

The seventh step to relationship building is **focused attention.** Focused attention brings us back full circle to the idea of listening. When you focus your attention on your prospect when he or she is speaking, you pay him or her a great compliment. You make him feel valuable, worthwhile, and important. You cut through the resistance, tension, and suspicion that accompany any new sales relationship. You put the prospect at ease by the very act of focusing your attention totally on him or her and on every word he or she is saying.

Your job is to be a relationship expert. It is to be a human relations specialist. Your job is to become one of the nicest, most enjoyable people in your field. It is to think carefully before speaking or acting, and diligently practice every behavior that can enhance the quality of the relationship between you and your customer.

If a person lives on a desert island, like Robinson Crusoe, he only has to satisfy himself. What other people think or feel doesn't matter because there isn't anyone else. But when you enter into the competitive arena of sales, your success and happiness depend on contributing to the success and happiness of others. You need to adapt your approach and style to accommodate whatever it takes to build and maintain a high-quality relationship of trust and credibility with your prospects and customers. And the more you practice these relationship skills, the better you get. The better you get, the more customers and prospects you have.

Above all, you will earn the respect, esteem, and admiration of everyone you work with, both inside and outside your company. You will win the acclaim of your superiors and the loyalty of your customers.

CREDIBILITY VERSUS MEGA-CREDIBILITY

Your level of credibility is the foundation upon which your success as a person and as a salesperson are built. Credibility is as necessary to human relationships as oxygen. Your credibility is taken into consideration by every person who makes any kind of a decision that depends on you in any way. You must have a minimum level of credibility even to get to first base in selling.

The level of trust and the quality of the relationship that exists between you and your customer are the critical variables in modern selling. They are the basic requirements without which nothing can take place. They are absolutely fundamental to building the confidence that allows a customer to become dependent upon you to fulfill your promises. Because of the element of risk and the fear of failure that enters into every buying decision, trust and credibility are essential for the transaction to go forward. The more the customer believes you and your claims, the lower will be his or her fear of failure and preoccupation with risk.

To get onto the playing field of sales, you need credibility. But to win in an intensely competitive market, you need more than that. You need *mega-credibility*. You need inordinate levels of credibility. You need credibility that is greater than that of your competitors and which is so high that it overwhelms the fears and doubts that would normally cause the prospect to hesitate, delay, or decide against a buying decision.

And here is one of the most important rules in selling, especially as it applies to mega-credibility: "**Everything counts!**" One of the marks of the true professional is that he recognizes that "the devil is in the details." It is the details that make you or break you, every single time. And with regard to the details, *everything counts*.

The principle that everything counts is one of the most basic rules for success in any area of endeavor. Everything you do, or don't do, from morning to night, counts. It adds up or it takes away. It helps you or hurts you. It contributes to your success or contributes to your failure. It moves you toward your goals or it moves you away from them. Nothing is neutral. Everything counts.

Wolfgang von Goethe, one of the most brilliant philosophers and writers who ever lived, said that the greatest discovery of his age was that of "double-entry bookkeeping." When he was asked why such a simple accounting mechanism would be so impressive, compared with all of the other great breakthroughs of his generation, he replied that its importance and beauty was in its simplicity.

Double-entry bookkeeping, he pointed out, was a metaphor for life. It enabled the development of the business system of that day because it was a method to account for every dollar flowing in and out of a business. All moneys could be divided into either debits or credits. From the simplest company to the largest organization, every single penny could be expressed on one side of the ledger or the other.

Goethe felt that life was very much the same. Everything that you or I do can be expressed on either the debit side or the credit side of our own personal ledgers. Every smart and helpful thing that you do goes on the credit side. Every foolish or thoughtless thing that you do goes on the debit side. A great life is a life with far more credits than debits. A poor life is one with far more debits than credits. It's extremely simple. It's unavoidable. It is clear to everyone. And everything counts.

Supreme Court Justice Oliver Wendell Holmes once wrote, "You can divide the world into two types of people: those who divide the world into two types of people, and those who do not." Well, I think you can divide the world into two types of people by looking at their attitudes toward the principle that everything counts. There are those who accept and believe that everything counts, and live their lives accordingly. These are the winners and high achievers in every area of life.

And then there are those who hope that it *doesn't*. These are the men and women who somehow believe they are going to achieve their goals without doing everything necessary to get there. They are the people who think they can climb the ladder of success without putting each foot solidly on each rung. These are the people who are always looking for shortcuts. These are the people who think that, if no one is looking, then it doesn't matter. These are the people who ultimately fail and then turn around and blame their situations on others. They ignore the principle that everything counts at their own peril.

This principle is vitally important in selling, where a major sale can be made or lost by one small thing that is either done or not done. A mark of the true professional is that he leaves nothing to chance. He thinks through every detail. He prepares thoroughly and he always keeps foremost in his mind the cardinal principle that everything counts.

Everything you do in the sales transaction either raises or lowers the fear and the perception of risk on the part of the prospect. Prospects are hypersensitive to details surrounding the salesperson. The mind of the prospect is like a computer that is rapidly adding and subtracting positives and negatives about the salesperson from the first contact. These impressions accumulate into a single perception that gives the prospect the confidence either to proceed or not.

Your job is to position yourself as the lowest-risk provider of your product or service, and this means that you must do everything possible to develop not just your credibility, but your mega-credibility in the eyes of your prospect.

HOW TO DEVELOP MEGA-CREDIBILITY

There are several areas of mega-credibility that have an impact on the prospect's total impression of you, your product or service, your company, and the idea of doing business with you. Just as an airplane pilot goes through a checklist prior to every flight, you need to put yourself through a checklist as well. And it is absolutely essential that you never attempt to fool yourself by hoping that the customer won't notice. Customers remember and record everything, and everything counts!

The first area where you establish high, medium, or low credibility is in your person, your appearance, your attitude, and your personality. First impressions are lasting. You never get a second chance to make a good first impression. The customer's mind is like quick-drying cement. The instant the customer meets you, he or she begins forming an impression that becomes indelibly marked on his or her mind. Once the impression is formed, it is very difficult to change it. The natural tendency of each person is to seek out more and more evidence to corroborate the conclusion they have already arrived at, rather than to seek out evidence to contradict it. This is just as true for you as it is for your customer.

In terms of your personal appearance, you must give careful attention to your dress, your grooming, and your accessories. Each day, before you start out, you should stand and look at yourself in a full-length mirror and ask yourself, "Do I look like a first-class professional salesperson for my company?"

Human beings are very much the same in this one area. We all judge people by the way they look on the *outside*. You judge other people this way and they judge you. It is useless to insist that people should judge you for your character and your personality, and ignore the way you appear. This is just not the way the world works. Since you largely control the way you look on the outside, people naturally assume that your dress, grooming, and accessories are choices that you have made to signal to the world the person you really are.

I will discuss the importance of dress, colors, grooming, accessories, and other items in a later chapter, but for now it is sufficient to point out that every item of your appearance either helps or hurts you in the sales conversation. Part of the Hippocratic Oath for doctors, from ancient Greece, says simply, "Do no harm." This should be your motto as well. At the very least, there should be no item of your appearance that could harm the impression of credibility and professionalism you wish to build in the customer's mind.

The second area of credibility you can affect has to do with your company. Customers are continually looking for ways to either include you in or exclude you out. They are looking for reasons to trust you and your offering or to pass it by. Every company has a variety of factors about it that can contribute to the building of trust and credibility, if not mega-credibility. It is your job to identify these positive features and point them out to your prospects in the course of your sales conversation.

The first three factors are the size of your company, the length of time it has been in business, and the market share it has of your particular product or service. Each of these can make a statement of stability and trust that will cause your prospect to more readily decide to do business with you.

If your company is large, for example, it can only mean that it has been successful over time at satisfying a lot of other customers similar to the one you are speaking to. Large companies almost always have an edge over small companies because their size suggests a proven ability to give customers what they want.

The length of time your company has been in business is important as well. Because of the wide number of choices for purchasing any product or service in our highly competitive market, customers are reluctant to entrust a buying decision to a new enterprise. Many small companies fail, as do junior salespeople, because they have no idea how long it takes to build up the necessary level of credibility to be taken seriously as vendors in the current marketplace. Many companies have to be around for two, three, or four years before they will be considered seriously by prospective customers.

If your company has been in existence for several years, this is a positive statement about your ability to satisfy customers satisfactorily. Sometimes, the longevity of your company can be enough in itself to give you the winning edge in a sales conversation.

Two businessmen from a Fortune 500 company and myself arrived late in the evening in Columbus, Ohio, prior to a day of evaluating training programs for their salespeople and staff. We were tired and hungry and as we drove into the city, we were wondering aloud where we could go for dinner. We didn't know the city very well and we didn't want to find ourselves stuck at a poor restaurant, after a long day of work and travel.

As we approached the hotel, I saw a restaurant on the same street. Under the name was this little sign, "Proudly serving the people of Columbus for 27 years." That was enough for us.

Without a moment's hesitation, we decided to have dinner at this restaurant. The length of time the restaurant had been in business was sufficient proof to us that it was a safe buying decision. With that one detail, the restaurant achieved mega-credibility.

Your company's market share is also a builder of credibility. If there are twenty-five companies in your market area and your company has one third of the market, this percentage is a good reason for your prospect to do business with you. If you have managed to achieve a high level of market share against your competitors, it means that you are obviously offering a product or service that has proven to be preferable to a greater number of people than your competitors have.

A salesman came into my office not long ago to make a presentation for the services offered by his firm. His approach was very effective. He opened by introducing himself, shaking hands, and sitting down. Then he asked, "Before I begin, may I ask you a question? Do you know *very much* about our company?"

Notice, he did not ask, "Do you know *anything* about our company?" He simply asked, "Do you know *very much* about our company?" This question triggered two reactions. The first was an admission that, "No, I don't know very much about your company." And the second was curiosity. Curiosity is one of the most powerful of all human motivations and this question triggered it immediately, like two electric wires coming together to create a spark.

With that simple question, he had control of the sales conversation and he had our complete attention. He went on to say something like, "Our company is the largest company of its size in our market area. We have been in business in the same location for twenty-two years and have grown from thirteen people to 230 people in the last decade. We also do about 30 percent of all the work being done in our field. And most of our work is repeat business with satisfied clients."

With those simple opening remarks he had taken himself, his company, and his services from minimum credibility to maximum credibility. He had answered the question, "Is it safe?" He had opened our minds and lowered our defenses so that we were immediately interested in how his previous clients had benefited, and how we might benefit as well from his services. We went from being resistant and skeptical to being open and receptive.

You've heard the old saying, "Put your best foot forward." You must always give this some thought at the beginning of a sales conversation, and then begin by highlighting some of the most positive aspects of your company.

The second area of corporate credibility has to do with your brochures, handouts, price lists, and business cards. Customers are sensitive to the visual aspects of your personal and material presentation. They are extremely aware of the quality of the materials that you use in your sales presentation. To your prospect, your sales materials are a reflection of the kind of company you represent, and the kind of products and services you sell.

Prior to visiting a prospect, be sure that you have a complete selection of brand-new sales materials. Be sure that you have an adequate supply of business cards. Be sure that your materials are stacked sequentially so that you have easy access to them in a logical order.

All true sales professionals prepare thoroughly, in detail, every single piece of paper that they are likely to show or leave with the prospect. They leave nothing to chance. Attractive materials might not make the sale, but poorly presented sales materials can very easily kill it.

I have met countless salespeople who have no business cards, or have business cards that have been written on, or that are tattered and frayed around the corners. I have seen salespeople pull out price lists and brochures that have handwriting in the margins, coffee stains on the bottom, and that have been scrunched up or folded in previous presentations and are still being used. Worst of all, I have seen too many salespeople go out on calls with incorrect or insufficient materials and find themselves unable to answer customer questions because their specification sheets are back at the office. In every case, they kick the chair out from under their own credibility and they make the customer wonder to himself why he ever agreed to an interview in the first place.

The third area of corporate credibility is telephone manners—yours, as well as the courtesy and helpfulness of the people the prospect talks to when he or she phones your company. Good telephone skills are absolutely essential to successful salesmanship. Many people do business together for years without ever meeting face-to-face because of the power of the telephone as a business tool. And very small differences in the way you carry yourself on the telephone can make very strong impressions on the customer's mind.

Whenever you phone a prospect, always be clear, honest, and direct.

Say something like, "Hello, this is Susan Jones, and I'm with ABC Company." You then go into the reason for your call.

If someone phones you, answer by saying, "Hello, this is John James, how may I help you?" Be upbeat and optimistic. Be warm and friendly. Make people happy that they took your phone call or that they phoned you back.

When you leave your office, be sure to tell the receptionist exactly how long you will be gone, and when you will be able to get back to someone who phones in. There is nothing more aggravating for a prospect than to phone a company to get in touch with the salesperson, only to have the receptionist say, "I don't where he is, and I don't know when he'll be back."

Be sure that the person who answers the telephone in your company has excellent telephone skills, which is what the very best companies in America do. And every telephone company gives regular courses to their corporate clients on telephone manners and courtesy. This is an extremely important part of credibility for impatient prospects who have a variety of suppliers to choose from. It cannot be left to chance.

The third major form of mega-credibility, which can be so powerful it can compensate for almost any other mistake you make, is what Robert Cialdini calls "social proof." Cialdini's research for his book *Influence* concluded that people are inordinately influenced by the choices that have been made by other people they consider to be similar to themselves. The average prospect concludes, "If someone else like me has bought this product or service, then it must be a good idea for me to buy it as well."

When a customer is considering a buying decision, he or she is looking for every way possible to minimize the risk inherent in any purchase. One of the fastest and best ways to lower this fear is by learning that many other people in the same situation are already using the product satisfactorily and are happy with their choice. This knowledge alone can eliminate the perception of risk from the customer's mind.

We are strongly influenced by hearing that anyone similar to ourselves has bought a particular product or service and is enjoying it. This is why one of the first questions we ask when considering any new product or service offering is, "Who else has done it?" This is another way of looking for proof that this is not a risky decision. And the more people similar to the particular prospect who have bought and used the product or service the higher the credibility of the salesperson and the company who is selling it.

For example, the most respected surveys of after-sale customer satisfaction with automobiles are conducted by the J. D. Power and Associates organization. They rank new cars in order, from those having the highest levels of customer satisfaction to those having the lowest levels in the three-month, six-month, and twelve-month periods after purchase. Any car that scores in the top ten on the J. D. Power ratings automatically has higher credibility among prospective purchasers than cars that do not.

In 1989, both the Toyota Lexus and the Nissan Infiniti, midlevel luxury automobiles, were introduced into the United States. As competitors, they had one goal in common: to win the J. D. Power award for quality and customer satisfaction. And they did. In 1992, they tied for first place for customer satisfaction among all cars sold in America.

This victory in the customer satisfaction survey had two powerful consequences. The first was that everyone who had ever purchased a Lexus or an Infiniti felt doubly satisfied at having made such a good choice. They probably told their friends as well what a fine car they were driving and how happy they were with it.

The second major benefit was that people wavering between the purchase of a Lexus or Infiniti or some other car were easily swayed into paying more for one of the higher-rated cars because so many others had already attested to how satisfied and happy they were. Today, more than 30 percent of new Lexus sales are repeat customers.

The fastest way to build credibility among skeptical prospects is with **testimonials** from satisfied customers. Testimonials are so powerful that they often make the sale all by themselves. A series of testimonials from respected purchasers can be all that it takes to brush aside fear and resistance and close the sale. After all, the customer thinks, if all these other people have made this buying decision and are happy with it, "How can I go wrong?"

The three main forms of testimonials are letters, lists, and photographs. **Letters** from satisfied customers are perhaps the most powerful of all sales aids. They cut through the clutter right to the heart of the decision. They make it clear that this is a good and safe product to buy. Often a prospect will decide to buy upon reading one solid testimonial from one respected person or company.

How do you get testimonial letters? There are a variety of ways that I've used over the years. All are effective. The first is simply to *ask* your satisfied customer for a testimonial letter. If you've been in sales for any time at all, you will have "sweetheart" customers, customers who like you and who will write a testimonial letter for you if you ask.

Tell them you need a nice letter that you can show to difficult prospects to reassure them that they are making the right buying decision.

If you get specific objections in your sales presentation, have your satisfied customer write a letter saying that he had this same concern as well before he purchased from you. Have the letter go on to say that he subsequently found that his concern never materialized.

For example, the kind of letter that I have obtained from my satisfied customers would say something like this:

"Dear Brian,

When you initially approached us with your product, I felt that your price was too high, compared to what others were offering. But after I decided to go ahead and buy the product from you, I found that the value of your product was far greater than the price. I'm glad I paid more because I got so much more."

Often, your customers are too busy to write testimonial letters for you. In this case, ask them if you can write the testimonial letter yourself and have them type it on their company letterhead and sign it for you. Almost every customer will allow you to do this because it saves them time.

Lists of satisfied customers are excellent ways to build mega-credibility. If you can make lists of your clients without violating confidentiality, they can be very impressive. When we were promoting our *Effective Manager Seminar* series, we assembled lists of dozens of major American corporations that had already purchased and installed the programs. And the more names we had of different companies in different industries, the more of our management training libraries we sold. It was very hard for a prospect to argue about the relative quality of the programs when hundreds of other corporations were already using them satisfactorily.

The third form of customer testimonial that contributes to mega-credibility is **photographs** of your product or service being delivered to, or being used by, one of your customers. "A picture is worth a thousand words." We tend to identify with characters in letters and people in photographs. The more of them you have, the more easily your prospects can identify with a satisfied customer. The more your prospect identifies with a satisfied customer, the more your prospect will want to be a satisfied customer as well.

A good testimonial—a letter, list, or photo—can overcome 90 percent or more of the sales resistance that a prospect might have in dealing with you. You should collect them as a regular part of your sales activities and use them at every opportunity.

One of the exercises that I recommend to the sales groups that I train is that they each set a goal to go out and get *two* testimonial letters in the next week from their satisfied customers. They then bring these testimonials back and share them with one another. They take each testimonial letter and use a yellow highlighter to emphasize the most powerful sentences. They then mount them in plastic pages, put them in three-hole binders, and carry these binders with them everywhere.

Many individuals and sales forces have been able to assemble ten or twenty testimonial letters together in binders, thereby arming every salesperson with a powerful weapon to build credibility and overcome sales resistance. When salespeople start using testimonials, their sales go up almost immediately. The content of the testimonials increases their confidence and their aggressiveness in prospecting and selling against competition. In fact, testimonials are so powerful, and used so regularly by top salespeople, it is said, "Salespeople who don't use testimonials have skinny kids."

The fourth major area where you can achieve mega-credibility has to do with outside **authorities and experts** who attest to the value and qualities of your product or service. Remember, a salesperson's assertions are not proof. The very fact that you are attempting to sell a product or service makes what *you* say about that product or service somewhat suspect in the mind of the customer. You are expected to build it up and tell the customer what a good product or service it is. You are even expected to exaggerate. You are expected to make sweeping statements about what your product or service will do and what good value it is. This is part of the selling game.

In fact, in law, there are three definitions of sales claims that turn out to be inaccurate. They are: 1) fraudulent misrepresentation; 2) misrepresentation; and 3) puffery. *Fraudulent misrepresentation* exists when the salesperson makes statements about the product or service that he knows are untrue. A sale can be set aside by the court on this basis.

Misrepresentation exists when the salesperson says things about the product or service that turn out to be untrue but that the salesperson did not know. He was acting in good faith. Sometimes this is called "innocent misrepresentation." A sale can be set aside on the basis of innocent misrepresentation if the customer relied on the salesperson's assertions and suffered a loss as a result.

The third category is *puffery*. When a salesperson says, "My product or service is the best in the world!" this is puffery. It is not a legal reason for setting a sale aside. According to the common law, salespeople are expected to "puff up" their products or services, to exaggerate them, to compare them favorably to anything else that is available. But it is not illegal. It is as expected of salespeople as it is expected by customers that salespeople will engage in it.

But when a *third party* says that your product or service is good based on an objective analysis, then it really means something to the prospect. Whenever you can get a credible outside source to testify that what you are selling is good and worthwhile, your credibility goes up in the customer's mind, sometimes to the point when a customer will drop all resistance and buy it immediately.

For example, any type of publication, magazine, or news story talking favorably about your product or service can exert a positive influence on the customer's thinking about what you are selling. Many people don't believe what you say about your product until they see something that has been written about it by an objective third party.

The best example of this is the magazine *Consumer Reports*, which is considered to contain honest, objective assessments of the relative quality of various products. Many people will not buy a product until they have checked it in *Consumer Reports*. If *Consumer Reports* ranks a product or service among the best in its category, that alone will lead to much higher sales. Many salespeople will carry a copy of *Consumer Reports* around with them to show how highly ranked their product or service is in comparison with their competitors'. Often this is all it takes to convince a skeptical prospect.

Another type of third-party endorsement is that of people who are respected for their expertise and knowledge in the field. I read an advertisement recently for a medicine that said, "Forty-two thousand doctors picked [this medicine] as the most effective pain reliever in America today."

Forty-two thousand doctors? How can anyone argue against the authority and expertise of forty-two thousand doctors? This is a very powerful argument for buying!

If there is a well-known person in your community who has bought and used your product or service, be sure to point this out when you are talking to a prospect. If the president of the Chamber of Commerce, the mayor, the president of a major business or industry, a leading sports or entertainment figure, or anyone else who is respected or looked up to by the customer has purchased what you sell, mentioning this fact builds tremendous credibility for you and your company and can often be the final factor that leads to the sale.

Another form of authority that greatly influences buying decisions is contained in the *symbols* of success and affluence worn or used by the salesperson. A salesperson who drives a beautiful car, who dresses well, and who carries an expensive briefcase exerts a strong influence on the prospect. The success and prosperity exuded by a salesperson extends to the product or service, and the company itself.

The fact is that people like to do business with other successful people and companies. That is why when salespeople win a sales award they often announce it proudly on their business cards. Would you like to buy a car or a house from a person just starting out, or from the top salesperson in the industry? Would you like to buy an investment from a person who doesn't look like he can afford lunch, or from a person who looks wealthy and successful? Remember, little things mean a lot, and *everything counts*.

The sixth area where you can develop mega-credibility has to do with the product or service itself. In fact, you can make it or break it in this area alone. If you can present your product or service as being absolutely *ideal* for the customer in every way, satisfying his or her most pressing needs of the moment, this factor can make the sale for you, holding constant for everything else.

You build greater credibility by showing the prospect that your product or service provides the exact benefits that he or she is seeking. When you build trust by carefully identifying needs, and then you show the prospect how his or her needs can be perfectly satisfied by the exact things that your product or service does, you can build tremendous credibility and overwhelm the strongest sales resistance.

When you can show your prospect that the value of the solution that your product or service represents to him greatly outweighs the cost of your product or service, you build credibility that is hard to deny. A client of mine recently paid $55,000 for consulting services for a medium-sized firm. When I commented to him that that sounded like a lot of money, he said, "I thought so, too. But they assured me that the payoff to my bottom line would be $150,000 in the first year once their systems were installed, and they were willing to guarantee it. How could I lose?"

It later turned out that the changes that the consultants made in the client's hiring, firing, and compensation systems actually saved the company more than $200,000 the first year. That consulting firm is now using the testimonial letter from this client to sell even more services to almost every qualified company they speak to. They have built their credibility to a high point by providing exactly the benefits that their customer needed and they are now using their reputation for results to build their business more rapidly.

Often, the critical determinant in a complex sale, from the point of view of the person who actually signs the check, is the bottom-line benefit to the company. Whenever you are selling a product or service to a business, you must be prepared to show the decision-maker that the product or service will eventually pay for itself. No intelligent busi-

nessperson contracts for a known loss. Businesses survive and thrive by making positive bottom-line decisions. Your job is to be continually looking for the different ways that your product or service can save or make money for the prospect in such amounts that it pays for itself over the life of the service. Your ability to do this gives you enormous credibility.

Another element that gives you and your product mega-credibility is your willingness to back what you say with guarantees and assurances. This is called "risk reversal." It is your showing the prospect that you are so confident that the product or service will do what you say it will do that you are willing to back it up by offering "complete satisfaction or your money back."

If your company gives guarantees and assurances, this is a powerful way for you to build the credibility necessary to win the sale. You can capitalize on the prospect's need for added assurance by offering your own guarantees, as well.

A salesman for a company that I had never dealt with approached me not long ago and gave me his presentation. He told me about how long the company had been in business and how rapidly it was growing because of its satisfied customers. He told me about the people who were using the company and were recommending the company to their friends. He told me about the quality of their products and how they maintained quality control. He told me about how committed they were to the absolute satisfaction of every customer they dealt with. And then he clinched the sale with these words, "Brian, in addition to all of the guarantees and assurances that my company gives on this product, I will give you my personal guarantee of satisfaction. I will personally do everything possible to make sure this is one of the best decisions you ever make. I really want you for my customer."

I am just as emotional as any other buyer and this was a powerful closing argument. I subsequently went on to spend thousands of dollars with this individual and his company over the following years. His closing argument eliminated my last vestige of skepticism and hesitation.

The final area where you can build tremendous credibility is in your sales presentation. This is so important that we will spend an entire chapter on it but let me give you the four key elements that add to, or detract from, your credibility in the presentation of your product.

First, when the presentation is **customer-focused and problem-centered,** you and your company have greater credibility than if you are talking about yourself and about the features of your product or service. The more you focus all of your attention, questions, body gestures, listening, and presentation on the customer's situation and needs, the more credible you are and the easier it is to buy from you.

Second, you build credibility when you skillfully **match your product features and benefits to the specific needs** that have been identified in your questioning and confirmed by your prospect. The more closely you can tie your product or service to the customer's actual situation, the more credible you are and the easier it is to buy from you.

The third area where you build credibility in the sales presentation is by your continuing to **focus on the relationship,** on the person. By the Law of Indirect Effort, when you continually reinforce the fact that you value the person and the relationship even more than you value making the sale, you build and maintain credibility. When the customer reaches the point where he or she is convinced that you care more about him than the sale, the customer will then want to buy from you and will look for every way possible to help you make the sale to him.

The fourth and final way to build mega-credibility in the sales presentation is for you to **accept complete responsibility for the sale.** It is for you to take upon yourself the responsibility to ensure that the paperwork will be completed, the product or service will be delivered and installed, and that it will be serviced and supported to the client's complete satisfaction. At the end of your sales presentation, you can say, "If you'll just authorize this, you can leave it to me and I'll take care of all the details."

As much as anything else, a prospect wants a trouble-free purchase. Once the customer has said yes to your offering, he wants to be able to turn to other things and get on with the rest of his life. The customer does not want to have to continually revisit the purchase decision because of unresolved details and unsolved problems. The customer wants to make the buying decision with complete confidence that this is absolutely the right thing to do and that he will never have any regrets for having chosen to do business with you.

SUMMARY

The essence of professional selling today is the building and maintaining of high-quality relationships, based on establishing a high level of trust and credibility with the customer. The job of the salesperson is to create and keep a customer indefinitely. You create a customer by convincing him overwhelmingly that you are the lowest-risk, highest-value, easiest person and company to do business with. You keep customers by delivering on your promises, fulfilling your commitments and continually investing in maintaining the quality of your relationships.

Selling today is based on the Golden Rule and the friendship factor. Treat every customer like a special and important person, exactly the way you would like to be treated by someone selling you a product or service. Be thoroughly prepared and knowledgeable. Be completely honest and straightforward. Be totally focused on helping the customer to make a good buying decision, just as you would like to be treated if you were the customer.

What makes the future of professional selling so bright is the fact that you are in the business of developing professional selling friendships. Some of the best people you will ever meet will start off as tough prospects that you will eventually convert into customers. Some of the best friendships you will ever form in your life will be the people who you help to improve their work and their personal lives with what you sell. The greatest joy that you will ever receive from your profession is the deep inner satisfaction that will come from knowing, that through your products or services, you are making a real difference.

5

THE PROFESSION

OF SELLING

You have one of the most important jobs in our society. Nothing happens for your company until you make a sale. Every other person in the company, from the president down to the janitor, is completely dependent on you for their employment and their income. Your ability to generate sales is the absolute prerequisite for the success of your business. Your effectiveness as a salesperson is crucial to determining whether your company will succeed or fail.

Selling is an honorable profession. Salespeople are the forerunners of progress, development, and growth throughout the entire economy.

It is salespeople who ultimately generate the markets for almost all other skills. When you make a sale, it has a domino effect that provides employment up and down the line for everyone else in society. Where there are no sales, there is no domino effect. It is salespeople who open new markets for products and services and whose work generates demand for land, labor, raw materials, capital, and technology. When sales slow down and stop, businesses also slow down and grind to a halt. According to Dun & Bradstreet, the number one reason for business failure is lack of sales. The number one reason for business success is abundant sales. And the effectiveness of your activities determines which of these it is going to be.

Every economic indicator or report in the newspapers and business magazines deals in some way with the level of sales in a particular company or industry. The various stock markets, the wholesale price index, the consumer price index, the commodity index, and so on, all refer to the quantities and prices of goods and services being sold at any given time. A softening in sales activity, or an actual decline, are indicators of trouble ahead for that particular product or area of economic activity.

Selling can be either an occupation or a profession depending upon your attitude toward what you do. It can be a low-paid way of carving out a living from paycheck to paycheck, or it can be one of the highest paying professions in our society. Your selling career can be a provider of bare sustenance or a high road to great success. There are salespeople who earn $10,000 a year and there are salespeople who earn more than $1 million a year. It is up to you to decide where you want your earnings to appear on this scale.

Top salespeople are among the most respected men and women in our society. Over the years, I have had the honor of working with thousands of men and women in sales who are leading their fields. I have files full of letters from salespeople in every industry who are creating wonderful lives for themselves by using the profession of selling as a springboard to the fulfillment of all their goals and aspirations.

In America today, more senior executives and presidents of Fortune 1000 corporations come from sales and marketing than from any other area in the company. Successful salespeople dine with presidents and prime ministers, movie stars and sports stars. Top salespeople become important people in their communities and have an enormous impact on their societies. Top salespeople are the spark plugs in the engines of social and economic progress. Their activities and successes define the American Dream.

The Mary Kay Corporation has single-handedly created more women executives earning $50,000 a year or more than any other company in America. And this has been achieved by educating them in the profession of selling. Women are forming businesses in America at three times the rate of men and the primary strength of these business owners is their ability to sell their products and services. For both men and women, the development of selling skills is the fastest and most dependable road, upward and onward, in American society.

Selling is a special field in that it is open at the bottom. Almost anyone can get into selling at the lower levels, and almost anyone does. It is easy to get a job selling something, somewhere, on some basis. There is no man or woman who cannot get a sales job under some circumstances. But from that moment on, it stops being easy.

A fatal mistake that most salespeople make is that they think it is as easy to rise in sales as it is to get into sales in the first place. Nothing could be further from the truth. Your first sales job gives you a tenuous handhold on the bottom rung on the ladder of sales success. From then on, it's up to you, and it takes tremendous dedication on your part to pull yourself higher.

In selling, as motivational speaker Zig Ziglar says, "The elevator to the top is out of order." You have to take the stairs. You have to rise on the basis of your own determined effort. There is no substitute for hard, hard work. And here is one of the most important rules of success: whatever got you to where you are today is *not enough* to keep you there.

Because anyone can get into sales, many people look upon sales as no more than an occupation. To them, it is just a job, a way of earning a living. The amount that you can earn for selling at the lower levels of the industry are average for the pay scales in that industry. Turnover is high, production is mediocre, and opportunities to earn high incomes are negligible. It is only when you begin to move ahead of the pack that the real opportunities begin to open up for you.

It is your attitude and your activities that determine whether you make selling an occupation or a profession. It is what you do every single day that is the critical determinant of the respect and esteem people have for you as a professional salesperson. It is you who makes your work honorable. It is not the company, the product, the service, the marketplace, or the competition. It is you personally who decides, every hour of every day, whether or not to make selling a noble activity that others look up to, admire, and respect. As a wise man once said, "Jobs do not have futures; only people do."

THE PROFESSIONAL APPROACH

A profession is an advanced occupation with a specific methodology and process. It is systematized and orderly. It has a standardized set of practices that are followed in sequence from the first step to the last.

In this sense, the profession of sales is like a combination lock, with a series of numbers that must be turned to, in order, for the lock to open. All the enthusiasm and energy in the world will not open a combination lock if you don't know the numbers or if you turn to the numbers in the wrong sequence. All the eagerness and ambition a person could have will not help him or her make sales in a tough market if he or she does the wrong things or does the right things in the wrong order.

Selling is a complex process of teaching, learning, influencing, persuading, positioning, and overcoming natural buying resistance to bring the prospect to the point where he or she becomes a customer. It is not easy. The very expectation that selling should be easy if you just see enough people can be harmful, if not fatal, to sales success. People who think something should be easy will always be demoralized and frustrated when they find that it isn't true.

You begin to move into the upper ranks of salespeople in your field when you start to approach selling as a profession. It is only when you stand back and look at what you are doing, and think about it seriously, that you begin to elevate yourself and your work to a higher plane. This is a case where the "longest way around is the shortest way through."

In 1905, a man named Frederick Taylor started a revolution in production processes that goes on to this day. It was called "scientific management" and he became the foremost authority in the world on this approach to manufacturing.

Frederick Taylor's idea was that the key to improving the quality and quantity of production was to break every job down into its individual activities and then train workers to perform these specific activities with a high degree of efficiency. Instead of a craftsman, like a cabinet maker, performing every part of the task from cutting raw wood through to finishing the completed product, workers were instead taught to perform a single function rapidly and well.

The scientific management process began with a careful analysis of the work to be done, the division of labor into specialties, and the establishment of a production process or production line that enabled large numbers of workers, like members of a fire brigade passing buckets of water from hand to hand, to work together to produce unprecedented quantities of products.

The idea of scientific management propelled America into the twentieth century and made her the greatest industrial power on earth in just a few years. Henry Ford was the first industrialist to apply it and he became the richest man in the world in the next ten years. The same organized approach to sales is the key to rapidly increasing your productivity as well.

The key words are "process analysis." Even though sales skills are primarily intangible and interpersonal, they can be subjected to process analysis in that the entire sale can be broken down into individual, specific activities that can then be analyzed and improved upon.

Millions of dollars and countless hours have been spent over the years observing thousands of sales calls conducted by salespeople at various levels of expertise. It is no surprise that this research shows that top salespeople sell in a specific way. Medium salespeople sell in a more random and haphazard way. And poor salespeople sell in a disorganized and self-defeating way.

Every activity of a professional salesperson, before, during, and after the sale, can be broken down and defined separately. It can be analyzed for its strengths and weaknesses. It can be compared against the behaviors of the highest earning people in that particular field. Each of these functions can then be vastly improved by learning and practicing the specific behaviors of other top performers in that area.

As we saw earlier, the Law of Cause and Effect says that for every effect there is a specific cause. It also says that if you can define the effect that you want (sales success) and you can trace it back to the cause (what other successful salespeople are doing), you can achieve the effect you want by duplicating the cause. There is no miracle to it. It is so simple, it is embarrassing. Yet the primary reason why salespeople underperform is that either they have not learned or they do not practice what has been proven to work by thousands and thousands of salespeople before them.

THE BASIC PROFESSIONAL SELLING PROCESS

In Chapter 1, we talked about how top salespeople view themselves as doctors of selling. As doctors of selling, like any doctor or professional, they follow a particular process in dealing with their prospects. This process follows the sequence from examination through diagnosis to prescription. It is rigid and unchanging and all doctors are adamant about following this process with their patients. It is the same in sales. Top salespeople follow a specific sequence of activities. They do not fall apart and vary their approach because their prospect is either negative or impatient. They see themselves as doctors, as total professionals in their field, and they conduct themselves in a professional manner.

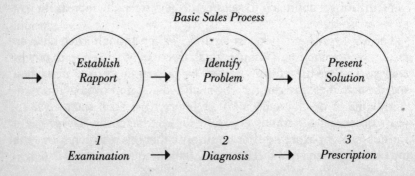

Basic Sales Process

For the sake of analyzing the sales process, the sale, in its simplest terms, has three basic parts. They are in order: (1) establishing rapport; (2) identifying the problem; and (3) presenting the solution. Like a combination lock with three numbers, the three parts of the sale must be covered in the correct order. Any attempt to open the lock, or to make the sale, by leaving out one of the numbers, or steps, or by getting the numbers or steps out of sequence, will lead to failure. The lock won't open; the sale won't be made.

As I said in the last chapter, the prospect cannot even seriously consider your offer until he or she is convinced that you are his friend and acting in his best interests. Therefore, you must take sufficient time to build a bridge of personal warmth and rapport between yourself and the prospect before you can go any further. This is the equivalent of the examination phase in the doctor-patient relationship. If you attempt to sell without taking the time to understand your prospect, he or she may be polite, but he will usually be uninterested in doing business with you. We will talk about how you accomplish this at some length in a later chapter.

The second part of the basic sales process is the identification of the problem. This is the equivalent of the diagnosis phase in the doctor-patient relationship. As a sales consultant, you are a problem-solver. The product or service you represent is a solution to a problem that the prospect has, or might have.

Both in establishing rapport and identifying the problem that your product or service can solve, you ask carefully prepared questions and you listen intently to the answers. You ask a certain number of personal questions to get to know and understand your prospect on a personal basis, but the majority of your questions are aimed at the prospect's problem or situation. It is only when you are addressing yourself to a real problem or "pain" being experienced by the prospect that he or she will see you and treat you as a professional rather than as just a salesperson.

The third part of the basic sales process, following mutual agreement on the definition of the problem, is the presentation of your solution, writing the prescription. Your job is to find problems for which your product or service is the solution or answer that the customer needs. The focus of your questioning and conversing should be on how your product or service can be acquired and used by your prospect in a cost-effective way.

In a proper presentation, the issue of price is dealt with at the end of the solution phase of the sales process. Until then, it is inappropriate and even counterproductive to bring it into the equation. Any discussion of price before the prospect has decided that he or she wants to enjoy the benefits of the solution will dampen, if not destroy, the sale.

Prospects almost always ask about price early in the sales discussion, but any discussion of price before buying desire has been aroused sufficiently is out of place. It is too early. It doesn't matter how much it costs if the prospect doesn't see it as the ideal solution to his problem. We'll be talking about how to deal with price resistance in a later chapter, but as a simple demonstration, can you imagine a doctor discussing and defending the price of an operation during the examination or diagnosis phases of the consultation? Of course not! Price is not even a real issue until the prospect has decided that he or she wants what you are selling.

BECOMING A SKILLED THINKER IN SELLING

The starting point of process analysis in selling is for you to think about these three phases of the sale. All top salespeople are excellent thinkers. They think before they act. They plan carefully before they speak to a prospect and they analyze carefully afterward.

Aristotle once defined wisdom as "an equal measure of experience plus reflection." People who grow wiser and more effective as they mature are those who take the time to reflect carefully on their experiences. They analyze them from every point of view. They evaluate them in terms of what they can learn from them to apply to future experiences. People who do not grow in their fields are those who may have many experiences but who don't take the time to reflect on them or to think about what they are learning from what they are doing.

Stand back from yourself and your work on a regular basis. Observe your way of selling and evaluate yourself on how effective you are in each of the areas of establishing rapport, identifying problems clearly, and presenting solutions effectively. This is the starting point of process analysis and it leads rapidly to greater sales success.

THE VITAL FUNCTIONS OF SELLING

If your car is running poorly and you take it into a garage, they will check it out thoroughly, moving from the most likely problem to the least likely. They will start with the carburetor, fuel pump, and fuel lines. They will move to the spark plugs, distributor points, and electrical system. Then they will look at the ignition, generator, and wiring. The mechanic knows that if each of these systems is functioning properly the entire car will work well.

Your body has a series of vital functions as well that are indicators and measures of life and vitality. An absence of any one of them fulfills the clinical definition of death. The first thing that happens when you go to a doctor when you are not feeling well is that the doctor checks your vital functions. A check of the vital functions often tells the doctor where the problem is. Proper functioning in each area is essential for healthy living.

There are vital functions in selling as well. The health of these vital functions determines the quality of your performance and the health of your sales career. Any deterioration in any one of these functions leads to a deterioration in your sales results. The cessation or poor performance of any one of these functions can lead to the death of your sales career. An important part of process analysis is for you to evaluate yourself in each of these areas for strengths and weaknesses and then make a plan to increase your overall level of competence in each area.

The **seven vital functions** of selling are: (1) a positive mental attitude; (2) good health and appearance; (3) complete product knowledge; (4) continuous prospecting and new business development; (5) presentation skills; (6) handling objections and obtaining commitment; and (7) personal management skills. These may vary from person to person, and from product to product, but in my experience these are the big seven that are vital to your achieving your full potential as a professional salesperson. An absence or severe weakness in any of these areas can be sufficient to undermine all your other efforts and doom you to underachievement and failure. For example:

1. The absence of a *positive* mental attitude is a *negative* mental attitude. If you are not positive and optimistic about your product or service and eager to show people how it can be helpful to them, they will not buy from you and you will soon be out of business.

2. If you do not appear healthy and presentable, looking like the kind of person that people want to do business with, your prospects will not want to buy from you. Looking tired or sick, or poorly turned out, can bring your sales career to a halt.

3. Without complete product knowledge you will lack the confidence and self-assurance enjoyed by high-achieving salespeople. If you cannot answer a question about your product or service, your prospect will lose confidence in dealing with you and you'll soon be out of business.

4. Sales success requires continuous prospecting and the development of new business opportunities. An inability to find new prospects and develop them into customers is probably the biggest single reason for failure in sales.

5. Your ability to make an effective presentation, moving from the general to the particular, arousing interest and desire, is a key skill of selling. Poor presentation skills can end a promising sales career.

6. Your ability to answer objections clearly and to obtain commitment to take action is the endgame of selling. If you do everything well except for this, you will still fail in your career.

7. The seventh vital function is personal management skills, your ability to plan and organize your activities so that you see the largest number of qualified prospects possible within a given period of time. An important reason for underachievement in selling in America today, in addition to poor sales skills, is poor time management, the failure to use sales time effectively. If this inefficiency continues for very long, your sales will drop below the critical level and you will be out of business.

You begin to increase your sales effectiveness by analyzing yourself in each of the vital function areas, very much the way you would take a medical examination to find out how healthy you are. A simple method of self-analysis is to give yourself a grade from one to ten in each area, with one being the lowest and ten being the highest. Once you have determined your own ranking, ask your sales manager to comment on your self-assessment.

Vital Functions	Score
Positive mental attitude	_____
Good health and appearance	_____
Product knowledge	_____
Prospecting skills	_____
Presentation skills	_____
Answering objections and gaining commitment	_____
Personal management skills	_____
Overall Rating (Divide total score by 7)	_____

EVALUATING YOUR SKILL LEVELS

Salespeople tend to be extremely individualistic in their orientation toward life. They don't like to take input from others. They don't like to ask for help. They dislike being evaluated by their managers. Because of this psychological aversion to criticism, they are reluctant to ask for the candid opinions of others to help them to improve.

But if your goal is to become one of the finest sales professionals in your field, you need to solicit objective feedback from people who are watching you perform and who are in a position to assess how well you are doing. You can make more progress in just a month or two by opening yourself up to feedback on your performance than you ever could by trying to figure out how well you are doing all by yourself. Superior people are always willing to accept input from others. Don't be afraid to ask!

Here is a powerful way to increase your effectiveness, and boost your sales and income. First, consider all the sales you are making today as the combined result of how well you are doing in all of the areas that contribute to sales effectiveness. Your current performance is the true measure of your current competence as a salesperson. This becomes your starting point, your baseline or benchmark.

Now, make a decision to improve by just 10 percent in each of the vital function areas. Decide that, over the coming year, you will learn what you need to learn and practice what you need to practice to become just 10 percent better in each critical area.

Determine to be 10 percent more positive and enthusiastic. You will be 10 percent better in terms of your health, fitness, and personal appearance. You will learn 10 percent more about your product and about competitive products. Do this in each vital function area.

Now, here's a question for you: At the end of one year, what will happen to your level of sales? If you become 10 percent better in each vital function area over the course of twelve months, how will this affect your total sales output? The answer is amazing and it is absolutely true. The understanding of this concept of incremental improvement can, in itself, revolutionize your career.

THE IMPACT OF INCREMENTAL IMPROVEMENT IN VITAL AREAS

Going back to the vital functions of the body, let us say for example that you go to your doctor and your doctor notices that many of your vital functions are poor because you are overweight, you have high blood pressure, a high cholesterol level, and you breathe poorly because you smoke. So your doctor instructs you to begin exercising by walking one or two miles each day. He or she feels that regular walking will, at the very least, improve the functioning of your heart, a key indicator of your health and vitality.

So you begin walking two miles each day. This regular walking will improve the functioning of your heart. But what else will happen? Your muscle tone will improve, your blood pressure will go down, your respiratory rate will improve, your metabolic rate will get better, and you will become a calmer, more relaxed person. *Any* exercise that improves any of your vital functions will tend to positively affect all of your other vital functions at the same time. Because your body is a system, everything you do affects everything else.

By the same token, anything that you do to improve yourself in any of the vital function areas of selling will tend to improve your abilities in all other vital function areas as well. Each function is interrelated and interconnected with the other functions. You will experience a compounding effect as you begin to improve in any one area. And the measure of your success will be that your sales will increase.

For example, let us say that you decide to increase your time management skills, and leave everything else constant for the time being. If, over the next twelve months, you use your time 10 percent more efficiently, and if you do nothing else in any other area, your sales will *increase* by 10 percent. This is because of the fact that, if you are making all the sales that you are making today with the way you use your time right now, and you increase the productivity of your

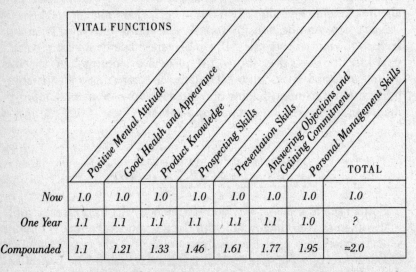

	Positive Mental Attitude	Good Health and Appearance	Product Knowledge	Prospecting Skills	Presentation Skills	Answering Objections and Gaining Commitment	Personal Management Skills	TOTAL
Now	1.0	1.0	1.0	1.0	1.0	1.0	1.0	1.0
One Year	1.1	1.1	1.1	1.1	1.1	1.1	1.0	?
Compounded	1.1	1.21	1.33	1.46	1.61	1.77	1.95	≈2.0

By becoming 10% better in each vital area over a twelve-month period, you can double your effectiveness and even double your sales.

time by 10 percent, your sales must increase by that same amount as well.

And if you become 10 percent better in every one of the seven vital function areas, the compounding effect, the multiplier, will almost double your sales, as you can see from the chart opposite.

Instead of it being an arithmetical progression, it becomes a geometric improvement. Each improvement compounds on each other improvement and affects all other areas. By the end of twelve months you would be 95 percent better overall and your whole life would be different.

Does this method work? Absolutely! Countless salespeople from every walk of life, all over the world, have used this simple method to drive their sales upward. It requires planning, persistence, and self-discipline, but it works if you apply it. In subsequent chapters, you will learn everything you need to know to achieve improvements in every area greatly in excess of 10 percent per year.

CRITICAL SUCCESS FACTORS IN SELLING

A craftsman is a person who is thoroughly skilled in every aspect of his trade. When you think of a master woodworker, you think of a person who is fluent with a wide range of tools, who is capable of transforming a piece of raw lumber to a finely cut, finished, and polished piece of furniture. A fine surgeon has a high level of expertise in every aspect of surgery, from the initial incision to the final suturing, and all the steps in between.

By the same token, an excellent salesperson is one who is familiar with every element of the selling process and who has developed an orderly plan to achieve a high level of competence in each activity.

The vital functions approach to personal improvement in selling is a fundamental building block of sales excellence. It is a natural extension of the basic selling process of establishing rapport, identifying the problem, and presenting the solution. The expansion of the sales process into the **critical success factors** of selling is the next logical step for you to take to move to the top of your field.

Every job, and every activity within that job, can be broken down into its critical success factors. Critical success factors are different from activities. Activities are the things that you *do* during the day. Critical success factors are the things that you *accomplish*, which can be measured and compared with previous periods.

Salespeople do not particularly like objective judgment or assessment of their performance. They don't like to be measured and evaluated. They don't like accurate numbers that tell them exactly how they are doing. They fear specific comparisons that might make them appear to be falling behind or falling below a particular standard.

However, it's not possible for you to grow and improve unless you carefully measure your performance in each definable activity. Just as champion athletes examine how each point of the final score was made, how every inch of the distance was run, and how every aspect of the play was made, you, too, must rigorously assess how well you are doing in every area as it affects your sales performance.

Critical success factors are those things you do that determine your success or failure. That's why they are defined as "critical." If you do them all well, you succeed greatly. If you do them poorly, you barely get by. If you do some well and some poorly, your overall result will still be poor.

These critical success factors are specific activities from which specific outcomes are expected. If you achieve the results required in each area, the sum total will be success in your field. If you fail to get results in a particular area, that *one* shortcoming alone can short-circuit your sales and your career.

Each critical success factor must be matched with a standard of performance. There must be a number attached to it. There must be a target to aim at. There must be some way to measure how well you are doing from one day to the next, from one month to the next. And a standard of performance should really be the standard of *excellent* performance. You've heard the old saying, "Aim for the stars! Even if you miss, you'll still hit the moon."

To achieve greatness, you must aspire to greatness. To achieve excellence, you must set standards of excellence and commit yourself to achieving them. In each of the nine critical success factors of selling that we will discuss, your goal should be to be outstanding. Anything less than a conscious commitment to excellence on your part becomes an unconscious acceptance of mediocrity.

The nine critical success factors in selling, which are an expansion of the basic sales process and a restatement of some of the vital functions, are the following: (1) prospecting; (2) getting appointments; (3) qualifying; (4) problem identification and clarification; (5) presenting; (6) answering objections; (7) closing; (8) follow-through and delivery; and (9) resales and referrals.

Each of these critical success factors must be carried out successfully before you can proceed to the next. And *all nine* must be carried out successfully for you to become a top salesperson.

Here is the important point: your *weakest* critical success factor determines the height to which you can use all your other skills. Your weakest skill sets the limit on your sales income. If on a score of one to ten, you are scoring at a ten on eight out of nine critical success factors, but you are only scoring a three on the ninth, that three will set the height of your sales performance and your income.

For example, if you are absolutely excellent at every part of the sales process except prospecting, that critical success factor alone will determine how many people you see and how many sales you eventually make.

If you are doing extremely well at everything but handling objections or closing the sale, those weak areas will determine exactly how many sales you make. Because your weakest skill area sets the limit on everything you accomplish, you cannot afford to be average at anything you do. You have no choice but to set high standards for your performance in every single aspect of your sales activities.

In my seminars, people often come up to me and object to this necessity to be excellent in every area. Many times, I've heard people say something like, "Isn't there some way I can be successful in selling without prospecting. I really don't like prospecting very much."

There will always be parts of your selling activities that you don't enjoy as much as others. This will almost invariably be because you are not particularly good in those areas. Whenever you do not feel yourself to be particularly competent in doing something, you feel uncomfortable in that area. As a result, you tend to avoid that activity as much as possible.

Many salespeople lose their jobs because of their inability to come to terms with the fact that becoming a top performer is not easy. Being the best in your field requires that you move out of your comfort zone to where you feel increasingly *un*comfortable. It requires that you push yourself to ever higher levels of accomplishment by learning new skills and then practicing them until you feel comfortable at a new, higher level of performance.

When I started studying selling many years ago, I would learn an idea from another salesperson, or read a book, or listen to a tape, or attend a course, and I would be determined to use that idea. However, I immediately found that the new idea didn't work. I would go out and call on a prospect and when I tried out the new approach, it would almost invariably fail to elicit the expected reaction. As a result, I would quit trying the new idea and revert to my comfort zone doing the same old thing as before.

The turning point for me came when I realized that I would have to practice a new method or technique at least *ten times* with prospects before I could honestly evaluate its efficacy. Prior to that, I would feel uncomfortable and inadequate with the new method. Therefore, my use of the method would not be an accurate measure of whether or not it was any good. Ever since then, I have realized that, as the saying goes, "If it's worth doing well, it's worth doing poorly at first."

Most people function at low levels of performance because they cannot endure the feelings of awkwardness and inadequacy they experience when trying something for the first time. Give yourself a chance. If you learn something that makes sense to you and that you feel can help you in your sales activities, force yourself to practice it several times before you pass a judgment on whether or not it is a good idea. You can become good at almost anything if you practice it long enough. It's up to you.

One of the most helpful techniques in improving your critical success factors is the concept of "benchmarking." This is the systematic process of measuring your performance against some other performance that is superior to your own, and then striving to bring your performance up to that level.

Many of the very best companies in the world are aggressively using benchmarking to upgrade their standards in every part of their businesses. The key to benchmarking in sales is for you to take each of the nine critical success factors and define a *standard of excellent performance*. This standard can come from the performance of the very best person in your organization in that particular area. It can also be a standard that you create, which represents your idea of the perfect performance. In either case, you define your standard so that it gives you a specific measure to compare your performance against on a daily, weekly, and monthly basis.

Begin this exercise in benchmarking by giving yourself a score from one to ten in each area of performance. This becomes your starting point. You then define clearly how you would be performing if you were getting a ten in that area. Every day you think, plan, and organize your activities so as to improve your performance against that standard. Remember, small improvements in performance can lead to extraordinary improvements in results.

I worked as a consultant with a large distribution organization not long ago. Every November, this company had a sales contest. Everyone who achieved a certain level of sales above their monthly average would win a trip to the Caribbean for a week that coming winter. Every year, after ten straight months of steady but unspectacular sales performance, one salesman would boost his sales dramatically in November in order to win this contest. After this had happened three years in a row, we sat down and analyzed his increased sales activity for the month of November. What we found was quite surprising.

This salesperson was calling on an average of eight qualified prospects a week and making an average of three sales a week throughout the year. During the month of November, however, he called on *ten* qualified prospects a week and made an average of *four* sales a week. Immediately after the sales contest, he went back into his comfort zone, and for the next eleven months he again called on an average of eight prospects a week to whom he made an average of three sales.

We asked him why he didn't maintain his November level of sales for the entire year. He replied by saying that he didn't feel capable of sustaining that level of effort. We then looked at his records and found that he was working less than one additional hour per day during November to achieve that twenty-five percent increase in sales.

What really got his attention was when we showed him that, because he was working on commission, that extra twenty-five percent of sales income he was generating in November, if maintained throughout the year, over a forty-year sales career, would give him ten extra years of income. Or, to turn it around, if he increased his sales by twenty-five percent and held them constant, he could make the same amount of money in thirty years that he would otherwise make in forty years. He could retire at the age of fifty-five rather than sixty-five. The extra few minutes per day, the extra two calls and one sale per week, would move him from being a good performer to being one of the top people in his organization. Little things mean a lot!

BENCHMARKING FOR EXCELLENT PERFORMANCE

You begin the process of continuous improvement using benchmarking by dividing the sale into its nine parts, or critical factors, and then defining the standard you are aiming for in each area.

Prospecting is the first skill area at the beginning of the sales pipeline. The continuous development of new business is the lifeblood of both the salesperson and the organization. Whether your company provides you with leads or you develop them yourself, your ability to prospect effectively and to keep your sales pipeline filled with prospective customers is the critical success factor on which all the others depend.

Let us define prospecting as, *"My ability to develop a sufficient quantity and quality of prospects to make sure I meet or exceed my sales goals in a timely and predictable fashion."*

Give yourself a score from one to ten on how well you are fulfilling this definition in your daily activities. If you find yourself with too few prospects or with your prospecting pipeline drying up and your being unsure where your next sales are coming from, you would give yourself a lower score. If you find that you have more good sales leads and prospects than you can possibly handle, you would give yourself a higher score. You might ask other people in your company what score they would give you, based on their familiarity with your work habits and your results. Once you have an accurate score, that then becomes the starting point for improvement.

Getting appointments is the second critical success factor in selling. It is different from prospecting in that many salespeople have lists of people or companies that are qualified to buy but they can't seem to get through to them to set up appointments. Your ability to get more appointments with better-qualified prospects is key to determining your success or failure in this profession.

Let's define getting appointments as, *"I have a well-developed system, using telephone, mail, and direct calling, to acquire as many qualified appointments as I need to be busy all the time."*

Evaluate your current sales activities against that definition and give yourself a score from one to ten. Use that score to determine whether this is an area where you need to upgrade your skills. Here, as in every other critical success factor of selling, your goal should be a perfect ten. That is the target you are aiming at.

Qualifying is the third critical success factor in selling. This is the ability to determine if the person you are talking to has the authority and the means to make a buying decision if he or she is sufficiently impressed by your presentation. It is amazing how many salespeople spin their wheels and waste their time talking to people who, for whatever reason, cannot buy even if they wanted to.

I remember working with a sales organization that sold services from house to house. When someone would answer the door, the salespeople would launch into a sales presentation that might last thirty or forty minutes. But often, at the end of the presentation, the person they were talking to would say, "By the way, I don't live here, I'm just visiting."

We taught these salespeople to use a very simple question that increased their sales by 30 percent. When someone came to the door, the salesperson would smile, introduce himself or herself and ask, "Do you live here?"

If the answer was yes, the presentation would continue exactly as before. If the answer was no, the salesperson would make arrangements to come back at another time. This simple change in the qualifying process saved a lot of wear and tear, and demoralization, on the salespeople.

You can use this definition for qualifying: "*I carefully qualify each of my prospects in advance to ascertain that the prospect has the ability to buy my product or service if he or she is sufficiently satisfied with my presentation.*"

With your ideal perfect score being ten, evaluate yourself and give yourself a grade based on your current experience in this key result area.

The fourth critical success factor, **problem identification and clarification,** can be stated as, "*I ask questions, listen carefully, and accurately determine the exact problem or need that the prospect has that my product or service can solve or satisfy in a cost-effective way.*"

Many salespeople get through the first three stages only to fall apart when they get face-to-face with the prospect. They talk too much, they listen too little, and they miss the messages that the prospect is sending. They make the unforgivable mistake of beginning to recommend solutions to problems that the prospect doesn't have. There may be faster ways to turn off a prospect to a salesperson, but not many.

Presenting skills are the fifth key result area, or critical success factor. After all is said and done, the sale is usually made in the presentation. It is during the presentation where you skillfully match what your product does to the exact needs of your customer, like inserting a hand into a well-fitting glove. It is in presenting skills, above all else, where top salespeople excel. Some companies even have other people perform all of the other functions of selling and save their very best people to come in at the critical moment just to give the presentation.

You can define presenting as, "*I present my product or service so skillfully that my prospect is overwhelmingly convinced that it will solve his or her most pressing need.*"

If you have done everything else well up until now, and you have prepared your presentation thoroughly, a very high proportion of your prospects will be ready to buy at the end of your presentation. Give yourself a score from one to ten on how well the above definition describes your presentation abilities.

Answering objections is the sixth critical success factor in selling. There are no sales without questions or concerns. Even if a person is totally sold on buying your product or service, he will still have misgivings and be unsure about certain aspects of your offering. Your ability to reduce his fears of making a mistake, to assure him that it is safe to proceed with your recommendation, is a key skill area where sales are won or lost.

Some years ago, an insurance agent made a presentation to sell me a million-dollar policy. That was far more insurance than I had ever imagined owning in my life. I told him that although I appreciated his work, I was already fully covered with my existing insurance policy. Even though he already knew the answer, he asked me how much it was. I told him, "$200,000."

He then asked me how I planned for the proceeds from the policy to be dispersed, should something happen to me. I told him that the money would retire my mortgage and pay off all my bills. Then he asked me this key question, "How long do you intend to stay dead?"

The question jolted me and got my full attention. As I thought about the question, he smiled and went on to explain that the amount of insurance that I had currently would be completely used up within a few months and my family would then be destitute. He said, "With that amount of insurance, you'll have to be back at work within six months. You obviously don't intend to stay dead for very long!"

Needless to say, that way of reframing my situation put me over the top. I went on to buy the policy, and others as well over the years, and I never forgot that example. He made the sale to me because he was practiced and skilled at answering one of the primary objections that anyone has with regard to the purchase of an insurance product.

Here's a definition of competence in answering an objection: "*I anticipate and answer each question or concern of my prospect in such a way that the prospect is satisfied with my answer and the objection is dropped and never brought up again.*"

How well are you doing in this area? Give yourself a score from one to ten. This is a critical success factor of professional selling, and it is so important that I will devote an entire chapter to dealing with various kinds of objections and how to handle them later in this book.

The seventh critical success factor in sales is **closing.** Closing is the way you overcome the natural tendency toward indecision and procrastination that arises at the end of any sales conversation, and in anticipation of any expenditure of money. Closing is the way you ask for a commitment to take action on your offering.

You can define closing as, "*I am both competent and comfortable in asking for the order. I am sensitive and aware of the correct time to request a commitment to action on the part of my prospect. I close easily and well and move on naturally to wrapping up the sale.*"

Getting a commitment to take action at the end of a professional sales presentation is a low-pressure, no-pressure procedure. It is the way you mutually agree that this product or service is the ideal solution, all things considered, to the specific need that you and the prospect have identified in the earlier conversation. It is the confirmation that you have matched the product to the prospect's needs skillfully and that you have answered any questions, or resolved any misgivings, that the prospect might have that might cause him or her to hesitate from going ahead.

Salespeople and prospects both dislike the closing part of the transaction. They are both tense and uneasy because of the combined fears of failure and rejection they experience. It is the job of the sales professional to master this part of the transaction so that it is relaxed and easy for both parties. Give yourself a score from one to ten based on how proficient you are in this area of selling.

The eighth critical success factor in selling is **follow-through and delivery.** This is where you take care of all the details, including the last-minute questions or concerns that the prospect might come up with before the sale is concluded. This is the area where you assure that your product or service will be delivered on schedule and installed satisfactorily so that your customer feels comfortable and happy with his or her buying decision.

Many salespeople make the mistake of thinking that when they have a signature on a contract and a check in hand, that the sale is over. The very best salespeople, however, realize that a sale can fall apart at the last minute if the salesperson does not put an extra effort into assuring the customer that he or she had made the right decision. Many problems, and even lawsuits, can be headed off by an astute salesperson who does not let go of the customer's hand when they have crossed the finish line.

You can define follow-through and delivery as, "*I follow up and follow through on every sale to make sure the product or service is delivered to the customer's complete satisfaction, leaving him happy and content with his buying decision.*"

Give yourself a score from one to ten, and give thought to how you could improve your performance in this area. It is a real sales tragedy to see a transaction fall apart at the last minute because the salesperson forgot that "It ain't over till it's over."

The ninth critical success factor is **resales and referrals.** This an area of performance where the top salespeople excel. This is where you take such good care of your customers that they not only buy more of your product or service from you, but they eagerly recommend you to their friends as well.

A referral is worth ten to twenty times a cold call or new lead. Top salespeople are very sensitive to the importance of satisfying their most current customers so that they create a "golden chain" of referrals from them. It is only when your customers are your salespeople as well that you can move into the ranks of the highest money-earners in your profession. Without your customers working for you, you have to start over, prospecting after every sale.

Give yourself a score from one to ten. Ask yourself, "How much of my business comes from resales and referrals and how much of my business is new?" If you are handling this aspect of the sale well, eventually most of your business will come from your satisfied customers.

CONTINUOUS IMPROVEMENT

This exercise in *sales process analysis* is the launching pad toward greatness in your profession. The very act of breaking the sale down into its constituent parts and then giving yourself a score on your performance in each area is the starting point of rapid progress.

Objectively analyze both your strengths and weaknesses. Develop a written plan to bring your scores up by one point (10 percent) in each critical area over the next twelve months. Above all, identify your *weakest* skill area and put that at the top of your list for self-improvement.

It is your weakest skill area, more than anything, that is holding you back. If you are not sure what it is, ask your sales manager. You can even ask your satisfied customers. Other people can always see you better than you see yourself and if you honestly ask for feedback, without becoming defensive or angry, the people around you can give you insights to your performance that can help you and that may save you months of hard work.

If all you did was to become 10 percent better over the coming year in each critical area, the overall effect on your sales results would be extraordinary. The Law of Accumulation states that "All great success in human endeavor is an accumulation of hundreds and even thousands of tiny events and activities that nobody ever sees or appreciates." A person who eventually becomes a great success in selling is a person who has invested countless hours in study and practice to become good at his or her craft.

An extension of the Law of Accumulation is the Law of Continuous Improvement. It is based on the "kaizen" principle practiced throughout Japanese industry. Kaizen means "continuous betterment." It is a companywide commitment to finding new and better ways to do things every day.

A personal commitment to continuous improvement is the hallmark of the superior salesperson. He or she is never satisfied with the status quo but is always looking for ways to do things better, even if it's just a tiny bit better.

Business author and speaker Tom Peters once wrote that, "The best companies are not hundreds of percent better in any area, they are just one percent better in hundreds of areas."

All great success in America is based on the Law of Accumulation and its corollary, the Law of Continuous Improvement. It doesn't matter where you're starting from or how long you've been in sales. At any time, you can begin putting these laws and principles to work in your own life. And as you get better, your sales and income will get better at the same pace.

It takes character, courage, and discipline to sit down and honestly analyze and evaluate your personal abilities in each of the key result areas of your profession. But if you have the strength of will to do it, and the determination to do something about it, your improved results can be spectacular!

As we proceed through this book, I will give you more ideas, methods, and techniques that you can use to perform better in the critical success factors explained above. The starting point of continuous improvement is for you to view sales as a profession, and to make a firm decision that you are dead serious about going all the way to the top. You must decide that you are prepared to invest whatever time and money is necessary to achieve your full potential in selling. Your desire for sales excellence must be so intense and focused that it will drive you forward, through and over all the fears, doubts, and uncertainties that hold most people back.

PROCESS ANALYSIS IN LARGE ACCOUNT SALES

The starting point of improving your performance in any area of human endeavor is for you to break the activity down into its constituent parts and then analyze them one by one. In large account selling, there are seven vital factors that must be present for you to be successful in making the sale. There are many more elements of selling that we will discuss in coming chapters, but these seven are essential. They all begin with the letter C. If you want to be the best at what you do, you must evaluate how well you are doing in each of these areas, and then make a plan and commitment to become better in each one.

The first vital key to success in large account selling is **clarity.** It is one of the most important single words in the vocabulary of success in any field, especially sales. Lack of clarity about what they really want is the primary reason people live lives of frustration and underachievement. Absolute clarity about what you want to accomplish is the primary reason that you succeed. Clarity is the essential starting point in the achievement of any goal.

In selling, you must be absolutely clear about *what* it is that you sell from the point of view of the customer. What *exactly* is the customer buying? What *exactly* does the customer receive? What *exactly* is the purpose of the purchase decision, as the customer experiences it? This seems like an obvious question but it is amazing how few salespeople can answer this question accurately.

A man in one of my seminars asked me how he could be more effective in selling office automation systems. He told me that he was frustrated because he couldn't even get appointments with decision-makers, let alone make presentations that would lead to sales. He felt as though he were banging his head against the wall.

So I asked him this question, "What exactly do you sell?"

He repeated his first statement, a little impatiently, "I sell office automation systems, computers, workstations, and networks that companies use to automate their administrative functions."

Again, I asked him, "But what exactly do you sell?"

He began to lose his composure. As if I had not been listening, he began to repeat himself, and said again that he sold, "office automation systems . . ." But then he suddenly realized that one of us obviously didn't understand either the question or the answer. And he realized that it was he.

So he said, referring to an earlier part of the seminar, "How do you mean?"

I asked him, "How exactly does a company benefit from installing your office automation systems? It is the benefit that the customer buys and pays for, not the equipment."

He said, "Companies that install my systems cut their costs, increase their efficiency, decrease their staff size, and save so much money that the systems pay for themselves within the first year, and sometimes within the first three to six months!"

Then I said, "What you sell then is lower operating costs, greater efficiency, and higher profits at a price that is self-liquidating so fast that the customer gets a very high rate of return on his investment in your products and services."

At last he understood. He had been so focused on selling from his personal point of view that he had lost sight of what he was selling from the point of view of the customer. When he recognized his error, he revised his approach completely and before the end of the seminar, he had already phoned and made two appointments with decision-makers in companies that he had been unable to get through to for months. As soon as he became absolutely clear about what he was selling, his sales took off.

In selling strategically, we'll examine several ways to assure greater levels of clarity on your part so that it is easier for your customer to buy from you. You need to be clear about who it is you sell to, the real decision-maker. You need to be clear about who or what is your competition. You need to be clear about how you present your product or service depending upon the position and responsibilities of the person you are talking to. The more clear you are about what, why, how, and who in your sales activities, the more focused and effective you will be.

The second critical success factor in large account selling is **concentration.** To be successful in sales, and in life, you must develop the ability to concentrate single-mindedly on *one* thing, the most valuable thing you could possibly be doing, and then discipline yourself to persist in that activity until you succeed, or until it is complete.

Focus and concentration are critical to success. Lack of focus and the inability to concentrate are the guarantors of failure. Being absolutely clear about what you are selling and who your best prospects are, and then concentrating all of your energies on developing those prospects into customers, is the fastest way for you to move to the top of your field.

Statisticians use the phrase "sample population." This refers to the number of people being examined in any type of survey. The larger the sample population, because of the Law of Averages, the more accurate will be the generalizations that can be drawn from surveying that population.

Your sample population of prospective customers includes everyone within your market area who can possibly purchase and benefit from your product or service. Among this population, there are small, medium, and large potential customers. There are small customers who can buy in a short period of time. There are medium-sized customers who take longer to decide. And there are large customers who often take a long time to make up their minds.

The largest customers are usually the hardest people to sell to. They are the whales of the customer population. If you catch a thousand minnows, all you have is a bucket of fish. But if you catch a single whale, it will be enough to fill your whole ship.

One of your primary concerns in business development is to "fish for whales." You need to analyze your sample population of customers and determine the biggest, best, and most important prospects. You then concentrate your energy and attention on eventually getting those customers for your business.

The third vital factor in large account sales is contained in the word **consultative.** To sell to large accounts, you must take a consultative approach. You must deal with your prospect as though you were an advisor, a counselor, a problem-solver, and a friend. You must be seen by your customer as a helper, a person whose primary concern is to help him or her make an intelligent decision in solving a problem or achieving a goal.

The consultative approach is very different from the standard sales approach. Traditional sales is based on talking; consultative selling is based on listening. Traditional sales is based on telling; consultative sales is based on learning. Traditional sales is based on technique; consultative selling is based on intuition and sensitivity. Traditional sales is based on getting the order. Consultative sales is based on building the relationship.

The top 10 percent of salespeople in every industry are viewed by their customers as friends and advisors. The customers rely on their recommendations in their purchase decisions. They view the consultative salesperson the same way they view a doctor, a lawyer, or an accountant. They see him or her as a professional who is acting in their best interests.

Courtesy is the fourth vital factor of the sales professional. It is the mark of the superior person. It is the outward expression of a salesperson who is inwardly at peace. Courtesy, kindness, and friendliness are the characteristic behaviors of the most successful people in large account selling.

Courtesy is very hard to fake. Either you have it or you don't. But the good thing is that you can become a polite and courteous person. By practicing courtesy with everyone you meet, from the time you wake up in the morning until you go to bed at night, you will become a more pleasant and enjoyable person in all your relationships.

It is important that you be courteous with everyone you deal with in a client company, no matter what their position. The president of a large company told me recently of a major sale that he and his company were about to enter into. But at the last moment, because of a fatal error made by the salesperson, they changed their minds and purchased the product somewhere else.

As it happened, it was summer and the president's daughter was working in the company, taking over for people who were away on vacation. On the day she was relieving the receptionist, the salesperson came in to finalize the details for this major transaction. The salesperson was always polite and friendly with the decision-makers when discussing the product, but in the waiting room he was rude and demanding with the receptionist. He made the mistake of treating her like an underling of no importance.

Just before he was to go in to meet with the president, she excused herself and went in ahead of him and told her father how the salesman had spoken to her. You can imagine what happened. The father asked his daughter to explain exactly what had happened, thanked her for filling him in, and told her he would take care of it.

When the salesman came in, the father told him that they had decided not to do business with him or his company. They did not appreciate his attitude and they did not want to do business with him or with an organization that believed in treating the staff of customer companies the way he had just treated the receptionist. He showed the salesperson to the door and ended the discussion. Unfortunately, this sort of rudeness happens every day in offices all over the country.

The top salespeople that I have met and worked with over the years all seem to make a special effort to be nice to everybody they deal with. Thomas Carlyle once wrote, "You can tell a big man by the way he treats little men." The biggest people, let alone salespeople, treat everyone alike. They are just as courteous with the taxi driver as they are to presidents and senior executives. They are polite and courteous with the people in their own companies and they are equally as courteous with the people in their respective client companies. Over time, they build such a large reservoir of goodwill that the inevitable problems and difficulties that arise in the purchase and use of any product or service are never allowed to disrupt the long-term strength of the relationship.

The fifth key to large account selling is **competence.** Inexperienced salespeople sell to inexperienced customers. Experienced salespeople sell to more experienced customers. Highly experienced and thoroughly competent salespeople sell to the top tier of high-level customers within an organization.

Competence is something that comes from learning and practice. It comes from making a complete commitment to your profession and by working every day to improve your performance and the knowledge of your business in some way.

Your level of competence, your expertise, is demonstrated as soon as you open your mouth for the first time with the prospect. Customers in large account sales can tell the difference between a junior and senior salesperson almost immediately. They can tell the difference in your manner, your appearance, and your approach. They can tell by the quality and intelligence of the questions you ask. Especially, you demonstrate your level of competence in the thoroughness of the preparation you have engaged in prior to the meeting.

You can increase the perception of competence that the customer has of you, and the likelihood of succeeding in the large account sale, by thinking through every detail of the sale in advance and by preparing thoroughly before you get face-to-face with the customer. Customers enjoy being sold by a person who really knows his or her business. And there is no way to increase your competence except by hard work sustained over a long period of time.

The sixth C in large account selling is **confidence**. Confidence is a by-product of effective performance. You feel confident to the degree to which you have thought through every element of the sale. You feel confident when you are absolutely clear about what you are selling and what it is that the customer really needs. You feel more confident when you are concentrating single-mindedly on high-value prospects and customers. You experience higher levels of confidence when you take the consultative approach, thereby lowering the fears of failure and rejection that make most sales conversations strained and uneasy. Your confidence increases when you are courteous and attentive to what your customer is saying and how your customer really feels.

Especially, you are more confident when you know that you are very good at selling and are capable of dealing with anything that might come up in the sales conversation. Confidence is something you need to work on every day to counter the negative influence of the doubts and fears that we all experience in dealing in uncertain markets with unfamiliar prospects.

Most of all, confidence comes from your absolute belief and conviction that your product or service is excellent and well suited to your prospective customers. Your conviction about the quality and value of what you are selling translates into the kind of constrained enthusiasm that makes you irresistible in a sales situation. The more you believe in the value of what you are selling, the more confident and optimistic you become.

The seventh and final success factor in large account sales is **courage**.

Winston Churchill once said, "Courage is rightly considered the fore-most of the virtues, for upon it all others depend." And Mark Twain wrote, "Courage is not absence of fear or lack of fear. It is control of fear, mastery of fear."

The quality of boldness, of fearlessness, of willing to go where you have never gone before, is a quality that is vital to your success in both selling and in life. When you have the inner strength and mental power to confront your fears of making appointments, asking straightforward questions, dealing with the customer's situation, and asking for a com-mitment to action, your sales success becomes inevitable.

SUMMARY

Selling is a far more complex area of human endeavor, and a far harder way to earn a living, than it has ever been before, except for next year, and the year after. You can earn a dime or you can earn a dollar. You can sell an average amount and live an average life. Or you can sell five times, ten times, or twenty times the average person and live an extraordinary life. The choice is yours.

The Law of Sowing and Reaping says, "Whatsoever a man soweth, that also shall he reap." What you are reaping today is a result of what you have sown in the past. You always get out what you put in. And you can never get any more out than you have put in. It is an iron law and it is immutable. But the good part of the law is that, whatever you put in, you will eventually reap. It will come back to you.

The secret to success in selling is to put in more than you take out. It is to go the extra mile. It is to always do more than you are paid for. It is to set the highest standards of performance and behavior for your-self, and then to strive ceaselessly to achieve those standards.

The aim of this chapter is to give you a series of targets to aim at. Your responsibility is to set clear standards in each area of sales performance. It is to define them, make them measurable, write them down, and then measure yourself against those standards every single day.

Pattern yourself after the very best salespeople you know. Look at the men and women around you who are at the top of their field and make them your role models. Ask them for advice. Read about their experiences and attend the courses they recommend. Listen to their audiotapes and watch their videos. Invite them out for lunch or dinner and listen to their insights and ideas. If you can, go out with them on sales calls and sit quietly to observe the way they interact with customers. Learn what they do that puts them at the top, and then practice it yourself.

Stand back and take a look at your sales performance, and every detail of what you do. Resolve this very day to begin improving in each of your critical success areas. Upgrade each of your vital functions. Set benchmarks or standards for yourself and measure yourself against those standards every day and every week. Perhaps the most wonderful part of your career in professional selling is that there is no limit on how good you can get at it except for the limits you impose on yourself.

6

MOTIVATING PEOPLE

TO BUY

Selling complex products to complex people in competitive markets is one of the most difficult and challenging things you will ever do. The process of persuading people to buy things from you is complex because people are complex. Each time you make a sale it is because you have accurately presented your product or service in such a way that it satisfies the predominant need or needs of your prospect. Whenever you fail to make a sale, it is because your presentation of the features and benefits of your product did not connect with the underlying forces that would motivate your prospect to buy. Your ability to correctly uncover the real buying motives of the people you speak to will determine your selling success as much as any other factor.

Selling is an essentially creative act. It requires that you go out into the marketplace and create business where no business existed before. Selling requires finding people who did not even know that they wanted or needed your product or service and then convincing them that they should pay good money to acquire it. It requires that you uncover the true motivating influences at work in the heart and mind of your prospect and then appeal to them effectively. Becoming more creative in your selling activities is critical to unlocking your potential in your sales career. If you can develop your creativity sufficiently to discover the real reason why someone would buy your product or service, there is nothing that can stop you from moving into the top ranks of sales professionals in your field.

Using your creativity to correctly identify buying motives will enable you to find newer and better prospects. Your creativity will reveal better ways to present and sell your product or service. It will enable you to find new and better ways that your product or service can be used to help people get more of the things they really want.

Creativity can help you structure your presentation to more effectively answer questions and overcome objections that impede the sales process. This quality will enable you to more rapidly convince your prospect that your product or service can satisfy his or her most pressing needs. By creatively analyzing what motivates your prospects to become customers, you can devise ways to sell more rapidly at every stage of the sales process.

Finally, creatively analyzing and identifying buying motives will enable you to overcome buyer resistance by enabling you to shift the emphasis of the sales conversation onto those areas where your product or service is obviously the superior solution to the problem currently experienced by your prospect.

Your success in selling will depend upon your ability to get to the heart of why your prospect would buy, and then to show your prospect that purchasing from you is the ideal solution to his or her real need.

WHY PEOPLE BUY

Each prospect you meet is facing one of three situations regarding your product or service. In the first situation, he has a clear problem or need and he knows exactly what it is. In the second situation, he has a problem or need, but he is not sure what it is or whether his problem can be solved by your product or service. The third situation is when your prospect has no need for what you are selling, even though either you or he may think that a need exists before you get sufficient information from him. The process of prospecting, which we will talk about later, is the process of discerning which of these three conditions exists before you invest a lot of your time.

Why do people buy? Why don't they buy? Why do people do *any* of the things they do? To answer these questions correctly, you need to understand human action and human behavior. Fortunately, because you are a human being yourself, you have *inside* information. You have an excellent reference source from which to draw. You can compare your behaviors with those of your customers and you will find that they are very similar, given similar situations.

In its simplest terms, people buy to alleviate *dissatisfaction*. All human action arises from a felt dissatisfaction of some kind. People act to alleviate this dissatisfaction by moving toward a situation of greater satisfaction. Every human action of any kind is therefore an attempt to improve conditions in some way. The primary motivator of all human behavior is the desire to be better off after the behavior than prior to the behavior. If the individual does not feel that he or she will be better off as the result of taking action, he or she will not do anything at all. Your prospect will say, "Leave your material with me and let me think it over," which is *customer-speak* for the words "Good-bye, I'm not convinced that I'd be better off with your product than I would be by keeping the money that it would cost."

You must always present your product or service as an *improvement* on what the prospect is doing at the moment. People do not like change. They fear it. They avoid it at all costs. But at the same time everyone is interested in being better off, or in an improvement of some kind. When you present your product or service as a natural extension of what your prospect is already doing at the moment, only a better way to accomplish the same goal, he or she will always be open to your offer. The words, "new," "better," and "improved" are among the most powerful words you can use in the selling of any product or service. They appeal to the basic motivator of all human action.

Because each person acts to improve his situation, every act is a *rational* act. It is based on the perception of the actor. It has an end in mind—improvement. It may or may not lead to the desired improvement, but it is always rational from the point of view of the customer. Customers do what they do because they believe it is the *best* way to get what they want under the best possible conditions.

Selling rule number one is, "The customer is always right." Rule number two is, "Whenever you are in doubt, refer back to rule number one." Your customer is always *correct*, based on his current information, on his or her perception of the appropriateness of your product or service to improve his or her condition. This is a foundation principle in understanding human behavior.

There is a good deal of discussion about the difference between "needs" and "wants." The customer seems to *need* one thing, while he or she *wants* something different. Sometimes, it appears that what the customer wants is not what he or she needs at all. Salespeople are often frustrated when it is clear to them what their customer should have but the customer doesn't seem to appreciate their insight and awareness. Salespeople then fall into the trap of attempting to convince the prospect that what they are selling is what the customer *really* wants, rather than what the customer is telling them. This striving to convince your prospect that your product or service is a more satisfactory improvement than what your prospect feels that he really needs or wants is usually an exercise in frustration on your part. We'll talk more about this later.

There is an ABC theory to explain human motivation. This theory says that all human motivation is based on *antecedents, behavior, and consequences*. Customers act based on their *antecedents*—their previous experiences and their current situation. They engage in *behaviors* to achieve certain *consequences*, usually an alleviation of dissatisfaction or improvement in conditions. The consequences are the results of the buying decision. This ABC approach is helpful in designing your sales presentation.

In terms of motivation, antecedents represent about 15 percent of the reasons people do things. The consequences, on the other hand, represent 85 percent of the reasons why customers buy. To put it another way, customers buy in anticipation of the consequences they expect as the result of the buying decision. For this reason, the more your sales presentation focuses on how much better off the prospect will be when he is using your product or service, the greater motivational impact your words will have.

Top salespeople always focus their sales presentations on consequences, on the ownership and enjoyment of their product or service. Average salespeople focus instead on explaining how their product or service works, or how it was developed, or how it compares with other products or services on the market. To put it another way, top salespeople talk about what it "does," while average salespeople talk about what it "is."

People buy the consequences they expect from owning and using your product or service. They do not buy the product or service itself. In the customer's mind, your product or service is a means to an end. It is the way the customer gets from where he is to where he wants to go. In that respect, your product or service itself has no emotional value. It is only the ends sought after by your prospect that have the power to elicit a buying decision.

This is why you've heard it said that people do not buy *products*, they buy *solutions* to their problems. They do not buy *services*, they buy ways to help them *achieve their goals*. Prospects do not buy the *features* of your product or service, they purchase the *improvement* that they anticipate enjoying in their lives and work as the result of those features. It is the anticipated benefits of ownership and enjoyment that are the key motivating factors in making any buying decision.

For example, people do not buy life insurance. They buy the feeling of security that they will enjoy knowing that their loved ones are properly provided for should something happen to them. People do not buy automobiles. They buy dependable and attractive transportation that gives them greater freedom to move around among the important activities of their lives. People do not buy computers. They buy the increased efficiency that enables them and others to get their jobs done faster, with greater accuracy and at lower costs. In every case, it is the customer's ability to envision a desirable future state brought about by your product or service that motivates him to buy it.

PRIMARY AND SECONDARY MOTIVATORS

There are *primary* motivators and *secondary* motivators. The primary motivators are the basic reasons a person would buy anything. These are the minimum requirements that your product or service must promise to satisfy if the prospect is even going to give you a hearing. A car must be drivable, a computer must compute, a camera must take pictures, and a training program must educate people and make them more competent. These are the basic minimums.

Secondary motivators are the reasons people will purchase *your* particular product or service. These are the added things that make the difference between what you are offering and what someone else is offering. They are the specific benefits that trigger the emotional responses that lead to the buying decision.

For example, in leasing commercial office space, the primary motivators will be the quality of the premises, the parking, the attractiveness of the building, the availability of nearby shopping for employees, and so on. The secondary motivators will be more subtle. They will have to do with the prestige associated with the building, the quality of the other tenants, the anticipated reactions of other decision-makers, colleagues, and customers, and most especially, the proximity of the office premises to the home of the chief executive officer. More than 80 percent of all offices are located within five miles of the president of the company occupying those offices. This is a subtle but essential motivational factor that is often the key to leasing industrial and commercial space. And every product contains these secondary motivators.

There seems to be a Law of Duality in many purchase decisions. This law states that "There are always *two* reasons for doing anything; the reason that sounds good and the real reason."

The reason that sounds good is the practical, logical, bottom-line reason that any intelligent, rational, calculating human being could agree with. People have an intense desire to appear to others to be doing the correct thing in every situation. The sales conversation, proposal, bid, and attempt to get the order will usually revolve around the reasons that sound good.

But, it is the "real reason" that usually triggers the purchase decision. The real reason is psychological and emotional in nature. It could even sound or seem irrational but it is the driving force nonetheless. Your first job in the sale process is to determine both the reasons for buying that sound good and the real reasons, and then show the prospect that both of these sets of reasons are provided for in what you are selling. The sale hangs on your ability to accomplish this.

All buying decisions are emotional because people are completely emotional in everything they say and do. They decide emotionally and justify logically. They usually make their decisions quickly, even instantaneously, and then spend a good deal of time rationalizing and justifying why they have decided to act in a certain way.

One of the reasons many women are moving to the front in selling is because they are often more attuned than men to the emotional factor in decision making. Men have a tendency to focus more on facts, figures, numbers, details, and rational arguments. Women more often look beyond the totally rational arguments to the real reasons a person would buy or not buy a particular product. That's why it's said, "Men have sight; women have insight."

You sell successfully to the degree to which you appeal to the correct emotion or subconscious need of your prospect when you present your product or service. You may make the sale because of your skill in doing this or you may make it because the customer himself concludes that your product or service satisfies his primary emotional need. But in either case, your customer buys because he perceives that the purchase will satisfy his *real* need better than any other use of the same amount of money at the present time.

. My friend Dr. Jim Newman suggests that you look at each person you are speaking to as if he or she had a chest full of buttons, all wired into different emotions. Imagine that some are *green* and wired into positive emotions, while others are *red* and wired into negative emotions. In your interactions with other people, you are pressing either red buttons or green buttons all the time. When you press the correct button, you get the desired response, and the other person reacts accordingly. Your job is to find the correct button to press to get your prospect to respond to you with a buying decision.

Each person has a series of green buttons. When you press any of these buttons, you trigger positive emotions, such as love, pride, respect, happiness, and security. Referring to a person's family, accomplishments, appearance, or merits will instantly trigger these kinds of positive feelings.

Each person has a series of red buttons as well. These are wired into negative emotions based on previous experiences. These red buttons trigger recollections of old fears, angers, resentments, and uncertainties. If you push one of them, the other person will instantly react with anger, fear, suspicion, or hostility.

These red buttons are connected to parts of our lives where we have a good deal of emotion invested, such as our personalities, our work, or our families. You can push one of these buttons and make a person angry by simply suggesting that she is not particularly competent at her work, or that he is not a good husband or father. The response will be instantaneous. He or she will immediately defend and attack.

Your job in the sale is to push green, positive buttons and avoid the red, negative ones, except when it specifically serves your purpose. Sometimes you will have to press a red button, to illustrate the downside of not purchasing your product or service, and then push a green button to illustrate the benefits and advantages of owning what you are selling.

The two major motivators are the *desire for gain* and the *fear of loss*. All buying decisions are motivated by one emotion or the other. You should attempt to structure your presentation creatively so that you use both motivators on every occasion.

For example, I purchased a new car recently. I wasn't planning to, as I was content with the car I was driving. But the garage told me it would require $3,000 worth of service work to replace the tires, realign the wheels, and do some other necessary repairs. The car was six years old and I knew that I could never get that money back out of it on resale or as a trade-in in the future. I *immediately* became a prospective customer. I decided to purchase a new car rather than fix the old one.

My *fear of loss* involved the $3,000 worth of expenses that I could never recover. My *desire for gain* was the expected pleasure of owning and driving a new car. The key buying factor during the test drive and the negotiation was the fact that the dealership had only one car left that was priced $2,000 below the new models on the lot. It was the car I wanted, in the color I wanted, with the accessories I wanted, and if I purchased it that day, I could get it for $2,000 less than the identical car would cost a week later. The twin factors of desire and fear combined to trigger a buying decision that very day.

Because all buying decisions are emotional, one of the most important things you do in the sales conversation is to determine the

emotional factors that are likely to influence the behavior of the prospect. You can only do this by asking questions skillfully and by listening
carefully to the answers. People are structured psychologically in such
a way that their chief emotional concerns are usually on the top of
their minds. Whenever we discuss any product or service, our primary
desires and fears relative to that offering surge to the forefront of our
thinking and control our attention.

In psychology, there is the term "Freudian slip," which refers to the
tendency of people in conversation to inadvertently blurt out what they
are really thinking. Often, if you listen carefully and quietly to a prospect talk about his or her situation as it relates to your product or
service, he or she will give you the emotional cues, clues, and words
that reveal his or her true emotional agenda. It is this emotional agenda
that you must satisfy in order to make the sale. Every customer has
one, and they will let slip in conversation the words that will enable
you to identify what it is. When you listen, you must be sensitive to the
words the prospect uses and make note of them to incorporate them
into your sales presentation later.

As you would expect, the customer reveals his or her true emotional
agenda by the use of emotional words. Emotional words are those that
are somehow charged with the electrical sparks of fear or desire of
some kind. The word "exciting" in reference to your product is an
emotionally charged word; the word "interesting" is not. When a customer uses an emotionally charged word or phrase, catch it, as you
would a flyball in baseball, and be prepared to toss it back a little later
in the conversation.

If your prospect says, "All I am concerned about is how it impacts
my bottom line," you could push his particular green button by later
saying something like, "This product will really *impact your bottom
line.*"

If you have correctly identified an emotional hot button, your customer will react, often physically. He will sit up straighter, lean forward, and become more animated. Sometimes, he will begin speaking
more rapidly and start telling you what he is most concerned about
with regard to what you are selling. Each time you repeat key emotional words, you increase your prospect's desire to buy from you.

HOT BUTTON SELLING

Professional salespeople become very skilled at determining which of
the invisible buttons on the customer's chest is the **hot button.** Once

they have determined the hot button, they continually press it throughout the presentation. They focus on this hot button in their proposal and they mention it repeatedly in their closing arguments. They ask questions about the hot button and they continually illustrate how this specific emotional need will be satisfied satisfactorily with this purchase decision.

The hot button is always emotional and almost invariably has to do with the respect and esteem of other people. If you are selling a home, an office building, or a car, or if you are selling an insurance policy, an investment program, or a computer networking system, in almost every case the prospect will be concerned about how he or she will be thought of by other people as a result of making this decision. American Express has an excellent advertisement that illustrates this appeal when they say, "The American Express Card: It tells people who you *really* are."

There are various questions you can ask to uncover the hot button in almost any sales situation. When you ask these questions hypothetically, your customer will answer you hypothetically as well. But the answer that your prospect gives you will be the key benefit you will have to demonstrate to get the sale.

Here are my three favorite questions for uncovering the real buying motive:

1. "Mr. Prospect, if you were *ever* to buy this product, what would you want it to do for you at that time?"

2. "Mr. Prospect, what would you *absolutely* have to be convinced of for you to go ahead with this buying decision?"

3. "Mr. Prospect, if this product or service was *free*, would you take it?" If the prospect answers, "Yes, if it was free, I'd take it," you pause and then ask, "Why?"

Once you have identified his hot button, you must focus on convincing him overwhelmingly that if he buys your product or service, he will "absolutely, positively" get the key benefit that he is seeking.

You should bring the whole sales presentation to hang on this one question. You must demonstrate that your product or service is the ideal solution to his or her problem, or the ideal way to achieve his or her goal.

We've discussed the Pareto Principle, the 80/20 rule. It says that 80 percent of the value of what you do will be contained in 20 percent of your activities. In addition, there is another rule that applies to selling called the 90/10 rule. This rule says that 90 percent of the buying decision will come to hang on 10 percent of the actual benefits that the prospect anticipates enjoying by purchasing your product or service.

Your job in selling is to find that critical 10 percent, that one special feature that is more important to your prospect than all of the other features put together.

For example, IBM, during its heyday, turned out some of the best trained and most qualified executives of any major corporation in America. Many of these executives were hired away into senior positions by client companies of IBM. Later, when these companies needed to purchase or upgrade their computers, the ex-IBM executives in their ranks always ordered their computer products and peripherals from IBM.

What was the hot button? The hot button was the high esteem and regard that these ex-IBM'ers had for their first company. IBM had been so successful at instilling within them a feeling of loyalty to the corporation that when it came to making decisions on computers, these former IBM executives always specified IBM products. It was almost impossible for rival computer manufacturers to get into a company where a former IBM executive had a key role.

An IBM salesperson, pressing the hot button in his or her discussion with an ex-IBM executive, would always refer to the fact that these products may not be faster than the competition and may not be cheaper, but they were from IBM. This argument invariably carried the day. The more people left IBM and went to work in other corporations, the more of a market there was in those corporations for IBM products because of this decisive hot button factor.

The critical determinant of the buying decision can be the *relationship* that exists between the salesperson and the customer. It can be the excellent *reputation* that the company enjoys in the marketplace. The hot button can be a *satisfied friend* or associate of the customer who has recommended the product or service highly. The hot button can be that the product or service is *immediately available* from your company and not available from another. The hot button can be something as simple as the *color* of a product or the *view* from a property. It can be the depth of *your understanding* of the customer's situation. It can be your *personal reputation* for having achieved similar goals or solved similar problems for other customers in the past. But whatever the hot button, it is the critical emotional factor that you must discover and press repeatedly if you are to make the sale. It is the specific need that you must satisfy.

MOTIVATORS VERSUS NONMOTIVATORS

Motivating people to buy your product or service requires not only that you know why they buy and how to appeal to their chief buying motives, but it also requires that you know why they don't buy and how to avoid focusing your efforts in areas where it will do you no good.

Frederick Herzberg, the psychologist and pioneer in motivation, made a major contribution to need theory in his studies of the factors that motivate employees to produce more or less depending upon the situation created by the company. He developed the concept of "hygiene factors versus motivational factors." Your understanding of the difference between these two, especially in today's marketplace where quality, value, price, and service are used interchangeably as reasons for buying, is absolutely essential for your success.

What Herzberg found was there were many things that management did for employees that did not seem to improve morale or increase production very much. If you created a clean working environment, with a comfortable temperature, ample lighting, comfortable furniture, with adequate coffee and lunchroom facilities, sufficient parking, and the proper equipment and materials to work with, these would have little lasting effect on employee productivity. Management was mystified. Although they spent a good deal of money to create a comfortable working environment it didn't seem to increase the volume of work being done.

Herzberg also looked at the role of financial compensation, health and pension benefits, vacation pay, bonuses, and the regularity and predictability of salary increases. He found that altering any of these could affect motivation and increase productivity temporarily, but then people would go back to performing at the same level as before the improvement. Management was at a loss to understand this behavior as well.

But as soon as they understood that a need once satisfied was no longer a motivator, it became clear. Herzberg called these satisfied deficiency needs "hygiene factors." He said that the existence of these factors did not motivate employees. They were the basic minimum requirements for effective work. He did find, however, that the *absence* of any one of these factors would be a demotivator.

In other words, if the company provided all of the factors that went into a good working environment, including satisfactory pay and regular increases, it did not motivate anyone to produce any more than they were already. But if the company neglected to provide any of them, this factor would be a demotivator that would lower the overall level of productivity.

Herzberg then went on to postulate what he called "motivating factors." These, it turned out, were all psychological and emotional. They were things like challenging work, interesting jobs, increased responsibility, positive interactions with peers and superiors, regular training and development to prepare people for bigger and more challenging tasks, being in the know about what was going on in the company, and having a variety of assignments. These all turned out to be motivators. The more of these that were included in a person's work life, the happier and more productive the person tended to be.

What Herzberg found was that motivators could be increased almost indefinitely. An entire work environment could be structured in such a way that productivity increased steadily over time. Herzberg found that men and women working in stimulating, happy environments continually performed at ever higher levels of output and quality.

The same principle applies to sales, as you shall see in a minute. Certain product attributes do not increase the attractiveness of your product or service, but if your product or service lacks them, you won't be able to sell at all. Certain aspects of your product or service and of those of your competitors are expected by the prospect, and are therefore no longer motivators. They are hygiene factors. Mentioning them as part of your presentation in an attempt to create buying desire has no effect on the prospect. If anything, mentioning things that the prospect expects as a basic part of your offering will bore your prospect or even demotivate him.

FOUR ASPECTS OF YOUR PRODUCT OR SERVICE

Theodore Levitt of the Harvard Business School has suggested that each product or service is divided into four parts by the prospect or customer. These four elements of your product or service affect the way the customer views you and your offering.

The first part of your offering, from the customer's viewpoint, is the *generic* product or service. This is the basic product. It is the absolute minimum. If you are selling photocopiers, the generic product is a machine that produces photocopies. If you are selling cars, the generic product is a vehicle that includes four wheels, transmission, drive train, and rear end, plus basic interior finishings. If you are selling telecommunications systems, the generic product includes all of the internal components and wiring necessary for the purchaser to pick up the telephone and call anywhere in the world.

The second element of your product or service is the *expected* product. This is the part of the product that may not be written down or described in your materials but that is expected nonetheless. Failure to deliver on the elements of your product or service that the customer expects can lead to dissatisfaction, canceled orders, and ruined business relationships. These expected factors are important and misunderstandings with regard to them can be serious.

For example, your customer expects that your paperwork will be completed correctly and your billing will be accurate. Your customer expects that his phone calls will be responded to in a timely manner. Your customer expects that the product or service will be delivered in proper packaging and by a polite and knowledgeable person. Your customer expects that you will be punctual for your appointments, presentable in your appearance, and dependable in fulfilling your commitments. These may not be written in your brochures, but failure to live up to any of these expectations will negatively affect the customer's opinion of you and your company, as well as of your products or services.

The third part of your product is the *augmented* element. These are the extra things that you include in your product or service, or the things that you or your company do, that go *beyond* expectations. It is in this area of exceeding expectations that you can set yourself and your company apart from your competitors. It is by doing the things that are beyond what the customer anticipates that you build high the levels of goodwill that lead to testimonials, resales, and referrals to other prospects.

Doing more than you are paid for, more than is expected, going the extra mile, are the keys to superior customer relationships. These are the things that surprise and delight your customer and that help build the long-term quality business relationships that are consistent with great sales success in every field.

The understanding of these three elements—the generic, the expected, and the augmented—of any product is essential to the way you position and sell against the competition. They are the natural applications of Herzberg's definition of hygiene factors versus motivational factors.

A new product or service may enter the market as an augmentation that satisfies needs and exceeds existing customer expectations. It can offer benefits that have not hitherto been available. Its very existence is its competitive advantage. Its unique ability to satisfy specific customer needs is the core reason for buying it. Its sales and marketing are based on introducing it to the greatest number of prospects in the shortest period of time. This is what happened with the first fax machines.

But in no time at all, competitors enter the field with similar products. What started off as new and different quickly becomes a standard feature. It becomes generic and has no power to influence or motivate. It is now a hygiene factor.

Each company moves to improve their product by augmenting it in some way. They add special features, terms, methods of acquisition, service options, and so on to differentiate their product from their competitors. However, as soon as one company introduces a successful innovation, rival companies either copy it or do them one better. In no time at all, the special added feature appears on all similar products. It soon becomes part of the expected product, and soon, as far as the customer is concerned, part of the generic product. As a hygiene factor, its presence does not help in selling the product, but its absence, or even its questionability, will hurt or possibly destroy the sale.

American Airlines was the first company to come out with frequent flyer miles. Frequent travelers signed up and began instructing their travel agents to book them more often on American Airlines so they could get more frequent flyer points for later use. When the other airlines saw the promotional success of frequent flyer miles, they began offering them as well. Soon every major airline had a frequent flyer program. And the competition began among the airlines to see which frequent flyer program could be made better for the flyers. Today, announcing a frequent flyer program would not impress anyone. If, as an airline, you don't have an advanced, convenient, easy-to-use frequent flyer program, you're not even playing in the same game as the major carriers.

The mistake that many salespeople make is to build their approach and their presentations around generic features that have no ability to motivate the prospect. You sell effectively by emphasizing the special features and benefits that are in addition to the generic and expected product, and that make your product or service particularly attractive when compared against your competitors.

The fourth element of the product defined by Leavitt was the area of the *potential* product. This is the area of creativity and innovation where product or service developers can add features to them to make them unique and different from anything in the marketplace. The potential of a product or service can be unlimited.

Excellent and attentive follow-up service, continued long past the sale, can be a form of augmentation of your product or service. Even little things mean a lot. When I purchased my new car recently the sales manager had one of his top salesmen take me to a gas station near the dealership and buy me a full tank of gas before I drove away. This may not seem like much. It cost about $22. But in twenty-five years of buying new and used cars, this was the first time I had ever driven away without an empty tank.

Since then, I have recommended two other customers to this dealer, both of whom have purchased cars costing more than $40,000 each. Was the $22 tank of gas a good investment on the part of the dealership? You bet it was! This small gesture went so far beyond the standard expectations we have of this industry that it generated enthusiastic testimonials to other potential customers.

Think about your product or service for a minute. What is the generic product that you sell? What are the various factors of your product or service that your customers expect, even though they are not spoken about or written down? How could you augment your product? How could you exceed customer expectations in the sale and delivery of your product or service? And finally, what are the areas of potential service where you can do things that satisfy your customers better than anyone else? All market and selling breakthroughs come from expanding in the area of the augmented and the potential product.

QUALITY, SERVICE, VALUE, AND PRICE

In my sales seminars, I often stop the class and ask this question, "Why should I, or anybody else, buy your product or service? What is it about your product or service that makes it the better choice for me over any other products or services like yours in the marketplace?"

Invariably, the majority of the people in my audience will answer, "Quality!" "Service!" "Value!" "Price!" The favorites are, "Quality and service!" "Quality and service!" "Quality and service!"

I call these the "parrot" answers. Just like a parrot squawks out, "Hello there!" "Hello there!" most salespeople parrot the words "Quality and service!" "Quality and Service!" "Quality and Service!" just like a parrot and just as unthinkingly. Salespeople have the mistaken idea that quality and service, or value and price, are reasons for buying a particular product. Based on everything we've talked about so far, you can see that this is silly, if not hurtful to your sales message.

The fact is that *quality, service, value, and price* are all hygiene factors. Their existence does not *increase* the desirability of your product or service, but their absence certainly *decreases* the attractiveness of your offering. They will not get you the sale, but if there is the slightest suspicion on the part of your prospect that they aren't included in your product or service, they will certainly lose you the sale.

Quality is not a reason for buying anything. Quality is only one of several factors that go into the buying decision. And because of enhanced consumer awareness of product availability, combined with the extreme competitiveness of today's marketplace, quality is a basic minimum for being in the market in the first place. It is a hygiene factor. Your customer assumes that your product has a minimum level of quality or you wouldn't even be in business.

From the customer's point of view the critical issue is *utility*. Will your product or service do the job that the customer needs to have done? Philip Crosby, founder of the Crosby Quality College and best-selling author on quality, defines quality this way: "The product does what you say it will do, and continues to do it without breaking down." The percentage of the time that your product or service fulfills that definition is its quality rating. The percentage of the time that your product or service breaks down or fails to do what it was purchased to do is your defect rating.

The quality must only be appropriate enough to satisfy the customer's needs. If this were not the case, then everyone would drive Mercedes-Benzes and Rolls-Royces. The key question is: "Is this the best choice, all things considered, to do the job that I need done?"

When you discuss and explain quality features to your prospect, you must show how and why they benefit this particular customer. You must show why they make your product or service more appropriate than any other product or service in satisfying this customer's specific needs.

Your product or service must be the most suitable for what the customer needs before quality enters the equation. If you lead with quality as a reason for buying your product or service, you will find yourself pushing a button of the customer that is not wired to anything. People are not motivated to buy because your product is high quality. People are motivated to buy because your product is the very best solution to their problem, and the quality of the product is only one of several motivators that can trigger the buying decision.

The service you provide for your product is not a motivator either. It is expected. Even excellent service is becoming expected. You cannot say that people should buy from you because you give "good service." Everyone gives good service. You will seldom find a competitor who will say, "Our product is good but our service is lousy."

Excellent service today is a hygiene factor. If there is any problem with prompt, attentive service once a customer has purchased a product or service, it will act as a demotivator. But the existence of follow-up service does not motivate. It is simply expected. Eventually, for service to have any meaning at all as a competitive advantage, your service will have to be continually better than that of the rival companies in your marketplace. You will have to keep raising your service standards just to stay even in the minds of your customers.

Value is also expected in today's market. Customers today both demand and expect the very highest quality for the very best price. You don't get anything extra for providing good value, or assuring the customer that he or she is getting good value. But you will lose out on the sale and the business if your customer has the slightest suspicion that this is not the highest value, all things considered, that he or she can get in making this purchase.

When you discuss value, you must explain, detail by detail, the various factors of your offering that constitute value. You must show how these are specifically relevant to your customer. You must show how your customer gains in convenience, or lower cost, or shorter downtime, or longer life, or greater speed, with the special features of your product or service than he or she would without them. You must also show how your product or service has specific benefits that your competitors lack that represent real added value to your customer.

Good price, or lower price, is another major reason that salespeople give for people to buy. Many salespeople think that if they tell the prospect that their price is really excellent compared to the competition that this will motivate the customer to buy. But remember, price is seldom the reason for buying anything. According to interviews with customers, fully 94 percent of all purchases in America are made on a *nonprice* basis. Even basic commodities, undifferentiated from one another, like grain, crude oil, and lumber, are often bought on a nonprice basis.

For example, Lawrence Steinmetz points out in his book *How to Sell at Prices Higher than Your Competitors* that gasoline is a commodity. It is undifferentiated in its composition. Yet, in any gas station, it sells at three or four different prices at the pump. There is the cash price, the credit price, the full-service price, and the self-service price. There can be a price difference of 20 percent to 30 percent for the identical liquid depending upon how it is sold. If price is not even the determining factor in buying gasoline, then it isn't in buying virtually anything else.

This is because price is also a hygiene factor. People assume that the price of your product or service will be fair and reasonable. A higher than reasonable price will serve as a demotivator of buying activity, but a fair price does not act as a motivator. It is just expected.

Prospects talk a lot about your prices. They question and complain about price. They also comment and complain about their business, their budgets, competitive prices, and availability of funds. But in the final analysis, when they decide to buy, they almost always make their decisions on a nonprice basis.

Neil Rackham, in his book *S.P.I.N. Selling*, quotes studies where customers were telephoned after they had turned down the product or service and given price as the reason. In 68 percent of cases, the customers admitted that price was not the *real* reason for not buying. It was something else. When they were asked why they told the salespeople that they couldn't afford it, they explained that that seemed to be the easiest way to get them to leave peacefully.

You can never motivate a person to buy a product or service that he doesn't want or need by cutting the price. Once the prospect has decided that he or she wants it, you may motivate him or her to act *now* by making price concessions, but you can seldom use price reductions to create buying desire.

Buyers are emotional. They buy from you depending upon whether or not you appeal to what really motivates them. They buy depending upon whether or not you have addressed their emotional agendas correctly. Customers buy because you have presented the benefits of owning your product in such a way that it satisfies their real needs. Customers buy because you have shown them clearly that their real problems can be solved and their real goals achieved most effectively by the use and enjoyment of your product or service.

DEMOTIVATORS AND SALES BLOCKERS

Not all people who can benefit from the use of your product or service are potential customers. There are several factors that can enter into the equation and block the sale. Sometimes you can detect and neutralize these factors and sometimes you cannot. At the very least, you need to understand what they are and be ready with intelligent answers for them if they arise.

You've heard the equation "No need? No sale!" What this really means is that the need may exist but it is not big enough. To buy anything, a customer must overcome the twin forces of habit and inertia. Unless your product or service addresses a pressing need that you have identified and demonstrated, the forces of habit and inertia will stop the prospect from taking action on your offer.

The force of habit will cause the prospect to continue using what he is using, or doing what he is doing, even though it is less satisfactory than your offering, because he or she is comfortable and sees no need to change. The benefits of your proposed solution appear to be too small relative to the inconvenience of uprooting the established way of doing things and starting something different.

Inertia refers primarily to laziness. People don't like to change, even if it represents an improvement. They prefer to continue doing whatever it is they are doing at the present. They continually seek ways to justify their current method of operation rather than seeking ways to make them better and more efficient. They often have a lot of ego involved in the way things are being done already.

Usually something has to happen to give them a jolt before they will consider switching to a different product or service. Sometimes, the only jolt that will move a complacent prospect to take action is a breakdown of their existing system simultaneous with your presentation of a superior product or service that makes sense in terms of quality, value, and service.

The prospect may not buy because he doesn't feel your solution is appropriate for him and his situation. It may seem like an ideal purchase decision to you, but it may seem unacceptable to the prospect. It may be inappropriate because of the cost, which the prospect is not willing to bear at this time. It may be inappropriate because of the different tastes of the prospect. If your product is not consistent with his or her particular aesthetic sense, he or she will have a mental block to purchasing.

It could be that the price of your product is simply too high for the financial situation of the prospect. I work with beginning salespeople who pay $200 for a suit and they are quite proud of their purchase. I work with senior salespeople who pay $2,000 for their suits and are equally happy with their purchases. But the $2,000 suit is simply not appropriate for the beginning salesperson. It may be worth every penny, but the beginning salesperson is simply not in that market.

Another common demotivator that blocks sales is that the prospect, or someone he knows, has had a negative experience with your company. This is a hard demotivator to overcome. Many companies have made the mistake of producing a poor quality product or service for a short time and then found themselves spending years overcoming the negative reputation they had created.

Customers today are gun-shy. Once they make a purchasing mistake, they very seldom ever go back to that company, and they seem to take great delight in making sure that none of the people they know purchase from that company either.

If your company has a negative reputation in the marketplace because of problems with earlier products or services, you may be able to overcome this block to the sale by admitting the mistake, accepting responsibility for the previous problem, and guaranteeing absolute satisfaction in the future, if the prospect will just give you another chance.

If everything else about your product or service makes it appear to be the most appropriate choice for the prospect, your willingness to accept responsibility and offer an unconditional guarantee can give you another chance to win that customer. People in general are quite forgiving when it comes to competitive enterprise. It is a trait of the American character to be willing to give the underdog a chance, especially if he or she accepts responsibility for the problems of the past and asks for an opportunity to make up for it in the future.

Another major demotivator that can block a sale, even if your product or service is perfectly appropriate to the prospect, is the existence of strong competition. The unfortunate fact is that often your competition has a product or service that is better than yours in some way. Often it is more approrpriate for this particular customer than yours would be. Customers today are the smartest, best educated, and most knowledgeable customers that have ever existed in all of human history. They know an immense amount about their needs and about what is available to satisfy them. Sometimes, they will conclude that what your competitor is offering is superior to what you are offering and there is no way that you will be able to change their minds.

When you are dealing with a prospect who you cannot move to purchase from you, use *reverse* psychology. Be extremely courteous and professional in everything you do. Thank the prospect profusely for taking time to consider your offer. Assure the prospect that you very much want the business and that you will do anything to satisfy the prospect should he change his mind. Tell the prospect that you would like to be considered as his second choice in case his first choice doesn't work out. Life is very long, and what goes around comes around. Many times, the prospect will decide to go with another company and then find that the other company cannot deliver what they promised. Your job is to position yourself as the immediate second choice.

You've also heard it said, "No urgency? No sale!" If you have aroused the prospect's desire high enough for your product, the urgency will exist naturally. But in many cases, your product or service is positioned in such a way that whether or not the customer gets it today, tomorrow, or next year doesn't appear to make any difference to him. Your job is to somehow put a deadline on your offer to get your prospect to make a decision sooner rather than later.

You need to develop that rare combination of eagerness plus patience. It must be very clear to the customer that you think he or she would be better off acting immediately. Simultaneously, you must be patient enough to realize that people often take time to make up their minds. When your customer is going slow on your offer, it is usually the time for *persistence*, but not insistence. It is the time for professionalism, not pressure.

If there is any way that you can give a special inducement to the customer for acting immediately, you should save it until the very *end* of the sales conversation. If you bring it up anytime before the customer has decided that he wants to own and enjoy your product or service, the inducement will be treated as part of the package and it will have no motivational or incentive effect to cause the customer to act at the end. Always save something for the final shove at the end of the conversation.

What *demotivators* exist in your selling activities? Why do perfectly qualified prospects decide *not* to buy from you? How could you neutralize or offset the most common reasons prospects give for not taking action on your offering? These are some of the most important questions you ever ask or answer in professional selling.

WHY BUSINESSES BUY

Businesspeople are the same as any other customer. They are motivated to act to satisfy the various needs that we have discussed. They are influenced by both hygiene factors and motivators when they consider purchasing your product or service. They are completely emotional. They act to improve their condition in some way. They only make buying decisions when they have a felt dissatisfaction on the one hand, and they are convinced that your product or service can alleviate it on the other.

In almost every case, a limited number of the benefits offered by your product or service, sometimes only one, will be critical in making the buying decision. Every business customer has a hot button that is unique to him or her, and it is your job to uncover that hot button and then to convince the prospect overwhelmingly that his deepest emotional need will be satisfied with what you are selling.

Businesspeople are motivated to buy by appealing to their most pressing needs in their current situation. Each businessperson, at each level, and with different sets of responsibilities, has a different set of needs that you must satisfy. They are all different, depending on what the businessperson is doing and the psychological dynamics of his or situation at the moment.

Gaining and keeping the respect of one's superiors and co-workers is a major motivator for business buying decisions. A correct purchase decision can earn him praise and approval. A wrong buying decision can open him to criticism and condemnation. A businessperson's position, promotability, and status are more important to him than the appropriateness or quality of what you are selling. You must be alert to this.

People at the lower levels of a business want, more than anything, to be appreciated and respected by their superiors. They want to be liked by their co-workers. They want to be seen as part of the team and to belong to their work group. Their buying decisions will be strongly influenced by how they feel people around them will react to what they do.

You have also heard the admonition "No authority? No sale!" Many businesspeople at lower levels of the organization have the authority to say no, but they do not have the authority to say yes. And because they are so concerned about being liked, even by the salesperson, they will seldom tell you that they do not have the authority to make the buying decision. They will ask for proposals and presentations, price comparisons and discounts, and feedback with modifications on your product or service, but they often do not have the authority to buy from you even if they like what you are selling.

When you begin a sales conversation in a company, with anyone, always ask, "Is there anyone, in addition to yourself, who will be involved in the final decision?" Be prepared to press this point until you get a definitive answer. Do not allow low-level decision-makers to waste your time. Your time is all you have to sell and you must treat it with care.

If lower-level decision-makers are concerned primarily with cost relative to competitors, middle-level decision-makers are more concerned with the performance of your product or service. Their basic need is to make decisions that enhance the performance and productivity of their areas of responsibility. This is their major concern. This is their hot button. This is what you need to uncover and address in your sales conversation.

For example, if you are talking to a sales manager, your entire focus must be on how your product or service will help his department increase the volume of sales. The respect and esteem of his superiors is determined by the volume of sales he and his salespeople achieve. You must focus all of your attention on showing him that his needs for security, belonging, and esteem can be met by using your product or service.

If you are talking to a midlevel administrative manager about your product or service, you must focus on his or her primary need to demonstrate improved performance and efficiency. He or she wants to be respected and esteemed by getting the job done faster, more efficiently, and at lower cost.

People always purchase a product in anticipation of how they expect to feel as a result of having this product in use in their organization. Will they feel better, more secure, more respected and esteemed, and more competent? Your job is to present your product or service, point by point, to demonstrate that the use of your product or service will fulfill these needs better than something else.

Always ask, in the relationship-building part of the sales transaction, "What are the exact outputs of your job?" "What exactly do you do? What exactly are you responsible for at this company?"

Each person has key result areas, the result areas for which he is primarily responsible. Successful performance in these areas determines his success in his career. You should find out the key result areas of the prospect you are talking to, and build your sales conversation around helping him do better at the critical success factors of his job.

You will find, when you ask, that many people are fuzzy or unclear about their key result areas. When you help them to better understand what they most need to accomplish, and present your product as an aid to achieving that goal, you will be viewed more as a consultant than as a salesperson. Be friendly and genial, and ask in a curious, interested way, "What is the most important thing you do here?"

Attached to each person's key result areas are standards of performance. These may be written or unwritten. This is how the person is measured in the important things they do. Don't be afraid to ask your prospect, "How do you measure that?" Or, "How do you know if you have done a good job in that area?"

In talking to businesspeople, you can always feel free to ask questions like, "What is the biggest single problem that you are wrestling with right now?" Or, "If you could solve any one problem in your work today, what one problem would it be?" If you then listen patiently to the answers, nodding, smiling, and encouraging the prospect to expand on his or her thoughts, the prospect will often tell you his primary areas of concern as they affect your product or service.

When you are dealing with senior executives, the top tier of any organization, their primary concern will be for the success of the enterprise as a whole. They are preoccupied with financial results. They think in terms of the bottom line. Their primary motivation is return on investment. They measure almost every product or service in terms of its ability to contribute to the financial strength of the organization.

Your job is to position your product or service as a financial solution to their most pressing problems. This can be done with almost any product or service. You can make a tangible product into an intangible and you can make an intangible product into a tangible. A photocopier, for example, can be presented as an intangible reducer of time and cost thereby increasing the bottom line. An insurance policy can be seen as a guarantor of continued business operations, thereby assuring no breakdown in the ability of the company to generate profits.

When you deal with a senior-level person, always explain your product or service in terms of the financial results, as a return on investment, that the prospect will enjoy from owning it. If you can s' your product or service will pay for itself over the life of its use generate a profit based on increased efficiency or reduced costs, you can show a return on investment in excess of the total price. This is how you persuade a senior decision-maker to buy from you.

"What here?"

When you are selling to retailers, their primary concern is for net profits. They want to know how much they make from each of your products they sell, and how fast they can make it.

You must show them that their primary need, that of profits from regular, rapid, and predictable turnover, can be met by carrying your products in their stores. If you can also show that your products lend additional prestige and beauty to their product assortment, you can often trigger the secondary motivators that push the prospect over the edge into becoming a customer.

When you are selling to businesses of any kind, you should be thinking of the doctor's question, "Where does it hurt?" Your goal must be to help your prospect take away his pain, satisfy his need, and achieve his or her goal. Your product or service must be positioned as a solution to his or her most pressing problems. You must discover his primary positive motivators, and emphasize them. Simultaneously, you must find out what would stop him from buying and eliminate them.

THE SALESPERSON AS MOTIVATOR

The sale can be made or lost by a single factor. Everything counts. Everything that you do, or don't do, either helps or hurts you. Everything moves you closer to the sale or moves you away. Nothing is neutral.

One of the most pressing needs of every customer is for a competent professional salesperson to help him or her make good buying decisions. Customers want a salesperson who is knowledgeable, experienced, and well informed. They need a salesperson who asks good questions and who listens carefully to the answers before making a recommendation for purchasing.

Customers today want the simple truth about a product or service. They want honest information from you about how it can help them improve their businesses or their lives. They don't want to be sold. They want to make up their own minds. They want to be helped to buy without any kind of high pressure.

Purchase decisions are often made because of the character and competence of the salesperson alone. The customer may not be able to sort out the conflicting claims of the various competitive offerings, but the customer can and will rely on his or her own personal judgment with regard to the character of the salesperson.

Usually, the greatest asset that a company has is a world-class sales force composed of top professionals who are capable of creating and maintaining long-term quality relationships with customers. And this means *you.* Perhaps your greatest single business asset is the quality of your personality and the completeness of your professionalism when you are with a prospect.

The customer needs the assurance of the salesperson in several ways. The customer's confidence increases and his fear of making a mistake decreases in direct proportion to the quality of the salesperson, in every respect. Your appearance, your dress, your comportment, and your demeanor are all essential parts of the sales conversation. Every element of your personal appearance should be designed to increase the confidence and the willingness of the customer to enter into a relationship with you and your company. The customer is reassured by a professional sales presentation, thoroughly prepared, carefully organized, and followed in a logical and sequential manner. Even the quality of the questions you ask, and the order in which you ask them, have an enormous bearing on whether the customer reaches the critical mass emotionally that is necessary before he or she can buy from you.

How the customer feels about you as a person is a critical issue in superior selling. Customers will pay more, for less, to buy from someone with whom they feel completely comfortable than they ever would in dealing with someone who made them feel uneasy for any reason.

WHY DO THEY BUY?

More than $1 billion is spent every year in America on market research. This research has one single purpose: to discover what people buy and why they buy it. The reason companies spend so much on this research is so they can advertise and promote their products and services more efficiently. They can structure their advertising appeals to the real needs that their products and services are capable of satisfying. They can minimize or eliminate advertising or promotional expenses that do not contribute to increasing sales.

As a top professional, you must also do market research on yourself. You must take the time to find out why it is that people buy your product or service from *you*. At the same time, you must find out why it is that people do *not* buy from you, or why they buy from your competitors. The reason for your market research is the same as the reason for market research conducted by large companies. It is so that you can spend more time with better prospects who can make buying decisions earlier and who can buy more of your products and services and recommend you more often to other potential customers.

Most salespeople do not know why their customers buy from them. I have asked thousands of salespeople if they could tell me the reasons they made the sales they made in the previous weeks and months. Most salespeople are simply baffled by the question. They start off by trying to tell me about the features and benefits of their product or service, then they shift to their customers, then to their competitors, then to the economy and back to the company and themselves, and finally they give up. They simply don't know why they are making the sales they are making.

Making sales without knowing *why* it is that people are buying, or not buying, is like shooting in a shooting gallery with your eyes closed. If you pull the trigger often enough (if you make enough calls), the odds are that you will hit something. But the odds are not very good that you will become an excellent marksman.

Because you accept total responsibility for yourself and your career, and you know that no one else is going to do these things for you, here is an exercise in *personal* market research that you can use to

dramatically increase your effectiveness as a salesperson. It is simple
and easy to perform. It will only take you two or three hours over
the next month. It will save you countless hours of hard work and
dramatically increase your sales at the same time.

First, make a list of your ten most recent customers. Write down
their names, addresses, and phone numbers. You probably know them
all on a first-name basis. You can select more than ten if you like, but
ten will be sufficient for this exercise. This list then becomes the basis
of your own personal market research project.

Second, telephone each of these customers. After asking them how
everything is going and establishing a certain level of rapport, ask them
the following question:

"We're doing some market research in our company, to find out how
we can serve our customers better. May I ask you a couple of quick
questions?"

(The prospect will almost invariably answer, "Sure.")

"I really appreciate your deciding to buy from me, especially knowing
that you had many other choices. Could you tell me, what was the *real*
reason you decided to buy from me rather than from someone else?"

Remain perfectly silent. Give the prospect time to think about why
he or she decided to buy from you rather than from someone else.

Listen carefully and write down every word that the prospect uses.
Listen for both the primary motivators (quality, service, value, price,
responsiveness, reputation of company, etc.) and the secondary motivators, the underlying emotional reasons why the person actually decided to buy. Listen for feeling words, those words that reveal the
strong emotional currents that run deep within the individual.

After you have interviewed ten customers, you will begin to notice
an overlapping similarity among their answers. If you are fortunate,
you will detect the critical reason why people are buying from you.
You will find that as many as eight out of ten of your customers have
the same reason in common. It may have to do with you, your company, the competitive market, advertising, or referrals and testimonials. Whatever it is, take some time to double-check your answers with
other people in your company and even call some of your customers
back to ask them again.

Your job is to develop a clear understanding of *who* you are selling
to and *why* they are buying. This understanding can help you pinpoint
your prospects and focus your sales presentation so as to dramatically
increase your sales results in a short period of time.

Not long ago, I was working with a major trucking company that
had expanded rapidly throughout the southeastern United States. This

company spent almost $3 million installing an extremely elaborate computer-based tracking system for the packages shipped on their trucks between the various cities they served. They felt that this investment would give them an edge in the marketplace and would dramatically increase their sales when their prospective customers heard about it.

But for some reason, they failed to do any market research in advance. They spent the $3 million on the computer system and then they advertised it widely and sent out their salespeople to tell their prospects about it. However, nothing happened. Their sales did not increase. If anything, their sales leveled off. The expensive upgrade of their computer tracking system had made no impact on the marketplace at all.

They called in a market research company, which brought their customers together in focus groups. The focus groups would sit around a table where they were televised discussing different trucking companies and the strengths and weaknesses of these trucking companies when it came to carrying freight from point to point. When they asked these customers what they thought about the fact that this particular trucking company had installed a very expensive tracking system for the packages they carried, the customers responded that they thought nothing about it. They didn't particularly care.

The researchers then explained that the purpose of the trucking company's new system was to ensure that if their packages were lost, damaged, or stolen, claims could be processed rapidly and their customers' losses could be corrected faster than that of any other company. How did they feel about that?

Again, the customers replied that they considered that system to be of little value. When they were asked why, the customers replied, "We don't want our packages lost, stolen, or damaged, and we are not impressed with a system that processes lost, stolen, or damaged packages faster than another trucking company that strives not to lose or damage our packages in the first place."

The researchers then asked the critical question: "What is it that you really want from the trucking company that you choose to carry your freight?"

Almost unanimously, the customers said, "What we want, more than anything else, is that the packages we ship are picked up from our facilities by a competent, courteous, nicely dressed person who fills out the forms correctly, and that when these packages are delivered to our ultimate customers, they are delivered by a competent, courteous person who fills out the forms accurately."

The answer was so simple that it took the trucking company executives aback. How had they missed this? What their customers wanted more than anything else was not higher technology, but higher *touch*. They wanted to deal with nice people at every step of the shipping process. With this information, the trucking company stopped advertising its computer system and started advertising and promoting the quality of its people. Their sales took off, and as far as I know, they are still growing.

Why do people buy from you? Why do they *really* buy from you? If you are shy about asking your customers, have one of the other salespeople in your company do the market research on your customers, and you do the same market research on his or her customers. But do not spend another day out beating the bushes in these competitive markets without knowing exactly *why* it is you are making sales in the first place.

The second part of your market research project is the flip side of the first. Phone ten people who either did *not* buy from you, or who bought from your competitors, and ask them similar questions. Start off by reducing their defensiveness with these words:

"Hello, this is John James, I spoke to you a few weeks (months) ago about our ABC system. I just wanted to call you and tell you that I very much appreciate your taking time to consider this system and I respect your decision to buy from XYZ Corporation (or to put off the decision until a later time.)

"I am trying to be a better salesperson for my customers and I would really appreciate it if you could tell me, 'What was the *real* reason that you decided to buy from XYZ Corporation?' (Or you could ask, 'What was the real reason you decided not to buy from me?')

"Every product has its strengths and weaknesses and it would really help me to know, from your perspective, what you felt were the strengths and weaknesses of my presentation."

The answers will probably surprise you. You will be amazed to hear your prospects tell you that they purchased from someone else because they did not feel that you had a specific capacity, which you may have had buy you neglected to tell them. You will find that prospects decided not to buy because you failed to mention a critical part of your offering that would have overcome their final objection. You may also find that the reason they didn't buy was because they did not feel comfortable proceeding with you and your company. Sometimes they will say that it was the price. If they say that price was the major objection, ask them this: "Aside from the price, what was the other major reason you decided not to buy from us?"

Don't be afraid to probe. This is serious business. Knowing why you are succeeding and why you are failing is the key to improving. Most people are so paralyzed by the fear of rejection and disapproval, or the fear of criticism, that they will go to any lengths to avoid asking a customer or prospect a straightforward question. Your focus must be on becoming the very best that you can be, and in order to do this, you must get accurate feedback on your performance.

SUMMARY

Top salespeople are committed to be the best in their profession. They are determined to pay any price, overcome any objections, or confront any embarrassment if that is what it takes for them to learn what they need to learn to move to the top.

By the same token, your ability to determine why your prospect really buys your product or service is absolutely essential for you to move ahead. It is only when you are crystal clear about the primary buying motivation of your prospect, and the deep subconscious needs that your product or service can satisfy, that you can begin to make better calls on better prospects, ask better questions, focus on getting better answers, and make better presentations that lead to bigger and better sales than you ever had before.

Most salespeople are in the position of the man in a dark room with the plug to the lamp in his hand. He is feeling around in the dark looking for the socket into which to put the plug, so that the light will come on and the room will be illuminated.

When you meet a prospect, you are operating in the dark as well. You are looking for the way to connect your product or service offering with the socket of the primary buying need of your prospect. It is only when you get your plug in the socket, when you present your product or service in such a way that the prospect feels that it is exactly what he or she needs at the moment, that the sale takes place.

When you take the time to think through and clearly identify why people buy, and why they buy from you, you will be on the road to greater and greater sales success! And how do you find out? You ask them!

7

INFLUENCING THE

BUYING DECISION

The sale is often made or lost within the first thirty seconds. People are inordinately affected by the suggestive influences in their environ-ment. Customers are often hypersensitive to the cues coming to them from the salesperson and from every aspect of his or her appearance and demeanor. Your prospects form a judgment about you in the first *four* seconds and they *confirm* it as soon as you open your mouth. The initial impression that you give them influences everything they do and say subsequently in their interactions with you.

Your ability to create a positive impression that triggers within your prospect a feeling of trust and confidence in you and your offerings is indispensable to your success in sales. For this reason, top salespeople in every field consciously and deliberately do everything possible to create an image of competence and professionalism in the first few minutes.

The moment the customer meets you, you make an indelible impres-sion. From that point on, the customer seeks information and proof to *validate* his or her first impression, while simultaneously *rejecting* information that contradicts what he or she has already decided to believe.

In a recent survey of personnel directors of large corporations, those people in charge of hiring for their companies, they were asked how long it takes them to make up their minds about a job candidate. They replied that, in all honesty, they make their decisions within thirty seconds of meeting the candidate. The time spent in interviews, background checks, and diagnostic testing are merely formalities. And they seldom change their minds. This is the same process that customers go through when they first meet you.

The subconscious mind functions as fast as thirty thousand times the speed of the conscious mind. It absorbs an entire series of sense impressions—sight, sound, smell, touch, and others—and blends them into an instantaneous gut-feeling that causes the prospect to either like and trust the salesperson, or not. Your primary aim therefore must be to do everything possible to *influence* this impression so that it is favorable to you and your product or service from the first moment.

The starting point of creating the kind of positive psychological environment where a sale can take place is for you to think through in advance the ideal impression you want to leave on the customer's mind. What emotions do you want to generate? How do you want to be *viewed* by the customer? If the customer were to come out into the waiting room, meet you for a few seconds, and then go back to his or her office and describe you to another person, what words would you want the customer to use?

One young salesman in my seminar told me how he got to the top of his organization. He had been about number twenty-four out of thirty salespeople in sales volume in his company for about four years. Then one day, something snapped. He decided that he didn't like being at the bottom of the totem pole. He decided at that moment to become one of the top salespeople in his branch.

So he asked himself, "If I were one of the top salespeople in the branch, what would I look like? How would I behave? How would I organize my day? What would I do, hour by hour, if I were one of the highest selling salespeople in this company?"

He then looked around him at the top people in his office. He observed the way they dressed and the way they worked. He had coffee with them and asked them questions about the way they planned their days and their weeks. He discussed them with his manager and with the other salespeople. He began to develop a composite picture of their activities, behavior, and appearance that he could use to compare himself with.

From then on, every morning before he started out, he would look in a full-length mirror and ask, "Do I look like one of the top salespeople in my company?" If for any reason he didn't *look* like a top producer, he would go back and change. He cut his hair shorter and improved his grooming. He polished his shoes and wore a better shirt and tie. He soon purchased better clothing so that, within a couple of months, when he stood in front of the mirror before going out the door, he could answer to himself, "Yes, I do look like one of the best salespeople in my branch."

Then, throughout the day, he would ask himself, "Is what I am doing right now *consistent* with being one of the best salespeople in my company?" When he was with his customers, he would ask himself, "Am I dealing with this customer and behaving as though I were one of the top salespeople in my organization?" He would review and reflect on every call and ask himself, "Am I doing everything possible so that my customers will view me as one of the top salespeople in my industry?"

Within a year, he was one of the top five salespeople in his branch. In two years, he was the second top producer, and in the third year he became the top-grossing salesperson, not only in his branch but in the entire region. And when I saw him and spoke to him, he looked every inch like one of the top salespeople in his industry, because he *was*.

To put the power of suggestion to work in your favor, compare yourself with the very best people in your industry. Look around you at the men and women you *admire* the very most and ask yourself what it is that they are doing or saying that is different from what you are doing or saying? Look at the pictures and stories of top people in newspapers and in magazines. Compare yourself with them and make them your role models. Let them set the standards to which you aspire. Always think of yourself as being among the very best in your industry and look for ways to improve everything you are doing. This is the real mark of a champion.

DRESS FOR SUCCESS

Ninety-five percent of the first impression you make on a prospect is determined by the way you dress. This is because in most cases your clothing covers 95 percent of your body. It is absolutely amazing to me how casual, and even poorly, many salespeople dress in their daily selling activities. It is almost as if no one has taken them aside and told them how important it is that they look the part of the professional salesperson if they want to be treated as a professional salesperson. Remember the words of Ralph Waldo Emerson, "What you *are* shouts at me so loudly I can't hear a word you are saying."

Shakespeare said, "Clothing oft makes the man." The reason that your clothing, your dress, is so important is because your clothing is *self-selected*. It is an expression of your personal preferences. Every item you wear is seen by others as part of a statement that you are making to the world about the kind of person you really are. When a person says that "people shouldn't judge me by my clothing," they are denying reality. You are openly *inviting* people to judge you by the clothes you choose to wear at any given time. You must therefore choose them with care.

Every salesperson should read at least one or two books on how to dress for success. John Molloy has written two excellent, well-researched books in this field, *John Molloy's New Dress for Success* and *The Woman's Dress for Success Book*. Start with these and then regularly read books and articles on how to dress even more correctly for a variety of situations. Image consultants charge as much as $1,500 a day to advise businesspeople on how to dress for greater power and influence with others, and you can get the essence of their very best thinking and research for just a few dollars in one of the books they have written.

In the meantime, remember that your choice of clothing and clothing style can make or break you. If you violate the specific rules of proper dress, you can be ruled out of the competition before you even open your mouth. In business, the most important impression that you make on a prospect is that you are trustworthy and reliable. The prospect must feel comfortable with you before he or she can seriously engage in a sales conversation with you. If the prospect has any mental block about the way you appear or come across, he or she will be unable to listen to you or to even take you seriously. They will be distracted by your appearance. Your sales message will fall on deaf ears. At the end of the conversation the prospect will mutter something about thanking you for coming in and show you the door. He or she will then never see you again.

People like to buy from people who are similar to themselves. The Law of Attraction is one of the most powerful influences in human behavior. People are most relaxed in dealing with other people who look the way they do, who are dressed similarly to them. They are also more relaxed when they are dealing with people whose dress is appropriate to the particular situation, whatever it may be.

For this reason, your dress should always be the best and most appropriate possible. If you are selling to law firms, you would dress very conservatively. You would wear dark colors and soft pastels. You would be more reserved and self-contained. You would dress in such a way that people working for law firms would be comfortable with you, and feel confident accepting your recommendations.

On the other hand, if you were selling grain dryers to farmers, you would dress more casually. You would still be neat and clean, but your dress would be such that farmers would feel relaxed chatting with you about their needs for the coming harvest season. In every case, it is your *customer* who determines the appropriateness of what you are wearing.

Here's an important point. Many executives or decision-makers who have made it in their businesses dress very casually to the office. Sometimes they wear cowboy boots or open-neck shirts with jewelry. They grow their hair long and are easygoing around their workplace. However, this does not mean that you should dress the same way. You have not yet *earned the right* to relax with regard to your dress.

If you try to match your customer by coming in with an open-neck shirt and a pair of jeans, he would not take you seriously. He would not be interested in your offer. In many cases, he would be offended that you would take the liberty of dressing down when you have not yet paid your dues.

For women in sales, this issue is equally important. When a woman has reached a position of power and authority in her organization, like the man, she may begin to relax a bit and dress more casually at work. However, if another woman, a subordinate or salesperson, attempts to interact with her by wearing the same casual dress, she will usually react negatively. If you have not yet earned the same right she has, or if she *perceives* that you have not yet earned the right, and you choose to dress down, she will discount you immediately. She will not be interested in dealing with you.

HOW DO THEIR ADVISORS DRESS?

When you are selling to businesspeople, dress as their *advisors* dress. Dress the way their bankers, lawyers, and accountants dress. Dress the way the professional people in their business environment dress. If you want to give advice to people about what to buy, you must look like the kind of person that they are accustomed to taking advice from.

Studies show that the higher a person's income, the more conservative and low-key you must be when you want to sell something to them. When in doubt, always dress *more* conservatively rather than *less*. Wear darker colors and muted tones in shirts and blouses. Be more reserved with accessories. Dress in such a way that you give an overall impression of being stable, solid, dependable.

For a man, the very best colors to wear in business are navy blue or dark gray. IBM was famous for years for its dress code. It said that you could wear any color of suit you liked, as long as it was blue, and you could wear any color of shirt you liked, as long as it was white. Thomas J. Watson, Sr., and his successors, were only too aware that 99 percent of the customers that IBM salespeople dealt with were senior businesspeople and conservative in orientation. They wanted to be sure that the impression left on a customer by an IBM salesperson was also conservative, reliable, and solid.

Navy blue and dark gray, with or without stripes, are also excellent colors for women to wear. In addition, women can wear hunter (dark) green. Neither men nor women should wear brown suits for business. Brown is considered a lower-class color. It may be appropriate if you are selling to farmers, garage mechanics, or owners of small tool and die shops, but brown is a weak color in terms of getting people to trust you and have confidence in your recommendations.

When dealing with *lower*-income customers, a salesperson is more influential when he wears brighter colors, especially blues, oranges, and reds. This is why the lower-level salesman stereotypically wears long hair, big ties, plaid jackets, bright pants, and white shoes. This is the typical dress for a low-brow salesperson selling to low-income customers who are more easily impressed by flashy appearance and fast talk.

But the more intelligent and higher-income your customer, the more low-key and intelligent your approach must be if you are to persuade him or her to buy from you.

THE CONTROVERSY OVER DRESS IN BUSINESS

There is an argument about whether or not it is still necessary to "dress for success." Let me lay this controversy to rest. The answer is yes! Conservative dress is absolutely essential in selling, and anything that you read or hear to the contrary is both self-serving and untrue. Let me explain.

There are wide-circulation fashion magazines for both men and women. These fashion magazines sell clothes that are primarily for social wear, for interaction between the sexes, and for social functions. These magazines depend for their survival on selling advertising. In order to sell the advertising, they have to have stories and editorials on the accompanying pages. To attract the advertising they write articles recommending casual, frilly, bright-colored clothing for people to wear in *every* situation, especially at work, and by extension, after work. However, these articles have been proven to be completely untrue.

In interview after interview, and study after study, researchers have found that in today's business world, the highest earning salespeople, both men and women, dress in such a way that their prospective customers take them seriously at first glance. They dress in a low-key, conservative manner so that they immediately gain and keep the respect of their prospects. Their appearance is calculated to raise their credibility and increase the level of trust between themselves and their prospects.

Their outward appearance is such that they are treated with respect by receptionists and secretaries, and their recommendations are more likely to be followed than those given by people who look as if they are on their way to a party. The bottom line is this: don't believe anything you read in a fashion magazine about what constitutes appropriate dress *unless* it makes conservative recommendations.

There is a simple way to prove that what I'm saying here is true. Just look around you at the top people in your field. Look at the pictures of the top people in any newspaper or magazine and you will find that, almost without exception, they look the part. If you are happy among the medium or low performers in selling, you can wear what you want. But if your goal is to be among the top 10 percent of salespeople in America, you must dress the way they do and dress in such a way that your customers look up to you and take you seriously in everything you say.

HOW MUCH SHOULD YOU PAY FOR YOUR CLOTHES?

The best rule for buying clothing is to pay *twice* as much money and get *half* as many clothes. It is better that you pay *more* than you feel you can afford for your clothing, but that you buy *fewer* articles. The reason for this is both practical and economical. It is practical because you look and feel more powerful when you are well dressed. It is economical because you will wear good clothing more often and therefore the *cost per wear* will be *lower* than if you buy cheaper clothing that you wear less often. In any case, you cannot afford to be cheap when you are selling to businesspeople and higher-income customers. Buy good quality clothes in natural fabrics such as wool or cotton.

As you go through your day, be alert to the way other people dress. Make mental notes about how various colors and fabrics go together. Look especially at the people who dress in such a way that you admire and respect them and learn from them. Determine to dress in such a way that people will look to you and refer to you as an example of how a top sales professional should look.

THE CANARY SONG

The customer's mind is like a microprocessor, rapidly taking in countless bits of information and assembling them quickly into a composite impression of you, your company, your offering, and the advantages or disadvantages of doing business with you. In addition to your clothes, your *accessories* are important in managing the perceptions of your client. They have a powerful suggestive influence on him or her in determining whether you are credible and trustworthy, and the right person to do business with. After your customer has taken his or her visual snapshot of your dress, the customer's vision, both conscious and unconscious, narrows and begins assessing you on the basis of your accessories and the secondary elements of your appearance.

The song the canary sings is, "Cheap! Cheap! Cheap!" People have a natural tendency to equate price with quality, and like a *halo effect*, to see everything the salesperson does and says in the light of the *perceived* prices of his or her accessories. If we get an impression of cheap we expand our perception of the salesperson and everything the salesperson offers as being cheap and of lesser quality as well. In choosing your accessories, it is better not to wear them at all than to wear obviously inexpensive items.

The economic theory of marginality says that all decisions are decided on the margin, on the basis of small, sometimes incidental factors that are often overlooked or ignored by the amateur. As we have seen, the customer never makes his or her decision solely based on the fact that your product will function efficiently and perform usefully for him or her. The customer makes his final decision based on far more subtle perceptions. And the quality of the individual items you wear or carry can make you or break you when it comes time for the customer to make the buying decision.

THE MOMENT OF DECISION

Imagine that your customer has to reach a buying temperature of 100 degrees before he or she is ready to say yes. Imagine now that you have brought your customer to exactly 100 degrees and your customer is ready to make the buying decision. At this critical moment, you lean forward and pull a cheap plastic pen out of your pocket for him or her to sign the order. The customer sees the pen and his guard instantly goes up. He wonders if your product or service is cheap as well. His perception of risk increases to the point where he pushes back from the table, and rather than making a mistake, he says something like, "Well, it looks pretty good, but why don't you leave it with me for a day or two so I can think about it."

You then find yourself back on the street, having lost the order because the customer heard the "canary's song" when he closely observed that particular accessory.

Human beings in general are intensely visual. There are estimated to be twenty-two times the number of nerves from the eye to the brain as from the ear to the brain. This means that what a customer *sees* has twenty-two times the impact of something that he hears.

Customers engage in *sorting* behaviors by the use of visual perception. That is, they divide incoming impressions into either positive or negative. In this sense, the human brain works like a binary computer, accepting or rejecting information, and classifying it on the basis of whether or not it is positive or negative. Your prospect is quickly evaluating everything about you, and adding it to one list or the other, the debit or the credit column. The more credits you have, the more credibility you have. The more debits you have, the less believable you become.

From your head to your toes, your accessories are making an impression, either positive or negative. If you are a woman, the prospect assesses your earrings, your necklace, your brooch, your watch, your rings, the buttons on your clothes, your belt, your purse, your scarf, your stockings, and your shoes. A man may be unfamiliar with these various items and unable to specifically identify what it is about the woman that he likes or dislikes, but the totality of a woman's choice of accessories makes an impression on him nonetheless.

If you are a man, your tie, your ring or rings, your watch, your pen, your belt and belt buckle, the crease in your slacks, your shoes, and your socks will all be quickly assessed and categorized by the person you are talking to.

Why is it that customers are so hypersensitive to the visual aspects of your presentation? It is simply because they are concerned about the element of *risk*. They are concerned about making the right decisions. They are afraid of being criticized for making a mistake. They have had enough experiences in the past where they ignored a critical cue and made the wrong decision, and lived to regret it. They don't want it to happen again. They are very much like personnel officers interviewing a lot of people. They are attempting to *exclude you out* rather than include you in. You must therefore do everything possible to be included, in the customer's mind, as a credible vendor of your product or service.

CHOOSING THE RIGHT TIE FOR MAXIMUM CREDIBILITY

A man's choice of tie makes a strong statement about his quality consciousness and his knowledge about dress. Men should only wear silk ties when they are selling. Polyester is unacceptable. It is cheap, and looks bad as well. Your tie should have two basic colors. The body of the tie should blend or contrast nicely with the color of your suit, and the design in the tie, or the highlighting, should match the color of your shirt. If you are wearing a blue suit with a white shirt, your tie should have a predominance of blue with a white design in it. This is classic business dress. Even a customer who doesn't know how to dress himself will recognize whether or not you are turned out appropriately.

You can wear more colorful ties as well, such as reds and yellows, as long as the design picks up the basic color of your suit. But in any case, your tie should not be so garish as to arouse comment or draw attention away from you and your message.

SHOES AND SOCKS SEND A MESSAGE

The color of your shoes and socks is also very important. In a recent survey, 84 percent of executives said they would not promote a man who wore scuffed or unshined shoes. Your socks should be darker than your slacks and of one color. They should be calf length and tight over your feet and ankles. Your shoes should invariably be black or, at the most colorful, burgundy, but this is taking a chance. The essence of excellent dress is that nothing about your choices in clothing or accessories draws attention. Nothing about your appearance must distract or disturb your prospect.

Interestingly enough, if you get into an elevator with a businessman, a likely decision-maker, he will first look at your face, neck, shirt, and tie, and then glance downward at your shoes. His eyes will come up and he will complete his assessment of you. In less than four seconds, he will have pigeonholed you. After that, you will have a hard time getting out of that category if it turns out to be inconsistent with what you are trying to achieve.

THE ELEMENTS OF GOOD GROOMING

Let us assume that you know everything we've talked about so far. You have crossed the first barrier on the psychological obstacle course to getting the opportunity to build trust and credibility with your customers. Your clothes and accessories have been carefully chosen and properly matched. You look like a professional salesperson in every sense of the word.

You now come to the next hurdle, that of your face, hair, and teeth. You can lose the opportunity to sell at this critical juncture if your appearance is not everything that a first-class professional would want it to be.

FACTS ABOUT FACIAL HAIR

For men, the issue of facial hair is often a sensitive one. If you don't wear a beard or a mustache, you don't think about it very much. But if you *do*, you tend to be easily offended when anyone says anything about whether your facial hair is appropriate.

Many studies show that facial hair is a detriment to success in any public profession. It is not that you cannot be successful. It is just that you could be far *more* successful if you were clean-shaven. In countless experiments where photographs of people are shown both with and without beards, the people with beards are identified as eccentric, artistic, reclusive, strange, different from the ordinary, professorial, academic, or creative types. A beard is considered a sign of eccentricity. Customers feel that it is too risky to deal with an eccentric person who may be representing an eccentric company. They would much rather hedge their bets by purchasing the product or service from someone who appears to be a little bit more trustworthy.

In addition, people with beards are felt to be "hiding something." The beard is registered unconsciously as a form of mask, disguising the individual's face and putting a division between the individual and the prospect. People just don't seem to trust people with beards as much as they trust people without beards.

In a recent seminar, a very hardworking but bearded salesman came and asked me if I had any advice for him. He seemed unable to get his new sales career underway. I told him that salespeople with beards are often frustrated and unsuccessful. It turned out that he had been wearing a beard for years, and as was to be expected, he was offended by my evaluation. I explained to him that this was not my *personal* opinion. It was a conclusion based on research that had been conducted for years. The dislike of facial hair is also the primary reason there are virtually no elected officials at any level of any government anywhere who wear beards.

This particular salesman got over his resentment at my comment on his beard, went home, and shaved it off. The very next week he closed a $30,000 sale, the biggest transaction of his life, to a customer he had been calling on for six months without making any progress. He was absolutely amazed at how differently he was treated when he removed his beard.

What about mustaches? Well, the research is clear on this score as well. A mustache is considered by most people to be a mark of *indecisiveness*, of weak character. It is as if the person could not make up his mind whether to have a beard or no beard so he compromised and grew a mustache. This is why mustaches are humorously, and sometimes derisively, referred to as "cookie dusters." This is not a compliment, even if it is rendered with a smile.

I have met countless men over the years who have seen their sales results improve measurably within a few days *after* they shaved off their beards and mustaches. It may seem like a small thing, but in selling, with competition fierce and customers nervous about any kind of risk at all, a beard or mustache can only get in your way. It is not personal, it is simply a fact of life.

KEEP YOUR HAIR THE RIGHT LENGTH

Once upon a time, a young salesman with a good product came to me for advice. He was not afraid of hard work and he was making a lot of calls with a well-priced product for business offices. But he wasn't selling anything. He was continually strapped for money and he was living in the basement of his parents' home. Could I give him any insights or ideas?

I saw his problem immediately. He had a long, shaggy *page-boy* haircut that came down to his shoulders. He was calling on businesspeople who were essentially conservative and risk-averse. It was easy making appointments over the phone, but the moment he walked into the customer's place of business, the customer went cold on him. The conversation was short and stilted, and he was turned around and sent back into the street within a couple of minutes.

I told him that if he wanted to be successful, he would have to cut his hair considerably shorter. He protested at this. He said that he liked to "do his own thing." I explained to him that that was all right if he wanted to load hay bales on a farm. But it simply would not do if he wanted to sell to businesspeople. He would have to impress them favorably just to get a chance to deliver his message.

He finally agreed to cut his hair but did a halfway job. He took off a few inches and had it trimmed to neck length. But at least it wasn't touching his shoulders. The very next week, he started to make a few sales. It dawned on him that there was something to what I had told him so he went back to his barber and had his hair cut even shorter. As his hair grew shorter, his sales increased. Soon, his hair was short and conservative and he was making an excellent living. He was on his way.

But then he made a fatal error made by many salespeople. He concluded that the reason he was succeeding was because he was such a wonderful person and because his product was so attractive. He felt that he could do no wrong. So he let his hair grow back out. And as his hair grew longer, his sales became fewer. Finally, his hair grew back to shoulder length and his sales dried up. His car was repossessed and he moved back into his parents' home. He laid off his one employee and the last time I saw him he was walking the streets in old clothing trying to get appointments. He refused to accept that his appearance was turning people off even before he got a chance to open his mouth. Sadly, this story is true for many salespeople.

TEETH ARE IMPORTANT TOO

When you look at a person, the very first thing you see is the totality of his or her clothing and accessories. Your eyes instantly move, within the first second, to their face, eyes, mouth, and hair. This complete overview takes place at extraordinary speed. Your attention then comes back and focuses in on the face, unless it is *distracted* by some element of clothing or accessories. Because it is uncomfortable to stare into a person's eyes, you invariably look at his *mouth* and nose, with occasional flicks upward, to maintain eye contact. If a person's mouth, for any reason, is not presentable, you become distracted when you are communicating with him.

A saleswoman I know had one front tooth that was too large for her mouth. Because of the size of her tooth, the prospect's attention immediately went to it, though, out of politeness, nothing would be said. The woman was extremely conscious of it, and would continually cover her mouth with her hand. When someone looked at her she would look away uncomfortably. The size of her tooth not only affected her self image and self-confidence, but it seemed to sidetrack her sales conversations as well.

Finally, someone was kind enough to tell her that she had a problem that a dentist could solve. She was courageous enough to go to a dentist and have the tooth shaved so that it eventually fell back into alignment with her other front teeth. As a result, she became more outgoing and confident. She no longer felt the need to be continually holding her mouth shut or holding her hand in front of her face. Her sales went up. Her whole life turned around.

If you have any doubts about the way your mouth appears to other people, have someone you know and trust tell you candidly what they think about your personal appearance. If you are uneasy about asking a friend or employer, go to your dentist and get a solid professional opinion. Having bad, dirty, or irregular teeth can cost you tens of thousands of dollars per year throughout you selling career, and you may never know why it is that your customers turn you off the minute that you turn on your smile.

SPECIAL CONCERNS FOR WOMEN

I have spoken to many women who advise other women on the best combinations of dress, cosmetics, accessories, and overall appearance for succeeding in business. Invariably, they have emphasized *one* critical point for women. In order to be taken *seriously*, the entire attention of the prospect during the sales call *must* be on the woman's *face*, and on no other part of her appearance. The woman salesperson must be dressed and turned out in such a way that the customer, man or woman, looks at her face and pays complete attention to what she is saying. The customer must see the saleswoman as a serious businessperson who is there to conduct an intelligent needs analysis and to make well-founded recommendations for the purchase and use of a particular product or service. The customer must not be tempted or encouraged to think of anything else.

When selling to men, women must realize that men are conditioned from infancy to see women in a particular light. When the male customer was a child, he looked into the face of his mother and related to his mother as his caregiver and supporter. If he had sisters, he related to them as boys relate to their sisters. As he grew up, women became friends and then girlfriends. Later they became lovers and wives. Men are conditioned by these many years of experience to react to women as they have in the past.

When a saleswoman calls on a male prospect, it must be immediately clear that she is neither mother, sister, girlfriend, or wife. The man must immediately see her as a *businesswoman*, visiting for a specific business purpose. This is why it is so important that women avoid the recommendations of the fashion magazines when they suggest that she can wear bright, trendy, or sexy styles. If a woman does this, the male prospect, as the result of a lifetime of conditioning, will relate to her as *other* than as a professional saleswoman. The sales conversation will usually go downhill from there.

THE SWEET SMELL OF SUCCESS

Another suggestive element for you to control is that of smell. This is another area where people are extremely sensitive. You can do everything right in terms of creating a powerful, positive appearance and then lose it all because you smell badly. Salespeople who are clean and fresh smelling tend to be treated better by everyone they deal with in their sales activities.

To be turned out at your best, and to utilize every possible advantage, you need to give special attention to your hygiene. You need to wash your hair and bathe thoroughly every single day. You need to use good shampoo and high-quality soap. You need to use an effective deodorant. And you must do this in the morning before you start out, rather than in the evening before you go to bed.

You should brush your teeth thoroughly and use mouthwash to clean your breath. Regular visits to a good dental hygienist are absolutely essential. If you have tooth decay of any kind your breath will have a foul odor.

Smoking especially gives a person breath that would turn a camel's head if the wind was right. If you do smoke, be sure to never, *never* do it in the presence of a customer. Many sales are lost this way. Non-smokers are often extremely offended by the very notion of tobacco usage, and they can smell a smoker from five feet away.

Smokers don't realize it but the cigarette smoke permeates their clothes and hair. When they meet with a prospect in a small room, the smell of stale tobacco seeps out of them and fills the air. It is something you can't hide.

If a smoker wants to be successful in selling, he must wash his hands, brush his teeth, use mouthwash, smoke outside so that the smoke is blown away as much as possible, and do everything he can to keep it a secret. Smoking alone can be fatal to a person's success in this profession.

At lunchtime, give some thought to the foods you eat and only eat foods that will not leave an odor on your breath. You should carry a toothbrush and toothpaste around with you and brush after eating. When in doubt, carry breath mints and suck on them prior to a sales meeting. Don't be reluctant to ask your friends how your breath smells. If you ask them openly and honestly they will tell you, and if they tell you that they can smell *anything*, you should go back to the sink and brush until you smell fresh.

The customer will seldom buy from a person who has offensive odors of any kind coming from any part of his or her mouth, skin, clothes, or feet. Many people decide against purchasing products and services they wanted on that basis alone. They simply do not want to get into a long-term relationship with someone who smells unpleasant.

THE SENSE OF SIGHT CAN MAKE OR BREAK THE SALE

The sense of sight is so powerful that you must manage every single item of your appearance, your presentation, and your product that the prospect can see and evaluate. You can never allow yourself the luxury of wishing or hoping that the prospect will not pick up on small details. Your purse should be carefully selected to match your clothing. Your briefcase should be the very best possible and look clean and presentable in every respect. Your sales materials should all be clean, well organized, and in the proper sequence.

Take some time before you call on a customer to perform a military-type inspection on every element of your appearance that your customer might see and evaluate. If you are in doubt, ask someone else. If anyone else has even the slightest concern about any part of the way you look, go back and *change* it. You must look both conservative and professional when you call on the prospect.

Remember, finding and getting a meeting with a qualified prospect is the most expensive and difficult part of selling. It is a tragedy if, after all your efforts, you get in front of a prospect and you lose your chance to sell because of your inadvertent omission of a critical part of your physical appearance and impression.

POSTURE AND POSITIONING

Imagine being a customer who goes out to the waiting room to greet a salesperson with whom he or she has made an appointment. The salesperson is leaning back in his chair with his legs crossed as if he were watching the Sunday football game. The customer immediately files this first impression away as he leads the salesperson to his or her office. The salesperson comes into the office, plunks down in a chair and slouches into a half-sitting position to begin the sales conversation. If you were such a customer, you would have already made the decision that you are not interested in whatever the salesperson is selling.

Again, because of the power of visual impressions, your posture is terribly important in a sales conversation. You must be aware of your body at all times.

There are a series of things you can do to ensure that you come across as the most professional and credible salesperson possible. The very first is for you to stand up and sit up straight as an arrow. Your back should be as straight as if there were a board strapped to it. When you get up to greet the prospect, imagine that there is a string holding your body from the top of your head pulling your head higher and making your body almost dangle from your neck. If you practice this element of posture, you will find yourself standing and walking in a more erect and regal way in everything you do.

One of the interesting discoveries concerning posture is that *lifting* your chin up changes your attitude and your physiology. The very act of raising your chin causes you to feel more positive, be more alert, and stand more erect.

Whenever a person feels good about himself, he invariably walks with his chin held high. When a person feels depressed, his chin drops. But we know from neurolinguistic programming that you can generate the emotion by assuming the physiology or physical structure that the emotion would generate. When you raise your chin and hold your head high with your shoulders and back erect, you look and feel like a winner. You are more positive, more alert, more optimistic, and more outgoing. And this positive impression is conveyed instantaneously to the customer.

When you sit in your customer's presence, avoid leaning against the back of the chair. Sit slightly forward so that your back is forced straight. When your customer talks, deliberately lean toward him or her. Pay close attention. Focus intensely on the customer's face, especially on his or her mouth and eyes. Keep leaning forward as though the customer were about to give you a priceless piece of information that he or she would only repeat once.

The very act of leaning forward increases the intensity of the conversation and the propensity of the customer to take you and your offering more seriously. He will tend to give you better and more complete information as he speaks. This is the fundamental art of listening that we talked about earlier.

When you are standing and talking to a customer, shift your weight forward onto the *balls* of your feet. This act of shifting your weight forward causes your energy to move forward and into the customer. The customer will actually *feel* the power of your energy and concentration by this subtle movement, even though he or she will not even be aware of it visually.

When your customer takes you into his or her office, your immediate next consideration will be the physical positioning of yourself relative to the customer. This can strongly influence whether or not you make the sale.

It is common for the customer to sit you down and then go around and sit on the other side of his desk. The desk then becomes a psychological barrier between you. It becomes a protection for the customer from you and from whatever you are offering. It is a physical representation of the suspicion and fear that the customer has of making a bad decision. Its very existence increases and reinforces the customer's resistance to your presentation. It is an obstacle that must be removed if at all possible.

I learned as a young salesperson that customers are amenable to coming out from behind their desks *if you ask them to*. They will also allow you to move around behind their desks and sit next to them. I didn't believe it initially, but from the first time I tried it, I was amazed at how cooperative customers could be. This is what I did.

When my customer sat me down on the other side of his desk and said something like, "Well, what can I do for you?" I would stop, appear a little bit embarrassed and flustered, and then ask the customer very politely if I could come around his desk and show him what I had brought for his or her evaluation.

The customer was always a little surprised and bemused, but never refused. He or she would say something like, "Well, sure, okay, what would you like to do?"

That was my cue. I would stand up and take my chair and drag it around the desk so that I was sitting next to the customer—on his left —and then lay out my materials on the desk in front of the customer and walk him through my sales presentation. They seemed to find it an interesting and intelligent approach to making a presentation.

Another thing you can do, which is much more acceptable nowadays, is to ask the customer to get up from his desk and to sit with you at a table, either in the customer's office or in another place. If you ask politely for a change of location so that you can more easily show the customer what you have brought, the customer will almost invariably agree.

You can say something like, "It would be much easier and far quicker if we could sit over here so I could show you some of the things I have brought with me."

When the customer agrees to move, remember to always position yourself to his or her immediate *left*. This way, you can show your materials easily, turning the pages toward the customer and keeping complete control of the conversation. If you have two customers, sit to the left of one customer and have the other customer sit to the right of the first customer. Avoid a situation where you are between two customers or across the table from them.

During the peace talks between Hanoi and Washington at the height of the Vietnam War, several months were lost while the North Vietnamese and Americans argued over the shape and structure of the tables and the seating arrangements of the various participants. It seemed to most of the world like a colossal waste of time. The war went on and people continued to die, but both the North Vietnamese and Americans recognized that the seating arrangements made a very definite statement about the relative power and authority of the different nations in the negotiations. And the North Vietnamese were adamant about getting an arrangement satisfactory to them before they began serious discussions.

You should remember the importance of sitting in the correct chair when you are moving to a different venue for your presentation. Always ask the customer where he or she would like to sit before you take your position. In a home, homeowners almost invariably have their favorite chairs and positions at the table or in the living room. You don't want to make the mistake of sitting in the chair that the decision-maker is most accustomed to.

In an office setting, if you move to a conference table, very often the key decision-maker will be accustomed to sitting at one end or the other. By allowing him to choose where he would like to be seated, you avoid making a subtle mistake that could unconsciously put the customer off and negatively predispose him or her to anything you say afterward.

MIRRORING AND MATCHING THE
CUSTOMER'S BODY LANGUAGE

Always keep uppermost in your mind that you are using these elements of the power of suggestion to create a favorable buying climate in the customer's mind. And absolutely critical is your ability to develop a high quality of *rapport* between yourself and your customer. This is essential. Without it, no serious selling can take place. Everything you do that makes the customer feel more comfortable in your presence will ultimately help close the sale.

As we've seen, we like people who are similar to ourselves. We like people who dress the way we dress and who are groomed the way we are groomed. We enjoy people whose interests, values, and opinions are similar to ours as well. And we also like people whose body language and gestures mirror and match ours, even if we are not aware this is taking place.

In mirroring and matching, you assume the same bodily posture as your customer, with a five-second *delay* after your customer moves. For example, if you were sitting at a conference table and your customer relaxed and leaned back to ponder what you had just said, you would wait about five seconds and then you would gradually lean back and *match* the same posture, as though the customer were looking in a mirror. If the customer straightened up and leaned forward, you would wait about five seconds and then gradually straighten up and lean forward as well.

After you have mirrored and matched the customer four or five times, you can then lead the customer into the kind of buying posture that equates to taking action. For example, a customer who is ready to buy leans forward, like a runner on the mark, waiting for the starting gun. After you have followed your customer several times, you can test whether or not you are fully attuned to your customer by leaning forward in the conversation. After a few seconds, if you have established a high-enough level of rapport, your customer will lean forward to synchronize his body language with yours. At that point, you can gently lead your customer, as you would lead a partner in a dance, into the postures of careful listening, paying close attention, and readiness to take action.

This technique of mirroring and matching is often used unconsciously by top salespeople. When they were videotaped in sales conversations, they would seem to follow the customer's movements for a certain period of time and then begin to lead the customer. When these salespeople were asked afterward why they did it, and what they were thinking at the time, they were almost invariably *unaware* that they had done it at all. They were mirroring their customer's movements as a natural part of their extreme sensitivity to the customer.

You can practice this technique with your friends and family until you get the hang of it. Often, by taking the identical physical position of the other person, you will actually get a feeling for what is going on in his or her mind. You will understand how he or she is thinking. You will often get an intuition of exactly what to say to satisfy the predominant concern that the customer has at that moment.

CREATING AN OFFICE ENVIRONMENT
CONDUCIVE TO BUYING

If your customer is coming to your place of business, give considerable thought to the surroundings that he or she will experience. There is a good deal of research on the effect of colors on emotions. For instance, a soft pink color tends to be soothing and is used in any physical environment where people are agitated, angry, or upset. A light blue color tends to be cool, calm, and businesslike and leads to more efficient thinking about the subject at hand. A gray color tends to be stern, conservative, and even more businesslike, and is used in banks and financial institutions.

Select your colors and the decor of your place of business with care. If necessary, call in an image consultant or an interior designer and tell him or her the exact impression that you want to make on the people who visit you.

Your surroundings should look successful, clean, light, airy, and businesslike. They should give your prospect confidence that this is a safe organization with which to do business. Everything should be neat and orderly. If you have magazines, they should be current and new. All waste baskets and trash should be out of sight. There should be nothing to distract your prospective customer from the image of success and affluence that you wish to portray.

THE MEDIUM IS THE MESSAGE

Dr. Albert Mehrabian, a communications specialist, has estimated that your communication is comprised of three elements: your words, your tone of voice, and your body language. His studies conclude that your words constitute only 7 percent of the total message that is received by the other person. Your tone of voice and the inflections you use constitute 38 percent of your message. Your body language, the total visual impact of everything about your appearance and posture, constitutes fully 55 percent of the message received by your prospect.

If you are talking on the phone to a customer, the influence of body language drops away and the importance of voice tonality escalates dramatically. That is why, in telephone conversation, you have to listen closely to the speed and rhythm of the person on the other end of the line and then match that person's conversational tone as closely as possible. If he or she speaks rapidly, you should speak rapidly as well. If her or she speaks slowly, with pauses, you should slow down and speak with pauses as well. The more you harmonize your way of speaking and tone of voice with that of your prospect, the more comfortable the prospect will feel with you and the more productive will be the conversation.

The words you use and the attitude with which you use them are all important in a sales conversation. Each has an impact on the other. There is perhaps nothing more influential in a sales conversation than the suggestive influence of a positive, smiling, warm, attentive salesperson. People like to be around positive, happy people. When you are enthusiastic about what you are doing, when you are friendly and cheerful and you look your prospect straight in the eye, you break down his or her natural resistance. You cause him to want to listen to you and learn more about what it is you have come to share with him.

Good salespeople seem to have a natural "other-orientation." They calmly and confidently *lean* into the prospect in a warm and kindly way. They create the kind of emotional climate that opens the prospect up, like a flower in the sunshine, by focusing in on the client with openness, honesty, and sincerity. They appear competent and professional. They are courteous and polite. They come across immediately as the kind of person that other people enjoy being around.

In addition, top salespeople choose their words carefully. Market research shows that the first ten to fifteen words of any sales message set the emotional tone of the subsequent conversation. Good salespeople think through and plan the words they are going to use. They plan the questions they are going to ask. They plan their openings to each sales conversation. They know their words will have a tremendous suggestive influence on whether this prospect considers them and their offering seriously. Their words cannot be left to chance, so they write them down and rehearse them, like a Shakespearean actor, before they go in to see the client.

On the other hand, poor salespeople have what my friend, sales trainer Jim Pancero, calls the "parking lot mentality." That is, they don't think about the prospect until they drive onto his or her parking lot, and they stop thinking about him or her as soon as they drive off.

When you first meet a prospect, you have an opportunity to reach in and make a mark on the customer's mind with the first words you say. Your job is to create such a positive impression that your customer's mind will open up and be receptive to everything that follows.

Your initial goal is to build expectancy. It is to make the customer feel happy that he has given you his time. It is to build the customer's anticipation of the sales message to come. And you can achieve all this by simply saying the words, "Thank you for your time. You're going to be very happy with what I have to show you." These words arouse curiosity and interest and open the customer to listening and paying serious attention to you.

When you sit down with the customer, it is very professional for you to say, "Before we begin, may I ask you a question?" When you ask for permission to ask a question, and the customer agrees, he or she is also agreeing to *answer* your question. And the more and better questions you ask, the higher the level of trust you will build and the better the relationship you will establish. You can take control of the sales conversation at any time by pausing and saying, "May I ask you another question?"

The words you use to open a sales conversation, and the way you use them, are too important to be left to chance. You should plan them thoroughly in advance, and then use them consciously and deliberately as soon as you get your first opportunity to make personal contact with the customer.

THE IMPORTANCE OF HOW YOU SPEAK

There is a direct relationship between the quality of your *vocabulary*, your grammar and diction, and the amount of money you earn in life. There are exceptions to this rule but not very many. In every study of word recognition and word usage, those men and woman with the best vocabularies tend also to be the best paid. It is something you can't hide. As soon as you open your mouth, people immediately evaluate you and classify you as either educated or uneducated.

As with most human behaviors, though, it is possible for you to improve your vocabulary, and thus your results. And you can do it fairly quickly.

When I was a young man, I didn't graduate from high school. I failed most of my classes in my twelfth year, including English. I eventually took correspondence courses and night school and went on to receive my high school diploma. In my thirties, I invested three years of hard work taking an MBA program, also at night school. In the meantime I read continually and built my language skills one word at a time.

Many people have had similar experiences. They did poorly in school and found themselves hampered by their lack of education when they started working. But they discovered that by a program of self-study that helped build their vocabulary, their incomes and opportunities increased. They became more effective in their interactions with more and better people. They were promoted more rapidly, and if they were in sales they sold more products to higher-income customers.

You can never sell *above* your own level of personal and professional development. If you are uneducated, you can only sell to uneducated people. If you wish to sell at a higher level, you must develop yourself to a higher level first. If you want to *have* more, you must first *be* more.

You can begin improving your vocabulary immediately by doing a few simple things. First of all, you must read at least *one hour* every day, in material that is both educational and informative. Novels and newspapers are written at about the seventh-grade level and that level is *not* sufficient for you if you want to go all the way to the top. You must read more challenging material that forces you to think. This material will almost invariably include words of subtlety and difficulty that you must master.

A word is a condensed thought. A word is a tool that you use to think and communicate more clearly. The more words you know and use, the better a thinker you become, the more articulate and intelligent you will be. You can actually increase your intelligence and become a smarter and more competent person by developing and following a plan to expand your vocabulary.

The first and most important step in vocabulary building is for you to always read with a dictionary at hand. Carry one with you. When you come across a word that you are not familiar with, immediately look it up. Underline it. Turn down the page or make a marking in the book. Look at the word later and review it two or three times. Attempt to use it in conversation or create a sentence with it. If possible, write it in a letter, a report, or even in your own personal journal. Do everything possible to make the word one of your personal possessions.

Many years ago, I found myself unable to understand many of the words I was coming across in my reading. I then did something that expanded my vocabulary very rapidly. I purchased a stenographer's pad, and whenever I came across a new word I would write it on one side of the page and then write a brief definition of the word on the other side. Once a week, I would take out the pad and read it through from beginning to end.

I started off with a few words and ended up with several hundred. Regular review of the words drove them deeper and deeper into my memory until I began to use them in conversation and in writing. As my vocabulary grew, I found that I could understand more thoughtful reading material and I was able to converse at a higher level as well.

There are several excellent programs available on audiocassette to help you expand your vocabulary. You can listen and learn, stopping and starting them in your car as you drive along. There are also excellent exercises in each issue of *Reader's Digest* entitled "How to Increase Your Word Power." These are available in paperback as well.

If for any reason your education has left you a poor reader, you can overcome it by taking remedial courses at your local high school, college, or Y. In a year or two of steady work, you can dramatically improve your reading skills and vocabulary. And your income will shoot straight up.

Each time you learn a new word, it will introduce you to, or expand your ability to use, as many as *ten* other words. If you simply made a decision to learn one new word each day and then found a way to use it in conversation, your vocabulary would grow at an exponential rate. If you were to learn one word per day and write it down on your stenographer's pad, you would learn 365 new words in a year. Those 365 new words would increase your ability to understand and use more than 3,000 *other* words. In a couple of years you would be one of the most articulate and well-spoken people in your industry or social circle.

And as your vocabulary improves, your ability to think more accurately improves at the same time. Your ability to communicate and persuade others improves as well. You will sell to more and bigger customers.

THE IMPORTANCE OF TOUCH

Human beings process information predominantly in one of three ways, visual, verbal, and kinesthetic. About 35 percent of the population processes information *visually*. They only believe it when they *see* it. They only understand it when it is presented to them in visual form. They are readers and they like graphs, diagrams, charts, brochures, pictures, and other visual representations that they need to get their minds around a particular idea or concept. They acknowledge your arguments by saying things like, "I see what you mean."

About 30 percent of the population are *listeners*. They process information that they can *hear*. They say things like, "That sounds good to me." They process information by talking about it. They enjoy conversations and discussions. They like to ask questions and if you give them your sales materials, they will ignore them while they talk to you. They will be interested in listening to what you have to say and in your tone of voice.

Another 30 percent to 35 percent of the population processes information kinesthetically. They experience things more with their *feelings* than by hearing them or seeing them. They are intuitive. They say things like, "That feels good to me." They like to touch things with their hands and fingers. They like to reflect on your message and listen to themselves before they make decisions. They are often slow to make up their minds. How they feel about you and your product is the critical determinant of whether or not they accept or believe your message.

Touch has a powerful suggestive influence on as many as one third of the people that you attempt to sell your product or service to. Although everyone is affected by the element of touch, these people are especially sensitive to the tactile nature of everything you do.

For example, when you meet a person for the first time you have the first opportunity to make physical contact with that person by shaking hands. I have worked with salespeople who did not understand the importance of a full, firm handshake. As a result, they were discredited the moment they held out their hand in a limp, clammy fashion.

Most people initially measure the character, integrity, and personal strength of another person by his or her handshake. A firm handshake, accompanied by a full look in the eyes and a smile, tells the other person that they have met a real human being who is there with an important message.

Many women especially have been brought up to believe that they do not have to shake hands unless the man offers his hand first. This is an archaic notion. In modern business, women need to shake hands as readily and as firmly as men do if they want to be treated as serious businesspeople.

I have met many women who mistakenly take the "halfway approach" to handshaking. Instead of shaking hands fully, they stick out the *ends* of their fingers, almost as if they expected the other person to kiss the back of their hand, and they wonder why the meeting gets off to a bad start.

In Europe, and throughout most of the European-influenced world, people shake hands every time they meet and every time they depart. It is as common as breathing in and breathing out. In America, shaking hands in business, fully and firmly, should be the same.

A man in one of my seminars had moved to the United States from India some years before. He was intelligent, well educated, and articulate. He was in sales and he asked me why it was that he was having so little success even though he was calling on so many prospects.

The minute he shook hands with me, I knew the problem. In India, handshaking is uncommon. It is not a part of the culture. Men and women who come from India, or other countries where they do not shake hands, find it an awkward thing to do. As a result, they generally do it badly. They hold out their hands self-consciously until the other person grips it and then they pull it away uncomfortably. He had no idea how off-putting this was to his prospects until I pointed it out to him.

He was a good student. Thereafter he practiced on every occasion, shaking hands firmly with everyone he met. He did it over and over until it became an automatic extension of his personality. And as you might imagine, his sales increased. He was soon one of the top people in his company. Little things do mean a lot.

You can use the power of touch to greatly increase your influence with the prospect. By touching the prospect appropriately, you will appear more likable and trustworthy.

Your body is divided into roughly three zones with regard to touch. The first is the "public" zone, the area from your elbows to your fingertips. The second is the "social" zone—your arms, your shoulders, and your back, which your family and friends touch or pat in passing. The third is the private or intimate zone, which is only touched by people with whom you are very close.

In selling, you can always touch a person in the public zone without offending. When you touch a person for *emphasis*, either on the hand or the lower part of the arm, he or she will perceive you to be a warmer, friendlier, more sincere and believable person. When you are showing a prospect around your premises, or giving a demonstration, and you gently touch the prospect on the elbow with your fingertips to guide him or her, you are felt to be a more likable and credible person. The prospect feels more comfortable with you.

Many years ago, before I read the research in this area, I would quite commonly reach out during a sales presentation and touch the back of the prospect's hand with my forefinger to make a point. I would say something like, "Now, here's something that's really important." And I would gently touch the back of his or her hand. I never knew why it was that I was so successful in selling to those prospects until I learned later that the prospect felt more comfortable dealing with me as a result of the touch.

And here's the interesting part. If you touch a prospect on the hand or forearm during the course of a sales conversation, 95 percent of prospects will *not* even remember it. They will not even be aware of your gesture. They will just know that they like you, feel more comfortable in your presence, and are more open to your message.

I'm not suggesting that you extend yourself or act unnaturally to reach out and pat the other person on the arm. What this power of touch means is that, if it is a normal and natural part of your personality, don't feel shy about gently touching the person's arm with your fingertips in the course of your conversation. You will be amazed at how much more warmly the other person responds to you. You will be perceived as a friendlier, more trustworthy person.

Another element of touch has to do with your sales materials. We consider quality items to be of higher value than inferior items. When your sales materials are produced on high-quality paper, with glossy stock or with heavy, textured covers, the customer feels that what you are offering is of higher quality.

One of the mistakes that salespeople make, and which is usually made by their companies, is to produce business cards on extremely thin paper. Sometimes, someone who is ignorant of the subject concludes that thin paper has some sort of *elegant* connotation. But in my experience, it is quite the contrary. A flimsy business card suggests a flimsy person, a flimsy company, and a flimsy product or service.

Your business cards should be as stiff as playing cards. You should be able to shuffle them and deal them. They should be crisp and hard and hit the table with a click. A business card of substance suggests that you and everything you represent is of substance as well.

SUMMARY

Customers are predominantly emotional, just as you are. They are strongly affected by the suggestive elements in their environment. They consciously or unconsciously record everything that they see, hear, touch, smell, and experience. They respond to the various factors that constitute a likable and trustworthy salesperson. They are quick to judge and once they have formed an opinion or an evaluation of the salesperson, they are slow to change their minds.

Customers quickly take in every aspect of your dress and they permanently record their impressions. They look at you from head to toe and they make a judgment about whether they should take you seriously. They expand that initial impression to everything you say, to your product or service, to your company, and to everything about you.

If they come to your place of business, their eyes sweep around and pick up everything. They see dirt on the floor and they notice the dates on the covers of magazines. They use their evaluations to decide whether this is the kind of place they want to do business with.

They scrutinize your accessories and look at your hair, skin, and fingernails. They evaluate your posture and every aspect of your appearance. They appraise your body language and your bodily odors.

They look at your business cards and your sales material. They listen to your vocabulary and your tone of voice. They watch your body language. They assess your attitude and your personality. Their minds are racing.

Like an airplane pilot before takeoff, you need to go through a checklist with regard to the elements of your appearance and behavior. You must stand back, look in the mirror, and ask yourself, "What kind of an impression do I want to make on this prospect?" "Does every part of my appearance and behavior contribute to that impression?"

Your most important job in professional selling is to build and maintain a high-quality relationship based on trust, credibility, and warmth. Your goal is to be liked by the prospect and to be believed in everything you say and do. Your talk should create an emotional climate around yourself and the prospect such that the prospect feels comfortable listening to you and accepting your recommendations.

Everything you do either helps or hurts to create this climate. Everything you do either moves you toward a sale or moves you away. One small mistake is all that it takes for you to lose a sale that you may have spent weeks putting together.

All top salespeople consciously and deliberately orchestrate every single element of their suggestive environments to make sure everything about them and their behavior causes the customer to feel comfortable and confident in dealing with them and about buying their products or services. This attention to the small details is a mark of the true professional.

8

PROSPECTING: FILLING

YOUR SALES PIPELINE

Nothing happens until a sale takes place, and "before you do anything, you have to do something *else* first." Before a sale takes place, above all, you must locate a prospect, someone who can and will buy within a reasonable period of time. You can be excellent at every part of the professional sales process, but unless you can find someone to talk to, your skills won't help you.

You are in the business of new business development. Your ability to find new customers determines your level of success, your ranking among your peers, your position in your industry, and your standard of living. You owe it to yourself therefore to become absolutely excellent at prospecting, and in this chapter you will learn how.

As we have seen, the biggest single obstacle to success, in every part of life, is *fear*. This is especially true when it comes to *prospecting*, to phoning or visiting strangers, or to self-promotion. The average person is unknowingly sabotaged by the fear of rejection, by his or her concern for the opinions or the approval of others. This fear of rejection can feed on itself until it literally controls a person's entire life.

To illustrate how powerful this fear can be as an obstacle to sales success, imagine for a moment that you or your company had hired a very expensive but absolutely excellent team of market researchers. Their job was to examine all the potential customers in your market area and determine, on the basis of sophisticated methodology, exactly *who* was most likely to buy exactly what you are selling.

Now imagine that, at the end of this research, they generated a list of *superb* prospects, people who were ready to buy *now*, this very day. They guaranteed that every single person on this list would buy from you if you asked them to, but the names were good for *this day only*.

If you had a list of guaranteed customers, every one of whom would buy immediately, but only if you called on them before the end of the day, what time would you start? How fast would you move? How long would you work? How much time would you take for coffee breaks or meals, or to socialize?

With a guaranteed list, you would probably call on every single person you could possibly reach. You would phone, fax, fly, and rush from appointment to appointment. You would call on people without appointments and you would make every minute count.

If you were guaranteed success, if you had no fear whatsoever of rejection or failure, of embarrassment or disapproval, you would be one of the most forceful, confident, powerful, and dynamic salespeople in your entire industry.

And the primary reason you don't act every day as though you have a guaranteed list of prospects is *fear*. That's how powerful it can be.

Just ask yourself, "How would I prospect, who would I call, what would I do differently if I was totally unafraid?" Whatever your answer, becoming *that* kind of person is your goal. The achievement of this goal will guarantee your success in professional selling.

Where does this fear of self-promotion come from? As we saw, this negative habit pattern is the result of a long process of conditioning, starting in early childhood. When you start selling, you bring this fear of rejection with you. And because you are inexperienced at prospecting, when you first attempt to call on new customers, you will do it poorly and get poor results. Unfortunately, it is natural that, if you try something and fail at it repeatedly, you will become tense and uneasy about trying it again. If you call on several prospects and they react negatively to you, you will feel hurt and angry. After all, you've got your ego fully involved. Your self-esteem is on the line.

When this happens, you move to protect yourself. You avoid exposing yourself to the same emotionally hurtful experiences. You make every excuse to avoid calling on "negative people," who unfortunately happen to be prospects, your only source of business and income. Soon, this avoidance behavior can become a habit. You may even start to hate the very idea of prospecting. This is normal and natural. It's what happens to most salespeople.

Not knowing *how* to prospect properly and well causes a person to do it poorly. When a person prospects poorly, he gets negative results. The negative results reinforce his fear and anxiety about prospecting.

He begins to cut down on his prospecting activity. He spends more and more time on nonprospecting activities, or calling on prospects who may be easy to talk to but who will never buy. He will spend much of his time *preparing* to make sales calls or visiting past customers so he can maintain a semblance of working while avoiding calling on anyone new.

The statistics indicate that there is a turnover of about *one third* of salespeople in America every year. This means that one third of salespeople are coming into the selling profession and one third of those already in the profession are on their way out each year. And the primary reason that people get out of selling and go searching for other jobs is because they can not endure the emotional stress of calling on new people unsuccessfully.

The good news is that just as fear and ineptitude reinforce each other, they can also eliminate each other. As you become smoother and more professional in prospecting, your fear of prospecting diminishes. You may never reach the point where you are *totally* fearless at prospecting. However, by learning to prospect well, you will master yourself, and master the prospecting process, to the point where you will be able to confidently generate all the new business you can handle.

The remarkable thing is that when you become an absolutely excellent prospector, you will have so many referrals from satisfied customers that you won't have to prospect anymore. One definition of a top salesperson is that "He or she is outstanding at prospecting, but never has to do it."

To increase your sales, you must spend more time with better prospects. By applying the systematic, professional process explained below and by continually analyzing your product and your market, you will generate a continuous stream of prospects that will keep your pipeline full and make you one of the best salespeople in your industry.

THE GOLDEN PROSPECT

Some prospects are better than others. In fact, some prospects are wonderful to deal with while others are a complete waste of your time. The starting point in spending more time with better prospects is for you to define clearly for yourself the *attributes* of an excellent prospect. Then your job is to find as many of them as possible.

There are several qualities possessed by an excellent prospect. The *more* of these qualities possessed by the person you are talking to, the more valuable this prospect can be to you in terms of immediate and future business. One of the most valuable things you can do in your initial conversation with the prospect is to ask the kinds of questions that enable you to determine your prospect's quality ranking, on a scale from one to ten, with one being low and ten being high.

First, a good prospect has a **pressing need** for exactly the product or service that you are selling. He has a problem for which your product or service is an excellent solution. Or he has an opportunity that your product or service enables him to take advantage of immediately. The more urgent the need or more pressing the demand, the lower will be the customer's price sensitivity or concern about the smaller details of the purchase. The more prospects you can find that have a clear and pressing need for what you are selling, the more and faster sales you will make.

For example, a company in the middle of its busiest season, during which a critical machine breaks down and cannot be repaired, is a prime prospect for the person and company who can sell and deliver this type of machine rapidly.

Not long ago, a young salesman selling construction materials lost a major order to a more aggressive supplier. But in the middle of the construction job, the supplier's workers went on strike. The customer was desperate and called the young man to see if his company could deliver quickly. They could, and even though their prices were slightly higher, the young salesman gained a first-rate customer who not only bought large quantities from him but who opened doors for him to other people who also became customers.

The second factor that makes for a good prospect is that there is a **clear cost-benefit relationship** between your product or service and the customer's projected use of it. The financial benefit in money saved or gained by implementing your product or service is obvious and measurable. The return on investment on your product is fast and significant. The customer can easily justify buying from you without a long process of evaluation. The sale can be wrapped up quickly.

When my staff wanted to buy a $1,500 collator-printer for my company, they showed me how this machine would save four to six hours a day of work of a person earning $1,800 per month. The machine would therefore pay for itself in less than sixty days. My company's return on the investment would be between 600 percent and 1,000 percent per year on the purchase price. The decision was a no-brainer. We bought it immediately.

When you are evaluating a prospect, you should be looking for opportunities to show the prospect that purchasing your product or service yields such an attractive payback that it makes no sense *not* to proceed.

The third attribute of a good prospect is that he has a **positive attitude** toward you, your industry, and your product or service. He has had positive experiences with you or with what you sell in the past. He is open and interested in your offering and is primarily concerned about how he can work with you to make the best buying decision. A prospect who is looking forward to enjoying the benefits and advantages offered by your product or service is one of the easiest of all people to sell to.

If you sell custom-tailored suits to a person who has always worn custom-tailored suits and who has no current supplier, virtually all you will have to do is assure satisfaction to get the initial order and to make this person an ongoing customer. The prospect is already psychologically predisposed to buying the product from someone.

The fourth attribute of a good prospect is that **a large sale is possible** to this prospect if your selling efforts are successful. If the prospect becomes a customer, he or she will buy a lot of what you are selling. This one customer can buy as much or more as several smaller customers. This is a very good customer to have.

The fifth attribute of a good prospect is that he or she is **a center of influence.** He or she is well respected by other people in the industry. A satisfactory sale to this person or company will lead to testimonials and referrals that will generate substantial follow-up business from other potential customers.

It is a very good strategy to select this kind of customer at the outset and then make every effort possible to get this person to buy from you and become a satisfied consumer of your products or services. The extra initial effort expended on this customer can give you leverage with other customers who know and respect him. This one sale can serve as a *multiplier* of your selling efforts.

For example, professional salespeople will quite commonly read the newspapers and ask around to get the names and organizations of the most respected people in the local business community. Often it will be the head of a large company or the president of the Chamber of Commerce. The top salesperson will then lay out a strategy to get that person as a customer. He will gently persist, for months if necessary, until that person buys from him. The salesperson will then make an extra effort to make sure this customer is highly satisfied with his purchase. With this customer's testimonials and referrals, sales then become possible to everyone who knows and respects him.

The sixth attribute of a good prospect is that he or she is **financially sound,** and prompt with payments. In the final analysis, a person is a good prospect only to the degree to which they can and will pay promptly for what they buy. When someone says, "He is a good prospect but he just doesn't have any money," the salesperson has missed the point of the entire selling profession, which is to sell something and get paid for it.

The seventh attribute of a good prospect is that his place of business or home is reasonably **close to your office** and your home. He or she is geographically located so that it is easy to call on him and easy to service him. There is very little time wasted in traveling to and from his location.

Many salespeople, in an unconscious attempt to avoid rejection, start working on prospects located at great geographical distances. All the time they are traveling to and from the prospect's location, they are fooling themselves into believing they are actually *working.* The fact is that a salesperson is only working when he or she is face-to-face with a prospect. And the more time the salesperson spends in the presence of qualified prospects who can buy within a reasonable period of time, the more sales he will make. Spending long periods traveling between prospects is one of the surest ways known to kill a sales career.

The most important question in evaluating a prospect is, "Is this a good use of my time?" Of all the prospects that you have, is this the *most valuable* prospect that you could be calling on, all things considered? Your measure is your return on energy. Does calling on this prospect represent the very highest payback to you for the mental, emotional, and physical energy that you are expending to convert this prospect into a customer?

You can only make your time more valuable by spending it with more valuable prospects. You can only increase your sales by spending more time with prospects who can be converted into larger and better customers faster than others. As you survey your market using some of the techniques we will discuss in this chapter, you must always discipline yourself to ask, "What is the most valuable use of my time right now?"

The greater the quality and quantity of prospects that go into the top of your sales hopper, or funnel, the greater will be the size and value of the customers that emerge from the bottom. Every choice you make with regard to the quality of the prospects you call on has an effect on your personal bottom line. The sum total of your choices determines almost everything that happens to you in your sales career.

PROSPECTING STRATEGY:
THE QUESTIONS YOU NEED TO ASK YOURSELF

The top 10 percent of salespeople are usually characterized as being more thoughtful than the other 90 percent. They take more time to think about what they are doing *before* they act. They carefully analyze and evaluate every part of their selling activities before setting forth. They ask and answer the critical questions that enable them to construct a prospecting strategy that leads inevitably to greater sales success than the average.

The better you think, the more sales you will make. And better thinking begins with asking and answering better questions. Good answers to well-framed questions enable you to focus your attention and channel your energies toward those prospects who most represent your major selling opportunities.

What Do I Sell?

The first question you must ask yourself is, **What exactly do I sell?** What *is* your product or service? What does it *do* for the purchaser? Imagine that your customer is at the other end of the sales pipeline. What comes out? What does he actually *get* as the result of purchasing your product or service?

As we have seen, the difference between the amateur and the superior salesperson is immediately evident in the way they answer these questions. The amateur tends to respond in terms of the qualities, characteristics, and features of the product or service. They focus on what the product or service "is." They repeat the specifications and descriptions of the product or service contained in their brochures and other sales literature.

The professional, on the other hand, focuses single-mindedly on the specific problems or goals of the prospect and shows how the product or service enables him to get what he really wants with the lowest risk and the highest return.

The professional focuses on what the product *does* for the customer in terms of improving his life or work. The professional talks about the end result, what emerges from the pipeline, rather than getting bogged down in the details of how the product is created, produced, and delivered. The professional deals with the what of the product rather than the why or how.

As salespeople, we sometimes become so involved in our product or service that we see it through our own eyes and then try to impose that vision of what it is on our customer. However, if you can put yourself aside and mentally project into the mind of your prospect and look at your product or service from his or her point of view, you will see more clearly what it represents in his or her life. What exactly is your product or service from the viewpoint of your *customer?*

Remember, people buy the feeling that they anticipate enjoying as the result of purchasing what it is you are selling. From our earlier discussion of needs, you know that your first job is to discern the exact need that this particular customer wants to satisfy by owning and using your product or service. What is it?

When I was consulting with a retail tire chain, their salespeople were focusing their efforts on convincing prospective customers that their tires were the best-priced. Inadvertently, they were encouraging their customers to make their decisions on the basis of price alone. Their prospective customers would then shop around and eventually find someone, somewhere who would sell them pretty much the same tire for a lower price. This was frustrating their salespeople and their management to no end.

After some discussion, we changed the focus of the sales presentation away from price toward safety and security. Instead of building the sales presentation around the price-quality relationship, we had the salespeople start the conversation by asking the customer how he used the car. Especially, would the tires be used on a car that drove children or loved ones from place to place?

If the answer was yes, and it almost always was, the salespeople would then direct the customer toward a higher-quality, higher-priced tire. They would explain the subtle differences in grip and dependability they would experience with a better tire when braking or cornering. They would explain how a higher-quality tire could make all the difference in saving the passenger's life in an accident.

Prospects who had been shopping around for the best price realized that their primary concern was really the safety of the passengers of the car and that it was well worth spending slightly more to ensure a higher level of security and dependability. This tire company went on to dominate the market by putting all their emphasis on safety as the critical determinant in tire selection, and then by backing this strategic position with their installation, service, and repair facilities.

If you have any doubt at all about what it is you are actually selling from the viewpoint of your customer, you are selling in the dark. You are playing "Pin the tail on the donkey" wearing a blindfold when you are talking to a prospect and trying to convert him into a customer. By not knowing exactly what you are selling, your sales activities will be random and haphazard, and largely a matter of chance.

Conduct the market research exercise I suggested in Chapter 6. Phone your last ten customers and ask them directly, "May I ask, why did you *really* buy my product or service from me, rather than getting it from someone else?" Probe your customers carefully and see if you can get them to tell you what it really was that caused them to buy. In contrast to what you were selling, what was it that they were *buying?*

If you ask this question of ten recent customers, you will learn that 60 percent to 80 percent of their *real* reasons for buying were similar. You will then know how to approach and sell *new* prospects more effectively. With this information, you will be ready to make a giant leap forward in your selling career.

Who Is My Customer?

The second question in strategic prospecting follows from the first. It is, **Who** exactly is my customer? Who is my *ideal* customer? Think back over the people who have purchased your product or service in the past and ask yourself, "What do my customers have in common?"

You have already done part of this work in defining your ideal prospect. But describing your ideal customer is something more. It requires that you ask more specific questions. For example, is your ideal customer male or female? What age is your customer? What is your customer's educational background? What is your customer's level of experience with your product or service? Is your ideal customer a first-time buyer or has he purchased your products in the past? What is your ideal customer's occupation? Income range? Number of years of experience in his or her job? Family situation? Position or level of authority in his or her organization? Type of personality?

Why Does My Customer Buy?

This is the most important question in selling. **Why** does my customer buy? What benefits does he seek? What is he attempting to achieve, avoid, or preserve by buying your products or service? Of all the possible benefits available to him or her from your product, what are the *specific* tangible benefits he is seeking? What are the intangible benefits? A tangible benefit is something the customer can touch and feel. It is something the customer can hold up and show to someone else. A tangible benefit has very much to do with how the purchase is viewed by others, and is very important. Describing the components and features of a product or service is how you point out to the customer the tangible benefits of purchasing and using it.

However, as we have seen, the intangible benefits are the *real* reasons the customer buys from you. The intangible benefits are largely emotional. They revolve around pride, status, security, admiration, and the respect of others, plus other factors that make the customer feel *happy* that he or she has purchased what you are selling.

A person who buys a Rolex watch will explain his purchase to others in terms of its gold case, its jeweled Swiss movement, the fact that it is waterproof to 330 feet and the tremendous accuracy for which it is famous. But none of these are reasons for buying a Rolex.

The real reasons, the intangible benefits, are the feeling of success, prestige, and status that a person gets when he or she wears a Rolex in the presence of people who are wearing less-expensive timepieces. It is the unspoken statement that "I have arrived!" that the customer is making that causes him to buy the watch.

What are the tangible benefits of buying and using your product or service, and what are the intangible benefits? What are the tangible and intangible benefits of dealing with you as a salesperson? What are the *obvious* payoffs of dealing with you, and what are the not so obvious payoffs?

Here is a simple exercise you can perform that I call the "3-3-3 analysis." This analysis consists of three answers to each of three questions flowing from the prospecting questions we've just discussed:

1. List three reasons why someone should purchase your product or service at *all*, from your company or from some other company;
2. List three reasons why someone who has decided to buy your product or service should buy it from *your* company rather than from some other company;
3. List three reasons why a prospect should buy your product or service from *you personally* rather than from some other salesperson in your company.

These are not easy questions. But if you don't know the answers to them so well that they are an integral part of your conversation with your prospect, you are going to have a hard time selling your product or service no matter how good it is. Think through and write the answers to these questions. Then review the answers with your manager or with someone else. Accuracy in this area is vitally important to the whole process of prospecting.

Where Is My Prospect?

Before you can begin prospecting, you must also answer the question, **Where** is my prospect?

Your specific responsibility is to sell as *much* of your product or service as you possibly can. To do this, you must identify the exact location of your prospects so that you can better focus your sales efforts. This enables you to increase your *return on energy*. You can see more prospects in a shorter period of time with a greater likelihood of selling to each of them. Calling on several prospects in a smaller geographical area is one of the keys to higher productivity.

In determining where your prospects are, you can look at your territory both vertically and horizontally. Vertically would mean tall office buildings within which you may have a series of prospects. Certain office buildings within your territory may be virtual beehives of prospective customer companies. For example, if you sell to law firms, an office building near the courthouse that is filled with legal firms can be one of your prime market areas.

Viewing your market horizontally refers to it being spread out over a wide area, covering a few blocks, a few counties, or even a few states, depending upon what you sell. Where exactly are your customers? The purpose of identifying them geographically is so you can shorten the amount of time it takes you to get from one to the other. The less time you spend en route, the more time you can spend face-to-face, where all the action is.

Also, when you ask the question, "Where is my customer?" you have to think in terms of the specific businesses or industries in which your customers are found. The principle of concentration dictates that you spend more of your time in those areas where more of your prospect companies are located. Many salespeople have moved to the top of their fields by specializing in a particular business or industry and then making themselves extremely knowledgeable about the needs and problems of customers in that industry.

A friend of mine is a salesman who is one of the highest paid people in the life insurance and estate planning industry. Early in his career he recognized that medical professionals represented a potentially lucrative clientele with a steady flow of high earnings to save, invest, and protect. He decided to specialize in the medical field and make himself so knowledgeable in that area that he would eventually become the financial advisor of choice to medical specialists in his city and beyond.

He invested two solid years studying the structure of the medical industry. He subscribed to their magazines, read the books written by the foremost authorities in the fields of practice management, and attended their conferences. He interviewed dozens of doctors and dentists to broaden his understanding of their unique situations and special needs. He submitted articles to the specialty publications that went to these professionals. Soon he was invited to speak at their annual meetings. Step by step, he built a reputation as an expert in financial planning for medical professionals.

It took him two years to earn the right to sell in the medical services industry but then his business took off. It grew by reputation and word of mouth. In another few years, he became one of the highest paid and most successful professionals in his industry. Even though his prospective clients were beset on every side by salespeople trying to sell them similar financial instruments, no one had his depth of insight into their particular needs. He differentiated himself from his competition by being the most helpful and valuable resource in financial planning to doctors in his market area. He paid the price and he reaped the rewards.

Often the answer to the question, "Where is my customer?" is found in the *position* that a person has within an organization. Perhaps the customer is located in a particular department or function of a large company. Identifying where your customers are located enables you to focus your sales efforts and make better use of your selling time.

As you can see, the answers to the questions about who and where often overlap. First you identify the company or organization, then the position, then the actual person. However, one of the most important things you do is to think about who and where your customers are likely to be in the *future*.

With businesses rapidly changing, expanding or contracting, and with the wave of restructuring sweeping over every competitive enterprise, the actual decision-makers are changing as well. The person who purchases the product or service this year may be completely different from the person who purchased it last year. You must keep abreast of these changes by continually asking questions and feeding the information into your personal data base.

For example, at the dawn of the computer age, the decisions to purchase computers were often made at high levels of the organization by senior executives. Engineers, consultants, and information specialists were involved in the selection and deployment of mainframe computers, computer terminals and computer services. But senior executives made the final decisions.

But with the advent of the minicomputer, the microcomputer, and desktop computer, plus the local area networks and the service providers that link computers through a department or a company, the decision making for purchasing computers and computer peripherals shifted to the office managers and the actual users themselves. Until salespeople became aware of this transference of buying authority, they were calling on the wrong people and making the wrong presentations. This situation may exist in your industry right now.

When Does My Customer Buy?

When does my customer buy? This is the next question in effective prospecting. Dr. Thomas Stanley's research into selling to the affluent concluded that affluent customers make certain purchases only once or twice a year, usually in conjunction with company year ends and tax filings. If they are approached by a salesperson other than through one of these windows of opportunity they are simply not interested. They are not in the market. They are not prospects.

When does *your* customer buy? Does he buy a year in advance based on budget projections? Does he buy on a seasonal basis? Does he buy or make purchasing decisions during a specific budget period? Does he buy throughout the year as his needs dictate? Knowing when your customer is most likely to buy your product or service is essential to your being in the right place at the right time.

The question about *when* also refers to the things that have to take place before your customer is in a buying frame of mind. Does your customer buy only when he is sure that others have purchased your product and are satisfied with it? Does your customer buy when someone he respects gives your product a testimonial or refers you to him? Does your customer buy only after your product or service has been independently tested and recommended by an outside authority?

Just as many people don't go to a movie until they have read a dependable review of it, many people don't buy a product or service until a publication they respect has recommended it. For example, many buyers will not consider a product until it has been reviewed favorably in *Consumer Reports*. How does *your* buyer make up his mind? What needs to happen for your customer to be open to your selling message?

Why Doesn't My Customer Buy?

This is a great question! Why **doesn't** my customer buy? To illustrate, think about the brake and the accelerator on a car. You can go faster by either stepping on the accelerator or by taking your foot off the brake. Reasons for not buying are the brakes in the sales process. You can often increase your sales immediately by removing the main objections to buying that cause your prospects to defer, delay, or reject your offer.

Customers are funny. They have reasons for buying and reasons for not buying. It's essential that you marshal all the reasons that a customer should buy and include them in your presentation. But it's equally essential that you identify the major reasons your customers hesitate, and deal with them effectively, regardless of whether your customer specifically brings them up.

Xerox saw their market share drop from 80 percent to 12 percent when the Japanese invaded the market with less expensive copiers that included more features and better guarantees. After struggling for several years, Xerox turned the tide against its competitors by guaranteeing complete customer satisfaction. If you purchased a Xerox photocopier and you weren't happy for any reason, they would replace the photocopier with a new machine, and keep replacing it until you were satisfied.

Simultaneously, the factory was instructed to manufacture machines of such quality that the replacements would be few. This strategy enabled Xerox to garner some of the highest customer satisfaction ratings for photocopiers in America and launched them firmly on the comeback trail in an extremely competitive market.

Xerox discovered that the primary reason customers *weren't* buying their machines was because of service problems. They increased their sales dramatically by removing the primary negative attribute while at the same time highlighting their existing positive qualities and features.

Who Is My Competitor?

Who is my competitor? Who am I selling against? Who does my customer consider as an alternative to my products or services? When I lose a sale to a competitor, why does it happen? Why does a prospect select my competitor, a competing product or service, over mine? What does he or she perceive to be different and better?

Thomas J. Watson, Jr., former president of IBM, once said, "We don't mind if people make mistakes at IBM. There's nothing wrong with that. But to make the same mistake over and over again without finding out why is unforgivable."

Here is a strategy for you. If you lose a sale to a competitor, wait for three or four weeks and then go back to the customer and very politely ask him why it was he chose your competitor over yourself. Be low-key, polite, and curious. If possible, examine the competitor's product or service and compare it with your own. Rather than being confrontational, instead put yourself in the customer's shoes and attempt to see the buying decision from the customer's point of view.

When Chrysler was going through its financial problems in the early 1980s, Lee Iacocca brought Japanese vehicles, renowned for their quality, onto the factory floors throughout the company. The Chrysler autoworkers were invited to inspect them carefully and told that these were what they had to compete against to save the company. Many of the autoworkers had never taken a close look at a Japanese car and were amazed at how well made they were. They realized for the first time the basis for the objections dealers were getting about Chrysler products. That began a quality revolution at Chrysler that goes on to this day.

What are the strengths and weaknesses of your competitor's products? How are they better than yours? What needs do they satisfy for the customer that yours do not, or do not *appear* to? What are your competitor's weaknesses? How could you downplay or neutralize their strong points while emphasizing or pointing out their weak areas? Most of all, how could you position your products and services in such a way that the areas where your product is better become the most important considerations in the buying decision?

The customer is always right. The customer makes his decision based on his *perception* of what is best for him. Your job is to show your prospect that there may be more than one version of what is best for him. You must show your prospect that there are *other* areas of importance to consider. Your job is to shift the emphasis of the decision onto the areas where your product or service is superior to that of your competitors. Your need is to position yourself as the *best choice*, given all the various factors involved in the overall buying decision. And from the very beginning, when you are prospecting, you need to know who and what your prospect might also be considering.

Who Are My Noncustomers?

Who are my **noncustomers**? Who are the customers who could benefit from my product or service but buy neither from me nor my competitors? The largest single market for any product or service is always the noncustomer. Just in every election, the nonvoter block is large enough to determine the outcome, in selling, the noncustomer represents the greatest selling opportunity.

There is often little or no competition for the noncustomer. They are usually ignored. If you can find a way to appeal to them, you can have the market all to yourself, for a while at least. When Steve Jobs and Steve Wozniak invented the Apple computer in the late 1970s, the leading experts from the huge, mainframe computer companies predicted that the total market potential for personal computers in the United States was not more than three or four hundred units. They concluded that it wasn't even worth pursuing.

Apple however had identified the noncustomer, the low-tech individual who wanted the benefits of a computer but who lacked the skill or patience to learn how to use one. Apple computers and the Macintosh satisfied this need. They began to sell by the thousands, and then the tens of thousands.

The major companies did a complete turnaround and plunged into the market with their own versions. The personal computer market exploded. By mid-1993, more than fifty million personal computers had been sold and they are being improved upon and made obsolete at a breathtaking rate. The entire world of information processing has been changed by bringing the noncustomer for computers into the marketplace—with a vengeance.

CUSTOMERS AND TIME

There are three types of customers with regard to the time that it takes for them to make buying decisions. Sometimes you will work with only one type and sometimes you will work with all three at once.

The first is the **short-term** customer. This customer is usually a small buyer or user of your product or service. He or she can make a decision and act fairly quickly. This customer does not need approval from a board or a committee. He or she usually signs the checks as well. This type of sale is relatively quick and straightforward. If you can demonstrate that your product or service will make a meaningful improvement in the life or work of this prospect, he or she will make a buying decision almost immediately.

For many salespeople, this is the bread-and-butter customer. Some companies sell only to this type of person. Their products or services do not require a long period of contemplation, evaluation, and comparison. The product is easy to understand and the benefits of owning it are obvious to the prospect. In selling, this type of customer represents immediate income. In prospecting, you should be working with several potential customers of this type if you want to achieve maximum sales volume.

The second type of customer is the **medium-term** customer. This is a smaller company or organization that has levels of management and multiple decision-makers. When you make a presentation to this type of prospect, and he or she *likes* the product or service, it must then go to other people or committees for final approval. However, since the organization is small, the approval process is fairly short. These sales are usually larger than those of the short-term customer. There are often opportunities for additional sales to the same customer. These sales tend to be lucrative for the company and the salesperson. Their potential size makes them important to the overall sales volume of the enterprise.

You usually have to make several calls on this type of customer. There will be delays in getting approvals and in arranging payment. There will be competition. You will have to work harder for this kind of sale and it will take longer to bring it to fruition. But because of its size, it is worth the effort. It is a good investment of your time.

The third type of sale is the **long-term** sale. These are large potential sales and are usually made to big companies or organizations. They can represent enormous dollar value or sales volume. These are the kind of sales that every salesperson and every company hopes and plans for. These are the size of sales that can represent a substantial portion of the company's business for an entire year.

The challenge with this large type of prospect is that the sale takes a *long* time to make. It is not unusual to spend two or three years working with a huge organization before the big sale finally comes through. These companies or organizations usually determine their expenditures for the coming year in the annual budget. If you approach the company after the budget has been submitted, you may have to wait a full year before your offering is even considered and approved as a new budget item.

You should fish for whales on a regular basis. You should be scanning and analyzing your territory and identifying the companies that represent this type of potentially enormous sale.

These sales are also the most difficult to make so you must be patient. It is common for you to work on a sale like this for many months and then lose it at the last moment for a variety of reasons over which you have no control. Every salesperson has had the experience of bringing a sale almost to closure and then losing it forever because of a merger, acquisition, new strategic plan, unexpected business conditions, new decision-maker, an aggressive competitor with a superior offer, a personality clash, misunderstanding, or something like the Gulf War that completely disrupts the buying process.

Here's a key point. On the one hand, you must work on these large sales whenever you can. You must call back over and over, gradually nudging the sale forward toward conclusion. But you must never, never, *never* hang all your hopes on this one big sale coming through at the last minute. "A great ship should never be held by a single rope, nor a great life by a single hope."

Like keeping the plates spinning in a circus act, you must keep small, medium, and large sales prospects spinning as well. You must have short-term, medium-term, and long-term prospective sales to ensure income today, income tomorrow, and potentially huge income in the future. But you must never allow the possibility of a big sale to deflect your attention from the hard, day-to-day business of keeping your sales pipeline full through continuous prospecting.

There is something perverse in the world of selling with regard to the big sale. I have seen it over and over, and every salesperson I speak to has, at one time or another, experienced the unfortunate situation where he stopped calling on new prospects and hung all his hopes and dreams on the one big sale coming through at the last minute. And the sad fact is that it *never* does.

Whenever you bet everything on one roll of the dice, on one big prospect, you will invariably be disappointed. But when you have lots of prospective sales in your pipeline, you will not only generate a steady stream of income, but the big sale will eventually come through for you.

FOUR TYPES OF PROSPECTS

You will be calling on four different types of prospects. The earlier you identify which of these you are talking to, the more productive will be your selling efforts.

The first is the **successful** prospect. This prospect is in a business, industry, or situation where things are going well. Business is good. Sales are increasing. There is predictable cash flow. The company is growing and adding people. The key decision-makers are busy, happy, and optimistic. The future looks terrific!

This is the easiest type of prospect to sell to if your product is appropriate. This type of prospect is succeeding and wants to do even better. This prospect wants to "plus" his or her situation. This prospect is open-minded and has the money to spend on a product or service that will enhance or improve his or her life or work. Your goal with this type of prospect is to demonstrate to him how much better off he could be with your product or service, as compared to his current situation.

For example, if you were selling telecommunications equipment, the focus of your approach to this prospect would be on how much more efficiently the company could run and how many more customers the company could serve by using your equipment rather than by continuing to use their current equipment. If you can show that your equipment would more than pay for itself in reduced mistakes, improved communications, and higher morale, the decision-maker will be very likely to go ahead.

The second type of prospect is the person with a **problem.** This person recognizes that something is wrong and is looking at a product or service such as yours to take away the pain. The problem is costing the company money and is creating dissatisfaction both externally among customers and internally among the service and support people. The decision-maker recognizes that something must be done.

As an example, your approach to a prospect with a problem of telephone delays, lost messages, irate customers, and poor communications internally and externally would be that the state-of-the-art telephone system you are selling would enable the entire company to function more smoothly and efficiently. If you can work with the prospect to identify the high cost of an inefficient system in terms of lost revenues, lost time, mistakes, and confusion, the decision-maker or decision-makers can often make a reasonably fast decision to purchase your offering.

As we know, often when you approach a prospect for the first time, he or she will say, "I'm not interested." This is to be expected. The prospect has no idea how much better off he could be if he was using what you sell.

In fact, you should be *glad* that he's initially not interested. If he were already aware of how much better off he could be with your product, he might have already arranged to buy it from someone else.

You respond to "I'm not interested" by saying, "That's *exactly* why I'm calling."

When the prospect asks you what you mean, you reply, "Most of our customers were initially uninterested in our product when we first spoke to them. But when they saw how we could help them, they bought from us and recommended us to others. I'd like to show you what we showed them, and you can decide for yourself if this can be helpful to you or not."

This approach usually triggers *curiosity* and will get you the appointment. From there, if the prospect can genuinely benefit from what you are selling, you have an opportunity to sell.

The third type of prospect is the **complacent** or satisfied prospect. This is the type of person who is happy with the way everything is going and sees no need to change. This prospect is not particularly open to considering your product or service, and isn't interested in rocking the boat.

It could be that this prospect does not see that the benefits from your product or service outweigh the costs and trouble of installing it. In too many cases in business today this prospect is an employee on a fixed salary who is more concerned with stability and the status quo than he is with innovation and improvement. Remember the old sayings, "No need? No sale!" "No urgency? No sale!" "No authority? No sale!"?

This is not a good prospect because he does not feel that he has any need for what you are selling. He feels no urgency to solve a problem or improve a situation. And he probably lacks the final authority to make the buying decision, anyway. Working with this type of prospect is usually frustrating and not a good use of your time. Unless you can see a way to magnify a problem or need that the prospect has, you are better off moving along.

The final prospect is the **negative** or difficult person who is often rude, insulting, and obnoxious. This prospect looks down his nose at salespeople and considers himself to be superior to them. This prospect is often convinced that your product or service is a waste of money even before you begin describing it to him. This is the kind of prospect that you spend no time with at all. As soon as you recognize that you are dealing with this type of prospect, you politely break off the sales conversation and get busy finding more of the first and second types of prospects.

PROSPECTS FROM HELL

The *worst* part of selling is dealing with difficult people. As a professional, you are accustomed to long hours, hard work, and the invariable ups and downs and disappointments of day-to-day selling activities. You can take these in stride. You win some and you lose some. You go home tired at the end of the day, but with a good night's sleep you are once more positive, optimistic, and ready to go. But only if you *avoid* spending too much time with difficult prospects.

The most stressful part of selling, and of life, is extended interaction with negative and unhappy people. Robert Ringer, in his book *Million Dollar Habits*, calls them "drain people." Others call them "toxic people." These are people who make you tired, angry, and frustrated just dealing with them for any amount of time. They have negative mental attitudes and they make little effort to be pleasant at all. Like a good detective, you must ask questions early in your prospecting to identify and sort out these people so that you don't spend a lot of time with them.

There are several characteristics of the *poor* prospect. The more of these characteristics possessed by a single person, the less likely he is to buy and the less valuable use he is of your time. Prospects with only one or two of these attributes can often be turned into customers. But if a prospect has more than three of them, you are probably just wasting your time.

The first attribute of the poor prospect is that he is a **generally negative person.** This is a real obstacle because the purchase of any product or service is essentially an act of hope and optimism, combined with faith. When you buy any product or service, you are usually looking forward to being *better off* in the future. You are anticipating feeling better about yourself and life as a result of having bought whatever it is. Buying *requires* a positive mental attitude. If a person doesn't have a generally positive outlook on life, they are not likely to buy anything, at least not from you.

In addition to being negative, the poor prospect is often critical of you or your product and difficult to get along with. He may have had a bad experience in the past or he may just be suspicious and hostile when approached by someone in sales. Whatever the situation, you need to accept that you are not a psychotherapist or a guidance counselor. You are not capable of analyzing or understanding the deep subconscious impulses that cause people to behave the way they do. The sooner you break off the conversation with an unpleasant person, the happier you will be and the more energy you will have.

The second attribute of a poor prospect is that it is **difficult for you to demonstrate the value of your product** or service to him. It is hard to show a significant cost-benefit relationship. The prospect can't see how or why he would be better off with your product or service than he is without it. At the same time, the poor prospect will complain and argue with you about your price early in the sales conversation. He will often compare your prices critically with those of your competitors, often those competitors selling inferior products or services. Since this tends to be both irritating and demoralizing to you, when you meet this type of prospect, you should just smile politely and go on your way as soon as possible.

The third attribute of a poor prospect is that even if you do make a sale to him it will only be a **small sale.** If you hang in there, like a boxer being pounded by a strong opponent, and you are eventually successful, the size of the sale and the commission will hardly have been worth the price you've paid.

The fourth attribute of a poor prospect is that there are **no opportunities for follow-up sales.** Once this prospect has purchased something from you, he or she will not be in the market for your product again for months, if not years. There will be no customer relationship upon which to build that you can leverage into additional sales.

The fifth attribute of a poor prospect is that he has **limited value in terms of testimonials and referrals.** Even if he does buy your product or service, you would not be able to impress another prospect with that fact. He may not be well known or well respected. He doesn't know other people who could use your product or service, and if he does, he won't give you their names.

The sixth attribute of the poor prospect is that **his business is not doing very well.** He complains continually about how bad business is and blames his competitors, the government, and whatever else he can think of. Because of this, he is not a good customer. He will complain and argue about price and then he will be slow to honor your company's invoices. You may have to go back to him a couple of times to get payment, and sometimes even have to repossess the product.

The seventh and final attribute of a poor prospect is that his **place of business is geographically distant** from your office. You have to travel to get there. You end up spending a lot of time in transit that would be better used calling on prospects closer to your office.

Remember, all you have to sell is your time. Calling on poor prospects is *not* the highest and best use of your time. They do not represent a good return on the investment of your energy. They tire you out and wear you down. And even if you finally make a sale, you get very little satisfaction. You are usually just glad it's over.

PROSPECTING TO THE TOP

The basic strategy of prospecting consists of planning and organizing so you *spend more time with better prospects*. When you do this, you will feel more positive about yourself. You will feel a greater sense of control over your destiny. You will feel happier in your sales career. You will feel like a *winner* more of the time.

Just as you would sort the good from the bad, the wheat from the chaff, in selecting items from a large population, you should be measuring and evaluating prospects from the initial meeting. One of the fastest ways to increase your sales is to spend more hours every day with the kind of prospect who can most benefit from the special features of what you sell, and who both recognizes it and is eager to learn more about it.

SOURCES OF PROSPECTS

Where do you find prospects? You begin by identifying exactly *what* it is you sell and how it improves the lives of individuals or organizations. You determine *why* people buy it and *what benefits* they can expect to receive from using your product or service. You clearly *define your ideal customer*, the person who can benefit most rapidly and measurably from what you offer. You then look around in the marketplace, as you would scan the countryside from the top of a hill, and begin picking out the people who fit your ideal customer profile.

Just as people give off hints and clues as to whether or not they are happy or unhappy, prospects give off clues to indicate that they are in the market for what you are selling. You are surrounded by prospects, as a fish in the ocean is surrounded by other fish, but you need to be alert and be able to recognize them when they swim past.

There are many information sources that give you the names, companies, occupations, and positions of prospective customers. Depending upon what you sell, the sources that follow can be of more or less help to you. But the wider the net you cast, the more fish you will catch. The more aware you are of more sources of prospects around you, the more likely you will be to keep your prospecting pipeline filled with people and companies who can purchase and pay for your product within a reasonable period of time.

Newspapers

Start with **newspapers.** You can find in your local newspaper hundreds of prospects. Many salespeople can keep busy year-round by simply *farming* the prospects whose names and advertisements appear in the daily paper. There are never enough hours in the day to follow up on all the leads that your local paper will give you every single morning.

If you recall our definitions of a good prospect, you will see immediately that when companies advertise in the newspaper, they are either successful and want to sell even more, or they are experiencing lower than expected revenues and they want to increase their sales. Since it is expensive to advertise, and it takes planning and foresight, advertisers have already identified themselves as being in a prime prospect category. A newspaper is one way that companies announce, "Salespeople everywhere! Call on me! I have problems unsolved, needs unmet, or opportunities that I am trying to take advantage of. If you have a product or service that can help me, I am obviously in the market with money to spend and the desire to improve my business!"

You must think about how your product or service can be useful and helpful to an advertiser in a cost-effective way. Then you call the advertiser, tell him or her that you saw their ad and that you have an idea that could help them be more successful in whatever they are doing.

You should study every newspaper story about an individual or corporation, especially in the business pages. Don't fall into the time-wasting trap of just reading the headlines, sports, and comics. Let the second-rate salespeople do that. You're a businessperson. You're the president of your own professional sales corporation. You read the newspaper to get information that will help your business grow. Your aim should be to see every story or mention of a business expansion or contraction as a possible opportunity to sell.

Every company that is growing or expanding to new premises is a new prospect. Every company with problems is a prospect. Every company that announces profits is a prospect. Every company that announces losses is a prospect. Whenever someone new is hired by a company, he or she will be anxious to make meaningful changes and will be open to new products or services to improve his or her area of responsibility.

Besides helping you prospect, another benefit of reading a newspaper is keeping current with what is going on in the business world. Regular reading will ensure that you are better informed than the nonreader.

When you meet with a prospect, it will become immediately clear to him that you are a knowledgeable and professional salesperson with a firm grasp of the dynamics of the current economy. This will create a higher sense of trust and confidence in your ability to help him solve his problem or achieve his goal. Daily newspaper reading for business information is indispensable for you in becoming one of the top salespeople in your profession.

The Yellow Pages

The **Yellow Pages** are an excellent source of prospects, for several reasons. First, it is expensive to advertise in the Yellow Pages. Advertisers therefore obviously have money to spend to improve their businesses.

Second, you must plan Yellow Pages advertising a year in advance and pay for it on a monthly basis. This requires good planning and a long-term commitment to succeeding in that business. Companies that advertise in the Yellow Pages, especially those with large insertions, are obviously aggressive about growing their businesses. Because of this, they probably have a variety of other needs as well.

When you have sold your product or service to a particular company in a specific industry, turn to the Yellow Pages and get the names of all the *other* companies in the same industry. If one company has been able to take advantage of the benefits of your offering, other companies in the same business may be able to take advantage of it as well.

Take your Yellow Pages and begin phoning each company. Ask for the decision-maker for your product and tell him or her that you are already doing work in their industry. Tell them you have an idea that could help them. Ask for a few minutes of their time. Go and see them and show them what you have already done for another similar organization. Many salespeople have built their careers by selling to and dominating a specific industry niche. And the more you sell in a particular industry, the more of an expert you become on the specific needs of that particular industry. The Yellow Pages can get you started.

Business Publications

Business publications are some of the best *condensed* sources of prospects ever produced. There are business journals and newspapers in virtually every major city in America. These publications regularly have special editions that list the community's twenty-five or fifty largest companies in a specific industry. They have annual editions that list prospects for every conceivable product or service. Almost every article they publish is about a local business or businessperson who is on the move. Their editorials are often full of advice, comments, and ideas that are of interest to businesspeople.

If you sell to businesses, you should subscribe to your local business publication immediately. You should read every single page the day you receive it. You should make notes on every business that might have a need for what you are selling. You should be fast off the mark and immediately telephone each company that looks like a potential customer. Many salespeople make their entire careers by following up on the stories, advertisements, and listings in their local business publications.

Often you can write articles for your local business publications. These should describe how your product or service solves a common business problem or helps companies achieve a common business goal. You may not get paid for the article but you can include your name, address, and company. This will often cause prospects to come to you.

You can then use reprints of these articles as part of your sales materials and to accompany your correspondence. When you become known as an authority in your field, prospects will be much more open to consulting with you for their business needs.

You should also subscribe to magazines like *Forbes*, *Fortune*, and *Business Week*. These not only give you specific information on individual companies and industries but they give you a broad approach to the economy and to industry segments as a whole. They enable you to converse intelligently and understand your customer's situation in greater depth. They are read and reviewed by most of the highest paid salespeople in America.

Trade Publications and Directories

Another source of prospects is **trade magazines** aimed at people in the industry to which you want to sell. If you want to sell to a specific industry, go to your local library and ask the librarian to get you the *Periodicals Index*. This book lists all the magazines offered for sale in the United States by subject, category, and topic. Find the names of the most popular publications in your prospect's industry and subscribe to them. When you get them, read the lead editorials and the major stories. These will keep you current with the major trends in that industry and enable you to speak knowledgeably about your prospect's business when you talk to him.

Other companies that sell to that particular industry will advertise in those trade publications. These advertisements will give you a sense of how to position your products or services when you talk to your prospects. They will alert you to the problems and concerns of people in that industry and give you the kind of language that you should be using in your prospecting and selling activities with people in the industry. As Yogi Berra once said, "You can observe a lot just by looking."

Your local library will also have business directories. These directories break the companies in your market area down by industry and give pertinent details regarding sales volume, history of the company, key executives, number of staff and offices, and a good deal of additional information that can help you determine what kind of a prospect a particular company might be. There is nothing so flattering to a prospect as a salesperson who comes in having done his homework and who obviously knows a good deal about the company already.

If you sell to a person in a company who belongs to an association, see if you can borrow or purchase the association directory that gives the names, addresses, companies, and positions of all the other members. Once you've sold one member of an association, you will find it easier to call on every other member of that same association in your territory. It is easier to get referrals, appointments, and opportunities to sell when someone with whom the prospect has something in common has already bought from you.

For example, if you were selling to the legal administrators of law firms, you could get the membership directory of all the legal administrators of all the larger law firms in your market area. Having sold effectively to one member, you could then call on every other member using your initial sales success as a point of reference.

Whenever you sell anything to anyone, be sure to ask the customer if he or she belongs to any business organizations or associations. If the customer answers in the affirmative, ask if you can borrow the membership list and perhaps even get a testimonial letter that you could use to open doors to other members.

Your local library will also probably have a copy of the U.S. *Industrial Outlook*, which contains information on 250 industries. Look through this and take photocopies of the relevant data, plus information on the companies that compete with your prospect company.

Your product or service is a solution to a problem that a company has, whether it is aware of it or not. Your job is to uncover the problem. A major problem that every company has is its competitors. Competitors determine the strategy of the company, its volume of sales, its sales margins, its level of profitability, and many other things. The more you understand about the competitive situation that your prospect company is facing, the more authoritative you will be when you eventually sit down with the decision-makers.

Since all companies are interested in growth and profitability, during your research you should be looking for the constraints to that growth and profitability. What problems is the company experiencing? What challenges exist in the marketplace? What is holding the company back from producing and selling far more of its product or service? What problems is the company facing for which your product or service is a possible solution? The clearer you are about the prospect's problem and the more relevant your solution to that problem, the lower will be his price sensitivity and the faster will be the buying decision.

Get the Standard and Poor's industry surveys from your local library as well. These surveys contain detailed financial information on large companies and their competitors. They show year-to-year comparisons for sales and profitability. The Standard and Poors can give you excellent insights that enable you to see your prospect company more clearly and structure your offer more effectively.

The *Value Line Investment Survey* is also available to show you facts, trends, and business projections for 1,700 companies nationwide. It is used by stockbrokers and financial analysts to get a quick understanding of the past, present, and potential future of any organization. The Value Line surveys have been around for more than fifty years and are highly respected sources of authoritative information on large companies.

Dun & Bradstreet

Dun & Bradstreet sells information on businesses. They can sort this information by industry classification and size. You may have to buy them in lots of one thousand, but once you are clear about what it is you sell and who it is that you can best sell to, you can quickly sort out a large number of high-quality prospects from the names and data they will provide for you.

Chambers of Commerce

Your local **Chamber of Commerce** is another source of information and business publications that contain prospects for your product or service. The most prominent and active companies in every community are members of the Chamber of Commerce and participate in its activities. One of their primary reasons for involvement is to gain regular exposure to other companies with whom they want to do business.

The Chambers of Commerce nationwide are essentially business networking organizations, and as such their membership rosters are gold mines of excellent prospects.

If your company is a member of the Chamber of Commerce, you are entitled to request copies of everything that the chamber produces for its members. If your company is not yet a member, encourage them to join so that you can tap into this valuable source of leads and referrals.

Leads, Leads Everywhere

Another obvious source of new prospects is referrals from your present customers. When you make a sale, immediately ask for the names of two or three other people the customer knows and would recommend. A referral from a satisfied customer is worth ten to twenty times the value of a cold call. When you are sent to a customer by someone he or she knows, you are in the position of piggybacking on the credibility and friendship of your customer. Your new prospect becomes an extension of your relationship with your existing customer.

You can also get good leads from your noncustomers. You should resolve to get two names from every prospect you speak to, whether he buys or not. At the end of the sales conversation, if it becomes clear that this prospect does not have a problem for which your product or service is the right solution, simply ask, "Could you give me the names of two or three other people who might be in a better position to take advantage of this offer?"

If you appear professional and friendly, the prospect will often refer you to other people he or she knows. Assure the prospect that you will use no pressure on his friends or associates and that he will not be sorry that he gave you the names. You merely want a chance to show them what you have just shown this prospect.

When you get a referral from your customer or noncustomer, and call on that referral, be sure to report back to the source of the referral. Phone or write and tell him or her what occurred. Thank him for his help and ask if he knows anyone else that you could call on. The average person has as many as three hundred friends and colleagues and either has their phone numbers handy or can get them on short notice.

Remember the golden chain: if you continually ask people for new names, call on the names referred, and report back to the source, you will often get a continuous stream of referrals that can turn into a steady stream of new business.

A saleswoman in one of my seminars reported that she had carefully tracked the success of this method and found that she had gotten seventy-three leads over a three-month period from a single prospect who never bought from her at all!

Be sure to tell your friends, relatives, and social contacts that you sell a particular product. Tell them what it does for a customer, and the kind of people who can most benefit from it. Ask if they know anyone who might be in the market for it. If you continually ask the people you know for advice and referrals, you will be surprised at the doors they can open and the business that will ensue from the prospects they refer you to.

Cold Calling Can Fill Your Pipeline

Cold calling is another way to get leads. It is both the first choice of the new salesperson and the final resort of the experienced salesperson. If you are starting out with no prospects and no prospect information at all, making cold calls on large numbers of prospects enables you to plunge into the business and get an intensive education on your product or service in a short period of time.

For the first ten years of my sales career, cold calling was the primary method I used to develop new business. It is often called "gut selling" and it requires tremendous courage, at first. But when you do it over and over again, your fear of cold calling diminishes and eventually vanishes. Finally you develop yourself to the point where you are not afraid of anything. You will call on anybody and any company at any time. You break through the psychological wall that separates the great salespeople from the average.

In my twenties, I traveled and worked all over the world, in Europe, Africa, Southeast Asia, and Latin America. Whenever I stopped to work, I would go out and find a job in commission sales, primarily because that was all I could get. In each case, I used a basic technique to launch my new sales career. I found later that you can use the same technique to turn a sales career around, or to launch it into outer space.

It's simple. It takes a little courage at first, but then it works better and better. Here it is: I would make one hundred sales calls on one hundred new prospects in the shortest period of time possible. I resolved not to worry about whether they bought or not. The purpose of this blitz was to thoroughly immerse myself in my new product by getting face-to-face with a large number of people who could ask me every question and give me every objection in the book. They would teach me, with their questions and concerns, everything I would need to know to sell successfully.

It always worked! By the time I had spoken to a hundred people, I had overcome all my fears of rejection and I could hardly wait to get out and make more calls. And something else happened as well. For the next *year*, I would be doing business with people I'd called on in my first thirty days. With this simple method of total immersion, I moved to the top of every sales organization I ever joined.

You can use this method to rejuvenate your sales career, or start a new one. Just decide that, in the next thirty days, you are going to go out and talk to one hundred prospects about your product. Don't worry if they buy or not. Your very decision not to worry, not to put any pressure on yourself, will have you selling at your best. You'll make sales without even trying!

When I was leasing office space, I would take the elevator to the top floor of an office building and prospect at every single office on every floor, all the way down to the ground. When I was selling mutual funds, I would go from building to building and office to office looking for executives who would talk to me. When I was selling office supplies, I would call on every single tenant in every office building and industrial park I could find. When I was selling soap as a child, I would knock on the door of every house in every neighborhood within two or three miles of my home. Every time I started selling a new product or service, I would deliberately push myself past the fear of cold calling by doing it over and over until I got into the swing of it once again. After that, I learned at a rapid rate and my sales soon took off.

The way to use cold calling in conjunction with your other sales activities is to take advantage of the fact that, when you are calling on a prospect in a particular building or area, the other businesses nearby may also be prospects. Follow the old selling adage and "Make one call *more* at the store next *door*."

After you have finished the sales visit on your first prospect, go next door, walk up to the receptionist confidently and say, "Hello, my name is Susan Smith with ABC Company. I was talking to Mr. Jones of XYZ Company next door about our new office automation equipment and it occurred to me that this company might be interested as well. Is there someone here that I could speak to about arranging an appointment?"

The gregarious instinct among human beings is very strong. When people hear that someone in a nearby office or building is considering purchasing your product or service, they become curious and interested in learning more about it, and you will often get an immediate hearing and sometimes even a sale.

Many salespeople have had the experience of making a larger, better sale to the person at the "store next door" than they made to the original prospect. And since it costs you nothing to ask, make a habit of dropping in on the adjacent businesses whenever you are finished with a call on a particular prospect.

PROSPECTING TO LARGE ACCOUNTS

There is a distinct difference between the quantity and quality of prospecting that you do. Each is appropriate depending on what you sell and the number of prospects there are in your territory. If you are focused on making small sales to many accounts, you require *one* type of prospecting approach. If your aim is to make larger sales to fewer accounts, your approach to prospecting will be very different.

When you are selling small products with a short sales cycle and a smaller dollar amount, the number of calls you make is the major determinant of your sales success. When there are thousands of prospective customers in your market area, your sales volume will depend on the amount of ground you cover, the number of doors you knock on, the quantity of people you see. There is a direct relationship, based on the Laws of Averages and Probabilities, between the number of people you contact and the number of sales you will make.

When you are selling a large product with a longer sales cycle and a higher price tag, there will usually be fewer prospective customers in your territory. Each of these prospects is valuable, and it is especially important not to waste them by poorly prepared sales activities. Each prospect must be carefully analyzed and a strategy developed to penetrate each account.

If you are selling photocopiers, every office is a prospect. Your aim is to see as many as possible. But if you are selling data processing systems for large companies, there may be only ten or twelve prospects for your product in your market area, so a different approach is required.

The key to success in the small sale is *activity and exposure*. The key to success in the large sale is *planning and strategy*. The first step of the planned approach is prospecting, how you will initially approach the customer. Because larger prospects are so few and so valuable, nothing can be left to chance. You must thoroughly research the prospect organization and the key decision-maker before you call to arrange your first appointment. You must earn the right to discuss the large sale with your prospect by doing your homework thoroughly in advance.

Because each large account is so valuable to the total potential of your sales territory, you must prospect *indirectly* to gather the initial information you require to proceed with the account. Indirect prospecting involves your contacting someone in the company, preferably in a department separate from the department into which you will be attempting to sell your product or service. Just like storming an enemy fortress, your first job is to get inside. You must find a "vendor champion," a person who knows how purchasing decisions are made within the company and who will help you by leading you through the political intricacies of power and influence that exist in every large sale.

If you are going to be selling to the manufacturing department for example, you may call someone in the *accounting* department. Ask to speak to the manager and tell him who you are. Ask for a few minutes of his time to get his opinion on something that you are thinking about proposing to the company. Tell this person that you are not sure whether what you are offering is appropriate for the company and you would very much appreciate his comments or observations.

In this preliminary prospecting call, you do not present your product or service or make any attempt to sell it. Simply show him the idea or benefits that companies are enjoying from using your product and ask if he sees any relevance or applicability to his company. All you want at this point is candid feedback.

A good strategy is to call the receptionist and ask for the name of the best salesperson in the company. When you get in touch with that person, tell him or her who you are. Say that you are a salesperson as well and that you feel your product or service could be very helpful to the company that the salesperson works for. Ask for help. Tell the salesperson that you are not sure who to talk to or how to go about approaching the company. Could he or she give you some help or advice?

Salespeople are usually the most helpful people in any organization. If they are top salespeople, they are invariably people-oriented, supportive, and more than willing to guide you themselves or recommend you to someone who can direct you through the intricacies of the decision-making process. If the salesperson doesn't know, he or she will often check around and get back to you and let you know exactly what is going on. Often the salesperson will introduce you to the person who can become your "coach" on the inside. Often the two of them will work together, like blockers to help you move the ball down the field.

The rule in large sales is that you should never attempt to approach the decision-maker until you have established a foothold at a lower level with someone who will guide you in the sale. You must find someone who will introduce you to the person with the problem that your product can solve. If you attempt to sell without a friend inside the company who knows how things are done, and who wants you to succeed, you will almost invariably fail. Since all large sales are competitive sales, your competitor may get into the account by the simple act of finding someone who can help him *before* he approaches the real decision-maker.

In a large account sale, the more people you know within the organization that you are selling to, the more likely it is that you will acquire the invaluable tidbits of information that enable you to position yourself against your competition and win the business. The starting point is for you to find your champion and then follow his or her advice as you proceed through the sale with the final decision-makers.

You start the prospecting process with large accounts by identifying exactly who they are and what they might buy from you. Make a list of every company that you feel might be worthwhile for you to call on. Create a fact sheet or a file on each organization, complete with all the basic information you can find from the Yellow Pages. If it is a publicly traded company, phone and ask for a copy of their annual report and their 10-K report, both of which contain detailed information on the activities of the business and their plans and financial projections for the future.

Go to your local library and ask the librarian to help you find trade magazines and articles that have been written on the industry. Begin to assemble a research file exactly as if you were thinking of buying the company and you wanted to learn everything about it in advance of your initial approach.

Once you have done your research and preparation, you are ready to begin. Whether your goal is a large or a small sale, many aspects of the initial contact are the same. It almost always begins with the telephone.

TELEPHONE PROSPECTING TECHNIQUES

The telephone is a business tool It is like a car, a credit card, a fax machine, or a calculator. It is something that you must learn to use fluently and efficiently. Fully 99 percent of your initial contact and subsequent follow-up with your prospects will be by telephone. Telephone proficiency can make or save you an enormous amount of money.

Many salespeople are uneasy about telephone prospecting because they don't know how to do it very well. Others have unconscious fears that paralyze them and hold them back, which we'll talk about below. Here are some ideas on using the telephone to prospect to your best advantage.

The first thing to remember is that when you telephone your goal is only to set up the appointment. You are not *selling* your product or service at this time. You do not even discuss what you sell on the telephone unless you can take an order for it at that moment, as in selling securities, where you don't have to see the customer to conclude the transaction. Other than that, you must resist the temptation to tell the prospect about your product and get into a sales conversation over the phone. If you do, you'll almost invariably kill the sale.

Instead, phone the receptionist and introduce yourself. Ask the receptionist a question like, "Who is responsible for making the decisions in this particular area?" The job of the receptionist is to pass you on quickly to the correct person. Be open, honest, and direct. Be warm and friendly.

If the receptionist is not sure who is in charge of purchasing the product or service you are selling, or if it's difficult to get past the secretary of the decision-maker, you can use a top-down strategy.

Phone the receptionist and ask for the president of the company. You will be put through to the president's secretary. Introduce yourself with the words, "Hello, this is John Jones of ABC Company, and I need your help."

Virtually everyone is willing to help another person if they ask for it. Tell the secretary that you have an idea that can help the company save or make money in the months ahead and you are not sure who the best person would be to speak to. As the secretary if that would be her boss, the president, or should you speak to someone else?

The secretary will almost always help you by doing one of three things. She or he will know who is in charge of that department and will refer you to that person, transferring you and introducing you at the same time. Or, she will ask the president who you should speak to and get his recommendation. In either of these first two possibilities, the next person you speak to will know that this referral is coming from the president's office. This will usually get you a respectful hearing.

The third thing she might do is put you through to the president himself (or herself) so you can explain the reason for your call and have the president decide how it is to be handled.

Whoever you speak to next, your job is now to sell him on the idea of giving you *ten minutes* of his time. It is not to discuss or sell your product or service. It is merely to get an agreement to meet with you face-to-face for ten minutes to determine whether there is any advantage to going further.

THE KEY QUESTIONS YOU MUST
BE PREPARED TO ANSWER

Every prospect has a series of questions in his mind that he may or may not ask but which you must answer nonetheless if you are going to be successful in getting the appointment, and eventually getting the sale. The very first question you must answer, before you even get past first base, is, "Why should I listen to you?" The prospect is busy and continually approached by people who want to sell him things. Why should he listen to you?

Your opening statement should deal with the idea, benefit, or result of what you are selling. It should go right to the other end of the pipeline and deal directly with the chief advantage that your prospect will enjoy as a result of using your product or service. For example, you could begin by saying, "I believe I have an idea that could save your company a great deal of money."

For example, when I was calling on companies to sell sales training programs, I would open by asking, "Would you be interested in a proven method for increasing your sales by 20 percent to 30 percent over the next six months?"

If your opening question is phrased properly, it will trigger the second question from the prospect that you must answer to be successful in getting the appointment. It is the question, "What is it?" If the person on the other end doesn't ask "What is it?" after your opening question or statement, it means that either your statement is poorly phrased or the individual is not a qualified prospect.

For example, if you ask, "Would you be interested in cutting your paper costs by 20 percent with no loss in quality or efficiency?" and the prospect replied with something like, "How much is it?" Or, "I'm not interested." Or, "That's not my department," this would simply be an indication that you had called on the wrong person. The words "What is it?" in response to your introductory statement are the indicators that you are on the right track.

When the prospect replies, "What is it?" you say, "Mr. Prospect, that's *exactly* what I would like to talk to you about, and I just need ten minutes of your time. I'll show you what I have and you can decide for yourself if it applies to your situation. You be the judge."

To arrange an appointment over the telephone you must assure the person you are talking to of four things: First, that he or she is the right person; second, that your visit will be short; third, that you will use no pressure; and fourth, that the prospect will be under no obligation. The words, "I just need ten minutes of your time and you can judge for yourself," cover three of the four requirements at once.

The busy prospect will almost invariably ask, "Can you tell me about it over the phone?" Or, "Can you give me some idea of what it is about before we get together?"

The temptation to answer this type of question is a trap that will almost invariably destroy any chance you have of getting to see this prospect personally. The minute you share any information about your product or service with him, he will respond by saying things like:

"I'm not interested."
"I can't afford it."
"I'm happy with my existing supplier."
"We don't need it at this time."
"We already have enough."
"We're not in the market right now."
"Business is slow."

And the other things you've heard repeatedly if you've been in sales for any time at all.

When he says, "Can you tell me a little bit about it?" you reply by saying, "I'd like to but I have something I must *show* you." As soon as you use the word "show" you trigger the motivation of curiosity. The prospect goes from asking you questions to, "I wonder what it is?"

If the prospect asks you to mail some information to him, refuse to do so. Instead say, "I'd like to but you know how bad the mail is nowadays. Why don't I drop it off to you personally. I'll be in your area next Thursday afternoon. Will you be there?"

Repeat, "All I need is ten minutes of your time, and you can decide for yourself if this is the sort of thing you are looking for." If he says something like, "I'm really busy and I don't want to waste your time. Why don't you tell me a little bit about what it is and I can give you an answer right now." You can reply, "Mr. Prospect, all I need is ten minutes of your time. Hundreds (or thousands) of companies are already using our products successfully and once you see it, you can judge for yourself."

Sometimes the prospect will say, "Okay. Why don't you call me next week and we'll set up an appointment." Don't let him get away. Reply quickly by saying, "Mr. Prospect, do you have your calendar handy? Why don't we set up a specific time and day right now? Would next Thursday around ten o'clock be all right for you, or would Friday morning be better?"

(Don't insult the prospect, and start your relationship off on the wrong foot, by using the old *alternative time close* for the appointment. Years ago, salespeople were trained to say, "Would Thursday at ten o'clock or Wednesday at two o'clock be better for you?" Today, this is immediately seen as a form of manipulation and it turns the prospect off to anything else you have to say.)

If the prospect says, "I'd like to set a time right now but I'm not sure if I'm going to be in town on Thursday."

You reply by saying, "Mr. Prospect, let's manage by exception. Let's set the appointment for a specific time right now and if for any reason you can't make it, we can change it at that time."

In making appointments over the telephone, there is a huge difference between being *persistent* and being *insistent*. Most prospects respect a person who is gently persistent in nailing down a specific time and date. What prospects resent is an insistent or pushy salesperson who seems to be too aggressive and not sufficiently respectful or accommodating. As long as you are pleasant and polite, you can continue asking for ten minutes and gently deflect any attempt to get out of setting a firm appointment.

The telephone appointment with the new prospect is like the kickoff in a football game. It is the starting gun of the race. It is the opening bell of the process that will or will not lead to a sale. It must be planned and practiced and thought through in detail. Good, solid professional prospecting is the springboard to all great sales success.

FEAR OF PROSPECTING

Fear of prospecting is an important reason that salespeople fail to reach their full potential. As we've seen, when people respond to us in a positive way, we feel good about ourselves. When people respond to us in a negative or critical way, we feel hurt and angry. If we get too many negative responses to our prospecting attempts, and especially if we dwell on them continually, we can eventually demoralize ourselves right out of the sales business. By repeating the experience in our minds, we can eventually become so fearful and uneasy about the idea of calling on new people that we will avoid the activity altogether.

Here's an important point. It is normal and natural for customers to be initially *un*interested in what you have to say. Their normal response will be "No!" They are busy with their work and preoccupied with their problems. Your presence, either by telephone or in person, is an intrusion on their train of thought and an interruption to their daily activities. Their first reaction will almost invariably be to say, "I'm not interested."

The first thing you need to learn in selling is that *rejection is not personal!* It has nothing to do with you. The prospect does not even know you well enough to accept you or reject you. The prospect is not even aware of who you are or what you do. He is totally involved with his own life and his own situation. *Rejection is not personal.*

Laura Huxley once wrote a book entitled, *You Are Not the Target.* The title says it all. Whenever you find yourself dealing with a difficult prospect, remind yourself of those words, "You are not the target." ("I am not the target!") Don't take it personally. Let negative responses from prospects flow off you like water off a duck's back. Smile, shrug your shoulders, and get on to your next call.

The important thing is not to be put off by a negative reaction of any kind. You will experience a certain number of nos for every yes you receive. In the very best of markets, with the best of products, you will be turned down four out of five times. In a moderately difficult market, you may be turned down nine out of ten times. In an extremely difficult and competitive market, your rejection rate may be nineteen out of twenty. You can do everything possible to diminish the number of rejections you receive but you can never eliminate them altogether. Many of your very best customers will initially reject your overtures when you telephone or call upon them for the first time.

You could even define yourself as being in the "rejection business" rather than the sales business. For every rejection you collect, you learn something that makes you better and smarter on the calls ahead. If you collect enough rejections, you will become smart and experienced and make enough sales to achieve all your goals. The more you get rejected, the faster you learn. The more rejected you are today, the more of a great success you will be tomorrow.

THE PAVLOVIAN FORMULA

Ivan Pavlov, the famous Russian doctor and researcher, was the first person to demonstrate the power of the conditioned response. He would show a hungry dog a piece of meat and when the dog salivated and lunged toward the meat, he would ring a bell. After doing this for several days, he could just ring the bell and the dog would salivate and look around eagerly for the meat. By presenting both stimuli together, either would stimulate instant recall of the other. The dog had developed a conditioned response to the sound that made its actions predictable whenever that stimulus was presented.

You are very much the same. You are conditioned to respond automatically to a great variety of stimuli. You smell a favorite food and your stomach rumbles. You hear a friendly voice and you smile. You see an enemy, or even think about him, and you become angry. These are all automatic responses learned by a process of repetition and reinforcement over a long period of time. As much as 95 percent of everything you do is determined by habit, either good or bad, helpful or hurtful. The good news is that you can deliberately develop constructive habits that are helpful to your life and your career.

By using a simple proven process, you can *condition* yourself to look forward *eagerly* to prospecting, just as the dog looked forward eagerly to meat whenever the bell was rung. You can train yourself to think of prospecting in a positive, enthusiastic way. You can teach yourself to look forward to the opportunity to contact new people each day. You can train yourself with the *prospecting habit* in such a way that your success in selling will be virtually guaranteed!

There are four steps to the process. You must repeat them continually until you have developed a new habit pattern, a new way of responding whenever you think of prospecting. Step one begins with **self-observation.** Imagine that you are thinking about prospecting, and even looking at the telephone. You feel yourself becoming tense and uneasy. You start engaging in avoidance procedures. You go and get another cup of coffee, talk to other salespeople, read the newspaper. In the practice of self-observation, you would stand back from yourself and observe yourself engaging in these evasive behaviors.

In Buddhism, this is called "detachment." It is the process of rising *above* and standing *apart* from yourself mentally to watch yourself engaging in a particular behavior. As you disassociate or disidentify from the fear-induced behavior, you separate yourself from the emotion as well. You can then observe yourself with greater calmness and clarity. You can even say to yourself something like, "Look at him, going through those silly exercises to avoid something as simple as picking up the telephone (or calling on a stranger)."

In the second step, you perform what psychologists call a **pattern interrupt.** This is like knocking the arm of the record player off the record. You knock the tape out of your mental recorder. You break your negative train of thought.

You can do this in one of several ways. You can stand up quickly and shake your hands. You can clap your hands together loudly. You can pinch yourself, or even say emphatically, "Stop!"

With a pattern interrupt, you break the continuous reel of repeatedly thinking about calling and being afraid of calling, and then thinking about calling and being afraid of calling. You interrupt the pattern and jerk the tape out of the player, or the record from the turntable. Your mind will then be *blank* for a few short moments.

In step three, you quickly put in a new tape and get the **feeling of success and achievement** from prospecting. You do this by thinking about a person you called who became a prospect and then a customer. You recall and relive the pleasure of making the appointment, presenting your product or service, closing the sale and shaking hands with the customer afterward. If possible, get a Polaroid photograph of the business card of your favorite customer you met prospecting, and put it in front of you so that you can see it before you call someone new.

With this feeling of confidence and satisfaction filling your mind, you immediately pick up the phone and call the first number on the list. Go through the prospecting script outlined above. Be calm, positive, polite, and professional. Don't worry about a thing. Whatever happens, happens. Do your very best, smile into the phone, relax, and thank the prospect for his or her time.

Step four is to give yourself an **immediate reward** for having made the prospecting call. This can be a sip of coffee, a piece of cookie, a slice of donut, a candy, or even standing up and stretching while taking a deep breath.

When you give yourself an immediate reward right after doing something that you have consciously associated with a previous success, you reinforce the pleasure of the activity. You train yourself to actually look forward to the reward. You see, think, and feel *past* the action of prospecting to the pleasure of the reward that you will receive when you complete the action.

In no time at all, when you think of prospecting, you will involuntarily smile and feel happy. Soon, the very idea of prospecting will excite and enthuse you. You will look forward to it. You will have developed in yourself a *conditioned response* to the idea of prospecting. You will no longer need an immediate reward to be enthusiastic about prospecting, just as Pavlov's dog no longer needed to see or smell the piece of meat in order to salivate. You will also "salivate" every time you think of calling on a new person to talk about your product or service.

PUBLIC SPEAKING

As I said in Chapter 1, psychologists have also found that certain fears are bundled together in the subconscious mind very much the way electric wires are bundled together. Two fears that seemed to be bundled together in this way are the fear of rejection as it applies to prospecting and the fear of public speaking as it applies to standing up and speaking in front of an audience. By short-circuiting or burning out one of these fears, you can short-circuit or burn out the other fear as well. If you overcome your fear of rejection, you will become more relaxed and confident at public speaking. If you become relaxed and confident in public speaking, you will overcome your fear of rejection.

One of the best investments you can make in your career and in your future is to learn how to speak on your feet. According to *The Book of Lists*, fear of public speaking is the *number one* fear of adult Americans, ranking well ahead of the fear of death. More people's lives and careers are held back because of fear of speaking in front of others than because of any other single factor. And you can get over this fear if you really want to.

The way to overcome almost any fear is by "systematic desensitization." This requires you to do the thing you fear over and over again until you finally reach the point where it no longer holds any fear for you. You desensitize yourself to the activity by constant repetition until your "fear muscle" is exhausted.

In 1923, Toastmasters International was formed in Irvine, California, to help businessmen and women become competent in public speaking. The founders recognized that fear of public speaking was holding many people back in their careers and in their lives. They developed a system that has been modernized for the years and which is now taught in every chapter worldwide of Toastmasters.

This process is very simple. The group sizes are kept down to no more than thirty people (when the chapter becomes too large, it splits and another chapter is formed). With this small number of people, at every weekly meeting, every member gets an opportunity to stand and speak in front of the group. Exercises are designed to facilitate this purpose. Once a week, week after week, members stand up and give a thirty-second, sixty-second, or longer talk to the group, which is greeted by support, applause, and good humor.

Within about six months of confronting this fear every week, a person moves from being terrified of public speaking to being a relatively accomplished presenter who can design and give a talk with very little advance warning. When a salesperson learns to speak proficiently on his feet, he becomes far more dynamic, confident, and outgoing in dealing one on one with prospects. As his public speaking ability increases, his fear of rejection decreases simultaneously.

In less than a year, by learning how to speak on your feet through Toastmasters International, or by taking a Dale Carnegie course, you can become one of the most positive and effective salespeople in your company, or even your industry. By eliminating your twin fears of rejection and public speaking, you will liberate yourself and begin moving rapidly toward full self-expression in your work and private life.

MENTAL REHEARSAL FOR PROSPECTING

Many salespeople are nervous and uneasy when they approach a prospect for the first time. Even if you have followed all the instructions above, and you have arranged for an appointment at a specific time and place, you may become so tense and uneasy that you fail to function at your best. Fortunately, there are a series of techniques that you can practice every day to ensure maximum effectiveness when you get face-to-face with a new prospect.

First and foremost, you should **prepare thoroughly.** You should do your homework and learn every detail that you possibly can about the company, its products and services, the particular prospect, his position and background, and the factors affecting the prospect's business in the current market. The more prepared you are, the more confident and relaxed you will be when you finally meet with the prospect.

Second, you should plan to **arrive about ten minutes early.** Not only does this impress the prospect, but it also gives you a chance or organize your thoughts and make your final preparations for the meeting to come.

Third, you can reduce your anxiety by **imagining that you are independently wealthy** and that you are calling on this prospect as a courtesy to him on behalf of your company. Think that you would very much like to have this sale, but it doesn't really make much difference to you. Develop a healthy nonchalance about the outcome of the sales meeting, and refuse to get wound up or worried about something that you may, or may not, do or say.

The most important part of preparing for your first call is **mental rehearsal.** I've discussed mental rehearsal in Chapter 4 and I'll just briefly outline it again here. It is the technique used by all gold-medal-winning Olympic athletes, and by most top professionals in every performance field. Top salespeople use mental rehearsal regularly to make sure they perform at their very best by drawing on their subconscious powers in the sales situation.

You have arrived at your appointment a few minutes early. To use mental rehearsal, sit quietly in your car or in a nearby washroom, and close your eyes. Breathe deeply and relax. Inhale and exhale slowly five to seven times. This exercise will lower your brain wave activity and drop you down into the creative alpha state. Your subconscious mind will now be ready for programming.

In this relaxed state, which takes less than a minute to get into, *visualize yourself performing perfectly in the upcoming meeting. See* yourself through your own eyes as calm, positive, relaxed, and in complete control of yourself and the meeting. *See* your prospect as relaxed, positive, and very interested in what you are saying. Visualize the meeting moving progressively from step to step and ending with the ideal result you desire, either a signed order or an agreement to move to the next step of the sale.

While you are visualizing *affirm* to yourself the words, "This is a great meeting!" Repeat these words several times. Combine the words with the mental picture to give you a feeling of complete success and happiness. Continue to breathe in a relaxed way while you visualize and affirm the ideal outcome to the sales conversation.

The key to this entire process is for you to *get the feeling.* Imagine how *happy* you would feel if this sales meeting turned out exactly the way you are imagining. Create in yourself *the feeling of pleasure* that would go with the achievement of sales success. Hold that feeling in your mind in combination with the mental picture and the words you are saying. Enjoy the sensation. Experience the pleasure of accomplishment.

Once you feel that click and you get the feeling that you would have if the sales call were a complete success, you release the whole experience, like letting the air out of a balloon. Then you let go of the thoughts, the mental picture, and the words. Open your eyes, smile, and confidently walk in to the sales meeting.

The first time you try this, you will feel remarkably relaxed and confident. You will be positive and smiling. You will feel warm and kindly toward the receptionist and the prospect. You will feel very much in control of the situation. You will seem to do and say exactly the right things throughout the sales meeting. You will emerge from the meeting in most cases with exactly the result that you programmed into your mind before the meeting began.

FACE-TO-FACE: THE FIRST MEETING

You have arranged your first appointment. The prospect has agreed to see you for a few minutes. The prospect is usually busy and preoccupied. You are a little nervous and uneasy. You have invested an enormous amount of time and effort to get this far. The prospect has other things on his mind and is eager to get back to his work and his problems. A window of opportunity exists and you must be fully prepared to take advantage of this opportunity before the window closes. You don't have much time.

You must remind yourself that you are not here to sell anything. Your job is to discover whether or not this person is a "suspect" or a "prospect". You have only one mission: you must find out whether or not this person has a problem or need large enough for your product or service to satisfy in a cost-effective way. Uncovering this gap is your main objective. You must not allow yourself to be sidetracked into discussing your product or service, or onto any other issue.

You know from the previous chapter on the power of suggestion in selling that people judge you very quickly. Your first job is to make a favorable impression on the prospect. You want to establish rapport, lower resistance, and open the prospects's mind to talking to you and listening to you. Everything you do from the first moment you meet the prospect either contributes to or detracts from this central mission.

When the prospect comes into the waiting room, or when you are shown into the prospect's office, the very first thing you do is to smile, look him or her in the eye, shake hands firmly, and say, "How do you do? It's a pleasure to meet you."

This opening immediately marks you as a serious businessperson worthy of respect and attention. It lowers resistance and arouses curiosity. It causes the prospect to begin to be interested in your reason for calling.

FOUR GAMBITS TO OPEN THE FIRST CALL

There are four gambits you can use in the first meeting to continue the process of lowering resistance and skepticism. The first gambit is to open with **gratitude**. "Mr. Prospect, thank you for seeing me. I know how busy you are and I very much appreciate your giving me a few minutes of your time. I'll be brief."

Whenever you *thank* anyone for anything, you raise their self-esteem and make them feel better about you. Whenever you say "thank you" for something that the prospect does for you, you cause the prospect to like and respect you more.

The second opening gambit is **building expectancy.** This is very powerful. It arouses curiosity and interest and arrests the complete attention of the prospect. You say something like, "You are really going to like what I've got to show you!" Or, "What I've got to show you could revolutionize the way you do business." Or, "Our company has developed a process that can cut your computing costs in half within thirty days!"

Whatever you say, it should trigger the unconscious response of "That's for me!" or, "I can hardly wait!" If you are talking to the person whose job responsibility includes deciding on the product or service you sell, he or she will be eager to find out more about whatever it is you are selling.

The third opening gambit is **reversal.** You can use this when you sense a high degree of resistance toward you as a salesperson. This prospect may have had some negative experiences with pushy, aggressive salespeople and is very tense about finding himself in a similar situation.

You use reversal by opening with the words, "Mr. Prospect, before I begin, I want you to know that I'm not here to sell you anything. All I want to do today in our few minutes together is to ask you a couple of questions to see if there isn't some way my company can help you achieve your goals.

If you really want to impress the prospect, prepare a written agenda of three to five questions that you want to discuss with him in the time you have together. Give the prospect one copy of the agenda and tell him that these are the areas you would like to explore. Ask him if that would be all right. If he says yes, you can open with these words, "Before we begin, may I ask you a question? What exactly do you do here?"

When you deflect the focus of the conversation away from trying to sell him something and onto a series of exploratory questions, and then you ask him a direct question about his work and career, he will almost invariably relax and open up. From then on, focus all of your attention on him and his situation. Ask good questions and listen attentively to his answers.

Perhaps the most disarming question you can ask to relax the prospect and get him or her talking is, "How did you get into this business (line of work)?" Most people are fascinated with their career paths and if you ask him about his, he will usually be happy to tell you about himself, giving you an opportunity *to listen and build trust.*

The fourth gambit you can use at the initial meeting is to start with a **problem.** The very best sales presentations, either live or on radio, television, or in print, begin with a statement of the problem and then move to the solution offered by the product or service. It is the same at the initial meeting with the prospect.

You can say, "Mr. Prospect, health care costs are increasing at a rapid rate at every company in your industry. Our company has developed a way to get them under control and keep their increase to the rate of inflation."

With an opening statement like this, your prospect should respond with those magic words, "What is it?" This response enables you to flow into the next part of the prospecting meeting by saying, "Before we get started, may I ask you a couple of questions?"

When the prospect give you permission to proceed with your questions, you begin the examination phase of sales consultation, learning as much as you possibly can about the prospect's situation before you move toward your diagnosis and prescription.

THE TWO-STEP SALE

Unless you are selling a small, inexpensive product, it is difficult, if not impossible, to make a sale in a single call. You will almost invariably have to call back on the customer at a later time to take the sale to a higher level. Knowing this, you should look upon every initial call as the first of two or more calls and make it clear to the prospect that that is the way you see it.

This approach lowers resistance, increases curiosity, and makes the prospect more receptive to your product or service offering when you present it.

You say, "Mr. Prospect, what I would like to do in our few minutes together today is to ask you a couple of questions and get a little information from you in this area. Then I'd like to go back to my office and discuss your situation with a couple of our experts. At a later time, if it makes sense, I'd like to get back together with you to show you some ways that we could increase your sales (or cut your costs)."

You can paraphrase or improvise the words for yourself. But by assuring the customer that this first visit is merely *exploratory*, you will cause him to relax. He will answer your questions more fully and make the meeting more fruitful.

You can use the interview technique of the journalist by asking a series of questions and writing down the answers in plain view. At the end of your meeting, you can thank the prospect for his time and tell him that you would like to get back together with him in about a week with some ideas and recommendations. Would that be all right?

Each of the gambits described above makes you look and sound professional. They are the starting points to building long-term customer relationships. They are businesslike and efficient, and respectful of the customer's time. Most of all, they enable you to determine in the first meeting whether this person is a prospect. This saves both of you a good deal of time and enables you to either focus your efforts more on this customer, or get to another prospect with greater possibilities.

SUMMARY

The starting point of successful selling is successful prospecting. If you can't find someone to talk to who can and will buy your product or service, and pay for it within a reasonable period of time, you never get a chance to show you personality or to use your other talents and abilities.

Because of the increasing fragmentation and complexity of our marketplace today, the process of prospecting is more difficult and challenging then ever before. You are surrounded by prospects who can and will see you and buy from you, but because of the competition, it won't be easy. You will have to plan and prepare thoroughly in advance and follow the procedures outlined in this chapter.

These techniques and approaches have been developed over many years and are all field-tested and proven. They are simple, practical, and effective. Learning and practicing them will give you a distinct edge over your competitors. Your job is to think about your product and your customer carefully. It is to continually expand your sources of possible prospects. It is to do your homework in advance and to train yourself to be eager to call on new customers. You must become fluent on the telephone. You must use mental rehearsal so that you perform at your best in the sales conversation.

Finally, in the initial face-to-face meeting, you must impress the prospect with the fact that you are a complete professional, the kind of person that he or she can trust and open up to. By becoming an excellent prospector in every sense of the word, you dramatically increase your opportunities to sell more and more of your products or services to more and more customers.

9

HOW TO MAKE

POWERFUL PRESENTATIONS

The sale is made in the presentation. To continue the footfall analogy, prospecting is the kickoff and the presentation is the way you move the ball down the field toward the goal posts. It is the equivalent of running, blocking, and passing. It doesn't win the game but it is impossible to make a touchdown or field goal without them, and that is what you do in the presentation.

Most salespeople feel they are good at presenting. They may not like the rejection that comes with prospecting, or the stress that comes with closing, but they enjoy the conversation with the prospect that happens in between. And because they think they are fairly good at it, most salespeople end up doing it *poorly*.

As we have seen, most salespeople's idea of an effective presentation is to tell the prospect all the good reasons why he or she should purchase the product or service, often repeating information from the brochure or reciting the recommendations of other salespeople. They feel that as a result of being presented with all of these wonderful features and benefits, the prospect will be so impressed that he will get excited and buy. These same salespeople then wonder *why* it is that they are soon back out on the street not knowing whether they have made any progress and wondering what they should do next.

Presenting is like doing surgery. Like surgery, it is complex and requires a good deal of preparation and knowledge. Often the survival of the patient, or the sale, depends upon the sensitivity and dexterity of the surgeon, or the salesperson. A single slip can cost the patient his life or kill the sale. It is serious business and good surgeons, like good salespeople, are very serious about it. They leave nothing to chance.

More than in any other part of the sale, the presentation is where you demonstrate your ability to perform as a salesperson. When you are presenting you are "on stage." When you begin the presentation, you are entering into the "arena" of professional selling. You are all by yourself and just as the things that you say will count for you, the things you forget to say will count against you. Your job is to plan, organize, prepare, practice, and rehearse your presentation skills to the point where you can be absolutely confident that if there is a sale to be made, you can make it if you get a chance to state your case.

To sell successfully, you must do *four* things, over and over. First, you must find people who are capable of buying your product or service (prospecting). Second, you must uncover the problem or need your prospect has that your product or service can satisfy (qualifying). Third, you must demonstrate to the prospect that your product or service is the best-choice solution to his problem, and it makes economic sense for him to buy it (presenting). Finally, you must answer his questions and get commitment from him to take action (closing).

Almost four thousand books have been written on the subject of selling, exploring the sales process from every angle. And every one of them aims at helping the reader to be better in these four areas. In the pages to follow, you will learn some of the very best ideas and practices ever developed for becoming excellent in making effective sales presentations.

GAP ANALYSIS

The fact that a prospect *can* buy does not mean that he *will* buy. Ability to buy and *willingness* to buy are two separate issues. Just because a prospect can be better off with your product or service doesn't mean that the prospect will purchase it from you, or from anyone. The prospect may need what you are selling, but need is not sufficient. For the prospect to buy, the need must be great enough, your product or service must be the best choice available, and your prospect must be convinced that he will be substantially better off making this purchase decision than he would be if he did not.

As a salesperson, you are in the business of **gap analysis**. You are a "problem detective." Your job, somewhat like a police inspector searching for clues, is to find problems for which your product or service is the ideal solution. In a way, your product or service is a key. You make calls looking for locks that your key will open. In the prospecting phase, you insert the key and find that it fits. In the presenting phase, you twist the key and open the lock. In the closing phase, you turn the handle and push the door open.

Like a *verbal* detective, the tools of your trade are questions. You use them to get appointments, uncover problems, discover gaps between where the prospect is now and where the prospect could be by using your product or service. You then show the prospect how much better his situation could be by owning and enjoying what you are selling.

There is an old saying: "No need? No presentation!" Before you begin your presentation, it must be clear to the prospect that there is a distance between where he is without your product (his current reality) and where he could be with your product (his ideal future condition). The prospect must recognize that he has a need that is unsatisfied or a problem that is unsolved. The prospect must also feel that the gap between the real and the ideal is large enough to warrant him or her taking action.

Buying desire is in direct proportion to the *intensity* of the buyer's need on the one hand, and to the *clarity* of the solution represented by your product or service on the other. This process of taking the prospect from cold to lukewarm to hot is accomplished by the skillful use of questions that uncover the gap and then expand it to the point where the customer feels impelled to take buying action.

THE FUTURE BELONGS TO THE ASKERS

Questions are the keys to buying success. There is a close correlation between the skillful use of questions and success at every stage of the buying process. Questions are important at the *beginning* in finding prospects and they are important at the *end* in gaining a commitment to action. They are essential during the presentation for clearly identifying the customer's problem and clearly demonstrating how your product or service solves that problem in a cost-effective way.

In a sales conversation, the person who asks questions has the control. The best salespeople are invariably those who confidently and deliberately control the sales process, leading rather than following. The quality of your questions and your ability to ask them in a logical sequence is what demonstrates to the prospect that you are a complete professional, knowing what you are doing every step of the way.

Questions *arrest* attention. They reach out and grab the lapels of the prospect and jerk him toward you. For the length of time that it takes a prospect to answer a question, you have his total attention. It is not possible for someone to answer a well-formulated question and think of something else at the same time. The prospect is drawn more and more into the conversation as your questioning proceeds. If your questions are logical, orderly, and sequential, you can lead the prospect forward toward the inevitable conclusion that your product or service is exactly what he needs.

Telling is *not* selling. Remember, the average person speaks at 125 to 150 words per minute, but the average person thinks at 500 to 600 words per minute. When you are talking, the prospect can both listen to you and think of several other things at the same time. The more you talk, the more time the prospect has to think of objections, criticisms, doubts, fears, and all the difficulties and details of his personal life. But the instant you ask a question and wait quietly for the answer, the prospect's entire attention is focused on you. He cannot think of anything else while answering.

It is easy for salespeople to talk about their products or services, repeating the things they have read in their brochures. That's why most salespeople spend most of their time doing it. But it takes considerable foresight, planning, and imagination—and discipline—to organize your presentation around a series of well-worded questions.

The basic rule is that you should *never say a thing if you can ask it.* If you must answer a question or make a statement, remember that the average person's attention span is limited. He cannot hear more than three sentences in a row before he goes into mental overload. At that point, his eyes will start to glaze over and he will be unable to absorb any more of what you are saying.

To illustrate the limited absorbent capacity of the human mind to a seminar audience recently, I picked up a pitcher of water and starting pouring it into a glass. As I spoke about the need to give the prospect a chance to think about what they were saying, I continued pouring until the glass filled up and the water began spilling all over the floor. I continued to talk and pour and spill water everywhere until everyone got the message. Prospects need time to absorb and consider your message. *Telling is not selling.*

As we saw earlier, the biggest complaint of purchasing officers of major corporations is that salespeople talk too much. And what they like most is the salespeople who listen carefully to them. The salespeople they buy the most from are those who ask good questions and listen intently to the answers. The salespeople they respect are those who are always seeking for ways to help them do their jobs better as purchasing managers with the products and services the salespeople are selling.

One powerful principle in selling is that *listening builds trust*. When you ask questions, you get an opportunity to listen. And the more you listen, the more the prospect likes you and trusts you. The more the prospect likes and trusts you, the more *open* he is to listening to you and to considering your product or service seriously. This is why the future belongs to those salespeople who are the very best at asking good questions and listening attentively to the answers.

Ben Feldman, the legendary insurance salesman from New York Life, was once written up in the Guinness Book of Records as the greatest salesman in the world. In his best years, he was selling more than $100 million worth of life insurance one on one, to individuals, by using what has come to be called the "Feldman method."

Feldman said that his method was based on two specific activities. The first was his ability to ask the "penetrating question." This is the kind of well-worded and skillfully delivered question that immediately grabs the attention and arouses the interest of even the most skeptical prospect.

Once, when a prospect told him that he was not interested in life insurance, that he didn't need it, and that he was prosperous enough to do without it, Feldman paused and then said, "May I ask you one question? Will your *widow* be able to dress as well as your wife?"

This type of question would often stop the prospect cold. He would immediately say something like, "What do you mean?" Feldman would then go on to explain that, because of estate taxes and death duties, according to experience and statistics, if something were to happen to the prospect, his wife would probably be out of money and dependent on relatives within three years.

By this time, he would have the prospect's complete attention. He would then ask further questions, looking for the gap or deficiency in the prospect's financial situation that the prospect was not even aware of.

The second part of the Ben Feldman method was "finding the idea," using financial planning instruments, to solve the problems uncovered and brought to the prospect's attention with the penetrating question. Many of the very best salespeople in a variety of selling fields now use this two-step procedure regularly in their sales activities.

Whenever a customer asks you a question, he or she is taking control of the sales conversation. Instead of replying, you should smile, relax, and ask a question in return. When your answer a question with a question, you are gently taking the control of the sales conversation back into your own hands.

THREE TYPES OF QUESTIONS TO MAINTAIN CONTROL

There are basically three types of questions that you can use to open a sales presentation, develop rapport, uncover the information you need to sell effectively, answer objections, and call for action. The first and most common of these three is the **open-ended question**. These are questions that cannot be answered with a yes or no. They are a way for you to subtly but firmly guide and control the sales conversation.

Open-ended questions begin with the words, "what, when, where, who, how, and why?" A question preceded by one of these demands an expanded answer, which gives you a chance to learn more of the things you need to know to make an effective sales presentation. Open-ended questions require lengthier answers that give you an opportunity to listen and build greater trust between you and the prospect.

There is no end to the questions you can ask. Some examples are, "*What* exactly do you do here? *How long* have you been using this particular product? *When* did you start production in that area of activity? *Where* are you experiencing the greatest number of problems with that particular service? *When* do you anticipate needing a greater capacity in that area? *How* are things going in this part of your business? *Why* are you doing it that way?"

You should carefully plan your series of open-ended questions before you visit the prospect. You should write and rewrite them so that they are well worded and they demand good answers. You can even give a copy of these questions to your prospect and tell him or her, "These are the questions I would like to go over with you at this meeting."

Open-ended questions are sometimes called *divergent* questions. They open up the conversation and cause the prospect's thinking to diverge and expand. With open-ended questions, you can explore every aspect of the customer's situation as you seek a problem for which your product or service is a solution.

The second type of question is a closed-ended question. Closed-ended questions start with verbs, such as "are, will, is, have, did, and even contractions such as "aren't, didn't, won't." This is often called a *convergent* question. It brings conversation gradually to a convergence on a single point or decision. It is answered with a yes or a no. You use this question when you want to begin narrowing the conversation and getting specific answers that lead you to a conclusion or a commitment.

You can use closed-ended questions to get more specific answers. "*Will* you be making a decision within the next two months?" "*Are* you considering changing your suppliers for this product?" "*Is* this the sort of thing you are looking for?"

A closed-ended question forces the prospect to take a position. "*Do* you like what I've shown you?" "*Does* this make sense to you so far?" "*Would* you like to get started on this right away?" You use this type of question when you want to get clear answers and bring the sales conversation to a close.

The third type of question is a variation on the first two and is called the **negative answer question.** This is when a no means a yes to your proposition. "Are you happy with your existing supplier?" If the customer says no it means that he is open to considering a new supplier. "Are you getting the kind of results that you expected?" If the customer says no, it means that the customer is open to considering your product or service as an alternative.

THREE POWERFUL WORDS IN QUESTIONING

In addition, there are three powerful words that you can use in your questioning of the prospect. Each of these words requires ever greater commitment, from the least to the most. They are a form of verbal jujitsu and you can use them as you proceed through the sales conversation, from the beginning to the end.

The first is the word **feel.** When you ask a person, "How do you *feel* about that?" it is a very *easy* question to answer. Everyone has feelings. They are soft and intangible. They are easy to talk about. It is almost impossible not to express a feeling if you are asked for one. When you ask a prospect, "How do you *feel* about the current business situation?" or "How do you *feel* about the recent election?" your question is completely neutral. It will nonetheless generate a completely *emotional* response.

The second and more definite word is the word **think.** When you ask, "Do you *think* this would be better than what you are currently using?" you are asking the person to take a much more definite stand. You are in fact asking, "On the basis of your knowledge and experience, would this be an improvement on what you are doing?" People are a bit more hesitant to answer a "think" question but they are much firmer in defending their position after they have.

The third expression is **In your opinion.** The word "feel" is soft, the word "think" is harder, and the words "in your opinion" are the most definite and specific of all. When you ask, "*In your opinion*, is this the best choice of products to solve this problem?" you are asking the prospect to take a definite stand. If he says yes, he has made a decision to buy. Once a person has stated his opinion on a subject, he is locked into it. He will then defend and justify his decision rather than change it.

Well-worded questions are powerful tools in every part of the sales process. The more of them you have and the better you use them, the more competent you will appear and feel, and the more sales you will make.

THE CUSTOMER'S UNSPOKEN QUESTIONS

The customer has a series of questions that he may not ask aloud but which you must answer nonetheless. These questions lurk in the back of his mind and affect his feelings and responses toward you. Your failure to answer even one of these questions can be fatal to the sales process. You can do everything right and still lose the sale because you walked away without satisfying the customer on one of these points.

In the previous chapter on prospecting, we talked about two of these questions. The starting point of every sales effort is to answer the question, "*Why should I listen to you?*" If this is not clear in the first discussion or meeting with the prospect, the sales process will stop and the prospect will not be interested in talking to or seeing you again. He is simply too busy to play a guessing game.

The second question, which should be triggered in response to your approach or introduction, is, "*What is it?*" If you do not arouse the customer's interest and curiosity about the benefits of what you are selling in the first meeting, the customer will probably not take the time to see you again.

I sometimes ask my audiences if they have ever heard of a "three-year meeting." People in the audience immediately laugh because they know exactly what I'm talking about. After failing to address these questions in the first meeting, they have been calling back on the prospect for as long as *three years* and have been told that he is in a "meeting." They continue to call and the secretary continues to tell them that he has just gone into a meeting or he has just started a meeting, or that he is away at a meeting.

This happens because the customer is busy and when you call, he tells his secretary to tell you he is in a meeting so that he doesn't have to be impolite and tell you that he is simply not interested. You missed the brass ring on the first chance and it doesn't come around again. You failed to answer the key questions to his or her satisfaction and you don't get another chance.

The third question, which you must address throughout the sales conversation, is *"What's in it for me?"* People buy for their reasons, not yours. When dealing with a salesperson, customers are only interested in how they can *personally* benefit from what it is you are offering. Everything you do and say must be geared toward answering this question in some way, or the customer will lose interest and begin wondering when you will leave.

The fourth question that customers never ask aloud, but which you must imagine he is thinking is, *"So what?"* Your company has been in business for fifty years. *So what?* You've been at the same location for twenty-three years. *So what?* Your products are used by many of the biggest companies in the country. *So what?* The answer to *"So what?"* is the same answer as to *"What's in it for me?"* Every fact or piece of information you give must be tied to a benefit of some kind for the prospect.

Imagine there is a spotlight above the desk between you and your prospect. Imagine also that every time you talk about the prospect, and *what's in it for him*, the light shines on the prospect. He is the center of attention. The prospect is smiling and happy. The prospect is curious and interested. The prospect is open and receptive. The prospect and his situation are in the spotlight.

But when you start talking about yourself, your product, its features and your company, the spotlight swings around and shines on you. You are the star, the important person, rather than him. The prospect is in the shadow. His personal concerns are now secondary. He soon loses interest. He becomes bored and impatient. The prospect wonders how long you will be staying. The prospect begins thinking about his other problems and begins planning what he will do as soon as you leave.

When you ask an open-ended question, or when you talk to the prospect about what's in it for him, the spotlight swings onto the prospect again and the prospect once more becomes the center of the conversation. Your job is to keep the sales spotlight on him at all times by continually phrasing everything you say to answer the question, "What's in it for me?"

The fifth question the prospect wants an answer to is, *"Who says so?"* (other than you). Your answer can make or break the sale because of the prospect's experience with sales and salespeople in the past. Every customer has been misled by salespeople, so when you call on a prospect and begin a presentation, you should always remember that this particular prospect has been subject to years of puffrey from salespeople in the past. Everything you say is somewhat suspect, no matter how honest, experienced, reliable, or trustworthy you are. You are a "salesperson." You are expected to put the best possible light on your product or service. You are expected to blow it up, to puff it so that it looks and sounds better than perhaps it really is.

Often you will deal with a prospective customer who seems cynical, negative, and disenchanted. He will respond to you with caution and suspicion. He will sometimes roll his eyes when you make a claim for your product or service. He has probably been burned so many times in the past that he is extremely careful about being burned again. No matter what you say about your product or service, he feels that he has heard it all before. The only question he has is, "How much of what you say is really *true?*"

So after you have answered the question, "What's in it for me?" the prospect wants to know, "*Who says so?*" Other than *yourself*, who else, preferably an objective third party, says that your product or service is as good as *you* say it is? You must be prepared to answer this question right out of the gate if you are going to get a fair hearing from your prospect. As long as it is only you making claims about your product, there will be an invisible wall of skepticism and suspicion standing between you and your prospect.

The sixth question is, "*Who else has done it?*" Nobody wants to be first. No one wants to be a guinea pig. No one wants to be alone in purchasing and using a product or service. The prospect wants to know, "Who else has done it, other than me?"

Human beings have a herd instinct. We feel there is safety in numbers. We are more convinced that a product or service is good when we learn that lots of other people have already bought it and are satisfied with it. We don't want to make a mistake. We don't want to pay too much or buy the wrong thing. We have a fear of failure. But when you can show us that lots of other people have bought your product or service and are happy with it, it answers both questions, "Who says so?" and "Who else has done it?"

TESTIMONIALS—THE KEY TO MEGA-CREDIBILITY

In selling, you need credibility to get a hearing with the prospect. But as we saw in Chapter 2, you need *mega-credibility* to make a sale.

You need to be believable just to be listened to, but you need to be *extremely* believable and trustworthy for a person to take the risk of buying from you.

As explained in Chapter 2, one of the most powerful ways of all to build mega-credibility is by using testimonials in your selling activities. Very often, a good testimonial is sufficient in itself for you to get the sale. The most powerful testimonials are those coming from people who are similar or familiar to the prospect. People are inordinately influenced by learning that someone else exactly like them has already bought and enjoyed a particular product or service.

You may call on a company to sell a piece of equipment. The executive you are talking to is uninterested in what you are offering. Then you say, "By the way, your major competitor across town just bought *two* of these."

Your uninterested prospect will sometimes do a 180 degree turn and say, "I'll take it!" As soon as a person learns that someone else that he knows and respects has already bought it, he will often make the same buying decision immediately. He doesn't need to hear any more. If it's good enough for someone *like* him, it's good enough for him.

Remember the three types of testimonial: the letter, the list, and the photograph. Letters are extremely powerful in influencing customers. A letter from a senior person on the letterhead of a well-known company or organization attesting to the value and quality of your product or service gives you mega-credibility when dealing with a new prospect.

If you have enough testimonial letters in a specific industry, you can almost go from company to company in that industry making sales. And the more sales you make to similar customers, the easier it is to make subsequent sales. Many salespeople have made a single sale to a single company in a large industry and then used that sale as leverage with a testimonial letter to sell to many other companies in the same industry, one after the other.

You should carry a three-hole binder with plastic pages containing your testimonial letters. You should highlight the key phrases in yellow so that the prospect's eye goes directly to them when he pages through your testimonial book. You should then add letters to this binder at every opportunity.

The second type of testimonial is lists of customers. If you sell your products or services to a lot of companies over a wide geographical area, put together a list of fifty or a hundred or five hundred names of companies, in alphabetical order, that are already using your product. If *hundreds* of companies have already carefully evaluated your product offering, and in a competitive market decided to buy yours rather than someone else's, how can *this* prospect go wrong? These are obviously sophisticated companies with careful purchasing procedures. If they have all decided, on balance, to buy from your company, then it must be a safe, intelligent thing to do.

Then there is the photograph of a happy customer taking delivery of, or using, your product or service. A friend of mine sells residential real estate. One day, after she had sold a house, she took a Polaroid of her customer happily putting a "Sold" notice on the "For Sale" sign in front of the house. She put this Polaroid photograph in her listing presentation booklet the next time she went to call on a prospect. When they got to the photograph, the prospect immediately asked about the picture. She wanted to know all the details. Where was the house? How much was it listed for? How long did it take to sell? What was the sales price? Where were the people going to move to? The entire focus of the listing presentation came to bear on the one photograph of a satisfied customer whose house this saleswomen had sold.

From that day onward, she carried a 35mm camera with her and took several photographs of satisfied customers in front of their homes with the "Sold" notices. She had the photographs reproduced in 8 x 10 size and inserted in plastic pages throughout her listing booklet. Her listings and her income both skyrocketed. Everyone who tried this method had the same experience. The photographs seemed to sweep aside all reservations that prospects had about listing their houses with the salesperson.

Testimonials of all kinds are so important that it can cost you sales and money every day that you call on prospects and attempt to make presentations without using testimonials. They should be a key part of building the mega-credibility that you need to win customers in competitive markets.

QUESTIONS THAT DEMAND AN ANSWER

Other questions that customers want to know the answers to are: "How do I personally benefit?" "What is the payoff for me?" "What does the product consist of?" "What exactly do I get as a result of buying from you?"

I used to sell to the presidents of major corporations. These men often controlled thousands of people and tens of millions of dollars. They had entire executive staffs reporting to them. They did business on the world stage. As a young man, I made the fatal assumption that, because they were so intelligent and capable in their fields, they would readily understand what they got when they purchased my product or service.

I was soon jerked back to reality. I quickly discovered that just because they were experts and kings of industry in their own areas, it didn't mean they knew anything about my business or my products. They turned me down even if they liked my product because they didn't understand it. I soon learned that competence is specific to a particular job. Ever afterward, I took ample time to carefully explain all the details of my product and exactly what the customer would get in exchange for the money he spent. You should do the same.

The final question that customers ask without asking is, "How do I get it?" Again, you must never assume that your customer fully understands how your product or service is manufactured, delivered, installed, serviced, maintained, or replaced. One of the reasons there are so many noncustomers for products and services in the personal computer industry is that tens of millions of adults who could benefit from personal computers have no idea how they would go about selecting one and learning how to use it. Most people who sell computers mistakenly assume that their major customers are people who are familiar with the complexities of the personal computer industry. However, the biggest potential customer population doesn't even know how to turn one on.

In your presentation, you can lose the sale at the last minute if you skirt quickly over the details explaining exactly how your product is delivered to the prospect and how he or she can use your product for maximum benefit and enjoyment. Prospects do not like to admit ignorance or feel stupid. Rather than telling you that they feel a little bit unsure about how to purchase or use what you are selling, they will instead say something like, "Well, why don't you leave it with me and let me think it over."

Of course, many prospects have bought and used your product or service many times in the past. They are completely familiar with how it works and they need no explanation. Their primary concern is whether your product or service is the best choice for their need at the moment. You don't need to go into detail on how to use it. In many cases, you can mail the product or service to them at their home or office, and they can take it from there.

A good question for you to ask in the early part of your presentation is, "Have you ever bought or used one of these before?" Later in your presentation, you should explain to the customer in detail how you and your company will make sure that the product or service is delivered and installed to the customer's complete satisfaction. If possible, you can offer to accept full responsibility for seeing that the customer gets exactly what he paid for in a form that enables him to take maximum advantage of it.

In *Fortune* magazine recently, customers of a large computer company that was experiencing declining sales and revenues were asked about their experiences with the salespeople from this company. These salespeople were some of the best-trained professionals in the world. They had been given eighteen months of intense training before they were allowed to make their first solo sales calls. They had an average of nine years of experience in the field, supplemented by hundreds of hours of additional training. And yet they were making the error of failing to answer this critical question: "How do I get it?"

The consensus of the large customers interviewed for the *Fortune* article was, "They come in here with big smiles and firm handshakes, ask us how everything is going, and then they leave without ever taking the time to show us how to use their products to run our companies better." And one by one, the large corporate accounts were shifting their business to the computer firms whose salespeople were taking the time to show them how to get the very best value out of their purchases.

DIFFERENT STROKES FOR DIFFERENT FOLKS

Different prospects require different approaches. Most salespeople tend to treat other people as if everyone were exactly the way they were. When they talk about their products or services, they talk about the features of it that they personally find most attractive. When they approach a new customer or make a sales presentation, they become so involved in themselves that they are almost impervious to the fact that each person they speak to is different in certain ways and may require a different conversational style.

There are four basic personality styles in selling. If you can imagine a box divided into four smaller boxes with a line running up and down in the middle and running side to side in the middle, you can imagine the four quadrants of personality.

The horizontal line in the middle goes from introvert on the left to extrovert on the right. The vertical line moves from task orientation on the bottom to people orientation on the top. This gives you four styles: 1) people-oriented/introvert; 2) people-oriented/extrovert; 3) task-oriented/introvert; and 4) task-oriented/extrovert. These four styles are also called the relator, the socializer, the analyzer, and the director.

The Relator Personality

The **relator** is the first style. This person is slower-paced, quieter, people-oriented, slightly indecisive, and is most concerned about being liked by others and getting along as part of a team. This person is very sensitive with regard to the effect that any product or service purchase might have on other people. When you talk to a relator, you must slow down, be patient and sensitive, and expect this person to need a lot of input and reinforcement from others for a buying decision.

The relator cannot be rushed. The relator becomes uneasy if you talk fast or if you insist on a quick decision. The relator is concerned about the opinions of others and gaining the approval of others both at home and at work. When you present your product or service, you should emphasize how popular the product is, how much other people like it, how well it will fit in to the way things are currently being done, and how much other people will approve of this buying decision.

Be warm and friendly. Be patient. These people are slow to make up their minds, but they eventually do.

The Socializer

The second personality style is that of the **socializer**. This is the person with the extroverted personality and the strong relationship orientation. This person is often overexpressive. This person likes to talk about himself and about you. The socializer type is highly achievement-oriented. His surroundings will be decorated with plaques, trophies, and awards. He is very much into power and influence.

This is often called the executive personality. This person likes to organize and coordinate teams of people to accomplish a particular

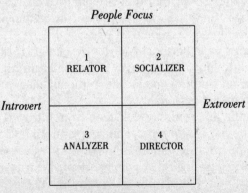

task. He is often highly imaginative, energetic, and conceptual. He bounces around a lot. He will make sweeping promises and commitments one day and completely forget them the next day. The socializer is most influenced by stories and testimonials about how other people have accomplished their goals by using your product or service.

To sell to this person, you need to pick up your pace as well. You need to focus on this person and be impressed by his or her accomplishments. You need to emphasize how your product or service will help him or her achieve greater success and recognition.

The Analyzer

The third personality style is the **analyzer**, the person who is introverted and task-oriented. This person is often found in accounting, administration, engineering, and computer programming. The analyzer is most concerned about accuracy and detail. He or she tends to be more concerned with getting the job done right than with anything else.

When you sell to an analyzer personality, you must be very specific about details. You must be measured and methodical in your presentation. You must provide proof and testimonials as to the accuracy of each of your claims. The analyzer only feels comfortable making a decision when he is absolutely sure that every base has been covered, every i has been dotted and every t has been crossed.

Our controller, for example, is an analyzer personality. In every test she takes, she ranks very high on "compliance." She sees her job as installing, following, and maintaining correct and accurate accounting procedures. When she was approached by a computer software company to buy their wares, her major concern was how their software could help her to produce higher-quality work in a shorter period of time.

When you sell to an analyzer, you must adjust your style. You must slow down and go through the details one by one. You cannot rush this kind of person for a decision. They need time to reflect and think. They will want to study your sales materials carefully and review your brochures with you before making a decision. They are very concerned about details.

The Director

The fourth major personality style is that of the **director**, the person who is extroverted and task-oriented. This person is usually found in entrepreneurial positions as well as in sales, sales management, and in other positions where specific, measurable results are continually in demand.

The director is most concerned about the bottom line, about getting the job done. He is impatient, direct, and to the point. He is not interested in details, but he wants straight answers. The director makes quick decisions and sticks to them. The director's only question is, "How will this help me do my job better and faster?"

The director likes to dominate every situation. He likes to be in control. He or she is invariably a leader and wants opportunities to perform at higher levels. The director looks upon your product or service as a possible springboard to higher levels of accomplishment. And this is how you must present it.

HOW DO YOU DETERMINE WHO THEY ARE?

You can usually tell what kind of a person you are speaking to by the kind of jobs they are doing, or the position they have in their organizations, and by their responsibilities. A human resources executive will tend to be a relator. An accountant will tend to be an analyzer. An executive in a creative field will tend to be a socializer, and an entrepreneur will tend to be a director.

You can also tell what kind of personality you are dealing with by the type of questions they ask. Relators will ask questions that revolve around how other people feel about your product or service, and how it will affect the people in their environment. The socializer will be interested in how your product can enable him to get better results from the people on his team. The analyzer will want to know exactly who has purchased the product before, and for what reason, and exactly what type of experience did they have? The director will be more concerned with increasing output and results than anything else, and his or her questions will be oriented to the bottom line.

As a professional salesperson, you will take the time to ask questions and listen carefully to the answers. By putting up your antenna and remaining sensitive to your customer, you will soon detect the kind of person you are dealing with.

You may also notice clues in the office or work space of each person. The relator will have plants and pictures of members of their family, and even cards and letters from their children. The analyzer will have a neat and orderly work environment with framed diplomas and certificates of their qualifications. The socializer, as I mentioned earlier, will have symbols of success and achievement. The director will often have a busy, even messy, working environment, with files and papers stacked on the desk, credenza, and floor.

The most important thing to remember about personality styles is that you must sell to people the way they want to be sold to. You must alter your approach and your selling style and get into step with the personality needs of your prospect. Everything you learned in Chapter 2 on relationships will serve you well in dealing with different kinds of personalities.

The Self-Actualizing and Apathetic Personalities

There are two additional types of personality that you will experience in selling. You will run into them on a regular basis though you will seldom see them described anywhere. They are the "self-actualizing" personality and the "apathetic" personality. They each represent about one in twenty prospects, or 5 percent of the prospect population. They have exactly opposite characteristics.

The self-actualizing personality is someone who knows exactly what he wants the minute you walk in. He has already done his research and his homework. He has a good basis of experience. He has thought it through. He is ready to make a decision immediately. He will ask you what you have, how it works, how much it costs, and how long it takes to get it. If what you have is what he wants and needs, he will make a buying decision immediately. He will give you a check, thank you for your time, and see you to the door.

After a sale like this, your head will be spinning. You will be amazed at how easy it was! You will almost feel as though you've *gotten away* with something. There will have been virtually no effort required on your part at all. You will think to yourself that, if you could talk to people like this, all day, every day, you would soon be rich. But remember, this type of self-actualizing buyer, who knows exactly what he wants and is ready to make a decision immediately, is very rare. Count yourself lucky when you occasionally run into one of them.

At the opposite end of the personality spectrum is the apathetic buyer. This is a person who is so far down that he has to look up to see bottom. This person is negative, cynical, bored, uninterested, and a real pain to deal with. He or she is a perennial tire-kicker, who never buys anything. You wonder why this person is even wasting your time.

Apathetic buyers are tiring and stressful to deal with. They drag you down. As soon as you realize that you are talking to one of them, you should politely disengage, thank him for his time, and get on to your next prospect as soon as possible. And from that point on, don't give him another thought. The apathetic buyer is the bane of the selling profession. And if you're not careful, he will cause you to doubt yourself and your capabilities.

BE YOURSELF

What I have discovered, in dealing with people of different personality styles, and different ways of processing information, is that if you relax and mentally prepare prior to each sales conversation, and then just go with the flow of your own nature, you will naturally synchronize your words and actions with your customers. You will do and say the right things at the right time, without trying.

If, on the other hand, you consciously try to be something you are not, you will feel uncomfortable. You will lose the natural spontaneity that builds and maintains high-quality relationships. Your behaviors will begin to verge on manipulation.

The minute you begin thinking about what type of person you are talking to and how you can adjust your personality to be more persuasive, you will start becoming insincere and unpersuasive.

It is important for you to be able to stand back from the sales conversation, almost like a third person in the room, and observe the interaction between yourself and your prospect. By thinking about your prospect for a few minutes after each conversation, you will develop an intuitive sense for the kind of person he or she is and for the little things that you can do to make him or her more comfortable in dealing with you. And this is all the effort you should make in modifying your personality if you want to continue selling at your best.

THE SALES PROCESS

Let's review the three basic parts of the standard sales process. They are: 1) establishing rapport; 2) identifying the problem; and 3) presenting the solution.

In the old school of selling, people were told, "Don't waste time with the prospect; just get right down to the purpose of your business!" However, we are now in a "high-tech market" that requires an equally "high-touch approach" method of selling. Any attempt to sell to a person without taking time to build a bridge will irritate him or her and ruin all your chances to make a good first impression.

The major aim of the rapport-building phase of the sales process is to get the customer to like you, to trust you, and to believe that you are acting in his or her best interests. It is to establish a certain level of warmth and confidence that causes the prospect to open up and be receptive to your message. If for any reason you cannot do this at the beginning of your first meeting, you should back off and arrange to return at another time.

A saleswoman was calling on a prospect one morning and arrived on time, ready to make an excellent first impression. She had initially contacted him by telephone and the conversation had been pleasant and professional. But when she arrived for the appointment, he seemed short-tempered, distracted, and fidgety. Instead of pressing forward with her presentation, she sensed that something was wrong and said, "I get the feeling that this is not a good time for us to talk. Would you feel better if I came back another day?"

The prospect, who was obviously going through this sales call out of a sense of obligation, immediately stopped and looked at her intently. After a few moments, he opened up and told her that a major customer had just called and canceled a large order, his boss was very upset, and on top of that, his secretary was out sick and he didn't know where anything was. He was really distracted, and he very much appreciated her sensitivity. She said, "I understand completely. Why don't I give you a call in a couple of days and let's set up another appointment at that time."

He was obviously very grateful. They shook hands and separated amicably. A few days later, he got back to her and they set up another appointment. This time he was relaxed, friendly, and in complete control. The rest of the sales conversation went smoothly and he became a long-term customer of this saleswoman and her company.

SELLING IN SEQUENCE—PRICE IN ITS PLACE

As we have seen, if the prospect asks you the price of your product or service early in the call, you should put off answering until later, especially since you know that giving him or her a price will likely end the sale. One very effective way to defer the price question is to simply say, "I don't know. There are several factors involved in calculating an accurate price and before I could tell you I'd have to ask you a couple of questions." Then, go into your prepared questioning sequence.

Unless your price is commonly known, or printed on all of your sales materials, do everything possible to put off the price discussion until later in the conversation. It is only when the prospect understands the full scope and benefits of your offer that price becomes relevant. If it arises any earlier, it may very likely become the focal point of the discussion and the rest of your meeting will be spent wrangling and arguing over how much your product costs and whether or not he can afford it or get it cheaper somewhere else.

STARTING OFF STRONG

One way to establish rapport, as we've seen, is to start off strong by telling him some of the most important qualities or attributes of your company. After you sit down, ask the prospect, "Do you know *very much* about my company?"

By using the words "very much," you will cause the prospect to say no. He may know *something* about your company, but he does not know *very much* about your company. And by asking the question, you have prepared the stage to answer it. You then give two or three qualities or accomplishments of your company of which you are quite proud and which are important for him to know in deciding who he is going to deal with.

A consultant made a presentation to our company recently by opening with that question, and this answer, "We are the largest single firm of our kind in the entire state. We have been in business for twenty-eight years and we are part of a worldwide group that includes 120 of the best companies in our industry. We have made our reputation by saving our customers at least $5 for every dollar we have charged in fees."

This was a very impressive, attention-getting opening. It distinguished him and his company as being serious players in this field and ultimately resulted in a large sale involving many thousands of dollars.

This consultant's presentation addressed three of the elements that will eventually have a major impact on whether the customer buys from you: your company size, how long your company has been in business, and your market share for your product or service.

The larger your company, the longer you have been in the same business, and the more people that are already buying your product or service, the greater the credibility that will attach to everything else you subsequently say. Your prospect will immediately recognize that he is dealing with a serious salesperson from a serious company with a long and successful track record of satisfied customers for the product or service you are there to discuss. This kind of first impression gives you the kind of mega-credibility that removes most of the prospect's skepticism in the first five minutes of the call.

Once you've set the stage, you continue to build rapport by asking two kinds of questions, personal and business. The more you ask a person about himself, and the more he gets the chance to talk about his personal life and experiences, the more he will relax and warm up to you. The more you listen intently as he talks about himself, the more he will like and trust you. By asking good personal questions and listening closely to the answers, you will be well on the way to establishing the kind of relationship that you will need later on to make the sale.

My friend Harvey Mackay, in his book *Swim with the Sharks*, talks about his "Mackay 66." This is a list of sixty-six personal questions that each salesperson must find the answers to in the first year of dealing with a new customer. At each meeting, the salesperson asks additional questions until the entire Mackay 66 is complete. From that point on, they virtually never lose that person as a customer. They know where he went to school, his favorite teams, the names, ages, and interests of his children, the birthday and name of his spouse, his anniversary, and a myriad of other details. They send birthday cards, flowers, tickets to sporting events, and other acknowledgments on a regular basis. They keep the customer for life by showing that they really care about him as a person, as well as a customer for their products.

However, a major mistake made by many salespeople is that they concentrate too much of their questioning on personal matters. This is because personal questions are both easy to ask and easy to answer. Customers love to talk about themselves, just as you do. You can ask personal questions for an entire hour and the person will expostulate at great length on his background, life, opinions, and experiences. At the end of your sales meeting, however, the customer is no better off than he was when the meeting started. He may have enjoyed the conversation, but he got nothing out of it. It was a pleasant interlude, but essentially a waste of time. And you have blown your big opportunity to begin transforming this prospect into a customer.

After a long conversation revolving around personal questions, the customer will be warm, friendly, and chatty as he shows you to the door. He will thank you for your time and promise to look at your sales materials. He will wish you well. And then he will go back to his office and he will never see you again. He will go into a three-year meeting. And it's not that he doesn't like you. He likes you just fine. But he has wasted a whole hour and he is too busy to risk another aimless hour of personal conversation with a stranger that leads nowhere and accomplishes nothing.

To build rapport you also need to ask business questions. These concern what the customer is currently doing in the area of the product or service that you sell. They are usually open-ended questions that start from the general and move to the particular. The purpose of asking them is to begin the process of finding a problem that your product or service can solve, or a gap that your product or service can fill.

When you ask business questions, you help the customer think better about what he is doing. You help him analyze his current situation. You help him begin weighing and balancing the pros and cons of the product or service that he is using and how it compares with yours. If the prospect has areas of dissatisfaction, your business-oriented questions help bring those areas to light. The more business questions you ask, the more the customer perceives you as a consultant, the more the customer senses that you are there to help him solve a problem or achieve a goal. As you ask good situation-oriented questions and listen carefully to the answers, you not only build higher levels of trust but you establish yourself as a professional who can answer the prospect's question, "What's in it for me?"

The approximate ratio for you to use is two business questions to one personal question. You start with predominantly personal questions and move gradually into asking predominantly business questions. Your questions move from the general to the specific. You ask something like, "What are you currently doing in this area?" And then, "How do you feel about the results you've been getting?"

The best salespeople ask twice as many open-ended questions throughout the sales conversation as the poorest salespeople. They develop a balanced dialogue with an easy ebb and flow of questions and answers. They are curious and interested, but they don't engage in interrogation. When they ask a question, they encourage the prospect to expand on the answer by nodding, smiling, and listening intently. They lean forward and nod agreeably to encourage the prospect to answer more fully.

Top salespeople practice a psychotherapeutic technique with their customers called "unconditional positive regard." This means that they remain completely nonjudgmental. They do not evaluate or judge anything the prospect says. They remain pleasant and supportive but neutral. They allow the prospect to say anything he wants, about anything or anyone, but they neither agree nor disagree. They neither feed nor starve the conversation.

Good salespeople are careful to avoid talking about subjects of an emotional or controversial nature, such as politics, religion, or their personal lives. If a prospect introduces these subjects, the sales professional will listen, acknowledge, and comment noncommittally. For example, the prospect could say, "Those idiots in Washington are going to ruin the economy!" You could reply, "You just never know what they are going to do next."

Top salespeople are invariably pleasant, positive, and easygoing. They are relaxed and smiling, and they sidestep controversial issues. They don't allow themselves to get distracted from the purpose of their call. They know that time is valuable and they do everything possible to avoid wasting it by talking about things that have nothing to do with their product or service. And if you don't feed a subject by getting embroiled in it and commenting on it, it tends to die away of its own accord. You don't want your time used up talking about things that don't help your sale.

PROBLEM IDENTIFICATION

Your ability to clearly identify the exact problem that your product or service can solve in a cost-effective way is the key to sales success. The two types of questions you use to help identify the problem and show that it is a large enough problem to be worthy of solving are *situation* questions and *meaning* questions. You probe with additional situation questions to get a deeper understanding of exactly what he is using, what he is using it for, and what shortcomings it might have. Sometimes people are reluctant to admit that their situations are less than ideal. They will say, "We're not really in the market right now, but we're interested in learning more about what is available for the future." Or, "We're quite satisfied with our current supplier but we like to talk to others just to keep current."

You would respond by saying, "Mr. Prospect, your current supplier, ABC Company, is an excellent organization. They've been in business many years and they are very successful with their products. However, we have an approach to this situation that is different from theirs and that is causing many of ABC's best customers to switch over to us. Let me show you what I mean."

You then go on to explain a relative strength of your company in the situation under discussion. Once you've done that, you go back into your questioning process to find out more about what it is the customer is doing and what it is he is really trying to accomplish in the particular area where your product is relevant.

What are their overall problems? What are their specific problems?

If they could change any one thing in that particular area, what one thing would it be? Keep probing and keep looking for the opening that shows you the problem you can solve.

The second type of question in this phase are *meaning* questions. When a prospect says that he has a problem with a piece of machinery or a business process, you ask questions such as, "What does that mean to you? How much does that cost you? How many other people does that affect? What is the real cost of production delays that occur when that machine breaks down? What are the indirect costs associated with a piece of machinery that doesn't work the way it's supposed to?"

Prospects are also motivated by the pleasure principle. They move away from pain and toward pleasure. They move from discomfort or dissatisfaction toward comfort or satisfaction. They only act when they feel pain. Your questioning is meant to reveal "where it hurts." Your follow-up questioning is aimed at taking a minor discomfort and turning it into a potentially major discomfort. It is to open the prospect's mind to his need to do something soon to solve this particular problem rather than letting it continue. By questioning skillfully, enlarging the problem, and by helping the prospect see your product as the ideal solution, you can create sales where no sales existed.

PRESENTING THE SOLUTION

The third phase of the sales process is presenting the solution. This phase includes the entire sales presentation. It is made much easier by the accurate diagnosis you have done in the problem identification phase. In the presenting part of the sales process, you show the prospect how your product or service can solve his or her problem in a cost-effective way. You show the prospect how he can achieve his goal faster and more dependably by using your product than he could by using any other, or than by using nothing at all. You show your prospect what your product does, how it works, and you answer that key question, "What do I get?" by bringing the whole presentation to bear on answering the question, "What's in it for me?"

I'll deal more thoroughly with the presentation process below. The most important thing for you to remember at this stage is that you must follow each phase of the selling process in order. You must first develop rapport by using good personal and situation questions. You go on to problem identification by asking more penetrating questions and exploring the real cost or meaning of the problem or gap you have uncovered. You proceed to the presentation of the solution once you and the customer are perfectly clear that a problem worthy of solving has been identified.

It is only at the end of this three-part process that price should enter the discussion. We'll talk more about how to deal with the price question in Chapter 10.

THE BUYING PROCESS

Just as you follow a specific sales process from beginning to end, every customer follows a specific buying process as well. This process may be conscious or unconscious. Since you are a customer when you buy things, you are well aware of this process, even if you haven't clearly articulated it in the past.

The buying process has three parts or stages. The first stage is when the customer realizes that he has a *need* for a particular product or service. Until the prospect crosses that line in his mind, he is not a candidate for what you're selling. Most people that you speak to initially have not crossed that line. They have no idea that they even need your product or service. This is why they say things like, "I'm not interested," or, "I'm not in the market," or, "I can't afford it."

The second stage occurs once he realizes that he needs a product or service to solve a problem or improve some part of his life. He then looks at what is available in the market and begins evaluating and *comparing various alternatives.* The more expensive the item or the greater the complexities of the purchase, the more information gathering and comparison the prospect will do before making a decision. Finally, in the third stage of the buying process, he resolves any lingering questions he might have about the choices available and *makes a decision.*

For example, when the average person buys a car, he first concludes or recognizes that he needs a new car. He then proceeds to the second phase and visits an average of ten dealerships before deciding upon the exact car he wants. He narrows the ten dealerships down to about three that offer the particular car he has decided upon. He then proceeds to phase three where he compares the three dealerships against each other on the basis of model, color, price, and trade-in value for his existing car, though not necessarily in that order of importance. When he determines which of the dealerships offers the best combination of these ingredients, he makes his buying decision.

As a customer, you will follow very much the same process whether you are buying a house, an accounting system, a new computer, a batch of chemicals, a machine tool, an airplane, or anything else. You recognize the need, compare among the options available, and make a decision. To sell effectively, you must get in step with your customer and sell the way your customer buys.

The second phase in the selling process, problem identification, corresponds to the first phase in the buying process, that point where both of you realize that the customer has a need. As you ask your prospect questions related to his current situation, you uncover a problem that your product can solve. You begin to create a mental gap between where the customer perceives himself to be and where the customer could be. You begin to create a sense of dissatisfaction or discomfort in the customer. As you widen this gap with your questions, you begin to point out the virtues and values of your solution and how much better off your prospect could be if he was owning and enjoying it.

Here's the rub. Very often you will open the prospect's mind to the awareness that he needs the product or service you are selling. You will go on to show how your product or service is ideal for his needs. He will apparently be convinced and you will feel that a sale is at hand. Then, unexpectedly, the customer will thank you very much, ask you to leave your materials and proposal, and suggest that you get back together again at a later time. He will show you to the door and thank you for coming in. What has happened?

What has happened is that the specter of *risk* has raised its ugly head. Customers don't buy expensive items without checking around to make sure they are getting the best possible deal. If you are not careful at this point, you can make a sale for your competitor. You can arouse the customer's desire to buy what you are selling and then the customer will call your competitors to get rival proposals. Instead of becoming the primary supplier of your product, you become just one more party to a bidding war.

In this second phase of the buying process, where the customer gathers as much information as possible so that he can evaluate the options and alternatives available to him to solve the problem, you have an excellent chance of winning the sale. But you must know what to do and you must do it well.

Your job is to help the customer make a good buying decision. To do this, at this stage of the sale, you must position yourself as a consultant and as a business advisor, rather than as a salesperson. You must 'sit down and work with your customer to help him define clearly what is important to him in this buying decision. A product or service may have a dozen features and benefits and be capable of doing many things for the customer. But from the customer's point of view, the decision will center on seldom more than three to five items.

THE LAW OF FOUR

The Law of Four says that most purchase decisions and negotiations revolve around the resolution of *four key items*. There is the *major* item that is most important of all and there are three *minor* items. The major item becomes the hot button or key reason for making or not making the sale. Your job is to help the prospect identify the three to five items upon which he will base his purchase decision.

When you or anyone makes a buying decision consciously, the first thing you do is decide exactly what you want to be included in the purchase. The second step you take is to organize the items by importance, from the most important to the least. Your third step will be to compare the various options available to you against the things you want and their order of importance, and your fourth step will be to make a decision based on this comparison. If you can help your prospect to complete the first two stages, you can often control the sale and make sure that, when the customer compares your product with your competitors, your product comes out on top.

If your customer decides that the most important item in making the buying decision will be a feature in which you are weak but your competitor is strong, you must show the customer that your areas of strength are really more important than he realizes. You must demonstrate to him that he gets what he really wants by choosing your product rather than that of someone else.

For example, if your customer says that price is his chief important priority, all things being equal, you would point out to your customer that there is a difference between price and *cost*. Price is the amount that you pay to acquire the item initially. Cost is the actual outlay over the life of the item. You may show that, although your price is slightly higher on the front end, the customer's total cost of owning this item over its lifetime will actually be lower because the higher quality assures fewer breakdowns and more consistent levels of productivity.

If your prospect says that speed of output is his greatest concern and your product is slower but more solid and durable, you would show your prospect that what he is really concerned with is the quantity of output over a given period of time rather than the speed at any given moment. You could show that your product, although slower, operates with fewer breakdowns and actually produces more units, with greater dependability, in a specific time period, than a machine that operates faster but which has more service problems.

It is important for you to demonstrate to your prospect that your strengths are what the prospect actually wants and needs, and your weak areas are not important to the buying decision. Because you know what your competitors are offering, you can discuss their relative strengths and weaknesses knowledgeably. You can point out that other companies (unnamed in your discussion) approach this product or service offering differently, but that, on balance, your product represents the best choice and the lowest risk for his particular situation.

When you know that your prospect is going to shop around before making a decision, the last thing you say to him before you leave is, "Whatever you do, your most important consideration should be . . ."

You then insert your **unique selling proposition,** your strongest point, your competitive advantage, and your area of excellence. You leave your prospect with the final thought that, whatever he does, his most important consideration must be just what your particular product does best. This will cause your prospect to remain focused on this particular element whenever he evaluates the offerings of your competitors.

The third stage of the buying process is the finalization of details, the resolving of concerns, and the answering of remaining objections. Again, the bigger the buying decision, the more likely it is that there will be small but critical issues unresolved at the point of making the final choice. You can have a sale 95 percent closed and still lose it if you fail to follow through on this endgame of selling.

If you have built a strong relationship at the beginning of the sales process, this will be where it counts the most. When you feel that your prospect is hesitating or hedging for any reason, you go back to him personally and ask him how things are going. When does he think he will be making a decision? Does he have any questions or concerns that you might be able to clear up?

If you don't get some kind of an answer, look him right in the eye and say something like, "Bill, what's the real reason you are hesitating on this purchase?" And then remain perfectly silent.

Very often, this will trigger the answer you are looking for. Whether it is small or large, follow up by asking, "What would it take to satisfy you on that point?"

This is called the "closing condition." Once he has given you this closing condition, and you have probed it to be sure that this is the real reason he is hesitating, your job is to provide him with what he needs to go ahead. If you can satisfy him on this point, you are ready to conclude the transaction.

THE HOT BUTTON IN SELLING

We've seen that there is a big difference between customer *wants* and customer *needs*. The customer may obviously need what you are selling, but not necessarily want it. The customer may want a particular product or service, but not necessarily need it. A need is often logical and measurable. A want is emotional and intangible. To make the sale, you must offer your product or service in such a way that the wants and the needs of the prospect converge on the same decision.

A person with a family may need a four-door car or a station wagon, but he really wants a sports car. He may need insurance to protect his family but he really wants a feeling of security. He may need a particular product or service in his business, but what he really wants is to own the product or service that the larger companies in his industry are already using. He may need what you are selling, but he may want to buy from the largest company in the industry. Many salespeople confuse these two and then become frustrated when the prospect does not respond to a presentation based solely on satisfying the prospect's needs.

The hot button, being emotional, can be triggered by an appeal to the prospect's desire for status, respect, recognition, prestige, or personal enjoyment. Some customers are motivated by wanting to be on the cutting edge, using products and services that are the most technologically innovative. These are their hot buttons.

Other customers want to be seen as creative, entrepreneurial, and advanced in their choices. Sometimes, the hot button can be the fact that the product or service offers greater speed, convenience, or savings. The hot button can be aesthetic in that the customer is motivated by the attractiveness or beauty of the product. Whatever it is, the prospect will reveal it to you if you ask questions skillfully and listen to the answers behind the answers.

Whether you are prospecting indirectly, to find a coach or champion in the organization who can guide you to the correct decision-maker, or whether you are speaking directly to the person who can purchase your product or service, in either case you must find out what interests or excites the prospect, what he really wants, and then concentrate on demonstrating overwhelmingly to him that he will receive that key benefit when he buys your product or service.

Whenever you talk to another person, he will be thinking about what is most important to him at the moment. If you listen carefully the prospect will often let slip the key words or phrases about your product that will guide you to the hot button. He will use emotional words in reference to your product that will give you clues to how he really feels about the various benefits your product offers. You must note these emotional words, even writing them down so as not to forget them, and work them back into your conversation as you describe your product or service in greater detail.

Customers use neutral or bland words to indicate that they are not emotionally involved in the sales conversation. They use emotional words when you have presented something that has touched a nerve. When a customer says, "This looks very interesting," he is saying that he is not very interested at all. But when a customer says that a particular feature or benefit is "fascinating" or "remarkable" he is saying that you are coming close to addressing his emotional agenda.

You can intensify his desire by using the same words later, by describing that particular aspect of your product as, "This is a remarkable breakthrough," or, "This is really fascinating when you think about it."

When you repeat his emotional words and phrases in your sales conversation, the prospect becomes more and more excited with what you are selling. And in every case, addressing the prospect's emotional agenda means talking to him about what he really wants, as opposed to what he needs.

Every person in every occupation has a set of emotional needs that go beyond doing their job well. These emotional needs almost always revolve around respect and recognition from their superiors. Whenever you describe your product or service in terms of how impressed others will be, how much more they will respect him for having made this decision, and how much better he will look to the important people in his business, you arouse greater buying desire and make the prospect think more and more about how he will personally benefit from buying your product or service.

How do you find the hot button? Sometimes the prospect is clear about the element of your product or service that turns him on. Sometimes he is unclear or uncertain. Sometimes he doesn't know, and you will have to discover the hot button before you can begin to press it repeatedly.

There are a series of questions that you can use to uncover this chief buying motive. You can work them into your sales conversation at appropriate times.

The Hypothetical Approach

The first is the hypothetical question. "Mr. Prospect, if *ever* you were to purchase this product, even five or ten years from now, what would you have to be convinced of *at that time* before you could go ahead?"

This kind of a question helps your prospect to think. His mind will immediately do a search, comparing and evaluating what he knows about your product or service with his life or work situation. His answer, whatever it is, will usually be his hot button. If you can then convince him that he will receive that particular benefit by purchasing *today*, you can often go on to make the sale.

For example, the answer could be, "I'd have to be assured that other people in my position in similar companies have already bought and used this product satisfactorily."

Your job will then be to demonstrate, through testimonials and references, that other people similar to him, in similar situations, have already bought your product and are happy with their decisions. By giving a satisfactory response to his or her answer to your hypothetical question, you will have removed the main roadblocks to the sale and pushed the hot button simultaneously.

The Magic Wand Technique

If the customer is hesitant, or resistant to your presentation, a second method you can use is called the "magic wand" technique. You say, "Mr. Prospect, if you could wave a magic wand and get exactly what you want, what would be the ideal outcome to you of buying this product?" Be quiet at this point and give the customer time to think. Allow him to reflect on your question and on his possible answer. When he does answer, probe a little further and ask questions like, "How do you mean?" or, "Exactly how would that affect you?"

By encouraging your customer to visualize and project forward to an ideal future state, using your product or service, you will often uncover the key benefit that you must convince him of to get the sale today. Prospective customers usually enjoy this process of visualing the ideal benefit or result of using a particular product or service. Of course, if he can't think of one, it will be almost impossible for him to buy what you are selling.

Measuring Your Progress

A third question you can ask to uncover the hot button is, "Mr. Prospect, let me ask you a question. On a scale from one to ten, with one meaning that you would never buy this product and ten meaning that you would take it right now, where do you feel you are at this moment?"

Almost anyone can answer this type of one-to-ten question with regard to how they feel about a product offering. If the customer comes back and says, "Right now, I'm at a one or a two," this means you have very little chance of making a sale. The customer is simply not in the market at this time. It is not a good use of your time to press the issue.

But if the customer comes back and says, "Well, I feel that I'm at about a five or a six," this means that the prospect is interested but still has considerable misgivings. You then ask, "Mr. Prospect, what would it take for you to be at a ten, right now?"

Again, remain silent. Wait and listen. If your customer can formulate an answer, he will tell you exactly what you have to convince him of at this moment to make the sale. He will give you the closing condition.

He might say, "Well, I would have to be assured that if it didn't work, I wouldn't be stuck with it."

You could then say, "If we could guarantee that you would be completely satisfied or we would take it back and refund your money, would you be willing to go ahead with it right now?"

The prospect will often agree to go ahead because you have satisfied his closing condition. You have removed his major objection and pushed his hot button with the key benefit that your product or service offers. At the very least, you will have a much better sense of what you need to convince him of in order to get the sale.

Give It Away (Sort Of)

Another technique you can use with a difficult prospect, especially someone who is resisting you on the basis of price, is to ask, "Mr. Prospect, would you take this product from us if it were *free*?"

This is such an unusual question that the prospect will be startled. He or she will think for a few seconds and then say, "Well, if it was free, I would take it!"

When he says this, you pause, smile, and looking the prospect right in the eye, you ask, "Why?"

You then remain silent and wait for his answer. If he gives you an answer, he will be revealing his hot button and telling you what he must be convinced of getting before he will buy your product.

For example, imagine you were selling an investment program. When you ask your customer the above question, he could respond by saying, "If it was free, I'd take it and put it in the name of my daughter to make sure her college tuition was covered by the time she finished high school."

You have touched the hot button. You now know the most important reason why he would buy this investment program. Your job is now to convince him that what you are selling is the very best choice for him at this time to achieve the particular goal that is so close to his heart.

Each time you explain how your program works, you mention the benefit to him and his daughter of that particular feature in terms of college tuition. Each time you mention his daughter and college, his buying desire will increase. By the end of your presentation, he will be eager to get started so that he can begin enjoying the feeling of having provided for one of his most keenly felt responsibilities.

Uncovering the Prospect's Buying Strategy

A final way of uncovering the prospect's hot button and overcoming his resistance is by asking him how he goes about making a purchase like this, or how he has done it before. You might ask, "Have you ever bought a product or service like this before?"

If he has, you then ask, "How did you go about making your decision? How did you know it was the right decision at that time? What steps did you follow to come to your conclusion?"

Every person has a buying strategy for particular products or services. It may involve listing the most important factors desired in the purchase, discussing it with other people, comparison shopping with a variety of suppliers, careful evaluation of the sales literature, negotiating the final terms and conditions, and so on. By asking the prospect how he has gone about buying a particular product or service in the past, either yours or something similar to yours, he will tell you the process that you must follow to sell him in the present.

People are creatures of habit. They do what they have done in the past and what they are comfortable with. They prefer the familiar way of working through a major decision and are reluctant to change. They get into their *comfort zone* and you must get into their comfort zone with them. You must present your product or service in a way that is consistent with how he has made decisions and how he has bought on previous occasions. By getting in step with your prospect and structuring your presentation so that it dovetails with the way he is most comfortable buying, you will find that making sales becomes easier and easier.

Many salespeople make the mistake of trying to sell without ever asking the prospect how he or she goes about making this kind of a decision. For example, a prospect might say, "Once I've decided I need a particular product, I get bids from at least three suppliers and then I have my team evaluate the bids before we make a final decision."

If you are the *first* vendor to talk to this customer, you might destroy your chances of making the sale by trying to get the customer to purchase your product before he has had a chance to evaluate the other two suppliers. You would be much better off by making an excellent presentation, encouraging him to check with other suppliers, and then close your presentation with the assurance that, "Whatever else you look at, I promise you that we'll take better care of you than any other company in the market."

When you close your meeting with this low-pressure, no-pressure ending, you will be investing correctly in a long-term relationship, building trust, and selling professionally—all at the same time.

The customer will often tell you what his hot button is by the kind of questions he asks. If he keeps coming back to a particular feature of your offering, asking for more details, or requesting more information on how other people have used and benefited from this particular feature, it will soon be clear to you what is most important to him.

Once you have found the hot button, you must bring the whole sale to hang on this one particular point. You must convince him overwhelmingly that if he buys from you, he will definitely get the key benefit that he is talking about. Whenever he raises other objections, you bring his attention back to this key buying feature as being the predominant reason your product or service is the very best choice for him among those that are available.

Another good way to press the hot button and to reinforce his desire for what you are selling is with what is often called the "relevant story close." The relevant story close or approach is based on the fact that people think analytically with their left brains but make buying decisions with their right brains. The left brain is stimulated by facts and information presented in a linear fashion. The right brain is stimulated by stories, anecdotes, and images. When you tell a story about another person who has used your product or service, or failed to use it, you activate the prospect's right brain and make a much stronger impression on him than all the sales literature in the world.

If you look at your own buying experience, you will find that the stories that salespeople told you about others who had bought the same product remain with you months and even years after you made the buying decision. You will have forgotten all the information contained in the brochures and product literature, but you will still remember the stories almost as vividly as if you heard them yesterday.

Whenever you want to reinforce the wisdom of the prospect buying your product or service, tell a success story about someone else who bought it and used it and was very happy as a result. If the prospect is hesitating you can say, "I understand your hesitation. You remind me of Bill Smith at ABC Company, who was also hesitant about buying our product. He decided to go ahead anyway and just last week he told me that it was the best buying decision he ever made. He said that the value and enjoyment he has received from our product greatly outweighed the small additional cost. He's now thinking of buying two more and has recommended us to several of his friends in the same industry."

Every company and every salesperson has success stories from people who have bought and used the product satisfactorily. One good success story can put you on the psychological five-yard line. People are more concerned about transferability of results than almost anything else when they make a buying decision. When they hear that someone else similar to them has bought and used the product, and is very happy with their decision, they often become eager to enjoy the same benefits themselves. When you weave into your sales presentation stories about other prospects who have used and enjoyed the particular features and benefits you are explaining, you raise the prospect's buying temperature toward the boiling point.

You can also use failure stories to motivate your prospect. If the prospect says he wants to think it over and maybe make a decision in the coming year, you can tell the story about someone else who also decided to think it over. You can then go on to explain how he called you back later and told you how sorry he was that he put off the buying decision. Or you can tell a story about a prospect who bought a cheaper product from someone else and how sorry he was later. A good failure story is often a stimulant that overcomes buying inertia and causes a prospect to move ahead on your offer.

By using relevant success and failure stories, you trigger the alternative buying motivations of *desire and fear*. People buy products either because of desire for gain or fear of loss. If you tell a success story and a failure story, you trigger both motivations in the same presentation. By illustrating your product through the stories of people who have bought and were happy, and comparing them with people who failed to buy and regretted it, you often overwhelm any hesitation that the prospect has and cause him to go ahead immediately.

IMPRINTING

A simple technique that you can use in conjunction with pushing the hot button and the relevant story close is called imprinting. This is when you repeat certain words and phrases during your presentation to program a command into your prospect's subconscious mind. These commands are combined with your sales message and often trigger a buying decision at the end of your sales conversation.

For example, a message you might want to imprint is "when you own." In your presentation, you could say, "*When you own* this product, you never have to worry about this particular problem cropping up." If one of the benefits of purchasing your product is that it deals with a particular problem each time it arises, this is a powerful sales message.

Another message you want to imprint is "buy it today." You could say something like, "If you *buy it today*, we can deliver it later this week and you can start using it this very weekend." Once a person decides they want to enjoy the benefits of a product or service, they almost immediately become impatient. They want it now. Urgency and speed of delivery become an important motivation to take action.

Or you may want to imprint the message "start using it." You could say, "After this machine is installed and you *start using it*, work that used to take two hours will take only twenty minutes." Your aim is for your prospect to be thinking about starting to use it as he listens to your presentation. This message predisposes him toward buying at the end.

In retail sales, you want to imprint the message, "take it with you." Many sales, even large ones, are made on impulse. While the person is there in front of you, you have the greatest likelihood of closing the sale. But if he walks away to think about it or to explore other options, your chances of getting him back and making the sale diminish dramatically.

You can say, "Why don't you *take it with you?*" Or, "If you *take it with you*, you can start using it as soon as you get home." Or, "The smartest thing would be for you to *take it with you*, today, and get started with it."

Please understand that these techniques are not ways of manipulating a prospect or trying get the prospect to do anything that is inconsistent with his or her best interests. They are simply proven ways to help you make a better psychological impression in the cluttered and competitive market where your prospect is bombarded with hundreds of commercial messages every day. These are ways to help your message stand out and stick in the customer's mind. The more of them you use, the more likely it is that the customer will end up buying from you, no matter what else happens in the world around him.

PRESENTATION TOOLS

Everything counts! Many sales are made or lost as the result of the salesperson doing, or failing to do, one small thing. Customers are busy, suspicious, and often unforgiving. They have a natural tendency to assume that a poor sales effort is indicative of a poorly run company and a poor product or service. They are afraid of making mistakes. And they often make mountains out of molehills. They are sensitive to details and constantly looking for indications that you are either the right or wrong person to do business with.

You've heard the little ditty many times:

> For want of a nail the shoe was lost;
> For want of a shoe the horse was lost;
> For want of a horse the rider was lost;
> For want of a rider the battle was lost;
> For want of the battle the kingdom was lost;
> Oh what a loss for one little nail!

Selling is a mental game. You do not load bales and tote hay to make a living. You think. Your stock-in-trade is your knowledge of your product or service and how it can be used to improve the work or life of your prospects. Like a doctor, your ability to apply your knowledge on behalf of your patient (customer) is what you have to sell. The more skillful you are at using this knowledge, the more sales and the more money you will make.

The first tool for successful presentations is through **product knowledge**. You must know your product cold, inside and out. You must be thoroughly conversant with every detail of your product or service, how it was designed, how and why it works, what it does, and the various applications to which it can be put.

You must be thoroughly familiar with your competitors' products as well. You must know what you are selling *against*. You must know the relative strengths and weaknesses of their products and services as compared with yours. You must have thought them through carefully and know exactly how to position your offering in such a way that your customer sees you as the best-choice provider of what you are selling.

Top salespeople make themselves absolute experts in the area of the product or service they sell. They study it continually. They read books, magazines, and articles on it. The take every course and attend every workshop they can find. They are determined never to find themselves in a situation where they are asked a question about their product or service that they cannot answer in complete detail. Top salespeople take it as a matter of pride that no one should know more about their product or service than they do.

The second presentation tool you need is **customer knowledge**. This is your in-depth understanding of the customer's situation and how your particular product or service can most help your customer to achieve his goals or solve his problems.

There is nothing more flattering to a customer than for him to realize that you have taken a good deal of time and trouble to learn about his situation and how your product can help him *before* you meet with him and begin to offer recommendations. On the other hand, there is nothing so irritating to a customer than to have a salesperson sit down and begin recommending a product or service before he has taken the time to thoroughly understand the situation the customer is facing.

A well-educated, well-dressed salesperson from a high-tech company called on me not long ago. Our company spends hundreds of thousands of dollars developing advanced, multimedia sales training programs. He arranged this appointment by going through someone else in our office and it had been scheduled several weeks in advance. He arrived on time, well dressed, well groomed, cheerful, intelligent, with a firm handshake and a pleasant personality.

After a few minutes of introductions and pleasantries, he launched into the purpose of his visit. He began telling me about the various things his company could do for my company to improve our products and services. He explained how advanced they were in video graphics, interactive learning systems, computer-aided teaching, and other skills that would be applicable to a training business. He spoke quickly, asking few questions. As I listened to him, I could tell from his comments that he knew nothing about my business and that he had made no effort to find out.

About ten minutes into the monologue, I stopped him and asked him, "How much do you know about this company and what we do here?" He stopped and immediately became flustered. He muttered and double-talked for a couple of minutes and then finally admitted that he wasn't sure what our business involved. I asked him if he had requested information from the person in my company who had set up this appointment. He told me that he hadn't. He had been too busy. Then he made the final mistake.

He said, "I would be very interested in learning more about what you do if we decide to do business together." What? Was he saying that he was not prepared to learn anything about my business *before* he made a sale to us? Yes, that's exactly what he was saying!

At this, I stood up and ended the conversation. I thanked him for coming in. He was a bit dumbfounded. As I showed him to the door, I explained to him that he was wasting my time to come in to talk to me about his services when he had no idea of my situation or business activities. I told him that he had violated one of the first laws of selling, "Know Thy Customer." I said good-bye at the door and suggested, as a sales trainer, that the next time he got an appointment with the president of a company he should make some effort to find out a little about the company.

My story is all too common. It is absolutely amazing how many salespeople call on prospects without having taken the time to learn something about him or her beforehand. And the bigger the customer, or the fewer the prospects in your territory, the more important it is.

Do your homework. Leave nothing to chance. Customer knowledge is an important part of your stock-in-trade. It is a vital part of what you have to sell. The quality and quantity of customer knowledge you have will determine the income as much as any other factor.

The *third* presentation tool is **thorough preparation** for the sales call. Many sales are lost every single day because the salesperson arrives at the customer's place of business without the necessary materials to complete the presentation and conclude the sale. The twin benefits of thorough preparation are that it not only gives you greater confidence in your ability to handle anything that might come up in the sales presentation, but it also gives your prospect greater confidence in you and your ability to satisfy his needs.

Do not overlook your briefcase during your preparation. It should be carefully arranged and neatly organized. You should only carry in your briefcase the things you need to make the presentation and make the sale. All other items should be left at home or in your drawer in the office.

When you open your briefcase, the customer will often glance inside to see how professional you really are. Your customer will assume that the organization of your briefcase is similar to the organization of your entire business. If your briefcase is sloppy and full of irrelevant materials, your customer will assume that your company is also sloppy and disorganized. Be sure to check and double-check everything in your briefcase before you leave the office. It will pay off in the long run.

Another critical aspect of preparation prior to the sales call has to do with the multi-call nature of complex sales. Because you will usually have to make several calls on the same person to make a single sale, *each call* must be planned and prepared in advance. You cannot simply go back and say the same things you said last time. Each call must build on the previous call. Each must have specific objectives that piggyback on the objectives reached in the previous conversations. There must be an obvious sense of forward progress on the part of the customer. You need specific, written call objectives, like goals, for every sales call.

Imagine that your sales manager was accompanying you. He is sitting in the seat next to you and he asks you, "Exactly *why* are we calling on this prospect at this time, *what* are we trying to accomplish, and *how* will we know that it has been a success?"

You should briefly write out the words that complete the sentence, "My objectives for this call are to . . ." At the beginning of the sales call, you should share these objectives with your prospect. Tell him exactly what you want to accomplish at this time, and where you hope to be at the end of this sales conversation. As I suggested earlier, a written agenda of your objectives, neatly typed out for your prospect to follow, is extremely impressive. It marks you as a true sales professional.

At the end of the call, take out your call sheet and quickly jot down every single thing you covered during your conversation. Especially, read your objectives for that call and ask yourself if you attained them. If not, why not?

Call objectives are like the rungs on a ladder. For you to get from the bottom of a ladder to the top, you must step on every rung. When you want to make a sale, there are a series of objectives that you must accomplish.

The fourth tool you need for any sales presentation is **timing and punctuality.** Once you have made all of the efforts necessary to get a definite appointment with a qualified prospect, you must protect this appointment against postponement or cancellation whenever possible. You should definitely confirm the appointment before you leave your office to make sure you are not wasting your time.

Salespeople sometimes fear confirming appointments because of the possibility that the prospect will cancel the appointment when they call. There is a simple way to deal with this challenge. Either do it yourself or have your secretary phone the prospect's office and ask if he is there. If the receptionist or secretary says yes, you then say, "Please tell Mr. Prospect that John Jones of ABC Company will be there for his appointment at ten o'clock as scheduled. Thank you very much."

The advantage of this telephone confirmation is that you remind the prospect that you have an appointment with him, just in case he has forgotten, plus you emphasize the importance that you place on this upcoming meeting. Your prospect will be much more likely to clear his calendar and create the time period that you require than he might have had he not heard from you.

Be sure to arrive for your appointment *ten minutes early*. If, for any reason, you are going to be delayed, phone in advance and ask for permission to come later. If you are really tied up with another customer, or are on the other side of town, ask to schedule another appointment and confirm the time and date at that time. Whatever you do, don't show up late and give the *idiot's excuse*, "I got stuck in traffic." This just makes you look foolish and undermines your credibility before you even start talking to the prospect about his problem and your solution.

The fifth presentation tool is **practice and rehearsal.** As I said earlier in this chapter, your presentation of your product is where you demonstrate your real skill as a professional salesperson. All top salespeople use a planned presentation. You could wake them up at three o'clock in the morning and ask for a presentation and they could get up and begin it, starting from the general and moving through to the particular to the close of the sale.

Top salespeople rehearse and review their presentations before they go in to see the customer. They take a few minutes to check all the details one more time. They review the customer's file so that they are aware of the pertinent information the customer has given them, or that they have gathered earlier. They are like star athletes going into competition, thoroughly warmed up, loose, flexible, and prepared to perform at their best.

The sixth and final presentation tool that can give you the winning edge in the sales conversation is **excellent health habits.** The quality of personal magnetism that you emanate as a salesperson affects the customer at a subconscious level and has a great influence over the eventual result of the sale. All top salespeople seem to be positive and energetic, alert and enthusiastic, bright and cheerful. The immediate impression they give to a prospect is that they are fully rested, primed for action, and ready to do business.

As explained earlier, the keys to building and maintaining high levels of energy and enthusiasm are diet, exercise, and rest.

I have met thousands of top salespeople and I have been amazed to discover how many of them have vigorous personal exercise programs. Many of the highest paid salespeople in America are marathon runners or triathletes, or engage in some competitive sport. And because they are so fit, they make a positive impression on their customers that exerts a powerful influence on the entire sales conversation.

Finally, you should get lots of rest, at least seven to eight hours a night, and go to bed early. When you go to bed early, you can get up early and plan your whole day before the average person even gets out of bed. In my studies of successful people over the years, I have never found anyone who was a late riser.

In addition to keeping yourself in excellent physical condition, there is one final physical exercise that you can do before you walk in to a sales appointment: deep breathing, which you should do as part of your mental rehearsal before *every* sales meeting.

You start by taking a few deep breaths. Inhale as deeply as you possibly can and push your diaphragm down with the inhalation. When you exhale, expel every bit of breath out of your lungs. Roll your shoulders forward and backward. This works the kinks, stresses, and nervousness out of the upper half of your body. Finally, shake your hands as though you were shaking water off the tips of your fingers. This action takes much of the stress out of your body.

The combination of breathing, rolling your shoulders, and shaking your hands gives you a feeling of being relaxed and in control. When you walk into the sales appointment, you will be ready to perform at your best.

THE PRESENTATION PROCESS

Once you have established a high level of rapport and trust, and clearly identified the major problem or need that the prospect has, you are ready to begin your sales presentation. You may or may not have found the hot button at this point but you remain alert for the kind of reaction from the customer that will indicate that you have touched the critical nerve. You are now ready to begin the formal presentation.

The best way to begin is to restate the problem or goal that you and the customer have mutually identified. "Mr. Prospect, your primary concern seems to be to maintain the quality and quantity of your existing production levels and to reduce costs at the same time. Is that correct?"

Before you begin your presentation, you must get agreement from the prospect that what you are talking about and what he is concerned about are the same thing. If you don't, you will be going down one road playing one tune while he is going down another, playing something else.

Your presentation should move from the general to the particular. You should begin by explaining how your product or service was developed to solve a particular problem or satisfy a particular need. You can explain different approaches that your company took to this situation and why you finally settled on this product or service as the very best of all possible solutions.

It is important that you get understanding and agreement at each step of your presentation. Inexperienced salespeople often rush through the presentation from beginning to end without inviting any feedback from the customer. But experienced salespeople divide the presentation into a series of discreet units, and tie a bow around each one as they go by asking for feedback and by the use of trial closing.

A trial close is something that can be answered by either a yes or no without ending the sales presentation. Examples of trial closing statements, which are often called "check closes," are:

"How does this sound to you?"
"Does this make sense to you so far?"
"Would this particular feature be useful to you in your current operations?"
"Do you like this color?"
"Will this be an improvement over what you are doing right now?"
"Is this what you had in mind?"

The basic formula for successful presentations that I have used throughout the years is summarized in three words, "Show, tell, and ask questions." Show the prospect a particular fact or feature, tell the prospect what it means to him in terms of a benefit, and ask a question to test whether this particular benefit is important to him. An excellent way to make a presentation is to write down each point, or use prepared pages that enable you to show, tell, and ask a question on each one.

As you move from the general to the particular, you move from simple facts and observations that are easy to agree with toward more complicated and specific conclusions that the customer must reach before he can agree to buy your product. At each stage, you check with the customer to make sure you are both on the same track. If at any time, your customer becomes reluctant or hesitant, stop your presentation and ask, "Do you have any questions or concerns about that?"

It is essential that you become comfortable with silences during the sales conversation. Most salespeople are so nervous and uneasy that they continually leap in with additional comments and never give the customer a chance to absorb the information being presented. Remember this: the teaching takes place with the words, but the learning takes place in the silences.

Whenever you ask a customer a question, either a partial close or a full close, or for any critical piece of information, you must remain perfectly silent afterward until the customer answers. Sometimes, the customer's mind will be racing as he formulates the correct response. You must wait patiently until the customer responds to your question. Otherwise, there is no point in asking questions at all, and they lose their force and effect in the sales conversation.

We are conditioned to answer when we are asked something. From infancy, our parents train us to speak when we are spoken to, to answer questions when we are asked them. As adults, we automatically answer questions when somebody asks us. We may not answer them aloud, but we answer them to ourselves. If the questioner remains silent long enough, the other person will eventually express the answer aloud.

For example, here's a question for you: "What kind of a car do you drive?" Without thinking, you instantly answered that question in your own mind. You immediately saw a picture of your car and you might even have thought simultaneously about how you bought it, what you like about it, where it is right now, and the condition it is in. The question itself triggered a whole train of thought, even though you never said a word. And it is the same with every question you ask your customers. They will answer to themselves even if they don't say anything to you.

You already know that features arouse interest while benefits arouse desire. When you describe a feature of your product, you must combine it immediately with a benefit for the prospect, with an answer to the question, "What's in it for me?"

A simple three-step method of proceeding through your sales presentation consists of describing the product feature, the product benefit, and then the customer benefit. The product feature is what has been designed and built into your product so that it is capable of achieving a particular purpose. The product benefit is why it makes your product better than something else, or nothing at all. The customer benefit is "what's in it for him," how he personally is better off by using it. You use the words, "Because of this . . . , you can . . ., which means . . ."

For example, in describing a wide-screen television, you might say, "Because of this rear-screen projection device [product feature], you can see from everywhere in the room [product benefit], which means that the whole family can enjoy movies at home [customer benefit]."

The most important part of this presentation method is contained in the words that follow, "which means . . ." You must continually link the features of your product into specific benefits that the customer will enjoy and that he considers important based on your earlier conversation. "Which means . . ." answers the prospect's unspoken question, "So what?"

The fastest way to kill a sales conversation is to describe features without linking them to benefits, or to talk about benefits that are of no interest to the customer. This is why you must be continually showing, telling, and asking questions. You must ask for regular feedback so that you can be sure that you and the customer are still on the same wavelength.

During the presentation, the power of suggestion is very strong. You use the power of suggestion by continually talking about how happy the prospect will be when he begins using your product. This is a form of "talking past the sale" and it is based on the fact that customers make buying decisions based on how they anticipate feeling when they are using and enjoying what you are selling. When you are creating vivid word descriptions of the pleasures they will experience once they have purchased your product, they begin to project themselves into the pictures as well.

For example, you could say, "Your staff will be so happy at how quietly this machine works and how little maintenance it requires."

"You will love the way this car corners and grips the road, especially on rainy days."

"With this computer program, you just boot it up, press the command, and you'll have all your sales figures for the previous day."

"When your customers see that you are using this process, they'll never think of buying from anyone else."

These positive, suggestive statements are so important that you must plan and rehearse them in advance. Your aim is to take your prospect, during your presentation, to the point that he is already thinking about acquiring and using your product. You want to "put him in the picture" and you do it by creating vivid, emotional images that describe the pleasure and satisfaction he will enjoy once he gets your product.

Where there are weaknesses in your product and there are strengths in your competitor's products, don't be afraid to point them out. You should assume that your customer is going to ask for a complete sales presentation from your most aggressive competitor and that this competitor will tell your customer everything about your product and its deficiencies. When you tell your customer in advance where your product might be weaker relative to a competitor's, your competitor gains very little from pointing out the same weaknesses during his presentation.

In addition, when you explain a weakness that your product has, you can also show that, based on what the customer really wants, this weakness is not important. Today, in our high-tech age, many salespeople push their products by telling the customer about all the extra features they have when compared to others that are available in the market. The smart salesperson comes in afterward and points out that the customer never uses those additional features anyway, so why pay extra for them? This type of approach can kick the chair out from under your competitor's strongest arguments. But you must be prepared.

MEGA-CREDIBILITY REVISITED

If you can imagine that your prospect has a *buying temperature* and the buying temperature must reach boiling point for him to purchase your product, you can think in terms of doing everything possible to raise that temperature.

Every time you present a benefit and the customer agrees that that benefit is important to him, his buying temperature goes up. Every time the customer says yes to a part of your presentation, his buying temperature increases. If you can skillfully guide the sales presentation in such a way that the customer understands and agrees at each step, his buying temperature will often go up to the point where he will come out and say, "I want it! How soon can I get it?"

When you present information on the size and quality of your company, and the great number of satisfied customers that you already have, you raise the customer's buying temperature.

When you present testimonials from satisfied customers attesting to the quality and value of what you are selling, the customer's buying temperature goes up. He or she believes you and what you are saying even more. His resistance and reluctance to buy diminish.

When you get your customer involved in the sales presentation by handing him things, asking him to move, and having him calculate numbers and figures, his buying temperature goes up. There is a direct relationship between involvement in the sales presentation and commitment to the outcome. The more the customer takes action during the presentation, the more likely he is to buy at the end. His actions prove to him that this purchase is a good idea.

Another major source of credibility is when you offer statements from authoritative sources as to the quality of your product or service, from clippings, magazine articles, or reviews in magazines like *Consumer Reports*. Whenever a respected outside authority compares your product to others and gives you a high ranking, it causes your customer's buying temperature to increase. Some people won't buy a product until a reliable third party has passed judgment on it and given it a high rating. And if appropriate to your product or service, use photos as well.

You can multiply the strength and power of your sales presentation by lacing it throughout with relevant stories, testimonials, and authoritative comments that attest to the value and quality of what you are selling. As the prospect's belief in you and your statements goes up, his natural skepticism and reluctance decline. At the end of your sales presentation, if you have done it properly, the customer will just about be ready to take action.

THE TDPPR FORMULA

In multi-call selling, at the end of a sales conversation, one of four things will take place. The customer will agree to buy, the customer will decide that he is not interested, the customer will suggest that you keep in touch with no definite date in mind, or the customer will agree to the next logical step in the sales process.

Your job is to keep the sale moving forward. It is to develop and maintain momentum. You must keep the initiative. Once you begin the sales process, you have to keep the ball rolling or it will come to a halt and your probability of making the sale will drop toward zero. The way you do this is by establishing a TDPPR.

TDPPR stands for **time, date, place, person,** and **reason.** If your sales manager asks you, "How is that sale going?" you should be able to answer by telling him exactly at what stage the sale is, and when your next time, date, place, person, and reason for an appointment has been set. If you leave a prospect without nailing these down, you will have lost the momentum in the sale and you may not have a prospect at all.

To make a complex sale, you must accomplish certain objectives with each call. At the end of each call, you will have enough information to go back and prepare for the next call. The next call may be on the person in front of you or on someone else to get additional information. Gradually, you will assemble all the information you need into a finished proposal that will become the basis of your final presentation to the customer.

At the end of each sales conversation, you should take the initiative by saying something like, "Based on our discussion, what I recommend is that we get together again toward the end of next week, by which time I'll have some numbers and comparisons for you to review before we go to the next step. How does that sound to you?"

Take out your time planner or your calendar and flip to the page and date you have recommended. As much as possible, be persistent in getting agreement to a specific time, date, place, person, and reason for the next call *before* you leave. Once you have it, repeat it back to double-check and guard against error.

Most prospects are extremely busy and even if they are good potential customers for your product, they are reluctant to commit themselves very far in advance. Be aware of this and insist that you set some kind of a TDPPR at that time with the option of changing it if something comes up. The prospect will almost invariably agree to set a specific time and date if he knows that it can be altered if need be.

SUMMARY

Your ability to set the stage and then present an interesting, informative, logical, and persuasive presentation is essential to success in selling. Studies show that you can be average in every other part of the sales process and still be very successful if you can make powerful presentations when you finally get in front of a qualified prospect.

You cannot leave a single detail to chance. Many sales are made because the salesperson mentioned one critical factor, or gave one convincing piece of evidence for the sales decision. And many sales are lost because the salesperson failed to do so.

You've heard the story about the man who stops a musician on the street in New York and asks him how to get to Carnegie Hall. The musician looks at him and says, "Practice man, practice." The key to giving outstanding presentations is the same. You must plan, practice, rehearse, and review continually. You must go over every detail of your sales presentation, from beginning to end, prior to every presentation you give. You must go in knowing that you are completely ready to handle any question or argument that the prospect could possibly think of.

It is common for a prospect to see you out of curiosity or politeness. Sometimes he will agree to meet with you simply because you have been professional and persistent in setting up the appointment. But he may come into the initial meeting with no interest whatever in purchasing your product or service. He is busy and preoccupied. His mind is somewhere else. His meeting with you is a duty that he must fulfill as part of his working day. His attitude toward your product may be neutral or negative.

Most sales in America start off this way: the positive, prepared salesperson meets the negative and uninterested prospect. But the professional salesperson is prepared for this. He is ready to take the prospect, one step at a time, through the process from skepticism about the product to complete conviction that this is exactly what he needs.

Establishing a friendly relationship, asking questions to uncover real needs, and then giving a thoroughly planned professional sales presentation is the key to turning the prospect around, from a doubter to a customer.

This is the business you are in. You talk to people who have no interest in what you are selling. They have no concept at all of how they could be better off by accepting your recommendations. Your job is to turn them from foe into friend. Your job is to convert them from a suspicious person into a committed customer. Your job is to use your personality and persuasive skills to build high-quality customer relationships that result in immediate sales and then continue with sales and referrals into the future. This is what you get paid for and there is no limit to how good you can become if you work at it.

10

CLOSING THE SALE:

THE ENDGAME OF SELLING

Selling is one of the toughest jobs in the world. There are no buffers between you and the reality of daily difficulties, delays, and disappointments. You often ride an emotional roller coaster, up and down, that never seems to stop. You are all alone. Like a front-line soldier, you must get yourself up every day and go out to where the bullets of rejection fly. You must continually deal with the possibility that all your sales efforts could turn out to be in vain through no fault of your own. And you must keep on going in spite of this because your profession of selling requires it.

Selling is hard. It always has been and it always will be. Even for the best and most experienced salespeople, it is a continual effort. You can make it easier by developing your skills in the critical areas of prospecting, presenting, and closing sales, but you can never make selling an easy profession. However, once you accept that selling is a hard way to make a living, it becomes a little easier. When you stop expecting it to be something other than it is, much of the stress goes out of it. As William James said, "The first step in dealing with any difficulty is to be willing to have it so."

Selling is also a wonderful profession. It offers opportunities for the average person that are unimaginable in most countries. Your potential earnings are beyond what 95 percent of the world's population could ever hope for or expect. You can eventually become financially independent. Five percent of self-made millionaires in America are salespeople who did their jobs extremely well.

Here's a question. If you worked at McDonald's behind the counter and a customer came up to you on the other side, what would be your probability of making a sale? The answer is that it would be about 100 percent! If a person drives to McDonald's, parks his car, goes inside, gets in line, and works his way up to the cash register, the chances of his buying something are 100 percent.

Now, how much can you *earn* working behind the counter at McDonald's? The answer is that you can earn the minimum wage, or perhaps a little more. That's all. When the sale is guaranteed, all the company has to pay for an order-taker is the minimum amount required to get someone in the current labor market. No matter how good a person becomes working behind the counter at McDonald's, he can never earn any more than the very lowest amount that McDonald's needs to pay to replace him.

As a salesperson, the reason you can make a wonderful living for yourself and your family, achieve your goals, and fulfill all of your aspirations, is because making the sale is difficult, often extremely difficult. And the longer the sales cycle, or the larger the dollar amount involved, the more that companies have to pay salespeople to do the work. When you are selling complicated or expensive products in a highly competitive market, and you do it well, you can become one of the highest paid people in your field.

You should get up every morning and give a silent prayer of thanks that selling is so difficult. If it was easy, the field would be flooded by amateurs and the amount you could earn would be greatly reduced. But because it is hellishly hard, by becoming very good at it, your future can be unlimited!

THE ENDGAME

In golf, there is a saying, "You drive for show, but you putt for dough." In selling, you present for show, but you overcome customer skepticism and gain commitment for dough. Your ability to answer objections and get the sale is the true test of how good you really are as a salesperson.

This is perhaps the most stressful and challenging part of the sales process. It is your ability to answer the questions the prospect puts to you and overcome his natural reluctance to make a commitment that wraps up the sales process. It is also the part of the sales process that salespeople dislike the most and which customers find the most stressful. This is why you must thoroughly plan and carefully prepare the endgame of selling so that you are completely ready to bring the sales conversation to its natural conclusion at the earliest and most appropriate moment. Fortunately, this is a skill, like riding a bicycle or typing, and you can learn it through study and practice.

Handling objections and closing the sale are two different parts of the sales process but they are so close together that in this chapter we will discuss them as a single function. Just as there are reasons why people buy a product, there are reasons why they don't. Often answering an objection or removing an obstacle is the critical element in making the sale. You can answer the objection and close the sale simultaneously. Objections can be turned into reason for buying. Just as there is a primary reason for buying a product, a hot button, there is a primary objection that stops the person from buying it. If you can emphasize the one and remove the other, the sale falls together naturally.

In selling smaller products or services where you can prospect and make a complete presentation in the first meeting, your approach to closing will be different from that required if you are selling a larger product in a multi-call sale that stretches over several weeks or months. In the shorter, smaller sale, the prospect knows everything necessary to make a buying decision at the end of your presentation. Your aim should be to answer any lingering questions and then ask for the order. In the larger sale, you may have to meet with the prospect several times before he or she is in a position to make a buying decision. You will have to be more patient and persistent.

If you make a perfect presentation, one that clearly explains the benefits and resolves all the doubts that a qualified prospect might have, the sale will often close all by itself, like a ripe apple dropping out of a tree into your hand. You will conclude your presentation, check to be sure that the prospect has fully understood the benefits and value to him of the offer, and the prospect will say something like, "It sounds good to me, how do I get it? Will you take a check?"

When you are dealing with a prospect who knows exactly what he wants and you structure your presentation so that you demonstrate to him that your product fills his needs perfectly, he can make a buying decision immediately and invite you to wrap up the sale. But this kind of result in selling is similar to a miracle: it's not that miracles don't happen, it's just that you can't depend on them.

You must go into every sales situation prepared for the likelihood that your prospect will have questions unanswered, concerns unresolved, and objections to be overcome. You must know a variety of ways to ask for the order at different points in the sales process, and you must be capable of recognizing which closing technique is most appropriate at any given time with any given type of prospect. Like a master craftsman, you need a variety of tools with which to do excellent work. The best salespeople are invariably those who are the most skilled in the fine points of bringing the sales conversation to a positive conclusion.

Your first job in the sales conversation, and throughout all of your interactions with the customer, is to build and maintain a quality relationship. It is to come across in a friendly way, to be warm, supportive, knowledgeable, and completely focused on helping the customer to solve a problem or achieve a goal with your product or service.

Because of the importance of *trust* in modern selling, you are never pushy, obnoxious, or overly aggressive. You never do or say anything that can be construed as manipulative. You never attempt to influence your prospect to act contrary to his best interests. Your job is to thoroughly understand his situation and to give good recommendations that enable him to make the right buying decision.

WHY THE ENDGAME IS DIFFICULT

There are several other reasons why the endgame of selling is stressful and difficult. First and foremost, as I have described earlier, is the *fear of failure* experienced by the prospect. Because of negative buying experiences in the past, over which you have no control, prospects are conditioned to be suspicious, skeptical, and wary of salespeople and sales approaches. They may like to *buy*, but they don't like to be *sold*. They are afraid of making a mistake. They are afraid of paying too much and finding it for sale cheaper somewhere else. They are afraid of being criticized by others for making the wrong buying decision. They are afraid of buying an inappropriate product and finding out later that they should have purchased something else. This fear of failure, of making a mistake in buying your product, is the major reason why people object, hesitate, and procrastinate on the buying decision.

The second major obstacle to selling is the salesperson's *fear of rejection*, of criticism and disapproval. You work long and hard to prospect and cultivate a prospective buyer and you are reluctant to say anything that might cause the prospect to tune you out and turn you off. You have a lot invested in each prospect and if you are not careful, you will find yourself being wishy-washy at the end of the sale, rather than risking incurring the displeasure of the prospect by your asking for a firm decision.

Another reason why the end of the sale is difficult is that the customers are *busy and preoccupied*. It isn't that they are not interested in enjoying the benefits of your product. It's just that they are overwhelmed with work and they find it difficult to make sufficient time available to think through your recommendations and make a buying decision. And the better they are as a prospect, the busier they tend to be. This is why you need to maintain momentum throughout the sales process and gently push it to a conclusion at the appropriate time.

The factor of *inertia* can also cause the sales process to come to a halt without a resolution. Customers are lazy and often quite comfortable doing what they are currently doing. Your product or service may require that they make exceptional efforts to accommodate a change or a new way of doing things. They perhaps recognize that they would be better off with your product, but the trouble and expense of installing it hardly seem to make it worth the effort.

The good news is that everybody you meet has bought, and will buy, new products and services from someone, at some time. If they don't buy from you, they will buy from someone else. You must find the way to overcome the natural psychological obstacles to buying and then hone your skills so that you are capable of selling to almost any qualified prospect you speak to. That will be the focus of this chapter.

THE ROLE OF OBJECTIONS IN SELLING

Objections are good. They are essential to the selling process. There are no sales without them. No matter how thorough your presentation, your prospect will always have unanswered questions and concerns that you will have to deal with before proceeding to the conclusion of the sale. He or she will be doubtful, hesitant or unclear. At the very least, the prospect will want you to know that he is astute and aware and not about to buy something without thoroughly understanding it.

Objections indicate interest. Where there are no objections, there is no interest. If you are talking to a prospect who sits there without moving, noncommittal, barely responding to your questions and ignoring your sales material, you're in big trouble!

Successful sales seem to have twice as many objections as unsuccessful sales. Sometimes, people express their objections in a critical or dismissive way, as though the shortcomings in your product are so obvious that no one could seriously consider buying it. If you are not careful when you hear an objection, it will feel a bit like a punch to your emotional solar plexus. You will feel disappointed, angry, or defensive. You will feel that your product is being attacked by the customer and your natural instinct will be to counterattack. But this is exactly the wrong approach.

If you were fishing in a quiet pond on a quiet day and you felt a gentle tug at the end of your line, you would immediately brighten up. You would instantly recognize that the tug represented a fish that was exploring your bait. The tug at your line would be the first suggestion to you that you might be about to catch something.

By the same token, when the prospect begins to take issue with your proposal, you should give thanks silently that you have finally aroused some interest, that you have triggered an emotional response and the sales process is under way. Instead of being set back by an objection, no matter how harshly it is delivered, you should be exhilarated. You now have an opportunity to begin moving the sale forward.

Objections also tell you how well you are doing in the sales process. They are a form of feedback from the prospect to you about your presentation and your product offering. They are signposts from the prospect that guide you toward the issues you must resolve and the assurances that you must give if you are eventually to make the sale. Objections reveal the hidden motives that underlie buyer behavior. When a prospect challenges one of your statements, he is saying that that part of your product is important to him and he wants more information in that area.

Additionally, the customer often objects to parts of your presentation to test the quality of the relationship that has developed between you. Just as customers ordinarily avoid complaining because they dislike the confrontation that complaining involves, customers usually dislike objecting because they don't want to antagonize the salesperson and get into an argument.

It is important that you create the kind of psychological environment where the prospect feels comfortable expressing any of his reservations to you about your product. It is only when the customer feels that he can freely express himself and ask you anything that he will open up and allow you to remove all his misgivings prior to concluding the sale.

Make it easy for your customer to object. Practice *unconditional positive regard*. Be positive, relaxed, and smiling throughout. Acknowledge and respect your customer's feelings and opinions. Whatever he says, treat it as a serious and thoughtful observation on your product or service. The more relaxed your customer becomes with you, the more likely that he will eventually buy.

THE LAW OF SIX

You will receive countless questions, concerns, and objections in the course of your sales activities. Some prospects will ask dozens of small and large questions affecting every aspect of your service, your business, the past, present and future, and a dozen other things. Your skill at answering these questions satisfactorily will determine whether or not you make the sale.

But no matter how many objections you hear, they can usually be condensed or clustered into not more than six categories. This is called the Law of Six. All of the objections will revolve around six major questions. Sometimes it will be two or three major questions, but it will seldom be more than six.

To determine the six as they apply to your particular product or service, you first write down every single objection that your customers have ever given you. If you work with other salespeople, you should do this as a group. It is best to have people throw out every objection they can remember hearing and have someone write them on flip chart pages. Tape the sheets up on the wall so that everyone can see them. Keep writing until no one can think of any more.

Once you have written down all of the most common objections, your next step is to categorize them, or group them together in clusters around a single main question. For example, you may find that the objections you hear most cluster around the following six questions: (1) price; (2) performance; (3) follow-up service; (4) competition; (5) support; and (6) warranties and assurances. These would become your six main headings and you would then list all the other minor objections under one of these headings.

You should define each major objection in about twenty-five words or less in the form of a question that might be asked by a demanding prospect. For example, under "performance" you might write the definition thus: "How can I be sure that your product will do what you say it will do and will continue doing it better and more efficiently than what I am already using?"

Do this for each of your six major objections or questions. Once you have defined them clearly, your job is to develop *bulletproof* answers to each of these questions. Your job is to plan an airtight, logical, powerful response backed by proof, testimonials, research results, and written comparison data. Your aim is to prepare yourself so thoroughly for that question that the next time it comes up, you can answer it so convincingly that it will never again be an issue in the sales conversation.

Here is a sentence completion exercise for you: "I could sell to everybody I spoke to if my customers never objected by saying . . ." Complete the sentence. What are the major reasons that your customers give for not buying? What are the major objections? What do you have to prove to a prospect in order to kick the chair out from under a particular objection completely?

The very best salespeople are those who have thought through the reasons their customers don't buy and who have then prepared such excellent rebuttals, backed by written proof, that when they hear the customer ask a certain question, they smile inside. They know within themselves that they are prepared to deal effectively with the most knowledgeable customer using the most difficult objections. For you to also be the best in your field, you must become so proficient at answering the objections you hear most commonly that you actually look forward to them in a sales conversation.

THE BASICS OF HANDLING QUESTIONS

There is a little poem that goes:

> For every problem under the sun
> There is a solution or there is none.
> If there's a solution go and find it,
> If there isn't, never mind it.

This should be your attitude toward objections. Always begin your sales conversation by assuming that there is a logical, workable answer for any reasonable objection that the prospect may have. If for any reason the objections is truly insurmountable, you should accept the situation gracefully and get on to the next prospect. In any case, you should remain calm, positive, relaxed, and friendly throughout the conversation, no matter what the prospect says.

There is a difference between an objection and what is called a "condition." An objection is a question for which there is a logical answer. A condition is a genuine reason why the customer cannot buy your product or service. There is no answer to it. There is nothing you can do about it. You just have to accept it and realize that this prospect is not a good candidate for your product.

For example, the prospect may say that his company is shutting down. This is a condition that makes it impossible for him to buy something that would be used by a growing business. Or the prospect may have just purchased an almost identical product with a five-year life. Or the prospect's company may own a supplier of the particular product or service and buy only from them. Whenever you find a condition, you will find an immovable obstacle to the sale.

It's interesting to note that most customers initially feel that their objections are conditions. When they have an objection, they often feel that it is a valid reason for not buying. When they put it forth as an objection, they feel that this is the end of the sales conversation. It is over. You should be aware of this and be prepared to show the prospect that his objection is not really a condition, it is merely an obstacle or difficulty for which there is a logical solution.

Some time ago, I was given a presentation for a life insurance policy by an excellent insurance agent. I was convinced that I should buy the policy and I asked him how much it would be. He said that it would cost $2,500 a year. At this, I told him that that was impossible. I did not have $2,500. As much as I recognized the benefits to me of having such a policy, there was no way I could buy it.

He then asked me if I could pay for it on a monthly basis. I was surprised, for every insurance policy I had ever bought I had paid for in one lump sum. I thought that all insurance policies were purchased with annual premiums. It had never occurred to me that you could buy an insurance policy on a monthly installment plan. When he asked me if I could afford $215 per month, I immediately agreed, signed the application, and I have been insured with him ever since. My condition turned out to be only an objection.

TIMING YOUR ANSWERS

When should you deal with an objection or provide an answer? This depends on many things. But there are basically five different times when it is correct to answer a question or objection posed by the prospect. The first, and usually the best, is **before the objection comes up** in the first place. This is called the "preemptive strike." If you know that you are going to get a certain objection in virtually every sales conversation, you bring up the objection in advance and kick the chair out from under it so that it is no longer sitting in the back of the customer's mind interfering with his concentration during your sales presentation.

For example, if your product is expensive relative to your competitors', and you know that the question of price is going to come up as a major objection, you would start your sales conversation by saying something like, "Mr. Prospect, before I begin, I want to tell you that our product is one of the most expensive on the market. Yet, in spite of our prices, hundreds (or thousands) of people like you purchase this product every single year. Would you like to know why?"

With this type of preemptive strike, the prospect cannot say later, "Your price is higher than your competitors'." You already told him it was.

We worked with a large telecommunications company not long ago whose sales were down. The salespeople were frustrated. They were demoralized and angry, and continually complaining about the company's pricing policies. The sales organization was convinced that sales were down because their prices were the highest in the market. In addition, their competitors had taken out ads in the paper showing price comparisons.

So we taught them the preemptive strike. We taught them to deal with the price question up front and then focus all of their efforts on answering the question, "Why do so many companies buy this product every single year?"

When the salespeople started doing this, their sales jumped to 165 percent of quota within thirty days. They started making sales to prospects who initially said, "I know your prices are the highest in the market, and I'm not interested." One woman walked out of a cold call that had started with these words carrying a $17,000 deposit on a $54,000 system. She reported that the entire process took forty-five minutes.

Whatever your major objection is, be prepared to hit it hard up front. Grab it and slam it to the mat. Eliminate it as an objection so that the prospect cannot come back later and use it as a reason for not going ahead.

The second time to answer objections is **when they come up early** in the presentation. Some objections need to be answered immediately, especially objections about the integrity of your company or the quality of your product or service. You can not proceed with a presentation with these questions left unanswered, rattling around in the prospect's mind. You must deal with them straightforwardly and completely, and to the customer's complete satisfaction.

For example, you sit down with the prospect and he opens by saying, "I've heard that your company doesn't honor its warranties and that a lot of your products don't work once they are installed."

Be prepared. When you hear something like this, you must handle it in a positive and professional manner. You must respect the customer's concern and then present convincing evidence to show that he is misinformed. He only has partial information or his information is completely wrong. Only when he is satisfied with your explanation can you proceed.

The third time to answer an objection is **during the presentation.** When you have presented your product often enough, you can anticipate certain objections coming up when you make certain statements or show certain elements of your product. You should be prepared to answer those questions convincingly with the very next step of your presentation. Anticipating and preparing for a customer's objection in your presentation makes you look like a real expert at what you are doing.

If you anticipate an objection and you are prepared to answer it but the customer doesn't bring it up, you can often say something like, "At this point, many people ask how it is that we can make such a claim. Here's the basis for our statement." The customer will be very impressed. You will have removed an obstacle that might have come up later in the presentation and derailed the sale. You will also have built your credibility with the customer and increased his confidence in doing business with you.

The fourth time to answer an objection is **later in the presentation.** Many objections are smokescreen or casual questions. They don't require a full-court press. You can simply say, "May I come back to that in a moment. I think you'll be very happy with the answer."

If the prospect says, "Sure," you can proceed with your presentation, making a mental note to touch on that point after you have clearly explained the main benefits of your product.

The fifth time to answer an objection is **never.** If an objection arises early in the presentation but is not mentioned again, let it pass. Very often prospects object or ask questions just to prove to you that they are paying attention. But the objection is not consequential. If the prospect doesn't mention it later, it usually means that it was unimportant or he has forgotten it.

Remember, in selling, timing is everything. There is a right time and a wrong time for everything you say. There is too soon and too late. As a professional salesperson, your job is to determine the time and to present your information and arguments in a logical sequence, with each building on the other. Stay loose, and only answer objections when the time is right.

RESPONDING TO OBJECTIONS

You should always handle objections diplomatically. When a person complains about or criticizes some aspect of your product presentation, you should listen attentively, pause for three to five seconds to carefully consider what the prospect has said, and then ask for clarification.

I've mentioned earlier that the very best question I have ever learned in sales is, "How do you mean?" Or, "How do you mean, exactly?"

This open-ended question is virtually impossible *not* to answer. Whenever you reply to an objection with this question, the prospect will expand on his concern and clarify the reasons for his objection. You can ask this question again and again, and every time you do the prospect will give you more information. In many cases, the prospect will answer the objection himself, if you give him a chance by feeding him this question.

You should treat objections as requests for more information. Turn the objection into a question. When the prospect says something like, "It costs too much!" you simply say, "That's a good *question*. Why *does* it cost that much?"

Compliment every objection. Treat it as an intelligent and thoughtful commentary on your product. The more you compliment a prospect for objecting, the more likely it is that the prospect will object again. He will eventually give you every misgiving he might have in considering purchasing your product or service. When your prospect objects for any reason, you can say, "That's a good question! I'm glad you asked that."

When you praise a prospect for asking intelligent questions, the prospect will feel more comfortable with you and will be motivated to ask additional intelligent questions. When you take the objection and rephrase it as a question, you take the negativity out of the conversation and turn it into more of a fact-finding exchange between you and the customer. Soon, the customer will be peppering you with "What about this . . ." and "What about that . . ." He will feel comfortable having you clarify every major and minor point that comes to his mind that may bear on purchasing your product or service. And the more questions he asks, the more likely it is that he will buy.

Another powerful phrase you can use to neutralize an objection and take control of the sales conversation is, "Mr. Prospect, *obviously you* have a good reason for saying that. Do you mind if I ask what it is?"

The power words in this phrase are "obviously you." Whenever you precede a statement with these words, you are saying that the prospect's concern is an intelligent and valid one and *obviously* based on a certain amount of thought. You compliment the prospect in a subtle way and you encourage him to elaborate on his concern. As the prospect elaborates on his concern, both you and he will understand the issue more clearly, and you will be better able to respond to it effectively.

Whatever the prospect says, hear him out completely. Listen patiently and attentively to the objection, even though you may have heard it a thousand times before. Resist the urge to jump in and knock it down with one of your well-prepared answers. Remember, for the prospect, this is the first time he has expressed this concern to you and it is important that you be respectful of his question.

An important reason for listening without commenting to his entire question is that often it will end up being a different question from what you expected. Many times the last 20 percent of any question or objection contains 80 percent of the value or importance of the objection. When you hear him out completely and then double-check by asking. "How do you mean?" you will be much more likely to understand and answer the real question that is on his mind.

Never forget that *listening builds trust*. Every objection or question that the customer gives you is an opportunity for you to build a deeper foundation of trust for the relationship that you must have in place when it comes time to making the buying decision.

Sales trainer Tom Hopkins says, "Objections are the rungs on the ladder to sales success." They are a vital part of the sales process and the way you respond to them will determine whether you get the sale.

COMMON TYPES OF OBJECTIONS

Customers object and ask questions in a variety of ways. Just as a boxer needs to know the various ways an opponent can punch so he can counterpunch effectively, you need to be able to recognize the different types of objections so you can answer them appropriately. The more familiar you are with the various ways that customers question the value of your offer to them, the more confident you will feel and the more competent you will be in the sales conversation.

General sales resistance. It's hard for us to accept, but customers don't particularly like salespeople. As the result of a lifetime of experience, they believe salespeople are pushy, loud, insensitive, aggressive, obnoxious, and dishonest. They see salespeople as a necessary evil, to be tolerated in the course of learning what products and services are available in the market to help them.

You should expect a certain amount of sales resistance the first time you meet a prospect. Don't be affected by it. Just remember that it's *not personal*. It greets every salesperson at the initial contact with this individual. You should smile, relax, and roll on into the sales conversation.

The way to deal with general sales resistance is to immediately change the customer's focus away from your trying to get him to do something and onto himself and his situation. Ask the customer about himself or introduce the reason for your visit with a strong statement concerning a common problem that he may be having and that your product or service can solve.

There is a famous story of the top salesman for Corning Glass who had the highest volume for selling safety glass for anyone in the country. When he was asked how he opened his sales conversations, he explained that he would walk in and ask, "Have you ever seen glass that doesn't shatter when it breaks?" When the prospect expressed disbelief in his claim, he would take a sample of safety glass out of his briefcase, place it on the prospect's desk, and whack it with a hammer.

The prospect would leap back to avoid the flying splinters, only to find that there weren't any. The salesperson would have his complete attention and the sale progressed rapidly after that.

He shared this method of selling safety glass with all the other salespeople at the national convention. From then on, they all went out with samples of safety glass and hammers to demonstrate it to their customers. But the next year, he was still the number one salesman in the nation. When they asked him how it was that he could still be selling so much more, even though everyone else was using the same technique, he explained that he had changed his approach slightly in the second year.

Now, when he went in to see a prospect, he would ask, "Would you like to see a type of glass that doesn't shatter even when you hit it with a hammer?" Then he would give the prospect the hammer and have the *prospect* break the glass.

The first ten to fifteen words out of your mouth set the stage. They either connect with the prospect's real concerns or they don't. You should plan your opening words carefully so that when the sales conversation begins, you are ready. Just as a professional speaker plans his opening comments word for word, as a professional salesperson you should plan your opening word for word as well. This is the surest way to lower general sales resistance at the very beginning.

Requests for information. This form of question or objection is exactly what you want. When you get these requests for information, you should welcome them and encourage him to ask more. "That's a good question. I'm glad you brought it up." Answer his questions thoroughly and then double-check with, "Does that answer your question? Is that what you want to know?"

Objective objections. These take place when your prospect challenges you on one of your claims or assertions regarding your product or service. He wants some proof or evidence of the statements you are making. He wants to know, "Who says so?" or, "What proof do you have?"

Remember, your assertions are not proof to your customers. What he wants is some other evidence that attests to the truth of what you are saying about your product. You should be prepared to answer this type of objection thoroughly and to his complete satisfaction before proceeding.

Subjective objections. This type of objection is aimed at you and tends to arise when you talk too much about yourself and your company. Very often, salespeople get carried away with personal stories and revelations and they make the mistake of thinking that these are of great interest to the prospect because the prospect is listening politely. Nothing could be further from the truth. The prospect is interested in himself first, last, and always.

When you talk too much about yourself, the spotlight is on you, not on him. He will often make comments like, "You must make a lot of money selling that product."

When you hear this sort of comment aimed at you, immediately switch back into an open-ended questioning mode and get the focus of attention back on him. Return to answering his implied question, "What's in it for me?"

Excuses. These are shallow objections that usually arise either because the customer is busy and distracted or because you have not captured his attention by addressing a problem or need that he has. You will hear statements like, "I'm really too busy to think about this now," or, "We're not really in the market at this time." Sometimes the prospect will criticize the color or packaging or fault some other small detail. But those objections are not the real reasons for lack of interest.

When you find your sales presentation in danger of being sidetracked with these shallow types of objections, defer answering the question and get back to asking the prospect about himself and his situation. "Good point, could I get back to that later?"

Show-off objections. You will often meet prospects who are, or who feel they are, extremely well informed about your product or service. They may have even worked in your industry before you did. They are proud of their knowledge and experience. And they want to be recognized for their expertise.

They may say, "I've had a lot of experience with that type of product," or, "I'm very familiar with your business."

When you hear something like this, be conciliatory. Tell him how happy you are to meet someone who knows so much about your business. Ask him for his advice. Ask him for his candid comments and opinions on what you are selling as compared to what else is in the marketplace. Treat him as you would a mentor or an elder statesman in your business.

One of the greatest of human desires is the need to feel appreciated. When you express respect and appreciation for the knowledge and wisdom of another person, he will like you and trust you and become more open to buying from you. Even if you know more than he does, keep your knowledge to yourself. Let him feel superior. Your job is to win sales, not arguments.

Malicious objections. Often you meet a prospect who is unnecessarily difficult. This has nothing to do with you. It has everything to do with his previous experiences with other people and other situations. There is nothing you can do about his behavior except to conduct yourself in a professional manner.

Sometimes the prospect will attack your product, your industry, or your method of doing business. "Most of the people who sell that product are just out for a quick buck." Or, "I got ripped off by somebody in your industry a couple of years ago, and it's not going to happen again."

Whenever you find yourself dealing with an unhappy person, there is a magic expression that you can use that comes from the Dale Carnegie training. It is, "I understand exactly how you feel. If I was in your position, I would feel the same way." These words often diffuse a person's negativity. Sometimes, all a person really wants is to be understood before they listen to you.

Psychologically, a person cannot pay attention to you or your presentation if he has even a single negative idea or thought in his mind. You must create an opportunity for him to express his unhappy feelings completely in order to clear the deck for your presentation. The best way for you to do this is by asking questions, listening, and being a polite and respectful person.

When a prospect begins to share a problem experience with you, recognize it as an opportunity to build trust. Encourage him to get it all out by asking questions like, "And then what happened? And then what did you do?" Keep saying, if you can, "If I was in your position, I'd feel the same way." The need to be understood underlies most close human relationships; it also accompanies good sales relationships. One of the statements used by customers to describe top salespeople in interview after interview is, "He really *understands* my situation."

At the very least, when a person is negative or difficult, refuse to react or respond. Be bland and neutral. Pretend not to have heard, if possible. Don't add your comments and put more fuel on the fire.

Unspoken objections. These are the most dangerous of all. They can kill a sale if you do not uncover them and pull them out of the customer at the appropriate time. They are like invisible shields that block you from making the sale, even though you can see it clearly. They are like gates in the customer's mind that shut, or drawbridges that are raised, against the very best points in your presentation. Many sales are taken to the 95 percent mark and then are lost because the salesperson failed to recognize or elicit the final unspoken objection and deal with it effectively.

If you have built an excellent relationship in the earlier parts of the sales process, it will be easier for you to get the prospect to give you the final objection. You can also use the "remaining objections close" to uncover his final concern.

THE REMAINING OBJECTIONS CLOSE

When the prospect won't proceed and won't tell you why, you ask, "Mr. Prospect, there seems to be some question in your mind that's causing you to hesitate about going ahead right now. Do you mind if I ask what it is?"

After you ask a question like this, you must remain perfectly silent. The only pressure that you are ever allowed to use in professional selling is the pressure of the *silence* in the room after you have asked a key question. If you leave the silence hanging there, the prospect will eventually move to fill the void by answering your question.

Acknowledge and compliment whatever question or objection he gives you as an answer. "That's a good question, Mr. Prospect, I'm glad you asked it. *And in addition to that*, is there any other reason why you might be hesitating about going ahead with this offer right now?"

Again, remain silent. Often the first objection is merely a smokescreen. The real objection lies further below the surface. If he gives you another objection, you acknowledge it and go on.

Continue asking, "And in addition to that, is there anything else?" until the prospect finally says, "No. That's my last concern."

It is almost as if the prospect will give you a series of smaller objections before he gives you the major objection. Prospects seem to know that once you have elicited their major objection and you answer it, they will have no reason not to proceed. They will often hold this final objection back from you just to avoid making a buying decision.

You then ask, "Well, Mr. Prospect, if we could answer that question to your complete satisfaction, would you be ready to go ahead right now?"

Wait until the customer says something like, "Yes, if you can take care of that concern, I don't see any reason not to go ahead."

You then ask, "Mr. Prospect, you tell me. What would it take to satisfy you in that area?"

The prospect's answer to this final question will be the *closing condition*. This is the final hurdle you must leap to get the sale. It is the final roadblock that you must remove. Once he has told you what it is, it is now your job to meet that condition to his satisfaction and then conclude the sale.

The prospect may say something like, "I would need to talk to two or three other people in my industry who are already using your product satisfactorily before I could make a final decision."

You could then say something like, "Mr. Prospect, rather than wasting time, let's make that a condition of the sale. We will write up the order exactly as we discussed it, subject to your speaking to two or three other people and being satisfied."

Instead of your going out and gathering names and numbers and bringing them back to the prospect, you can ask for the order immediately with the prospect's signature subject to his following up on the references you supply sometime over the next three to seven days. Always attempt to confirm the sale at that moment, even if you have to make it subject to the fulfillment of another condition. You will be much more likely to get and keep the sale this way than by attempting to come back later.

THE LOST SALE OR DOORKNOB CLOSE

When you have completed the sales process through to the end of your presentation and the customer will still not buy, and will not tell you the reason, you can use the "lost sale" or "doorknob" technique to find out what's holding him back.

You have nothing to lose. If you leave the prospect's presence with neither a commitment nor clarity concerning his major objection, the sale is essentially dead. You will not get back in again. By the time you reach your car in the parking lot, the prospect will probably have forgotten your name. So here's what you do:

You use reverse psychology and instead of continuing in your sales efforts, you begin to politely disengage and depart. You say, "Mr. Prospect, thank you very much for your time. I really appreciate your talking to me. I hope we can get back together at a later date."

As you say this, you pack up your materials, close your briefcase, get up, shake hands, and start for the door. The prospect, seeing that you are leaving and that he is no longer under any pressure to defend or explain, will begin to relax, like a person letting out a deep breath. His thoughts will begin to turn to what he will do after you leave. His focus of attention will drift. He will be in the situation of a boxer putting his hands down thinking that the match is over.

As you reach the door, you put your hand on the doorknob, as if to go, and then, as a seeming afterthought, you turn to the prospect and say, "By the way, Mr. Prospect, just before I go, I wonder if you could do me a favor? It would really help me with my other customers if I know exactly where I went wrong in my presentation to you. What is the real reason you decided not to buy?" And then remain perfectly silent, smiling.

Usually the prospect, now completely relaxed, will finally give you the real reason, like throwing you a flower. He will say something like, "Well, my real concern was that I don't see how we could justify the cost based on our current level of activities."

You then take your hand off the doorknob and say, "Mr. Prospect, that's my fault. I obviously didn't explain that part of our program completely. If I could just take another minute, I'll show you exactly what we do in that case and I think you'll find that it answers your question perfectly." You then return to your chair, open your briefcase, take out your materials, and begin selling again.

You will be amazed at how many sales you will save with this simple process. I get letters and comments from people all over the country on this method. One young salesman in my seminar told me recently that he closed the biggest sale of his life with this simple technique.

OTHER TYPES OF OBJECTIONS

Last-ditch objections. You will hear these in the final moments of the sales presentation. The prospect has decided to buy and, like a fish on a hook, he is wriggling and squirming a little. He will ask you things like, "How do I know I'm getting the best price?" Or, "Is this the best deal I can get?" Or, "Are you sure I'm doing the right thing here?"

Your job is to smile and to assure the prospect that he is doing the right thing: "You are making an excellent decision! This is a very good choice. You're going to be very happy with this."

Don't let a last-ditch objection put you off. Be pleasant and polite but continue wrapping up the details of the sale and concluding the transaction.

Whatever objections you get, you can continually control the sales conversation with the magic phrases, "How do you mean, exactly?" and, "Obviously you have a good reason for saying that; do you mind if I ask what it is?"

Remember, the person who asks questions has control. When you respond to a question with a question, you are staying in the driver's seat of the sales process. And every time you ask a question and require the prospect to elaborate on a concern of his, you get another opportunity to listen, to build trust, and to improve the relationship.

PRICE AS AN OBJECTION

Let's now turn again to the issue of price. The question of price arises early in almost every sales conversation. "How much is it?" leaps out of the prospect's mouth even before he knows what it is you are selling. And no matter what it is you are selling, or at what price, his initial reaction is something like, "It's too much. We can't afford it. We don't have the cash. Business is down. Sales are slow. We can get it cheaper somewhere else. We're not in the market. We weren't expecting to pay that much. It's not in our budget. Leave me some information. Let me think it over. Call us back in a year or two."

It drives you crazy. No matter what the price is, it is more than the prospect expected to pay. It is always higher than expected. And if you're not careful, first you will get into a discussion about price, then an argument, and then you will spend most of your time wrangling about the price differences between your product and that of your competitors, and what the customer is willing to pay.

But remember, *willingness* to pay and *ability* to pay are two separate issues. People may not be initially willing to pay a certain amount but that doesn't mean they are not capable of paying that amount if you can convince them that the value to them of what you are selling is greater than the price you are charging. This is your main job in the sales process.

As we have said, price is seldom the sole reason for buying or not buying anything. As mentioned earlier in follow-up studies to customers to ask them *why* they bought a particular item, fully 94 percent mentioned nonprice items as being the most important single determinants of their decisions. When customers are interviewed after they have turned down a salesperson, by telling the salesperson that they couldn't afford it, 68 percent of them admitted to independent researchers that price was not the determining factor. It was something else. They told the salesperson that price was the issue because they had found with experience that that was the easiest way to get rid of him.

Why does one product sell for more or less than another? It is because of *differentiation*. A product sells for more or less than a competing product because it is different from the competing product in one way or another. In the perception of the customer, it is worth more, or less. It is always the customer in the marketplace who eventually decides what the product will sell for. The price the company puts on the product is merely a guess at what the customer will eventually pay. Sometimes it is accurate and sometimes it is not.

Only products that are undifferentiated in any way are sold solely on the basis of price. Price is the determining factor in the decision only when products are so identical to each other that the customer cannot tell them apart. And even then, this is not always true. Your job is to find the ways to differentiate your product on the basis of nonprice factors and then concentrate your sales presentation on the benefits your prospect receives aside and apart form the actual price he pays.

Sometimes I ask the people in my sales seminars if they would like me to prove to them that low price is seldom the major reason for buying anything. When they nod and agree that they would like to have proof of this, I then ask them this question, "Is there anyone here in this audience who has a single item of clothing or accessories about their person that they purchased solely because it was the cheapest available?"

In an audience of a thousand or more people, there is usually not a single person who has a single item that they purchased solely because it was cheaper than anything else available. Every single item owned by every single person was purchased for a nonprice reason. The only time that a customer purchases on the basis of price alone is when the salesperson has been incapable of explaining the reasons why the prospect should buy it other than the attractiveness of its price.

Everyone asks about price because money is the single common denominator in our society. We use money and prices to orient ourselves in our commercial universe. It enables us to analyze and compare all products and services with all other products and services. We like to know the price because it gives us a certain measure of comfort to know where a particular product ranks among the various products available.

It's not that we, as customers, are indifferent to money. It's just that once we know how much something costs, we then go on to make our buying decision based on other factors. Your job as a salesperson is to find out what those other factors are likely to be and then bring the whole weight of your sales presentation to bear on those factors.

PRICE IN ITS PLACE

In the last chapter we saw that the Law of Four states that there are usually four reasons why a person buys a product. There is the main reason, or the hot button, and there are three minor reasons. One of the minor reasons may be the price in comparison with other items, but it is never the major buying factor. It is never the critical element that determines the outcome of the sale, one way or another.

As we talked about in prospecting, if price comes up early in the conversation, you should defer it to a later time. Like a matador steps aside when the bull charges, you should step aside and let the price question go past you. As we saw, usually the very best way to do this is simply to say, "Mr. Prospect, I know that the price is important to you and I'm going to cover it thoroughly. Could I come back to that question in a few minutes?"

If the prospect insists on knowing the price immediately, you can tell him that *you don't know* exactly what it would cost before you ask him a few questions. "If I could ask you a couple of questions, I could give you an answer that is accurate to within a couple of dollars. For example, I would need to know . . ."

When I was attempting to set up appointments on the telephone, I would get through to the right person and introduce myself by saying, "Hello, Mr. Prospect. This is Brian Tracy. I'm from the Institute for Executive Development and I was wondering if you would like to see a way to increase your sales by 20 percent to 30 percent over the next six months?"

Because I was talking to sales managers and sales executives, people who are both busy and impatient, they would almost always come back with, "How much is it?"

I discovered early that if I gave them the price of my training services, they would immediately say, "I'm afraid we can't afford that at this time. Send us some information in the mail and we'll get back to you if we change our minds."

I soon resolved not to give any information about my services or to make the slightest mention of price when I was setting up the appointment. This is how I did it. When I called up and introduced myself and the prospect asked, "How much is it?" I would quickly say, "Mr. Prospect, that's *the best part!* If it's *not exactly right* for you, there is *no charge?*"

This almost always stopped him cold. There would be a silence on the line and then he would say, "What do you mean, no charge?"

I would then reply very firmly, "Mr. Prospect, whatever I show you, if you don't like it, you are not going to buy it, are you?"

He would say something like, "You're darn right I'm not!"

I would then reply, smiling into the phone, "And Mr. Prospect, if you don't buy it, there is no charge. It won't cost you anything. And all I need is about ten minutes of your time to show you what I've got and you can decide for yourself if it makes sense to you."

This wording proved so successful that I could eventually get four out of five, or nine out of ten, appointments cold calling out of the Yellow Pages. I quickly built a million-dollar business in sales training using this method. And it works equally well face-to-face.

A saleswoman friend of mine in Chicago, who makes more than $150,000 a year on straight commission in a highly competitive industry, deals with this price question all the time. A couple comes in and one of them immediately asks, "How much is this going to cost?"

She turns and gives her best grandmotherly smile to the prospect and says, "Honey, if you don't like what we have, you're not going to buy it, are you?"

One or the other member of the couple always says, "Well, no, we're sure not."

She then says, "And honey, if you don't buy it, it's not going to cost you anything is it?"

They both nod and agree that this is true. She then says, "Why don't we first find you something that you really like, and then let's see if we can't get it for you at a price that makes sense. What do you say?"

She is one of the most successful salespeople in her field because she knows how to gently deflect the price concern at the beginning so that she can deal with it thoroughly later, but only after her prospects have decided that they really want to own what she is selling.

When a customer is insistent on knowing the price before he will listen to your sales presentation, another way you can derail his questioning is by asking, "Mr. Prospect, is price your *only* concern?" or, "Are you going to make your decision in this area *solely* on the basis of price?"

Sometimes he will respond by saying, "Yes, I'm really concerned about getting the very best price possible."

You then come back with, "Mr. Prospect, are you going to make your decision solely on the basis of the lowest cost product irrespective of attractiveness, convenience, quality, durability, service, follow-up support, guarantees, or the expected life of the product?" (You can select the strong points of your product and company and insert them in this sentence.)

Only one customer in twenty will say yes when you pose the question this way. By asking this question, you will help your prospect see that there are other critical factors that he should consider in evaluating your offering and comparing it with others. You will be doing him a great service by helping to expand his vision to include everything that should go into a good buying decision.

Neil Rackham, in his book *Major Account Sales Strategy*, writes that junior purchasing managers for large organizations are usually most concerned with getting the lowest price possible from suppliers. However, *experienced* purchasing agents have learned that the lowest price item often creates more problems than it solves. Senior purchasing agents are more concerned, based on their experience, with getting the most appropriate and highest quality product than they are with the lowest price product. And they always seem to make better decisions for their companies as a result.

By the same token, experienced buyers, including yourself, have learned that a higher quality item often turns out to cost less in the long run. That is why it has been stated repeated that, "If you can afford to buy quality, you cannot afford not to buy quality."

There is a substantial difference between price and cost. Price is the amount that it takes to purchase the item in the first place. Cost is the amount that is put out to own the item over its projected life. It's important that you point this out carefully to your prospects, especially those who seem to be most concerned about the initial price. Something that starts off at a low price may end up having a high cost.

Something that has a high price may end up having a lower overall cost. The customer's concern should be for the total dollar outlay over the life of the product, not just the amount that it takes to get it initially.

For example, let us say that you buy a $50,000 car and drive it for five years. Because it is of such high quality, it's trade-in value may be $25,000. It has therefore cost you $5,000 per year, or just under $500 per month to own the car, exclusive of insurance, service, and gasoline costs.

On the other hand, you could buy a $15,000 car that begins to fall apart as soon as the warranty expires. By the second year, the cost for parts and service could be eating you alive. By the end of the third year, the car could be in such bad shape that it would be better to scrap it and get a new one. Your actual dollars out of pocket for the $15,000 car could end up being substantially greater than for the expensive car and you would have had all of the headaches and problems associated with it as well.

This is the key to dealing with the price question. When you are selling a more expensive product, you must think it through and present it to your prospect in terms of its cost over its serviceable life. You must use good numbers and solid mathematical reasoning to divert your prospect's attention from the initial price tag to the real value and cost of what he gets.

No one is likely to pay more for what appears to him to be the identical product or service. Your ability to differentiate your product from those of your competitors and then to show your prospect that the value he receives more than offsets the additional price he pays is your key to succeeding in this part of the sale.

YOUR PRICE IS TOO HIGH

We know that what is important is not the price objection itself but the *real reason* behind the price objection. So whenever a person challenges your price, instead of arguing, you must probe and investigate to find out what the prospect really means.

The first question you might ask is, "Why do you *say* that?" Sometimes the prospect has no reason at all. Sometimes he objects to any price on the basis of habit. It is a knee-jerk reaction. Whatever you do, don't overreact. Just ask politely and curiously, "Why do you say that?"

Maybe he doesn't want to buy right now so he will object to any price. I've had experiences with customers who object to any price because they are really not interested in buying what you are selling. If your product costs $500 and you offered it to him for $5, he would still complain about the price. He may be short of cash or in a real financial bind. He may not be considering an additional cash outlay, no matter how attractive your product or service is. If this is the case, you can ask, "When do you think you will be in the market? What will have to happen before you seriously consider this offer?"

Or when the prospect complains about your price, you can ask him, "Why do you *feel* that way?" As I said earlier, people are usually very open to telling you why they feel a particular way. When you ask him why he feels that your price is too high, he will usually tell you. His reason may be firm or flimsy, but it is the *reason* that you are looking for, rather than the mere objection on the basis of price.

Sometimes your prospect wants to maneuver you into quoting a lower price. It is common for some businesspeople to grind salespeople as a form of sport. Or it may be customary in their own businesses to quote high and sell low and they feel that this is the same in your business.

People also hate to leave anything on the table. If they feel that, by negotiating, they can get a better price out of you, they will be absolutely determined to negotiate. And if there is the slightest thought in their minds that they have not brought you down as low as you can go, in many cases they won't even buy at all. So find out if the price objection is a negotiating ploy and be prepared to deal with it accordingly.

By the way, you should never offer a price concession or a discount until after the prospect has made it clear that he wants to buy your product or service. You should never use a price reduction to arouse buying desire. It is too early in the process. A discount is like a trump card that you can use at the critical moment to push the prospect over the psychological edge. But if you use it too soon, you will have nothing left to give when you come to the end of the sale. You can actually lose the sale by offering a lower price before the customer has decided that he wants to own what you are selling.

The basic rule in selling is that *buying desire reduces price sensitivity*. The more he wants it, the less sensitive he is to the price. When his desire is white-hot because of your ability to show him the tremendous value he will receive, he will become determined to buy it and small differences in price will not stand in his way.

PRICE VERSUS VALUE—THE PROSPECT'S PERSPECTIVE

When you meet with your prospect for the first time and begin discussing your product and its price, your prospect has a particular way of viewing the discussion. From where he sits, your price seems *high* and your value seems *low*. Because you have not yet had a chance to build value, your price seems out of proportion to your offering.

Imagine two balloons. One is large, the other is small, and they are connected by a thin tube. When you meet the prospect, the first balloon, with a P for price on it, is huge, and the second balloon, marked V for value, is small. Whichever of the two you talk about, grows. If you talk about price from the very beginning, the price balloon grows by withdrawing air from the value balloon. But if you talk about value, the value balloon grows and the price balloon shrinks the same way.

As you describe the benefits of owning your product in detail, and especially when you press the customer's hot button, the value balloon grows and the price balloon shrinks. If you have correctly identified the prospect's problem or need and focused your entire presentation on how your product or service can help him, by the end of the sales conversation the value balloon, in the customer's mind, will be substantially larger than the price balloon, and the customer will be ready to buy based on the merits of your offering rather than on its price tag.

Continued price resistance is a clear indicator that you have not yet answered the question, "What's in it for me?" in satisfactory detail. You must focus more on selling, and you are only selling when you are describing the specific benefits that the customer will enjoy from owning and using your product.

SHOWING THAT YOUR PRODUCT
DOESN'T COST TOO MUCH

My friend Alan Cimberg says that the smallest, weakest customer can reduce the biggest, strongest salesperson to jelly by leaning forward and saying, with reference to the product, "It costs too much." Salespeople are often dismayed and frustrated to hear this comment from a prospect. They have little control over pricing. The price is what it is. They can't change it.

There are several things you can do to diminish his concern about your apparently higher price. One of the simplest responses to "It costs too much" is to ask, "How much *too much* does it cost?" You need to know the amount that is at issue. Ask, "How far apart are we?"

When your prospect is comparing the price of your product or service with that of a competitor, you don't have to deal with the whole amount. You only have to justify the difference between what you are asking and what your competitor is asking. If your product costs $1,200 and your competitor's product costs $1,000, the amount at issue is $200. Your job is to first of all explain that he gets more than $200 in additional *use value* from your product in comparison with that of your competitors. Second, you must reduce the $200 to a meaningless amount by showing that, in comparison with the benefits he receives, it is inconsequential.

One way to do this is to spread the additional $200 over the life of the product. If the product lasts for a year and there are 250 business days in a year, you can show that $200 divided by 250 works out to 80 cents per day. This is a small amount for a large benefit.

For example, when we signed a five-year lease for our new offices, we contracted with AEI Music to install a $21,000, four-channel music system throughout our offices. I knew from my research that gentle, classical music playing in a work environment lowers stress, improves morale, reduces absenteeism, and fosters creativity among the staff. Since salaries and wages are the biggest single costs of operating my company, I felt it was a good investment, but $21,000 was a lot of money for a small company employing fifteen people.

I could easily have said, "It costs too much." The amount at issue was the full $21,000, because the alternative was nothing at all, with no financial outlay. So how did we justify spending that kind of money? It was relatively easy. We broke the amount down and spread it over not only the five years that we would be in these offices, but also over the number of people who would benefit from a musical environment.

Here's how it worked: $21,000 divided by five years works out to $4,200 per year. Let's say that the average of the salaries paid in my office is $2,500 per person, per month. Each person works approximately 172 hours per month. With these numbers we could cost out this musical system to see if it could be justified.

Dividing $4,200 per year by 12 months works out to $350 per month, and $350 per month divided by 15 people works out to $23.33 per person, per month. When you divide that amount by 172 hours, it works out to 13.6 cents per person, per hour. On that basis, we could clearly see that this was a good business decision. The improvements in morale and the increased productivity that occur when people work in a musical environment more than offset the cost. A 1 percent increase in output, or decrease in mistakes, pays for the entire system and a little more besides.

Whenever you are selling a product or service that has a useful life, you must be able to explain it to your customer in these terms. When you break it down to the smallest common denominator, you can reduce the importance of the price to the point where it is only one of several factors that enter into the final decision.

THE FEEL, FELT, FOUND METHOD

The final way to deal with objections of any kind is the "feel, felt, found" method. The power of this familiar method is that it tells a story about your product that activates the right brain of the prospect and makes the kind of impression that leads to a favorable buying decision.

Your prospect says, "I can't afford it," or, "Your price is too high," or, "It costs too much." You respond by pausing, smiling, and then saying, "Mr. Prospect, I understand exactly how you *feel*. Others *felt* the same way when they first looked at our prices, but this is what they *found*." You then go on to tell a success story of a customer who was initially concerned about the high price but who went ahead anyway, and how happy he was as a result.

Whether your customer's price objection is a knee-jerk reaction or a substantial concern, he still wants to be listened to seriously and treated respectfully. It is important to him that you take the time to understand his concern and his feelings. The words, "I understand how you feel," are the way you tell your prospect that you really care about him and about helping him improve his situation. When the customer feels that you really care, he will begin to relax and open up. He will freely express to you his worries and concerns. As the sales conversation proceeds, he will begin telling you everything he can to help you help him make a good buying decision.

YOU GET WHAT YOU PAY FOR

There is one final approach that may be helpful to you if your customer keeps coming back to the issue of price. Sometimes a customer can be fixated on the cost and, as a result, he won't let you bring your presentation to bear on the value he receives. In this case, you can try the following.

Ask him gently, "Mr. Prospect, let me ask you something. Did you ever get something for nothing?"

Remain silent. Give him time to answer. He will eventually admit that he has never really received anything for nothing.

Follow this answer by asking, "Mr. Prospect, did you ever get anything cheap that turned out to be good?"

Again, you must wait patiently for an answer. He will probably admit that he never has managed to buy something cheap that turned out to be valuable.

You then say, "Mr. Prospect, isn't it true that you get pretty much what you pay for?"

This is one of the great truths of buying and selling. When you present it in this fashion, your customer will almost invariably have to agree that what you have said is true. In life, you do get what you pay for. You don't get something for nothing. You don't get something good at a low price. Whenever you have tried to save money by buying the cheaper item, you have usually ended up regretting it.

You end with these words, "Mr. Prospect, our product is very fairly priced in an extremely competitive market. We may not be able to give you the lowest price, which you probably don't want anyway, but we can give you perhaps the very best overall deal on this type of product in today's market."

The virtue of these words is that they are almost always perfectly true. Your prospect will recognize that you are being completely honest and straightforward. He will also realize that your price is not going to budge. This is not an auction. You are not holding up your product and then soliciting bids or offers from interested parties. You are there to sell a good product at a fair price and the critical issues to be decided revolve around the appropriateness of your product for helping him solve his problems or achieve his goals.

CLOSING THE SALE

The fears of failure and rejection surge to the forefront of the minds of the prospect and the salesperson at the moment of decision. Money and ego are at stake, for both. The close, or moment of decision, is such a traumatic event for both people that it seldom happens. Fifty percent of all sales calls end without the salesperson asking for the order or for some sort of commitment to the next step in the sale.

In study after study, it has been shown that 90 percent of sales take place after the fifth call and the fifth time that the salesperson asks the prospect to make a commitment. The same studies show that most salespeople give up after the first call. Less than 10 percent of salespeople persist in their efforts with the prospect long enough for a sale to take place. That is why the top 10 percent of salespeople open 80 percent of the new accounts and earn 80 percent of the commissions payable in any industry.

We've seen that at the opening of the sales call, the relationship is paramount. It is the most important single factor. It is what gets you to first base. Every single element of personal and professional preparation must be focused on building trust and developing a friendly relationship where the customer likes you and believes that you are acting in his best interests. This must take place before you can move forward.

Throughout the sales process, your main job is to present yourself as a warm, friendly, knowledgeable, competent, and helpful sales consultant. The bigger the product, the more money involved, the more often it is that the prospect will have to interact with you before he reaches a critical mass psychologically, and feels confident enough to proceed with the purchase decision.

For the salesperson, the sales process begins with the initial contact. But for the customer, the sales process begins with the buying decision. Up to the point of saying yes, the customer is independent of the salesperson. He can accept or reject his offers, evaluate his proposals, compare his product with competitors', and decide to buy or not to buy. Before buying, the prospect can take you or leave you. The prospect is completely *free*. But from the moment the prospect signs the sales order and issues a check, he becomes a customer. He is now dependent on the salesperson and his company for the delivery of the product or service and the fulfillment of all his promises, and prospects don't particularly like to be dependent upon other people, especially salespeople.

Because of the complexity of modern selling, the sale goes on after the sale. Once you have closed the transaction, it is just the beginning. You must then make sure that the product or service is delivered and paid for, installed and operating, and that the customer is happy and satisfied. You must make regular public relations calls to make sure that the customer remains happy with his decision. In many cases, a sales relationship begins that can continue for years.

At the moment of making the final decision, the customer is in the position of entering into a "business marriage." Up to now, you have been "dating," conducting a business courtship. You have been going back and forth evaluating each other while the customer decides whether he wants to get involved with you for the long term. Whereas the relationship was important in the beginning of the sales process to get it started, the relationship becomes critical at the point of deciding whether or not to buy what you are selling.

It may seem too harsh, but every refusal to buy is, to some degree, the customer telling you that he doesn't like or trust you enough. A refusal by a qualified prospect to proceed with your offer is a statement that he does not have sufficient confidence in you or your company to enter into a long-term business relationship. More sales are lost for this reason than you could possibly imagine.

Almost every major decision, of any kind, is stressful. When you ask a prospect to give you a large amount of money and commit to a course of action that may take place over several months or years, the customer cannot help but wonder, "Am I making a mistake? Is it safe?"

Some people say that closing is unnecessary. They say that closing techniques are part of an earlier era of selling and sales training. They say that if you make an excellent presentation that is clearly focused on the customer's exact problem or needs, the sale will take care of itself. But this is simply not true.

The greater the possible consequences of the purchase decision, the more likely it will be that politics, bureaucracy, fear, and paralysis will set in as the sales process comes to a climax. Even if you have a fabulous relationship with the customer and all the associated decision-makers, you must be prepared, like a surgeon, to act with sureness and dexterity at the critical moment. You must be prepared to ask for the order.

I remember sitting in a boardroom with the president of a large corporation. He was surrounded by his senior executives. I had done everything correctly up to this moment. I was there to make the final presentation, close the sale, and get the check. The amount involved was $3.5 million, and I knew he wanted what I was selling. But at the end of the presentation, he started to back off. He suggested that we delay a final decision. He deferred to the executives around him and they concurred that this was a big step and perhaps they should study it a little more.

Up to this time, I had focused on presenting the facts, the details, and benefits of the offer. I assumed that they would speak for themselves. I suddenly realized that the sale was slipping away. Something that I had worked on for almost a year was moving beyond my grasp.

I remember leaning forward and locking eyes with the president, ignoring everyone else in the room. I lowered my voice, and said,

"Lyle, you know everything you need to know to make a decision right now. We have answered all your questions and satisfied all your requirements. You are not the only company that wants this deal, but we want to do business with you instead of the others. To close this transaction today, I need a check from you for three million, five hundred thousand dollars, and I need it now."

There was complete silence in the room. We were both watching each other, eyes fixed, like gladiators in the ring. Neither of us looked away. After what seemed like forever, even though it was only about thirty seconds, he smiled to break the tension and then turned to his chief financial officer and said, "Why don't you get him a check while we sign these papers!" The deal was done, the sale was closed.

On another occasion, the same thing happened to me as a customer. A salesperson had visited me, analyzed my needs, prepared a proposal, reviewed the proposal with me, and gotten my agreement that what he was offering satisfied all my requirements. The following week, he called and said he would like to drop in to our new offices and see how they looked. Perhaps he could have a cup of coffee with me at the time?

After I had given him a tour around our offices and we had sat down across my desk, he asked me if I had any questions or concerns about the proposal. No, I told him, it looks fine. I appreciated him putting it together. I was looking forward to reading it through more carefully when I got some more time.

I remember him leaning across the desk toward me and saying, "Brian, if this is exactly what you need, and you have no further questions, then I will need a deposit check from you for nine hundred fifty dollars, right now."

He was polite but firm. His gaze never wavered from mine. He was friendly but absolutely clear about what he wanted. I looked at him for a while, while he looked at me. Finally, I smiled, called my controller, and asked her to prepare a check in the amount he had requested.

Here's the point. In both cases everything had been done correctly. The president of the other company wanted the product, just as I did. We had no further questions or objections. We looked forward to enjoying the benefits of ownership. We had no reasons not to buy. But if I hadn't asked the president, or if the salesperson hadn't asked me, we wouldn't have bought. We would have continued to procrastinate and delay, maybe even indefinitely.

Customers like to be asked. More than that, they *need* to be asked. One of the major weaknesses in business today is that salespeople will carry the sales process through to the final moment and then pull back for fear of offending or antagonizing the prospect. You've probably read the words of George W. Cecil, who wrote, "On the Plains of Hesitation, bleach the bones of countless millions who, at the Dawn of Victory, sat down to wait, and waiting, died."

Customers both like and respect the salesperson who asks for the order. They do not want to be taught, told, or talked down to. They want to feel as though they are making up their own minds. They want good advice and counsel, and they want to be helped to make the best buying decision possible. They want a friendly relationship with a professional salesperson and they want to feel confident that they are doing the right thing. But after all of that, they want you to ask for the order.

TEN CLOSING REQUIREMENTS

"Before you do anything, you have to do something else first." Before you ask the customer to make a buying decision, there are a series of bases you much touch. Any attempt to bring the sales process to a conclusion with even one of these elements missing can cost you the sale.

First, the customer must **want** what you are selling. The customer's buying desire must be aroused sufficiently before you ask him to make a decision. The customer must have told you clearly that he likes what you have shown him and he must have expressed a desire to enjoy the benefits of your offer. If you attempt to get a decision from him prior to this point, you may turn him off and kill the sale.

Second, the customer must **believe** in you and your company. The customer must trust you and be convinced that you and your company have the capability to deliver on your promises. In your presentation, you must have made it perfectly clear to the customer that you are a sound and reliable organization to deal with.

Third, the customer must **need** the product or service you are selling. It must be obvious to both you and him that the product will help him to solve his problem or achieve his goal in a cost-effective way. Top salespeople will refuse to accept a sales order from a customer if they are not convinced that this is what the customer genuinely needs, even if the customer wants it and has expressed an interest in buying it.

One of my graduates, the top salesman for a radio station, spent a good deal of time analyzing the needs of a prospective client. He then gave him a presentation that called for $48,000 worth of advertising over a four-month period. The customer, wanting to save money, said that he liked the proposal but he only wanted to spend $25,000, and could the salesperson write it up for that amount?

My friend refused to take the order. He told the customer that the partial budget he was suggesting would not be enough to give him the type of frequency that he required to get the advertising results for which he was booking the time in the first place.

The customer couldn't believe it. He was a sharp businessman and he asked the salesman, "Are you refusing to take my money?"

The salesman told him politely that he could not, in good conscience, accept the order knowing that it would not give the client the results he was expecting.

After the salesman left, the prospect phoned the general manager of the radio station and told him his story. He said, "If that salesman won't sell me the time, I want to buy it directly from you."

The sales manager had worked with this salesman for several years. He was intelligent enough to reply, "This is the best salesman in this station, if not in the entire city. If he refuses to take your order, then we refuse to take it as well. We thank you very much for your interest but we won't take your money if we feel that this advertising campaign will not give you the results you are expecting."

The client was dumbfounded. In a vigorously competitive market, with advertising salespeople calling on prospects daily, here was a station that was turning him down for a substantial order because they didn't feel that it was what he needed. He couldn't believe it!

After thinking about it for a couple of days, the client called the radio station and had them send the salesman back. He accepted the $48,000 proposal as written, and gave him the necessary deposit check. He told the salesman that he had concluded that if they believed so strongly in the effectiveness of a program of this size, they must know what they were doing. And they did. Over the next four months, the advertiser traced almost $500,000 of new sales to that radio advertising campaign.

Fourth, the customer must be able to **use** it. Top salespeople will not sell someone a product that the customer is not capable of using to its best advantage. They won't sell a computer or computer software to a person who is not computer literate. They won't sell advanced sports equipment to an amateur. They won't sell complex machinery to a small operation. Top salespeople always take time to make sure the customer can get the very maximum value out of what they are selling.

Fifth, the customer must be able to afford it. The customer must not only have the money but must be willing to part with it. The customer must have sufficient funds to be able to buy the product without ending up strapped for cash.

This is a double-edged advantage. By making sure the customer can afford it, the salesperson makes sure his company will be paid for the product or service once it is delivered. At the same time, the salesperson makes sure the customer will continue to be solvent even after having paid for the product.

Sixth, the customer must completely **understand** the full nature and scope of the offer. The customer must be clear about what he is getting and why, and how to use it. The customer must understand the obligations he is entering into and the ramifications and consequences of the purchase. The salesperson must patiently walk the customer through these steps so that the customer absolutely knows what he or she is getting into with the purchase.

One of the biggest obstacles to the closure of a sale is fuzzy understanding. This occurs at the moment of decision when the customer realizes he is not quite sure about what it is he is buying or how he is going to use it properly. As a result, he may hesitate or delay. One of your responsibilities as a salesperson is to double-check and be sure that the customer is clear about your offering.

Seventh, the salesperson must be **eager** to make the sale. He must be positive and confident about the benefits that the prospect will enjoy and must be determined to help the prospect enjoy them.

In my company alone, we spend millions of dollars each year buying products and services from salespeople and outside companies. It continually amazes us to see the number of salespeople who make the calls and go through the motions but who don't really seem to care whether they make the sale or not. And because they don't seem excited about our buying, we don't get excited either. We procrastinate on the buying decision and often we don't buy at all.

Eighth, the salesperson must have **sound closing skills.** The only way you learn anything is by practicing, over and over, and this includes closing skills. One of the best things you can do is to write out your closing arguments and questions on paper and then practice them in front of a mirror. You should try your closing techniques with your children and your spouse. You should use them in your personal and business life. If you remember that a closing technique is simply a way of helping a person to make a decision, you will actually find it enjoyable and fun to practice different methods.

With my children, at their bedtime, if I tell them to go to bed they will argue and protest. But if I ask them, "What time do you want to go to bed—nine, or nine-thirty [the alternative close]?" they will immediately choose nine-thirty. When nine-thirty comes they will march off to bed like little soldiers. They were "closed" without even being aware of it.

Ninth, the salesperson must be prepared to **hear a no and continue selling.** You must be willing to ask for the order and be put off, either with an objection or a delay to another time.

Finally, the salesperson must be prepared to **remain silent** after asking the closing question. The very best salespeople are masters in the use of silence during the selling conversation. Not only are they extremely good at listening to the customer and absorbing what he is really saying, but they are also skilled at remaining perfectly quiet after they have asked a key questions of any kind.

The longer the silence goes on after you have asked a closing question, the more likely it is that the prospect will buy. But the person who speaks first usually loses. If you break the silence, out of nervousness, the customer will sense an opportunity to procrastinate on the buying decision or come up with another objection that cannot be answered at this meeting. It takes tremendous discipline to sit quietly while the prospect mulls over your question, but it pays off in the end.

The president of a large insurance company, who had worked his way up from the ranks of insurance salesman, sat through a complete presentation for a several-hundred-thousand-dollar computer system to automate their entire operations. At the end of the presentation, the computer salesman, who was an expert at his business, asked the closing question, "When would you like us to get started?"

The president smiled at the salesman and sat back in his chair, never removing his gaze from the salesman's face. The salesman sat quietly, unmoving, and without saying a word. The two of them sat there, much to the discomfort of the other people in the room, for fully five minutes with neither one moving or speaking. At the end of five minutes, the president looked at his watch, smiled, and said, "That's the best I've ever seen; you've got the business!"

It turned out that the president had briefed his staff prior to the meeting and told them to remain silent after he had been asked the closing question. He wanted to see how long this salesman could sit without wavering. His standard was five minutes. At the end of that period, he was ready to proceed. He knew he was dealing with a world-class salesman.

FIVE ERRORS TO AVOID WHEN CLOSING THE SALE

There are five common errors that salespeople make in the course of the sales conversation that can derail or destroy a sale to even the most qualified prospect. It is important that you be aware of them and that you avoid them at all costs.

The first is **arguing.** When you argue with a prospect, you are indirectly telling him he is wrong. People hate to be told they are wrong, especially when it is obvious that they are. They dislike people who point out their errors.

Always be agreeable in a sales conversation. If the prospect challenges your claims for your product, use the "feel, felt, found" method and say something like, "I understand how you could *feel* that way. Others *felt* the same way when we first showed them this aspect of our product. But this is what they *found* when they started using it."

Your job is to win a customer, not win an argument. Unless the customer questions the integrity of your company or the quality of your products, let it pass. Focus on what the product can do for him, and ignore the rest.

The second error that salespeople make is expressing **personal opinions,** especially those of a religious or political nature. You may feel very strongly about your beliefs, but you should remember that other people may feel equally strongly about theirs. Customers like to buy from people who are similar to themselves. If it turns out that you are vocal in taking a position that is opposite to that of your customer, he will probably not want to buy from you. Never assume that the customer agrees with your particular set of beliefs.

A third error that salespeople make is **knocking the competition.** Shakespeare wrote, "The fragrance of the rose lingers on the hand that casts it." The fragrance of whatever you throw seems to linger on your hand, and when you are selling, the fragrance seems to hover around your product. If your competition is not mentioned, you shouldn't mention them either. Never discuss them by name. Never bring them up to compare your product with theirs or attack them for any reason.

If your customer says something about buying from your competition or talking to your competition, you should acknowledge his remark by simply saying, "ABC, Inc. is a very fine company. They've been in business for a long time and they do a good job for their customers."

By speaking well of your competition, you will indirectly be speaking well of *yourself* and your product. You will look and sound good to your prospect, especially if your competition has said something derogatory about you or your product in a previous meeting.

If your prospect is going to buy from either you or a particular competitor, and he needs to know why he should choose your product instead of the other, you can undermine the competition indirectly. Instead of attacking them by name, you can instead attack their methods or processes as being inadequate or insufficient to solve this customer's specific problem. You concentrate on showing that the approach or structure of your company is superior to that of others in dealing with the needs of this customer.

The fourth error to avoid is **overselling.** This happens when you say that your product can do something it cannot. It verges on the border between puffing and misrepresentation. Since the element of trust is the critical catalyst that makes the sale come together in the end, you cannot afford to do or say anything that might shatter that trust.

In fact, *understatement* in selling today is probably more impressive than overstatement. Instead of your saying something exceptional about the capabilities of your product, you can tell about an experience enjoyed by one of your customers. Put the words in someone else's mouth. It's much easier for a customer to accept and believe a positive remark if it is someone other than you who has said it.

The fifth error to avoid is **assuming authority** that you don't have. This occurs when you tell the prospect that you can arrange a discount or speed up a delivery schedule and then it turns out that you can't. When you have to go back to the prospect and confess that you were unable to deliver on your promises, you undermine your credibility and weaken the trust bond on which the entire sales relationship depends.

Not only must you do things right, but you must avoid doing things wrong as well. If it doesn't help, it hurts. Recall the Hippocratic oath: "Do no harm." It's a good rule to follow.

OBSTACLES TO CLOSING

An important reason salespeople fail to make sales is **negative expectations.** These occur when the salesperson makes a negative prejudgment of the prospect. He decides that the prospect isn't really going to buy and that he is just wasting his time. He overreacts to the prospect's questions about price or about the capability of the product to do what he says it will do. The salesperson loses heart. The energy and conviction go out of his sales presentation. As he gets toward the end of the meeting, he has already given up on this prospect and his mind is on what he's going to do after the sales call.

The antidote to this thinking trap is to always assume that the prospect is going to buy. Don't be put off by his questions, complaints, or objections. Continue being pleasant and cheerful and focus on him and his situation. Talk to him about himself and the problems he is facing. Rise above any negative signals that the prospect gives off. At the very least, be natural and easygoing.

Selling has been defined as a "transfer of enthusiasm." The sale takes place when the enthusiasm you feel for your product is transferred into the mind and heart of the prospect. It is like an electric arc. The more power and conviction there is behind your belief and enthusiasm for what you are selling, the more the energy *arcs* from you into your prospect. When your prospect becomes as enthusiastic about your product as you are, the sale is made.

One of the top salespeople I know is blind, having lost his eyesight in an auto accident after be began selling. But he didn't' feel sorry for himself and he didn't give up. When he got out of the hospital, he went back to work. He had his secretary dial his calls for him. Even though he couldn't see, he could still talk and interact with his clients, setting up his appointments and arranging to see people.

When he went out to see a prospect, his secretary would go along to guide him. She would position him in front of the prospect and sit off to the side. Because he was blind, he just assumed that the prospect was happy to see him and eager to buy his product. He spoke with excitement, enthusiasm, and conviction. If the prospect objected or asked questions, he assumed that these were simply observations on his product and he answered them positively and completely. He would then go on to ask for the order.

The secretary reported that, in many cases, the prospects were not particularly interested. Their body language and facial expressions were negative. They looked at their watches, glanced away, tapped their fingers, and even signed their mail. But the blind salesman couldn't see his prospects so he continued talking exactly as if the prospect was eagerly hanging on every word. Eventually his enthusiasm and conviction wore them down and they bought.

The second obstacle to closing is **lack of sincerity.** This happens whenever a salesperson is thinking more about the sale and the commission than he is about the prospect and his situation. Prospects can pick up a lack of sincerity across a crowded room. The instant you begin thinking about what's in it for you, rather than what's in it for him, the prospect will sense that he is like a canary in a cage and you are like a cat on the outside, salivating and thinking about how good he will taste. The prospect will turn off to you immediately and lose all interest in your product and presentation.

The third common obstacle to selling takes place when you and the prospects are on **different wavelengths.** For some reason, you don't seem to communicate. It may be because you have different backgrounds, different levels of education, different interests or philosophies. You may have a different personality style and orientation toward life and people.

When you find yourself in a situation with a qualified prospect with whom you do not seem able to connect, instead of pressing forward and trying to make the sale regardless, you should have the maturity to back off. Don't ruin the prospect for your company. Turn the prospect over to someone else who may be better attuned to him. Say, "Mr. Prospect, you have a unique situation that I think our company can really help you with. I would like to get an expert in this area to talk to you and see if we can't help you achieve your goals."

The prospect will be flattered and the relationship will be saved. You then go back to the office and get another salesperson who you feel will communicate better with this prospect, and send him or her back. You will be amazed at how many sales you can save this way, and if everybody in your company engages in this form of reciprocity, you will all do better than you would by trying to force a sale on an unwilling prospect.

The fourth block to closing the sale is often a **personality clash** between you and the prospect. A basic rule in selling is that you cannot sell to a person you don't like and the prospect cannot buy from you until he likes you. He won't buy until he is genuinely convinced that you are his friend and that you are there to help him. If these conditions don't exist, no sale will take place, no matter how qualified the prospect or how appropriate your product.

If you find that you don't particularly like a prospect for some reason, don't blame the prospect or take it personally. It happens. Throughout your life, you will meet an enormous number of people with whom you don't get along. You will meet people you don't particularly like in selling as well.

But if the prospect seems to be a good candidate for your product or service, break off the conversation gracefully and make every effort to save the prospect for someone else in your company. Have other people in your company do the same thing for you. One company I worked with increased their sales 30 percent the very first month they instituted a new policy that called for two salespeople to see every prospect before giving up on him. It was amazing how many prospects were open to buying from one person while being closed to another.

BUYING SIGNALS

As explained in Chapter 7, only 7 percent of the customer's message to you is in the form of words. Another 38 percent is in his tone of voice. But fully 55 percent of his message is conveyed by his body language. His message is transmitted largely by the way he moves and the things he does with his hands, face, and eyes. If you are sufficiently observant, the prospect will actually tell you how you are doing in the sales conversation. He will also tell you when he is ready to make a decision. If you pick up on his cues, you will know exactly when to ask for a buying commitment.

The first and most obvious clue comes when the prospect, after you have presented your product, asks you about the **price and terms.** How much does it cost and how can he go about paying for it?

When you hear a question like this, immediately stop presenting and make an attempt to conclude the transaction. Answer the question with a question of your own. "How soon do you need it? How many will you want at this time? Will you want it delivered here, or to your home address?"

The second type of signal is when the customer asks you for **more details** about some aspect of your product. This often indicates that you have hit the hot button. The prospect will be curious and interested, even fascinated by the particular aspect of your product or service that attracts him the most. When you begin to hear those detailed questions, bring your arguments to bear on that particular element of the product, how well it works, how much he will enjoy it when he owns it. Say something like, "This is one of the most popular aspects of this product. In fact, if you really like it, I can probably have one of these out to you by the end of the week."

The third signal is when the customer asks about **delivery.** How long does it take to get it? You can confirm that this is a buying signal by asking something simple like, "Would you want it delivered to this address?"

If he confirms that this is where he wants it delivered, he has decided to go ahead. Or, you could ask him, "How soon do you need it?"

Whatever time schedule he gives you, he has decided to purchase your product. You should stop your presentation at that point and begin wrapping up the sale.

The fourth way the customer signals to you that he is ready to buy is by adjusting his posture or changing his **body language.** There are two positions that the prospect goes into when he is ready to make a buying decision, the *tea kettle position* and the deep-thought position, or *chin rubbing.*

In the tea kettle position, the prospect leans forward, with one hand on his hip and his arm on his knee. If you can imagine his head being the spout and his hand on his hip being the handle, you see where the tea kettle image comes from. This is the "ready" position, like a runner at the mark ready to spring at the starting gun. When you see it, shift your body forward into a similar ready position and ask, "Would you like us to get started on this right away?"

The second position that indicates that a buying decision is coming is deep thought, or chin rubbing. Sometime during your presentation, the prospect stops and his hand leaps to his chin. His head declines. He becomes lost in thought.

According to research, chin rubbing has a 99 percent predictive value. When the hand goes to the chin, and the customer becomes lost in thought, he is almost invariably thinking about how to purchase your product. He no longer sees or hears you. You should stop talking and sit quietly, until his hand comes down from his chin. When his hand comes down his head will come up and he will make eye contact with you. The answer is yes.

When this happens, as soon as the hand comes down and his eyes make contact with yours, ask a closing question. "Where would you like it delivered? We could send it out Friday, or would Monday be all right with you?"

Another way you know that it is time to ask for the order is when the customer begins **calculating numbers,** working out how much the product costs, how the price can be justified, how much the use of the product or service will add to revenues or detract from costs, and so on.

When the prospect is calculating numbers, remain silent. Don't interfere with the process. He can't calculate and hear you at the same time. After he has finished calculating the numbers and he looks up at you, ask, "Which one of these would you prefer?"

Customers also signal buying readiness by **sudden friendliness.** This happens when the customer shifts from being resistant or standoffish to suddenly being warm and friendly. He begins to act like a host. He will ask questions like, "By the way, have you seen our offices? Would you like another cup of coffee? Do you have any children? How long have you lived in the city?"

When the prospect shifts into a friendly mode, it means the tension of decision making has been broken. He is now relaxed and ready to go ahead. To confirm that this is what has happened, you should smile, and ask a closing question. "Which color do you prefer? Where would you want it delivered? How soon do you need it?"

The final signal that the prospect has reached the end of the road is when he begins asking smokescreen objections. These are questions like, "How do I know I am getting the best deal? Are you sure this is the right one? Is there any flexibility with regard to the price?"

The customer offers this type of objection only after he has decided that he wants the product and he can afford it. He is ready to make a buying decision. He is like a man slipping toward the edge, grasping at straws as he moves toward the point of no return.

You should always reassure him that he is making a good decision. "You've made a good choice! You are really going to be happy with this once you start using it."

THE SOUNDS OF SILENCE

We've seen that the biggest single complaint about salespeople is that they talk too much. Men especially tend to speak louder and faster when they are nervous and they fear rejection. Many salespeople have been told that because they have the "gift of gab" they would be great in sales. Old stereotypes like Robert Preston in *The Music Man* or George C. Scott in *The Flim Flam Man* have led many salespeople to believe that the essence of professional selling is talking people into buying things by jamming as many words as possible into as short a period of time as they have.

Nothing could be further from the truth. Every single day, thousands of salespeople talk themselves out of sales by going on long after the prospect has decided to buy. Finally, the prospect gives up waiting and mutters something like, "Well, leave me this material and let me think it over." And soon, the salesperson is back on the street, unsure of what exactly happened.

You can talk yourself out of a sale, but it is almost impossible to *listen* yourself out of a sale. Good salespeople are comfortable with silence. They let the customer do the talking. While the customer is talking, they are busy listening and building trust. They are observing the customer's movements and mannerisms. They are looking for clues that will give them feedback on what the customer is really thinking and what the customer really wants.

As an exercise, you should take time on a regular basis to observe other people, both the members of your family and the people you work with. Notice the clues and cues they give off in small bodily movements and tiny changes of facial expression. The more sensitive you become to the thoughts, feelings, and behaviors of other people, the more capable you will be of confirming the sale when the critical moment arises.

SEVEN CLOSING TECHNIQUES

There are supposed to be more than one hundred different closing techniques. I've read as many of the books and articles on closing as I could find over the years, and I have tested every closing technique that made sense to me. Just like at a smorgasbord, each salesperson has to select those techniques with which they are the most comfortable and which prove to be the most effective for them.

Some of the most popular closing techniques go back to the last century. There is the "puppy dog" close, where you let the prospect try out the product or service for a while until he becomes so attached to it (as he would to a puppy dog from the pet store) that he decides to keep it.

There is the "Ben Franklin" close, where you have the customer draw a line down the center of a page and write the reasons in favor of buying down one side of the page and the reasons for not buying down the other.

There is the "sharp angle" close, where you take an objection and turn it into a reason for buying. Prospect: "I can't afford the monthly payments." Salesperson: "If we can spread them over a longer time and get them down, then would you take it?"

There is the "walk away" close, the "take away" close, and the "today only" close. Then there are the variations and combinations of the basic closing techniques. I heard one sales trainer not long ago give a twenty-one-step method that he assured the audience could be used for closing any sale of any product or service whatsoever. The only problem with it was that by the time he got to step number seven, most people had already forgotten steps one and two.

As a professional, you are a low-pressure, no-pressure salesperson. You do not do or say anything manipulative that might damage the fragile bond of trust upon which your selling relationship is based. Everything you do with your customer is up front, straightforward, and on the table. You never use a trick or a technique that might cause the prospect to feel that he was being made to act against his own best interests. You never attempt to manipulate a prospect in any way.

Consistent with the above principles, here are seven ways to bring a sales conversation to a favorable conclusion and maintain a quality relationship afterward.

The first is the **invitational close**. This is simple, low-key, classy, and powerful. You use it at the end of a sales conversation to conclude the transaction. It is preceded by a trial close such as: "Mr. Prospect, do you have any questions or concerns that I haven't covered up to now?" Or, "Mr. Prospect, does this make sense to you so far?"

You ask these questions to be doubly sure that the prospect has no final objections lurking in the back of his mind that would block the closing of the sales process. You then invite the customer to make a buying decision by saying, "If you like what I've shown you, *why don't you give it a try?*"

Inviting the customer to buy is very powerful. This is a gentle way of nudging the customer into taking action. "Why don't you give it a try?" If you are selling services, you can ask, "Why don't you give *us* a try?"

If you want to be more bold and direct, you can simply ask, "Why don't you take it?"

One of my seminar graduates doubled his sales by changing his wording in the endgame of selling. After his sales presentation he would ask the prospect if he had any additional questions or concerns. If the prospect said no, he would then ask, "Well, if you like it, why don't you take it?"

He was amazed to find that many prospects could not think of a good reason not to go ahead with his offer immediately. Both his closing ratio and his income soared.

The second popular method is the **directive close**. This is sometimes called the **assumption close**, or the **post-closing technique**. It is one of the most powerful of all closing techniques and it is used by top sales professionals in every industry. It is used to change the focus of the customer's thinking away from the decision of yes or no to the ownership and enjoyment of the product.

Its major virtue is that it allows you to keep the initiative, to maintain control of the selling process, and to wrap it up at your own pace. It is also very simple.

At the end of the sales conversation, you ask a trial closing question like, "How does this sound to you so far?" If the prospect agrees that it sounds pretty good, you say, "Well then, Mr. Prospect, the next step is . . ."

You then go on to describe the *plan of action*, or what happens from this point forward. You get out your sales contract or order form and begin filling it in. You say something like, "Well then, the next step is that I get your authorization and a check and get it back to my company. We will be out in three days to begin the initial planning and we should have the entire process installed and working by the third week of next month."

In each of these first two closes, the customer can either say yes and help you conclude the sale, or he can ask any questions that he might still have. If, for any reason, the customer still objects, you answer the objection completely and then ask for the order again.

A customer at the end of the sales process is very much like a pot of water boiling on the stove. It is as hot as it is going to get. If you take it off the stove, it will begin to cool. If you leave it off the stove for any period of time, it will go stone cold, as though it were never heated up at all. Customers are somewhat the same. If you do not ask for the order at the end of the sales process, whether it is after one call or several calls, you run the risk of the customer cooling down, changing his mind, and even forgetting why it was that he was so eager to make the purchase in the first place.

The third technique is the **alternative close.** This is often called the **preference close.** It is based on the fact that people like to have choices. They don't like to be given what may sound like an ultimatum, to either buy it or not buy it. To apply this technique, you structure your close by saying, "Which of these would you prefer, A or B?"

With the alternative close, whichever one the customer selects, you have still made a sale. You should always try to give the customer two choices. Even if you are selling a single product, you can give him two choices with regard to payment, or delivery, "Would you like this delivered to your office or to your home address?"

"Will that be MasterCard or Visa?"

"Would you like the XYZ 26 or the XYZ 30?" And so on.

The fourth closing technique is the **secondary close.** This is extremely popular. It is a way of helping a customer make a big decision by having him make a small decision first. Instead of asking the customer to go ahead with the product or service, you ask a question about a peripheral detail, the acceptance of which means he has decided to buy the larger product.

"Would you want this shipped in a wooden crate, or would cardboard be all right?" "Did you want us to include the drapes and the rods in the offer?" "Did you want the standard rims or would you like the customized racing rims on the car?"

In each case, if the customer agrees to or chooses the smaller item, he has indirectly said yes to the entire offering. People often find it easier to agree to small details than they do to making a larger commitment. This is also called the **incremental close,** where you get commitment bit by bit to the entire offer.

The fifth closing method is the **authorization close,** which is commonly used to conclude even multi-million-dollar transactions. At the end of the sales conversation, you simply ask if the prospect has any questions or concerns that haven't been covered. If the prospect has no further questions or concerns, the salesperson takes out the contract, opens it up to the signature page, places a check mark where the customer has to sign, and pushes it over to him saying, "Well then, if you will just authorize this, we'll get started on it right away."

The word "authorize" is better than the word "sign." A check mark is better than an X. Offering to "get started right away" is better than sitting there hoping for the best.

A variation of the authorization close is the **ultimatum close.** You use this when you have been going back and forth with the prospect for some time. You have invested a lot of time and effort with this prospect and you don't want to lose it, but the prospect will not say yes and he will not say no. You need to get a resolution so that you can either close the sale or get on to other prospects who represent greater opportunities to sell.

To use this closing method, you call the prospect, whom you have seen several times, and arrange to see him once more. When you arrive, you sit down and say these words, "Mr. Prospect, I know how busy you are. We've been talking about this product for some time now, and either this is a good idea for you, or it's not. If it is a good idea, we should make a decision right now and get on with it. And if it's not a good idea, your time is too valuable for us to continue talking about it. If you'll just authorize this, we'll get started on it right away."

Push the completed sales contract across the desk, lay your pen on top of the contract next to the check mark, smile, and sit perfectly still. This technique has about a 60 percent probability of success, and the prospect will eventually sign the contract and buy the product. But you must sit silently and be patient.

In the other 40 percent of the cases, the prospect will push the contract back, say that he has decided not to buy it after all, and end the discussion. In either case, the discussion is over and you can get on with the rest of your sales activities.

The sixth closing technique is the **order sheet close.** It is very simple. At the end of your sales conversation, you take out your order sheet or sales contract and begin filling it out. If the prospect does not stop you from filling it out, he has decided to buy. You can confirm this buying decision by asking one of three questions: "Mr. Prospect, what is the correct spelling of your last name?" or, "Mr. Prospect, what is your correct mailing address?" or, "Excuse me, what is today's date?"

In each case, once you have asked the question, poise your pen over the sales contract and look down at it until he answers. Don't look up. Wait patiently, silently. When he gives you the correct spelling of his name, his correct mailing address, or today's date, and you write it down on the sales contract, he has decided to buy. You can then write up the rest of the order and conclude the sale.

The seventh and final closing technique is what I call the **I want to think it over close.** This is the only way I know to save this kind of lost sale. You know by now that when the customer says, "I want to think it over," he is really saying good-bye. You know from your own experience that customers do *not* think it over. They do not sit there carefully studying your brochures and price lists with a calculator and a pen.

On the other hand, as many as 50 percent of the people you speak to are probably ready to buy at the completion of a professional sales presentation. They just need a little push. They need some help. A buying decision is stressful for them. They are tense and uneasy, and afraid of making a mistake. They may be right on the verge of saying yes and they need the professional guidance of an excellent salesperson to push them over the edge. But if you accept the "I want to think it over" at face value and depart, you will probably never get a chance to see them or to sell to them again.

This is how you use it. When the prospect says, "I want to think it over," you appear to accept it gracefully. You smile agreeably, and begin packing your briefcase and putting your materials away. As you do, you make conversation with these words: "Mr. Prospect, that's a good idea. This is an important decision and you shouldn't rush into it." These words will cause the prospect to mentally relax. He sees that you are on your way. His resistance will drop as soon as you stop presenting and trying to sell.

You then ask, in a curious tone of voice: "Mr. Prospect, *obviously you* have a good reason for wanting to think it over. May I ask what it is; is it the money?"

Remain perfectly silent, watching his face. Smile gently. Take a deep breath and let it out slowly. This is a critical moment.

Again, you have nothing to lose. If you leave, you have lost this person as a prospect forever. The worst thing he can say is that he has no particular reason but that he still wants to think it over. However, in many cases, he will reply by saying one of two things. He will say, "Yes, I'm concerned about the cost." Or, he will say, "No, it's not the money."

If he says, "Yes, it's the money," you immediately ask the questions that deal with concerns about cost or price. You ask things like, "How do you mean, exactly? Why do you say that? Why do you feel that way? How far apart are we? Is price your only concern, or is there something else?"

If he says, "No, it's not the money," you reply by asking, "May I ask what it is?"

Again, you remain perfectly silent while you wait for his answer. In many cases, he will think about it for a few seconds, even a minute or longer, and then he will give you his final concern or objection. He will finally tell you what is really on his mind. He will tell you the real reason he is hesitating about going ahead.

If you can now satisfy him on his final condition, you can go on to conclude the sale. You can say, "Mr. Prospect, what if we could do this . . . ?" Or, "I think there is a perfect answer to that question." The sale is once more within reach.

The very best salespeople take nothing for granted. They review their sales presentations prior to every meeting with the client. They listen attentively when the client is speaking and they watch for clues to indicate what the client is thinking and feeling. They are always alert for the signal that says that the customer is ready to make a buying decision. And once the customer has indicated a desire to buy, they step forward boldly and ask for the order.

FINAL THOUGHTS ON THE ENDGAME

Handling objections and closing the sale are intertwined. They are inseparable parts of the endgame of the selling process. Your ability to answer questions and resolve concerns satisfactorily is what gets you down to the five-yard line in the game. But it is your ability to ask for the order that gets you the touchdown.

The world belongs to the askers. Because of their fears of failure and rejection, most people are reluctant to ask for the things that they want and need. They suggest, imply, and hint but they are reluctant to ask and be told no.

Much of your success and happiness in life will be determined by your ability and your willingness to ask for the things you want. Learn to ask positively. Ask cheerfully. Ask politely. Ask expectantly. Ask for information. Ask for appointments. Ask for the reasons people hesitate and ask for the real meanings that lie behind customer statements.

Most of all, ask for orders. Ask for customers to make decisions after you have gone though all the work of bringing a sales transaction through to the last step. As the Bible says, "Ask and it shall be given unto you, for all who ask receiveth." Courage and boldness are the fundamental qualities of the top salesperson. Salespeople who reach their full potential are those who have overcome their fears and developed their courage to the point that they are willing to march bravely forward in the face of the blazing guns of continuous failure, frustration, and rejection.

Dorothea Brande, in her wonderful little book *Wake Up and Live*, described the secret of success that turned her life around. It was simply this: "Once you have decided what you want, *act* as if it were impossible to fail, and it shall be!"

There are no limitations upon what you can accomplish in the profession of selling except the limitations you place on yourself by your own doubts and fears. When you practice acting boldly and behaving as if it were impossible to fail, you will soon make the quality of courage a fundamental part of your character where it will serve you all the days of your life. Your success in selling will then be guaranteed.

SUMMARY

I started off as a laborer. I spun my wheels for several years before I finally got into commission sales, peddling items from door to door. I started with no education, no skills, no friends, no money, no opportunities, and no contacts. From that limited beginning, by learning and practicing the ideas I've written about in this book, I've been able to go from the bottom of each sales force I've worked with, all the way to the top. I have been able to move from cheap boarding houses to a beautiful home on a golf course. I've gone from eating in cheap cafes to dining in the finest restaurants in the world. And so can you.

I don't consider myself to be a *great* salesman. I have met men and women who could sell circles around me. But I am a professional salesman. In the long run, I have been able to outperform and outsell virtually every salesperson I've ever met, and many I've never seen, because I have followed a logical process of professional selling, as described in this book.

You don't have to be a "super salesperson" and leap tall buildings with a single bound. But you *do* have to take your profession seriously and study it as a doctor or lawyer would study his or her profession. You do have to be attentive to the details, because you are talking about products or services that affect other people's lives. You have to work on yourself as hard as you work on your craft. You have to study, learn, and grow on a daily basis. You have to accept that everything counts. You have to commit yourself to becoming one of the finest salespeople of your generation.

And when you do all this, the future that lies before you will be virtually unlimited. There has never been a time or place in all of history where an excellent salesperson could live a finer life than he or she can, right now, right here, in our economic system. There are no limits to how far or how high you can go in the profession of sales. As you become better, you will sell to more and better customers. You will be paid more and more. You will earn the respect and esteem of the people around you. You will take complete control of your own life and your own destiny. You will be able to take charge of everything that happens to you. You will be able to achieve levels of financial independence, success, satisfaction, joy, and self-fulfillment greater than you could ever imagine.

Nothing that has happened before can have any effect or bearing on what you can make happen in the future. As Shakespeare wrote, "What's past is prologue." It doesn't matter where you're coming from; all that matters is where you're *going*.

I look forward to hearing from you, or seeing you personally at my seminars. In the meantime, don't just *have* a good day, go out there and *make* it a good day! Good luck.

APPENDIX A

Brian Tracy—Speaker, Trainer, Seminar Presenter

Brian Tracy is one of the most popular professional speakers in the world. He addresses more than 100,000 men and women each year in private and public talks and seminars. His fast-moving, informative, and entertaining seminars on personal success, sales, leadership, and motivation draw capacity audiences across the country.

Brian Tracy speaks regularly for corporations and associations at annual meetings and conventions. He has addressed the executives and staff of hundreds of organizations large and small, carefully customizing each talk to the specific needs of the audience. His clients include Ford Motor Company, Federal Express, Southwestern Bell, Northwestern Mutual Life Insurance, IBM, Million Dollar Round Table, United Van Lines, Culligan, Baxtor-Travenol, Blue Cross/Blue Shield, Domino's Pizza, Arthur Andersen, Hewlett-Packard, and many others.

If you are interested in having Brian Tracy speak to your organization, please phone 619-481-2977 to request a complete information kit, including an audio and video demo tape, biographical data, and client list, or fax 619-481-2445, or write to:

BRIAN TRACY INTERNATIONAL
462 Stevens Avenue, Suite 202
Solana Beach, CA 92075

APPENDIX B

Brian Tracy International

Brian Tracy has produced more than one hundred audio and video learning programs covering the entire spectrum of human and corporate performance. These programs, which have taken more than twenty years of research and experience to develop, are some of the most effective learning tools in the world.

These multimedia training programs are used in companies and organizations large and small to improve managerial effectiveness, increase sales, and empower individuals to achieve higher levels of performance. They have been translated into fourteen languages and are presented in thirty-one countries.

Each program is designed to ensure rapid learning and immediate results. Using a unique video-assisted format with Brian Tracy personally instructing each part of every program, combined with a special facilitation process including exercises, role plays, self-analysis techniques, and audiotape reinforcement, each student emerges from the training at a new level of performance.

The training programs can each stand alone, or they can be combined into a training series presented over several months for maximum impact. Each program is content-rich and designed to be custom-tailored to the specific needs of the individual client.

The Phoenix Seminar on the Psychology of Achievement

This seminar/workshop, based on the principles taught in *Maximum Achievement*, is perhaps the most powerful exercise in personal and corporate transformation in the world today. This video-assisted, person-centered workshop empowers individuals to achieve at their maximum potential. They emerge with a greater sense of clarity, personal responsibility, and commitment to themselves and the organization.

Participants become more positive, purposeful, and self-directed. They learn to set goals, organize themselves for greater effectiveness, and function as members of high-quality teams.

The Phoenix Seminar program consists of twenty-seven sessions with detailed workbooks, instructor's guide, exercises, and audiotape reinforcement for each person. It is fairly easy to present and enjoyable to take. It can be given by certified in-house facilitators or by outside professionals.

Professional Selling Skills—The New Psychology of Selling

This is the world's best-selling audiocassette program on sales. Since it was upgraded and put into a video-based training format it has been called, "The most effective professional selling course ever developed."

The power of the course lies in its simplicity, stripped of theory and jargon, based on twenty-five years of selling on the street. Participants, even experienced professionals and university graduates who've been selling for some time, are amazed at how well the ideas taught in this course help them make more sales.

Individuals and corporations report immediate and sustained sales increases of 10 percent, 20 percent, and 30 percent per year after participating in this program. It has rapidly become the foundation training for many organizations. It is flexible, economic, and relatively easy to install.

Professional Selling Skills—The New Psychology of Selling includes thirty-five sessions with application exercises that allow the course materials to be tailored to the needs of the client company. Preprogram analysis includes a survey of the company's salespeople, sales managers, customers, products, services, and the competition. Based on this information, the course is organized around specific needs to solve specific performance problems.

The seminar is given over a three-day period in a classroom setting. It can be facilitated by certified in-house personnel or by outside professionals. Sales results are immediate, measurable, and long-lasting.

Advanced Selling Skills—The New Psychology of Selling II

This is the graduate program for the experienced professional who sells complex products or services in a rapidly changing, cost-sensitive, highly competitive marketplace.

Advanced Selling Skills is a state-of-the-art, modern sales training program that brings together the most helpful ideas and sales methodologies ever developed to assist salespeople with multi-call, multi-decision-maker selling. It blends twenty years of research with a lifetime of practice to create a thoroughly practical, nontheoretical approach to selling in a tough, sophisticated market.

This is the perfect complement to *Professional Selling Skills*. It is a multimedia program with twenty-four sessions on video, accompanied by individual workbooks, application exercises, and audiotape reinforcement. It can be conducted by certified in-house personnel or by outside professionals.

Strategic Planning for the Sales Professional

This unique program virtually ensures that each salesperson achieves his or her sales quota on schedule and on budget. The ten parts of this program are designed to take each person through a strategic planning process for the upcoming sales period. It shows them how to set clear goals and make detailed plans. It also shows salespeople how to organize their daily, weekly, and monthly activities to achieve dependable, predictable sales results.

This approach to planning exactly how sales goals are to be achieved is both powerful and effective. Salespeople emerge with greater clarity, purpose, personal determination, and higher morale. *Strategic Planning for the Sales Professional* virtually guarantees a high return on the company's investment in sales training, marketing, advertising, promotion, and product development.

The seminar is designed to be conducted over one or one and one half days by in-house facilitators or outside professionals.

Superior Sales Management

This is the cement that holds all the sales efforts of the company together. It ensures that the company enjoys maximum sales results. According to McKinsey and Company, the job of the sales manager is the *pivotal skill* in the sales organization. Increasing the skill of the sales manager can do more to increase sales volume faster than any other change the company can make.

Superior Sales Management is the most complete, practical, powerful course on sales management ever developed. It turns average sales managers into excellent sales managers almost overnight, showing them how to improve sales results immediately.

Superior Sales Management covers twenty-four topics, from recruitment, interviewing, and selection to training, managing, motivating, delegation, and discipline.

This course is the key to building a world-class salesforce that can outperform the competition in any market. It should be required for every sales manager at every level of experience. The effect on the sales of the company are out of all proportion to the efforts of installing the program.

Superior Sales Management is designed to be facilitated over three days with video assistance, workbooks, application exercises, and audiotape reinforcement. The course can be conducted by in-house instructors or outside professionals.

Time Management for Results

This program takes a total approach to teaching people a philosophy of time management that changes their attitudes toward time and time usage. It is a total approach to life management that brings about immediate increases in efficiency and effectiveness.

Participants learn how to set goals and priorities, eliminate time wasters, overcome procrastination, and concentrate for maximum effectiveness.

Graduates of this course emerge more positive, more focused, and with greater energy and commitment to getting the job done. They learn how to gain two extra hours per day of productive time, with lower stress and higher feelings of personal pride.

This multimedia program includes twelve sessions with audio, video, and workbook accompaniment. It is easy to present, easy to participate in, and it can be conducted by either in-house or outside facilitators.

Achieving Personal and Corporate Excellence

This is an informative, skill-building, and thought-provoking one-day seminar on personal and corporate effectiveness that brings immediate results.

Participants learn the twelve dimensions of personal performance and productivity. They learn about quality, service, ethics, teamwork, and individual responsibility. They learn about accountability, communications, goals, and priorities.

This course is the ideal foundation program for improving productivity, performance, and morale in the organization. It gives everyone a common language and common denominators for resolving individual differences.

Achieving Personal and Corporate Excellence is a multimedia workshop designed to be conducted over one day. It consists of twelve sessions with workbooks and audiotape reinforcement. The course can be facilitated by in-house instructors or outside trainers.

Brian Tracy International Consulting Services

BTI's professional consultants and facilitators are trained and certified to install the training programs described above in companies of all sizes.

BTI services include consulting, diagnostics, customizing of each program, facilitation, and follow-up services to ensure retention and application.

BTI offers train-the-trainer programs for each of the seminars and workshops described above. In-house personnel can be trained to customize any of these programs for internal presentation.

For information on BTI programs and services, please phone 619-481-2977, or fax 619-481-2445, or write to Brian Tracy International, 462 Stevens Avenue, Suite 202, Solana Beach, CA 92075

APPENDIX C

Advanced Selling Strategies

To continue your personal and professional development, you may want to acquire additional materials. Here's how:

1. Catalogue of audio and video learning programs for continual reinforcement and skill development. No charge. Phone, fax, or write and we'll send you a copy.

2. Poem, "Don't Quit," 8 x 11, suitable for framing. No charge. Phone, fax, or write.

3. Relaxation tape, twenty-two minutes (same one used in our seminars): ten powerful affirmations with music, plus full script and detailed instructions for making your own tape with your own goals. Price: $10, including shipping and handling.

4. Goal-setting and achieving workbook, "30 Day Action Planner" with complete step-by-step Masterplan for designing a blueprint of your ideal life, complete with special reinforcement exercises to "lock in" the goal-achieving process. Price: $10, including shipping and handling.

5. Information on Brian Tracy seminars and workshops, corporate presentations, public appearances, and video-assisted training programs. Phone, fax, or write.

6. Correspondence: if you have any personal questions or observations, please write to me and I'll respond personally.

I welcome your success stories and experiences applying these ideas to your life. Good luck!

BRIAN TRACY INTERNATIONAL
462 Stevens Avenue, Suite 202
Solana Beach, CA 92075
Phone: 619-481-2977
Fax: 619-481-2445

Listen to Brian Tracy speak on selling and other important topics. His audio and video programs available from Nightingale-Conant include:

- **The Psychology of Selling**   **6 audiocassettes 1651A**
  Learn the proven techniques that separate the real superstars from all the others.

- **Advanced Selling Techniques**   **6 audiocassettes 10660A**
  Master powerful new strategies, tactics and techniques. This is a completely new sales-training program for experienced professionals.

- **Advanced Selling in Action**   **4 videocassettes 10670V**
  This is a complete, four-volume video "seminar" that gives you all the new selling ideas guaranteed to place you in the top 10% of all salespeople.

- **The Psychology of Achievement**   **6 audiocassettes 5031A**
  This all-time best-selling program reveals the specific techniques you can use to become more successful than you ever thought possible.

To order programs or request a free catalog, call **1-800-525-9000.**

NIGHTINGALE-CONANT CORPORATION
7300 NORTH LEHIGH AVENUE
NILES, ILLINOIS 60714
1-708-647-0300 • 1-800-323-5552

INDEX